D0174791

The Regressed Patient

The Regressed Patient

L. Bryce Boyer, M.D.

Jason Aronson, Inc.
New York and London

10 9 8 7 6 5 4 3 2 1

Library of Congress Cataloging in Publication Data

Boyer, L. Bryce.
The regressed patient.
Bibliography: p. 305
Includes index.
1. Schizophrenia—Addresses, essays, lectures.
2. Personality, Disorders of—Addresses, essays, lectures. 3. Regression (Psychology)—Addresses, essays, lectures. 4. Psychotherapist and patient—Addresses, essays, lectures. I. Title. [DNLM:
1. Regression (Psychology)—Collected works.
2. Psychoanalytic therapy—Collected works.
WM 193.5.R2 B791r]
RC514.B64 1983 616.89′82 82-24363
ISBN 0-87668-626-9

This book is printed on acid-free paper with a life expectancy of 250 years.

Manufactured in the United States of America.

To my wife, Ruth,
to my children, Sandra, Dewey, and Kim,
and to my analysts, Anna Maenchen and Robert E. Westfall

Contents

Preface

This book details principally the evolution during the past 35 years of my understanding and treatment of patients who suffer from characterological, borderline, and schizophrenic disorders. At the same time the 14 papers included here reveal much about my development as a person, a researcher, and a psychoanalyst, important information for those who believe with me that the nature of the developing interpersonal relationship of the patient and the therapist is of incalculable significance for the outcome of treatment. In that sense, the volume is autobiographical. Further, this preface adds personal information which will enhance the reader's understanding of the nature of my interaction with patients and how I have come to think as I do about their care. These remarks illustrate also how my career has served my personal needs.

It became apparent to me early in my clinical years that the nature of the interaction between the patient and the therapist, including both its real and its transference-countertransference aspects, is of even greater importance in the treatment of regressed patients than in that of their neurotic counterparts. Consistent with this viewpoint, some 20 years ago I became sufficiently courageous to specify some of my developmental conflicts and their resolution in the article reproduced here as "Psychoanalysis in the Treatment of Schizophrenia" (Chapter 4). In that essay I present two opinions I had held for a number of years which were then considered to be heretical and unwarranted by a large majority of North American psychoanalysts, namely, that the treatment of choice for many people who suffer from such disorders is psychoanalysis in as near classical form as can be applied and that a main obstacle to their therapy is unresolved countertransference. Today, I am convinced that these opinions have been amply justified.

Younger practitioners can scarcely know the degree of hostility accorded by North American analysts to therapists who sought to experiment with the psychoanalytic treatment of regressed patients. Freud's self-acknowledged equivocal stand that psychoanalysis is applicable solely for the treatment of the transference, as contrasted to the narcissistic, neuroses was taken as an inviolable dictum; his having himself used orthodox analysis throughout his career not only in the treatment of what would now be named borderline conditions but even with people whom he overtly designated as psychotic was ignored (Binswanger 1956). To be sure, psychoanalysts whose thinking was influenced by Klein, Fairbairn, and Bion were then advocating the treatment of regressed patients by psychoanalysis with few or no parameters, but their theoretical positions and their technical applications were overlooked or ridiculed in the United States. It would be years before "respectable" North American analysts began to consider the possibility that some of the ideas of the so-called English School warranted serious study (see, for example, Kernberg 1972a). Today, of course, their thinking is acknowledged widely as important in current object-relations theory and its technical implications, but when I began my psychoanalytic training and practice, the structural theory and ego psychology were in their ascendancy and I remained ignorant of the positive aspects of the theories of the abovementioned "School" until I was writing the historical chapters for my first book on the psychoanalytic treatment of regressed patients, coauthored by Peter L. Giovacchini (Boyer and Giovacchini 1967). Thus, during the years in which my clinical experiments led me to hold the unorthodox positions described, I did not have the emotional support of the knowledge that others advocated psychoanalysis with few or no parameters in the treatment of some schizophrenic and borderline patients as well as many of those suffering from severe characterological disorders. To my knowledge, the idea that unresolved countertransference issues might be a major if not in some cases *the* major cause for the failure of the psychological treatment of such patients was first published by me (Chapter 4), an idea which is widely supported today (Epstein and Feiner 1979, Giovacchini et al. 1975, Racker 1968, Searles 1979).

It is my belief that I also introduced a second important idea that is now commonplace. Not infrequently, the borderline or psychotic patient early in treatment presents heavily cathected derivative material which expresses oedipal conflicts. Extrapolating from current object-relations theory, therapists now generally hold that to interpret such material in a triadic relationship context is contraindicated because it serves to mask pregenital fixations and developmental failures and to defend against their analysis. Those data must be worked through in a dyadic relationship context before triadic relationship conflicts can be understood meaningfully by the patient. I wrote in 1961 (Chapter 4), in 1966, and again in 1977 (Chapter 7) on an empirical basis of the inadvisability of dealing with such material by making Oedipus complex–oriented interpretations (see also Ornstein and Ornstein 1975; Rosenfeld 1966a; and Volkan 1976, 1982).

The degree of hostility with which my ideas were greeted, especially in the organization where I received my psychoanalytic training, stunned me. Previous offerings, written while I was yet a candidate, had been acclaimed. Thus my first psychoanalytic presentation, "Christmas 'Neurosis'" (Chapter 11), had been selected by Sandor Lorand for inclusion in *The Yearbook of Psychoanalysis* as one of the ten best contributions to the literature of 1954; and my second, "Maternal Overstimulation and Ego Defects" (Chapter 1), had been published in the prestigious *The Psychoanalytic Study of the Child.* I was literally so naive as to believe that because my ideas as presented there were accorded respect, my other speculations would be treated similarly.

From my earliest exposure to psychiatric patients, I found that the understanding of the symbolism of dreams and symptoms and the primary-process–dominated verbal and nonverbal communications of psychotics came easily to me. From the outset, I found myself comfortable with most regressed patients. But that understanding and comfort had a special life-history background.

When I was 5 years old, and shortly after the birth of my only sibling, a brother, my father left our home. Thus, my extremely emotional and erratic mother became my sole parental focus. Even earlier I had found that the principal rival I had for her daytime interest was a dream book, a dictionary of arbitrary meanings ascribed to manifest content, which enchanted her. To attract more of her attention, I persuaded her to teach me to read it. We had long discussions which stemmed from our shared and separate reading of the dream book. My persisting absorption with symbology is reflected in the final five chapters of this volume. When my father abandoned our family, I turned to the teachings of a highly moralistic church for support in my efforts to be good and responsible, introjecting its precepts with exaggerated stringency. As would be expected, I developed an early and abiding interest in all varieties of folklore, mythology, and religiomedical practices which has led to many publications, including Chapters 13 and 14 (see also Boyer 1978, 1979, 1982; Boyer et al. 1978; Hippler et al. 1974).

My interest in learning to comprehend the meanings of symbols, whether verbal, written, or conveyed by body language and symptoms, had a more profound basis. As a child, urgently needing consistent affection, I was literally forced to develop the capacity to understand and communicate meaningfully with my mother, whose personality disorder was highly complex. Predominantly, it was characterized by hysterical and depressive traits; her superego was hyperpunitive but also allowed periodic antisocial activities. There were transient regressions of various kinds, such as severe paranoid episodes which sometimes included uncontrolled physical violence, and syndromes which included hysterical combined with psychosomatic elements. Her distortions of the truth led to my distrust of the oral or written word from a tender age and a profound need to learn for myself, empirically. These events had a profound and complex effect on my choice of career and on my relationships with my patients.

Surprisingly, even before my latency period I was able to understand in large measure the meanings of my mother's verbal and nonverbal behavior, whether expressed in everyday communications or by her psychotic, hysterical, psychosomatic, or antisocial episodes. I had also learned how to avert or avoid her rages, which were directed physically toward males and particularly against me. It can be no coincidence that during the years of my working with disturbed patients, I have been able to assess the seriousness of potential assaults. Not only has this capacity enabled me to avoid dangerous attacks, but it has made it possible for me to observe relatively dispassionately patients' threatening behavior and to use it for analytic purposes, as illustrated in "Working with a Borderline Patient" (Chapter 7) and "Analytic Experiences in Work with Regressed Patients" (Chapter 9).

No doubt it is by now apparent to the reader that my becoming a psychiatrist had as its main unconscious motivation the curing of my mother. I did not know that until I underwent in 1959 and 1960 a second period of personal psychoanalysis while seeking to remove a countertransference obstacle which had created unsurmountable impasses in the treatment of some patients (Chapter 4). Some 16 years later I realized that a secondary motivation had been to protect my brother and myself (Chapter 7).

For many years I recognized that my capacity to work with regressed patients was somewhat unusual. I assumed that to have such an ability necessitated an exposure to and mastery of conflicts engendered by actual early experiences with important parental figures who suffered from regressive syndromes, a position which seems to be inferred in others' writings (Langs and Searles 1980). I no longer hold that view. I have come to know several psychoanalysts who have consummate skill in treating such patients and whose backgrounds were much more conducive to secure ego and superego development. Additionally, I have been serving as supervisor for three and a half decades to psychiatric residents and private therapists, many of whose patients have fallen in the borderline to psychotic range, and have observed that their personal analyses combined with teaching enabled them to develop a progressively greater capacity to work effectively.

As would be expected because of the early separation of my parents, much of my professional life has been devoted to bringing into consonance phenomena that appeared to me to belong together but were treated generally as though they were disparate. In medical school I decided to become an internist after my initial interest in psychiatry was dampened by the disrespect accorded it by the professors of other disciplines in the medical school I attended and by the sterility of the mechanistic approach offered by the psychiatric faculty. However, during my last year of qualification to take the National Board examinations in internal medicine, I became convinced that the vast majority of the disorders from which my patients suffered were predominantly emotional, despite the position taken by my teachers. In consequence I switched to the study of psychiatry as a specialty. However, the nondynamic position taken by my teachers was a dominant factor which led me to turn to psychoanalysis as a means to bring internal medicine and the psychosomatic effects of unconscious conflicts into harmony.

Other efforts to reconcile the apparently disparate followed. From the outset of my psychoanalytic training I was taught Freud's view that the nature of the transference reactions manifested by patients who suffered from what he named the "narcissistic neuroses" made them untreatable by psychoanalysis per se. Yet my personal observations made that position untenable and from the middle 1950s onward, that disparity had been resolved to my personal satisfaction. But, of course, my professional pursuits had not changed my past, and I turned in another direction to symbolically reconstitute fantasized harmony in my childhood.

In my latency period, my happiest days were spent during summers when I was sent to live with my maternal grandparents of pioneer stock who resided on the edge of an Indian reservation. I was awed by the Indians' costumes and by their stoical and dignified behavior during parades and ritual performances. I came to believe that one of my grandparents had Cherokee forebears but that there was gross shame attached to such a possibility. In fact, I was confused when I witnessed the contempt accorded red men by the whites in the farming community. Nonetheless, my fascination led to curiosity and to a later inclination to do anthropological research. This was furthered by my wife, Professor Ruth M. Boyer, a professional anthropologist. In 1955 I began preparations for fieldwork, and since 1957 I have been engaged in research of a combined psychoanalytic and cultural anthropological nature, conducting joint studies with her and other anthropologists and psychologists in a number of areas worldwide. Our principal ongoing project has continued for 25 years with a group of Apaches living in New Mexico.

The research with the Apaches was designed to study the interactions among social structure, child-rearing processes, and personality organization; my charge was to determine the latter (Boyer 1979). My primary methodological approach during the first two years of the project, which included continuous residence on the reservation for 15 months, was to practice psychotherapy in which I almost limited my activities to interpreting transference and resistance. My skills in working with regressed patients proved to be most useful inasmuch as the modal Apache personality consists of a severe characterological disorder predominantly manifested by impulsive, hysterical, and paranoid traits combined with a diminished capacity to develop deep and abiding emotional ties. In general, my Apache patients were benefited. They were relieved of nightmares, phobias, psychosomatic symptoms, and drinking problems and helped with sadomasochistic involvements, at least temporarily. Reciprocally, my work with the Apaches increased my ability to treat regressed patients in my private practice.

Two anthropologists devoted their activities to the study of social structure, and Ruth Boyer investigated child rearing, residence patterns, and folklore. It was possible through nightly discussions to recount the day's discoveries and to raise and check hypotheses.

Two phenomena early became apparent to me, namely, that expressive culture is the study area that offers the greatest promise in showing the interactions we seek to understand and that the vast majority of anthropologists, even cultural anthropologists, and of folklorists hold the study of personality development and psychology itself to be almost irrelevant in the study of man and his works. Of course, there were then glaring exceptions to this position, such as Devereux, La Barre, Muensterberger, and Róheim, and since then there has been a gradual shift of attitude so that today an ever increasing number of anthropologists and folklorists are seriously applying dynamic psychology to their understanding of human behavior and expressive culture. Since my own fieldwork collaboration with anthropologists, a number of other psychoanalysts have undertaken similar studies, such as Freeman, Foulks, Morgenthaler, and the Parins (Boyer 1978, 1980).

After a few years of such cooperative research, I demonstrated to my own satisfaction, on the basis of actual fieldwork rather than the armchair research of prior psychoanalysts, that psychoanalytic theory can be applied cross-culturally. I then turned to yet another, and my latest, area of interest in which to bring illogical disparities together—the transcultural application of the Rorschach test. With few exceptions, cultural anthropologists have held that the Rorschach test provides no dependable information in field research. To me, such a position is as untenable as that which holds the psychology of the individual to be unimportant in the study of society and even expressive culture since, like expressive culture, Rorschach protocols reflect projections of personal conflicts and their resolutions. However, examples of the results of that research are not germane to the present volume although they have led to a number of contributions (Boyer and Boyer 1972; Boyer et al. 1964a,b, 1967, 1968, 1978, 1983a,b; Day et al. 1975; Klopfer and Boyer 1961) and a comprehensive monograph is in preparation.

The foregoing highly personal data will enable the reader to understand better not only the development of my thinking and technical approaches to the treatment of regressed patients but also the selection of papers included in this volume. As I write this preface I become aware of a certain stubborn persistence in my intellectual pursuits. Perhaps the pioneer spirit of my ancestors penetrates deeper than I have known.

Acknowledgments

I wish to express my gratitude especially to my teachers Drs. Gustav Bychowski and Bertram D. Lewin whose encouragement and counsel helped to sustain me early in my maverick endeavors, and to my peers Peter L. Giovacchini, Harold F. Searles, and Vamik D. Volkan for their continued support.

Part I

Technique with the Regressed Patient

1

Maternal Overstimulation and Ego Defects

The infant is born with a physical and physiological status which makes the perception of stimuli less efficient than subsequent growth will potentiate. In *Beyond the Pleasure Principle*, Freud (1920a, pp. 33–34) chose to call the high perceptive threshold of organisms a stimulus barrier. He stated, "The mass of excitations coming up against it [the *Reizschutz*] will take effect only on a reduced scale; towards what is within, no protection against stimuli is possible." Concerning inner excitations, he continued, "There will be a tendency to treat them as though they were acting not from within but from without, in order for it to be possible to apply against them the defensive measures of the barrier against stimuli." He defined trauma as "such external excitations as are strong enough to break through the barrier against stimuli" and further stated that "an external trauma will undoubtedly provoke a very extensive disturbance in the working of the energy of the new organism." The implication that internal stimuli which accumulate will likewise cause trauma in the same sense seems strongly indicated. To quote further, "The flooding of the psychic apparatus with large masses of stimuli can no longer be prevented: on the contrary, another task presents itself—to bring the stimulus under control, to bind in the psyche the stimulus mass that has broken its way in, so as to bring about a discharge of it."

It is outside the scope of this chapter to outline possible steps in and requirements of the process of the neutralization or binding of libidinal and aggressive drives. Their essential features, so far as our current stage of knowledge is concerned, are covered by the series of theoretical articles written by Hartmann, Kris, and Loewenstein (Hartmann 1939a, 1950, 1952; Hartmann and Kris 1945; Hartmann et al. 1946, 1949; Kris 1950a, 1954; Loewenstein 1950).

Freud (1924) stated that neurosis is the result of a conflict between ego and id and that, analogously, psychosis is the result of a disturbance between the ego and its environment. He (1940) thought that the conflict with reality and the subsequent break with reality could be traced either to the features of reality itself or to increased pressure of the instinctual drives, and that an ego which reacted in such a manner to the rivalizing demands of id and reality on the ego must have already been disturbed. Hartmann (1953) added a third possibility, suggesting that for some reason the ego's role as a mediator between the drives is impaired: "Either the defensive countercathexis of the ego, or those ego functions that maintain the contact with reality, may be incompletely developed or weakened. Thus, while a break with reality could ensue in all these situations, 'conflict with reality' can, as to its causative impact, only be evaluated in relating outer frustration not only to the instinctual, but also to the ego aspects of the situation" (p. 179). Thus, there is an increasing tendency to conflict and the ego is incapable of dealing with it by the usual methods. The reader is referred to Rapaport's paper, "The Conceptual Model of Psychoanalysis" (1951a), for further clarification of this point.

Bergman and Escalona (1949) described five children who were markedly hypersensitive to external stimuli. Four of the five revealed congenital physical abnormalities. Quantitative and qualitative hypersensitivities to stimuli in the visual, auditive, gustatory, equilibratory, and temperature spheres were demonstrated. The mothers of these children strove to protect them from outer excitations and to relieve their inner tensions. The maternal roles were in the form of what could be termed a supplementary barrier against stimuli. Nevertheless, the children described became psychotic. Bergman and Escalona suggested a hypothesis to be investigated, stating "that the infant who is not protected sufficiently from stimuli either because of a 'thin protective barrier' [*Reizschutz*], or because of the failure of maternal protection, may have to resort for such protection to premature formation of an ego. When this premature ego breaks down, possibly as a consequence of trauma, the psychotic manifestations are thought to set in" (p. 347). The implication was clear that ego defects would result also if the *maternal* protective barrier were too "thin"; this could be the result of "maternal deprivation" which might lead to an increase of tension through not removing excessive external stimuli or not satisfying drives; or, on the contrary, the mother, through her handling of the infant, may herself add excessive stimuli to the precarious balance.

Spitz's (1946, 1949, 1950, 1954, 1955a) observations of infants developing anxiety at about eight months of age apparently indicate that "at this stage at which the Ego is still nonexistent, its defense functions are partly replaced by an exceedingly high perceptive threshold which acts as a biological stimulus barrier . . . this stimulus barrier will serve later as a model for certain Ego functions in the nature of defense, more specifically those on the lines of repression. But before that can come to pass the threshold must be progressively reduced and finally disappear, to be replaced by Ego functions" (Spitz 1950, p. 138). His now famous illustrations of hospitalism (1945, 1947) can be justifiably interpreted to mean not only that the stimulus barrier begins to recede in its effectiveness during the third month of life but that inadequate protection from traumatic stimuli through the administration of care and handling by mothers during the crucial period when the biological protection recedes, results in a lack of psychical and physical maturation and development. Some analysts, as M. Sperling (1955), believe that psychosis is largely the result of outright maternal rejection. She saw this phenomenon as the fundamental difference in the mother-child relationship between the psychosomatic pattern and some psychotic patterns of response. The literature is replete with references to deleterious effects on children of maternal neglect and rejection (Aubry 1955; Gelinier-Ortigues and Aubry 1955; Klimpfinger 1950a,b; Langford 1955; Mohr et al. 1955; Morrow and Loomis 1955).

In the schizophrenic the ego's role as mediator between id and reality is impaired. The defensive countercathexes or those ego functions that maintain contact with reality are incompletely developed or weakened. What is most obviously lacking is the organized, ego-integrated stability of the defenses, compared to what is found in normals and neurotics. Primitive defensive mechanisms are more characteristic, such as turning against the self, reversal into the opposite, and the detachment of libido. Such defenses are those which do not utilize large quantities of neutralized aggression in countercathexis (Hartmann 1953). Unneutralized or deneutralized aggression is absorbed by the superego and turned toward the individual or may be directed externally (Nunberg 1920, 1932; Pious 1949).

Defenses against the without as well as the within develop in close interconnection with object relations (Arlow 1952, A. Freud 1949,

Hartmann 1953, Kris 1950a).[1] Trouble in the development of object relations may interfere with growth of stable defenses which may again stultify development of object relations. Distorted object relations predispose to schizophrenia. One decisive factor on the side of the ego is the level of neutralization. In dedifferentiation of the ego, more differentiated forms of object relations can no longer be maintained. Self-object and ego-id relations run parallel. Withdrawal of object cathexis may well lead to loosening of ties with reality. The dedifferentiation of reality testing may be related to deneutralization; inner reality as well as outer reality become distorted.

The communication between mother and infant during the early period of babyhood is a subject pregnant with difficulties. In the book by Ruesch and Bateson (1951) no chapter is devoted to relationships between mothers and infants; their index contains neither the word mother nor the word infant. However, one facet of the hypothesis of this study involves an assumption that a mother can communicate demands to a nursling.

We know that in this earliest relationship cooperative actions are required on the parts of mother and baby for such a basic phenomenon as survival. Escalona (1953) cited the case of a mother whose eager baby was simultaneously unable to suck. Therefore she cupped the infant's face in her hand, adapted herself to his breathing, and took over the job of moving his jaws. It was six weeks before this "division of labor" could be abandoned. Escalona suggested the possibility that "the importance which breast feeding can have in the developing mother-child relationship is anchored in the fact that breast feeding required mutual interaction of a delicate kind, mediated by bodily processes in both mother and child" (p. 200). The ability of the child's regulatory mechanisms to handle the problem of belching, his sensitiveness to stimuli awake and asleep, his levels of innate activity: all these and numerous other phenomena bespeak the great variability of the individual child. They limit the kinds of behavior which can be used in his care. Then there are the mothers. Some for various reasons reduce physical contacts with their children to a minimum. Others

[1]The importance in all living systems of four points more or less directly indicated in this brief review pertaining to one facet of the development of an infant in his environment can be found in the illuminating paper of Beach (1954). The four are: the interaction between the organism and the environment, the sequence of development, the importance of time phases, and the ways in which development can be held back or made to increase, depending on the environmental influences.

cannot leave their babies alone. The reasons for both types of maternal behavior and the varying intergradations are legion in the psychic structures of the mothers. If we recall the innumerable degrees of skin sensitivity, to mention only one facet, with which babies are born, the potential problems of interactions and adjustment unfold before our eyes. The mother has the upper hand in determining the kinds of behavior on the part of the infant she will accept and encourage. Likewise, through varying degrees of handling of the infant in all spheres, she will communicate through her muscular tension, her noises and expressions, her approbation or disapproval of the child's actions. Among his first memory traces will be the communicated attitudes of the mother. Spitz (1946) indicated that most probably muscular tensions and the degree of smoothness of motion employed will be more significant during the phase when the ego has not yet developed to the stage of the smiling response. The personal demands of the mother can be made known to the nursling through all her means of care for him. This we know from clinical observation. The precise mechanisms involved still remain mysterious.

Obviously, internal levels of stimuli and thresholds of perceptive sensibility will interact in diverse ways with excitations from the environment. A child with a low threshold to perception who has an average inborn level of impulses (Fries 1944) will more easily perceive tension or sharpness in the mother through his tactile, auditory, visual, proprioceptive, and perhaps gustatory receptors. Her permission of ingress of light and colors will affect his psychological state. Her neglect to relieve his tensions through the means at her command will result in higher states of frustration. The child with a higher stimulus barrier and average impulse tensions will be less perceptive to both inner and outer excitations. He will be better able to tolerate relative neglect and handling which is not gentle or is chronically increased because of maternal factors. There is no need to enumerate the possibilities which offer themselves. Even this rough description of means through which mothers can communicate their demands to the tiniest infants suffices to remind us what will be necessary for the child to develop the basic sense of trust to which Erikson (1950) referred and on which so much depends for the development of object relations and ego growth.

A striking example of what may be relatively permanent effects of early childhood perceptions is to be found in the case reported by Seitz (1950). A girl of 2½ years was seen because she pulled hair from her head and held it near her lips while she was nursing from a bottle and held in her mother's arms.[2] Such behavior had begun during rather strict toilet training at the age of 18 months. She had been weaned before she was 3 weeks old. Seitz suspected that her mother's aureolae were hirsute. Such was true. A nipple was constructed with human hairs projecting from around its base. When the child was given the bottle and the hairs were brushed against her mouth, she stopped plucking her hair.[3]

Eventually, no doubt, observational studies will be employed which can convincingly test the hypothesis of Escalona and Bergman. Studies of family interaction have revealed that the parents' unconscious desires exert extreme influences on children (Jackson 1954, A. M. Johnson 1953, Szurek 1954). However, just how to go about testing their hypothesis presents difficulties. It is risky, at best, to attempt to extrapolate backward into infancy data received from adult patients. Nevertheless, this is what will be attempted in the material to follow.

To recapitulate, the infant is born with a physical status which makes the perception of stimuli much less efficient than later growth will make possible. A baby possessing such a relative inability to perceive excitations can be thought of as having an inborn stimulus barrier. During the period in which the *Reizschutz'* efficiency diminishes, object relations develop. The primary development of such object relations is with the mother or her surrogate. Before the nursling can adequately perceive and both defend itself against and utilize stimuli to its advantage, the ideal mother serves as a supplementary stimulus barrier. Infants whose mothers supply deficient protection during this period develop ego weaknesses and inadequate differentiation of ego and id. If we consider an equation similar to mathematics, the situation would be: stimulus barrier plus maternal protective barrier plus growing psyche yield normal ego development. On the other hand, ego development would be disturbed if the stimulus barrier or the maternal protective barrier be deficient—and all possible gradations of both phenomena may exist in individual situations—or if the strength of the child's drives be unusually increased. That such varying intensities of drives exist seems to be demonstrated by the observations of Fries (1944) and Wolf (1953). It follows that if the infant has or has not a "normal" stimulus

[2]Hallopeau (1889) coined the term "trichomania" or "trichotillomania" for compulsive hair-pulling.

[3]Studies of psychophysiological responses to the environment have been conducted by a number of investigators. Although the references given here are to studies which included some children of slightly older ages, they seem applicable (Mangham and Tjossem 1955, Ripley et al. 1955, Tjossem et al. 1955).

barrier and drive potential and the mother adds traumatic stimuli to those to which the baby is optimally subjected, the net result might be similar.

It is the hypothesis of this study that a mother who adds to ordinary stimuli during this early period of ego development contributes to inadequate ego growth. A fragment of the case history of a woman suffering an acute catatonic state will be employed. From it, I hope to demonstrate that this mother added problems of her own to the child, was overrigorous in communicating her demands to the baby, thus adding stimuli for which the child was not ready, and that the mother's shrill, constant nagging resulted in a specific sphere of overstimulation. The effect on this child, as I interpret the situation, was a flooding of the immature psyche with stimuli both from the child's frustrated desires and from the side of harmful external stimulation. This particular mother provided overgratification in the feeding sphere. The combination of these phenomena resulted in growing dependency on the mother and confusion of identities, that is, inadequate development of ego boundaries. Later separation threats resulted in this woman's unconsciously perceiving the love object who might be lost to be her mother, and perceiving his or her parts to be mother's parts. Such traumata contributed to the development of her psychosis.

Case Material[4]

History

Mrs. P. was the 26-year-old daughter and only child of immigrant, uneducated Italians. Her mother was a garrulous, shrill, controlling, nagging, opinionated woman who seldom stopped talking.[5] No arguments could sway her. She spent her life interfering with others' affairs,

[4]Although the information regarding the parents and the girl's life history included in this presentation were obtained initially from the anamnesis offered by the patient, no data are included which have not been confirmed by a reliable informant, a sister of the mother, and, in large part, by the mother herself.

[5]Galvin (1955) has presented evidence that the mother of a schizophrenic does not enjoy being a woman and wants continuing control of her child. The control typically has a secret quality. The mother of Mrs. P. was such a woman, with a slight modification. Her control of Mrs. P. was obvious to outsiders and to herself, but the control urges were quite successfully rationalized. That is, her daughter was incapable of some decisions; therefore it was necessary for mother to make all her decisions.

directing her husband and daughter. She was nosy and gossipy. A hypochondriac, much concerned with her own bowels, she had odd, fixed ideas about food and health-giving mechanisms. Her conscious goals in life were headed by the acquisition of money. As a child, she had experienced a hard life and felt deprived in many ways. She had had little food and no opportunity to rest in the daytime. Mrs. P.'s father was a lazy, taciturn janitor who, despite loud, cursing protestations, submitted to his wife's intense domineering. His mother had been similar to his wife. Mrs. P.'s mother had married him because she had not been asked by anyone with more money. She had held him in conscious contempt. During the years before Mrs. P.'s birth, mother worked and accumulated money.

Mrs. P. was unwanted except as a device. Her mother had feared she would lose her husband and so became pregnant to keep him. Just before the child's birth, the mother ceased her work as seamstress and saleslady to devote her life to her daughter's care. Until Mrs. P. was somewhere between 3 and 6 months of age, she was breast fed whenever she whimpered and often when she did not. Weaning was the result of loss of milk, according to the mother. Mrs. P.'s version was different. She had heard a family story stating that one time her mother had nursed her on church steps. Someone had looked "strangely" at the scene. Thus mother stopped nursing her daughter because of fear of the evil eye. Even after the weaning, Mrs. P. was never allowed to get hungry. Though she was constantly handled, the baby was never sung to. Her father was considered too clumsy to care for her. During infancy and early childhood, she was force-fed and became quite fat. She was completely toilet trained for soiling and wetting somewhere between 12 and 18 months. As soon as Mrs. P. was old enough to be fully awake part of the time, mother set her sleeping patterns. Even though the baby was not sleepy, mother lay and held her as mother slept. In later preschool childhood, this pattern annoyed Mrs. P., but she had no choice. She judged the sleeping to have been done when mother wanted to nap. All the girl's activities were prescribed. Her likes and dislikes were ignored. Her clothes were laid out for her every morning until she graduated from high school. During her preschool years, mother took her to the toilet, pulled down her panties, frequently actually fed her, dressed her, bathed her, and so forth. Mrs. P.'s chief memories of her childhood before she went to school were concerned with her mother's insistent, nagging instructions and her own frustration because she was not allowed to do things herself, such as housecleaning, cooking, and sewing.

When Mrs. P. started school, mother abruptly returned to work. Her parents left before she awoke. A neighbor woman came in, dressed her, fed her, and sent her to school. She went to the neighbor's for lunch and was fed whatever mother had dictated. As soon as school was over, she ran to the neighbor's and sat there until her parents returned from work. She had withdrawn into friendless loneliness. During the week, she was dressed unbecomingly. She was supposed to have been fat and was fat. On weekends, she was lavishly clad and exhibited to mother's relatives.

After high school graduation, she became a clerk-typist. She continued to live at home. Now mother's attitude changed precipitously. Mrs. P. was to be gaudily dressed, wear makeup, and flirt with men, to seduce them to the altar. She was instructed to marry a monied Italian Catholic. According to Mrs. P.'s understanding, this meant that he was to have been a philanderer, brutal sexually, require her to be just a housewife, and insist on her having many children. Through her lifetime, she had heard nighttime noises and fights and had decided men were bestial. She had listened to mother's complaints of lack of sexual gratification and father's similar protestations. She decided that to keep a spouse, one must be sexual. But she considered her father to have been her mother's asexual son. She attempted to comply with mother's demands to find the right man, but failed. She met a soldier who was not Catholic, Italian, or rich. They kept company for two years. He made no overt sexual advance and had no interest in marrying her. He just came around. He criticized nothing she did or wore. When she was with him, she was pleased at the absence of nagging criticisms and directions. His voice made her feel "full." She built up romantic fantasies. When he left without bidding her farewell, she frantically sought to find him. She began to imagine sexual experiences and went uninvited to her boss's apartment to start an affair. She thought the man's landlady was cold and suspicious, however, and fled. She was soon a sleepless, immobile hulk.

She was hospitalized for three months and given electroconvulsive and insulin coma therapies. Following her release, her mother's efforts to dispose of her through marriage redoubled. Mother now more than ever had the helpless child she herself had wanted to be, but the disadvantages apparently outweighed the pleasures derived. Mrs. P. met and married a man like her father, an Italian Catholic, lazy and taciturn. He was the antithesis of the prescribed partner. In her fear she would lose him, she became pregnant with the thought he could not then leave her. With a baby inside her she felt more whole than before. With her son's birth, however, she felt empty and unreal. Three months later, on New Year's Eve, a woman enthusiastically kissed Mr. P. Mrs. P. became intensely anxious, demanded frequent sexual relations, and rapidly regressed into another catatonic state which was similarly treated. During the next year she was more markedly dependent on her mother. Simultaneously, mother was more dependent on her. At times, Mrs. P.'s solicitude for her son was strong; at times absent. The boy was never restricted by anyone. No toilet training was undertaken, nor had it been at the time of this writing although he was over 2 years old.

Fourteen months after her second acute psychotic episode, her husband injured his back. Her fantasies that he might die resulted in terror and marked preoccupation with having intercourse. Unable to use his penis successfully as the substitute for the breast which would dissolve the feared separation, she very rapidly reverted to catatonia.

Treatment

She was hospitalized under my care. She was found to be mute and motionless. She obeyed commands but displayed no initiative. When food was brought near her mouth, her gesture inquired whether she should open her mouth. She let the food lie in her mouth until she was told to chew and swallow it. Her behavior was that of a small child who has been taught she must have permission and orders to act. She had to be told to take down her panties to urinate, to relieve herself into the toilet, and so on. Against my wishes but for reasons that need not be discussed here, electroshock therapy was begun. It had no discernible effect during the two weeks of its administration. For the first week of her hospitalization, she refused to acknowledge my presence. One day after I suggested that she was angry with me because she felt I had betrayed her, a dramatic episode transpired. I sat by her bed for 30 minutes. No word was spoken. She looked constantly and inquiringly at my face. After 25 minutes, her eyes rolled from side to side, with her gaze focused on my eyes, nose, and forehead. I had the strong impression that she was imitating a nursling. The next day she voluntarily left her bed when I entered the room. She said she had heard a man's voice during the night, saying "Baa, baa, baa." The sound reminded her of a cow. She began to point to various objects and name them. Her speech was monosyllabic, and her tone was inquiring and approval-seeking. The naming behavior continued for two weeks. Her need to be instructed regarding actions did not change.

Two days after her last (ninth) electroshock treatment, which had no observable effect, she began to speak short sentences. She revealed falsification of identity with other women in her three-bed ward. Her speech showed sexual curiosity and confusion and a desire to be handled like an infant, all expressed in symbols. The next day she had again withdrawn into silence. I said she had left me in anticipation that I would leave her after she had revealed sexual curiosity. In the following interview she became talkative once more. Intermixed with the naming, pointing behavior, she spoke with such words and innuendos that I understood the presence of a desire to feel my body and know whether I had sexual reactions similar to her own.

Until this time her hostility had been handled by utter passivity which forced others to do things for her and seemed to ridicule her mother, in effect saying, "See what a bad mother you are, you've taught me nothing." There were also the withdrawal maneuvers. However, she now mentioned some realistically annoying actions of nurses and other staff members. I answered by stating that the nurses and doctors were responsible to me, that she did have to obey them but did not have to like the compliance. With this assertion of my power, willingness to accept responsibility, setting of limitations, and permission for her to be angry, she smiled and called me by name for the first time.

Because Mrs. P. still refused to eat unassisted and because she requested insulin therapy, subcoma doses were given. For three subsequent interviews, she continued to talk of confusion about identity and obligations. She began to test whether she could wheedle and cajole for unreasonable promises. When I was quietly firm, she laughed. Then she reproached me for not seeing her more often. She said her husband had promised her candy, but she thought he would not bring it. Understanding this to be a request for a gift of candy from me, I ordered a pound box of chocolates to be given in my absence. She ate all the candy within an hour. From that moment her behavior altered startlingly. Now she ate enthusiastically and socialized with the other patients. She was active and pleasant. She greeted me by name. No further hallucinations were admitted. She felt refreshed after sound sleep. The change in her actions was truly noteworthy.

Ten days before a planned absence, I informed her I would be gone for about a week. Her immediate response was withdrawal. As soon as I told her where I would be and gave her permission to call, contact was reestablished. The next time I saw her, she complained she had always been constipated. She did not want laxatives. She requested a lettuce salad. I inquired whether she wanted a lettuce salad from her husband. Her firm reply was, in that case, she'd take pills. Then she made an open, but apparently offhanded, request that I bring her a miniature doll from my trip. Instead of agreeing to give her the baby so directly, I told her I would order lettuce for her. With a happy smile, she promptly fell asleep. After a few minutes, she awoke and told me her baby slept at 6:30, 10:30, and 2:30. She soon amended her statement, averring he had done so before her second hospitalization.

Before I left, she asked permission to have sexual relations with her husband and then denied she wanted them. Previously, as will be recalled, when she said she wanted candy, she first stated she wanted it from her husband and then denied the wish. On the day of my departure, she pleaded with me to return safely because she felt she would regress into psychosis and be immured forever should I not.

A brief evaluation of the preceding vignettes seems indicated. The oral gratification of the candy insured her of my good will. I did not fear her introjection of a part of me. She could then take into herself her concept of me and behave both as she thought I did and as she thought I wanted her to. With my threatened withdrawal, the introject was ejected and psychosis supervened. However, told that although I would be absent physically, she could make a part-object of my voice, the good object was reintrojected. The subsequent material could be interpreted to mean she perceived all gratifications to be the same. Conversely, any refusal was felt to be the original trauma, epitomized by the withdrawn breast. The gratification of her request for the lettuce meant that she was permitted to eat things of mine, perhaps parts of me, that she could safely express aggression, namely the feces, that I accepted her since I did not reject her wish to give me feces, and that I gave her permission to have sexual experiences, that is, produce a baby. The baby was in the first instance my gift to her, but her falling asleep upon the granting of her wish meant that in return for my giving her the lettuce-baby,[6] she was giving me a baby—herself. Her messages before my departure confirmed her wish to have sexual experiences, really again with the aim of taking my penis-breast-milk into her and preventing or removing the separation.

To continue the story: Upon my return she had no use for me. When I suggested she was angry with me for having gone, she laughed,

[6]See Sechehaye (1951) for a discussion of the role of "symbolic gratification" in the treatment of a schizophrenic girl.

sighed with relief, and requested permission to come to the office after she left the hospital.

Mrs. P. summarized, I think, material which supports the thesis of this study. Following her hospitalization, she commuted to my office alone from another city and was seen twice weekly, vis-à-vis. Three months after office visits were begun, she reported spontaneously in one interview: "My husband is trying to make me ill, now. He's told me he wants a divorce. He tries to provoke me with his voice and his words." I asked why she obeyed his commands.

> That voice scares me. It leaves me completely alone. It's the same as when Tom [her soldier who left] disappeared. Maybe I'll get sick. It takes him out of me in every way possible. I put him completely into my mind when we married. I felt blank and lost after Tom left. With him I had grasped something human. I feel emptied out with that voice. So I mind him. But then he does it other ways. He gets my opinions and then ridicules me. He dances close to other women. When he did that that New Year's Eve, it emptied me out. Then we had relations and his body was next to mine and he was inside me with his body but that didn't make me feel full even though my body felt full. I got that full feeling from Tom's voice. Like in the hospital. My husband said I said the candy made me well. It was your voice. Even when you said the wrong things. Your sweet, purring voice, like a cat. It babies me in my mind. It says, "You're a nice girl. You've got a nice figure." You like me and that makes me feel well. You just want to help me for myself. You don't try to make me do things for you.
>
> I'd rather live with my husband, even like he is, than to return and live with my parents. That's horrible. Inside of me I couldn't get away from them. Now I don't let my mother's voice go inside of me. It's not my husband made me sick. It was my parents' voices. I want to be empty of them. They didn't give me a full feeling after Tom left. Instead it was a dominating feeling. I had to do what's best for them and not for me. I was supposed to solve her problems. Marry the kind of man she wanted to marry. She didn't want to do housework or cook or sew, so she wouldn't let me learn. She had no interest in *me*. I could have stood on my own two feet if she had taught me to do things for *me*.

Discussion

The anamnestic material from Mrs. P., her mother, and her aunt reveals that mother was hostile to this girl and minimized her needs. The girl's wants were ignored and mother's were heeded. Mother could not let the child be separate and bound her through feeding experiences (among others). The type of feeding experience, while gratifying in one way, should be considered as overgratifying, that is, frustrating. The girl was not permitted to learn to be hungry. Food shoved into the mouth in the absence of hunger adds unnecessary stimuli, perhaps similar qualitatively to an enema administered in the absence of an urge to defecate. Such an interaction between mother and child could result in the youngster's defensive development of an ego-alien identification. In short, mother kept Mrs. P. helpless. The disregard of the child's own wants resulted in unceasing inner tensions which she learned to attempt to handle according to mother's formula, through the mouth or other orifices which could be equated with the mouth, the anus via enemas, the vagina via intercourse, and the eyes and ears. There are hints that her skin itself was utilized as a similar orifice. Although there were denial actions, she seemed also to remove separations by skin contacts. The historical material obtained from the girl's memories and other stories obtained reveal a clear utilization of the daughter by the mother to solve the problems of the latter, at least during and subsequent to childhood. Confusion as to identity ensued. Not only did she and mother constitute a symbiotic psychological syncytium, but in this woman persisted a fusion of roles of men and women as well as of mothers and children, even after her overtly psychotic episode was no longer present.

In the hospital she acted like a hyperobedient little girl whose apparent willingness to comply disguises ruling through helplessness. After I interpreted her anger at me, she convincingly imitated a nursling. She hallucinated my presence, acting in accord with the primary model of thinking mentioned by Rapaport (1951b). She transiently regressed to a preverbal state. Then came a prolonged reliving of the period of babyhood in which the infant learns to talk. Her behavior at that time revealed a clear object confusion and a simultaneous listening for verbal clues. She expected to be told everything she was to do or think. Subsequently appeared confusion about bodily functions and differences. When I called her attention to reality, that I was her doctor and unafraid to accept my own identity and responsibility, she was relieved and understood I would not add my problems to hers. When I gave her the candy as well, without telling her I had sacrificed myself and she should feel guilty, as was mother's wont, she introjected a new figure to mime on the one hand, and behaved as she thought I wanted her to, on the other. The lettuce-doll episode was a dramatic illustration of the thesis that, for an orally fixated patient, every frustration and every gratification are perceived as oral experiences.

Granted that no certain evidence is present to indicate that the mother superposed her wants upon the infant Mrs. P., there are indirectly derived data, obtained through repetition of her infancy, if my conviction be accurate, during her hospitalization. I am indebted to a suggestion of Bertram D. Lewin, with which I agree, that the fact of my conviction that this is a reliving phenomenon, although subjectively received, should nevertheless be considered as additional confirmatory evidence.

The interview which was reported in detail, plus the fact that each time I saw her after she left the hospital she referred to mother's voice and its frightening aspects, combine to suggest a specific means through which this particular mother added traumatic external stimuli to the baby: that of the voice, its quality and amplitude.

That she grew up with ego defects is clear. Among them was inadequate development of ego boundaries. To retain identity at all, she had to feel she had someone or a part of someone inside her. With each threatened separation, she returned to mother in actuality and/or sought reunion through a man's penis as a source of milk. It is less obvious to me whether she developed premature ego segments, as hypothesized by Bergman and Escalona (1949).

If this material is considered from the standpoint of the stimulus barrier, the hypothesis tested appears to have been confirmed. It may be that a specific manner in which the infant's stimulus barrier was broken was through the agency of the mother's voice.

In his thoughtful discussion of this study, Wangh (1955) called attention to a publication of Spitz (1955b) which appeared after the present study was written. I shall quote from Wangh's discussion notes, but shall not attempt to answer the important theoretical question raised, since I do not feel qualified. Instead I refer my readers to the article of Spitz mentioned above and to Hartmann's "Contribution to the Metapsychology of Schizophrenia" (1953). Dr. Wangh stated:

> Dr. Spitz, in his recent paper, "The Primal Cavity," has thrown new light on his concept of the stimulus barrier. His view seems to me to raise the question as to whether this concept is at all necessary when we are trying to formulate intrapsychic hypotheses. Perhaps we may well consider it to be supplanted by that of countercathexis. Dr. Spitz writes, "The newborn is incapable of perceiving the outer world . . . the sensorium is not yet functioning, in terms of the dynamic viewpoint, the newborn has not yet cathected it . . . the stimulus barrier is not to be understood as an obstacle in the path of the reception of stimulation originating in the environment. It is to be understood as consisting in the uncathected condition of the sensorium." I ask then: can we not assume that

parallel with the gradual cathexis of the infant's sensorium, countercathexis too develops in the same way under normal circumstances. Possibly the latter with a temporal lag to the former. This would mean that we could think of a gradual transition from the uncathected to the cathected and then to the countercathected state of the sensorium. Cathexis and countercathexis would be necessary for optimal function in the same manner that agonists and protagonists in the muscular system make for orderly functioning. Following this line of thought we would then have to say that the mother of Dr. Boyer's patient interfered with the establishment of countercathexis in the course of the infant's development. I would recall to you Dr. Hartmann's (1953) views on the defective countercathexis in schizophrenia. He states: "These countercathectic energy distributions are essential, for instance, for the acceptance of outer reality. Without them, not even the separation of inner and outer world can come about." I would add here, not that of self from nonself.

[Dr. Wangh made other comments which seem to demand further information and perhaps speculation from the present author. He went on:] The mother in Dr. Boyer's case treated her child as a part of her own body, her own self. And so it is most interesting to find the patient felt herself to be such a part, needing completion. This completion she achieved only when her boy friend or his penis was in turn available as a part object. She also felt completed when she was pregnant. Then she was "full." Her identity was established. That the feeling of fullness was acquired through the combined oral and auditory route is most intriguing. The voice becomes an introject. Dr. Spitz traced the common pathway of orality and the visual sensorium. Here, we may have a common path of orality and the auditory sensation. Optic overstimulation we can avoid by some physical mechanisms: we can close our eyes or avert our gaze aside from reinforcement of countercathexis. Is it not possible that in the case of auditory overstimulation we need an extraordinary amount of countercathectic energy in order to avoid traumatization? The infant cannot plug its ears. Hence the great vulnerability of this perceptive route and therefore the frequent finding of auditory hypersensitivity of schizophrenics?

Mrs. P. had, so far as I know, no visual hallucinations. She reported only two hallucinatory experiences during the time I saw her, although she said she had heard indistinguishable noises and words when previously hospitalized. Following an interview in which she revealed through symbolic language a desire to feel my body to determine whether I had sexual reactions similar to her own, she reported she had spent the night with her (nonexistent) brother. Their bodies had been near each other all night. No sexual relations occurred. The identity of the man in bed with her was overdetermined. At one time she said it was her son. None of her relatives, to my knowledge, had blue eyes. I do. The man who lay with her and whose body filled her through tactile contact, she thought, even though she denied having seen him at all, had blue eyes. This hallucination, so far as reported, involved tactile and proprioceptive spheres. I assume that enteroceptive sensations were likewise involved. In the hallucination which succeeded the episode of imitating a nursling, the total related content was that she heard a man's voice saying "Baa, baa, baa." Although this hallucination appeared to fit the primary model of thinking delineated by Rapaport (1951b), it is possible that more was involved. It may be that her confusion of names contributed to her using the sound of a sheep to represent the sound of a cow. Nevertheless, one might speculate whether her sheeplike behavior and her attempts to make sheep of her mother surrogates through her helplessness contributed to her word confusion. It would appear that this particular sort of behavior on her part involved both primary and secondary autonomous agencies, similar to those utilized for explanation by Brenman (1952) in her discussion of the psychodynamics of the teasee and emphasized by Hartmann (1953) and Rapaport (1951a). Be that as it may, in this case we have what appears to be primarily an auditory hallucination.

Paraphrasing Spitz (1955b), Wangh (1955) stated:

> Lewin (1946, 1948, 1950, 1953a,b) . . . deduces logically that if a regression occurs from the visual imagery level at which the dream functions, then there should be memory traces older than these pictures. Thus, as I do, he sees these memory traces "more like pure emotion," made up of deeper tactile, thermal and dimly protopathic qualities which are in their way "memory traces" of early dim consciousness of the breast or of the half-sleep state. And, if I read him correctly, he believes it is to this level of integration that the subject regresses in the so-called blank dream. It follows that the level of regression involved in the Isakower (1938, 1954) phenomenon harks back to an earlier period, that which precedes the reliable laying down of visual mnemic traces or at least to a period at which a significant number of visual mnemic traces has not yet been accumulated. I would be inclined to say that while

the regression of the dream screen goes to the level of the mnemic traces laid down somewhere between the ages toward the end of the first half year and reaching to the end of the first year, in the Isakower phenomenon the regression reaches to the traces of experiences preceding this period. Obviously these age ranges represent extremely wide approximation.

In the case reported by Seitz (1950), tactile memory traces appeared to play a role in the little girl's action of putting hairs around her mouth while nursing, despite her having been weaned at two or three weeks. This case is so startling when we consider the diffusion of sensations experimentally observed—or, stated differently, the relative absence of sensorium cathexis during such early stages of life—that we must wonder whether indeed all the necessary information is available to us for making a clear statement regarding the meaning of Seitz's findings. All the same, the case is temptingly suggestive. If it occurred in the manner there described and there are no further important data which should be employed in its interpretation, the significance is that at least some infants do indeed develop strong memory traces of sensory perceptions and integrate them with phenomenological Gestalten at very early ages, although we are generally inclined to agree with Spitz (1955b):

> The sensations of the three organs of perception—hand, labyrinth, and skin cover—combine and unite with the intraoral sensations to a unified situational experience in which no part is distinguishable from another. This perceptive experience is inseparable from that of the need gratification occurring simultaneously and leading through extensive tension reduction from a state of excitement with the quality of unpleasure to quiescence without unpleasure. *We do not postulate any memory traces, be they even unconscious, of this situational percept of the newborn* [italics added]. (p. 227)

But to return more directly to the issue at hand: in the hallucination in which Mrs. P. slept with a man, one of the men in the condensed figure was her therapist, at that time her clearest mother surrogate. She was then deeply regressed. The perceptions involved in the hallucination appeared to be primarily tactile, proprioceptive, and, perhaps, enteroceptive. We know that in the case of Mrs. P. and her mother, much bodily contact was employed during her infancy. It may very well be that the level of her regression is indicated by the fact that previsual elements were at least predominantly employed. It could be that even in later periods of her infancy, such sensorial phenomena were of more importance than visual. In the case of the "baa, baa, baa" hallucination, we have no direct evidence to enable us to conclude that more than auditory perceptions and their projection contributed to her model of primary thinking, as there illustrated. We would assume that, if it was an episode of primary ideation, the absent mother surrogate was the object of an aim, namely, an aim to be held and nursed. Thus, indirectly, we could guess that proprioceptive, tactile, and enteroceptive perceptions were involved.

Spitz (1955b) has already called attention to the importance of the labyrinth in the nursing situation:

> When we lift the newborn from his cot and place him in the nursing position, we set in motion in the labyrinth a neurophysiological process of a very special nature. This process is a gravity-induced shift of the endolymph within the labyrinth, resulting in two sensory stimulations of a completely different nature. . . . The pressure of the endolymph on the lining of the semicircular canals results in changes of the equilibrium sensation; the same pressure will simultaneously provoke auditory sensations in the organ of Corti in the cochlea. . . . The sensations connected with the stimulation of the semicircular canals will be dizziness and vertigo, those connected with the stimulations of the Corti organs will be auditory, probably vague rushing, murmuring, roaring noises which may be similar to the sensation described by Isakower and Lewin. (p. 224)

It would appear that the case of Mrs. P. might give us information to substantiate a hypothesis that under special situations of infancy, in which certain auditory stimuli are repetitively associated with the experience of being mothered, they may become more clearly and persistently accentuated facets of the oral sensorium. It might, as Wangh suggested, give us some clues as to why in schizophrenics it is not unusual to find great vulnerability in the auditory sphere.

Summary

According to one formulation, the physical status of the newborn makes the perception of stimuli less efficient than later growth potentiates. Freud formulated the concept of the stimulus barrier. As the *Reizschutz*' efficiency diminishes, object relations develop; the primary figure of importance in the development of object relations is the mother or her surrogate. Before the nursling can adequately perceive stimuli, the ideal mother serves as a supplementary barrier against traumatic external and internal excitations. Infants whose maternal protective barriers are deficient develop ego weaknesses and inadequate differentiation of ego and id. If the stimulus barrier or the maternal protective barrier is deficient, or if the drive strength of the child is unusually increased, ego development may be disturbed. It follows that if the infant has or has not a "normal" stimulus barrier and drive potentials and the mother *adds* traumatic stimuli, ego development might be abnormal.

A fragment of the case history of a catatonic woman provides information which can be interpreted to mean that her stimulus barrier was broken by the mother's adding external stimulations and failing to relieve inner tensions by adding her problems to the child's and using the baby to solve her own problems, specifically through continual auditory excitation.

Certain speculations are made which lead to a tentative conclusion that under certain conditions of mother-child relationship in infancy, the accentuation of auditory stimuli cause an unusually strong bond between the Gestalt of being mothered and the auditory sensorium, that is, the development of a strong link between oral and auditory sensorial spheres.

2

Uses of Delinquent Behavior

In this chapter I present material selected from the lengthy analysis of a man whose psychosexual development was fixated at the level of the oral incorporative mode. The psychoanalytic treatment was concluded some 30 years ago and the great level of improvement which had been attained has persisted. The fragment will be used to illustrate: (1) how he employed delinquent behavior to maintain a sense of personal identity and avoid the anxieties of depersonalization, and in the service of sadomasochism; and (2) to substantiate a hypothesis that fixation of unneutralized energies to cardiorespiratory experiences during his infancy contributed to failure of ego development and formed a fundamental basis on which later symptoms and behavior were formed.

Case Material

History

Mr. X. was a 35-year-old single Jewish social worker. When he appeared requesting psychoanalysis, he was suspicious and disheveled. He complained that he lived with a divorced mother, did not love her, but could not bring himself to leave her, believing that she needed him so desperately that she would commit suicide were he to do so. He was preoccupied with thoughts that his penis was too small and disturbed because his fantasies of glory were dysmensurate with his actual accomplishments. He had chosen me for an analyst because he had heard I was interested in art and literature.

His parents were immigrants, and his childhood was spent in a ghetto slum of a large eastern city. A withdrawn, lazy, ne'er-do-well father contributed almost nothing financially to the family. He spent his meager earnings on his personal appearance and entertainment which included solitary attendance at musical events, dances, and houses of prostitution. An imperious hypochondriac, he scorned his wife and daughters and had little use for Mr. X. The mother was hard-working and self-sacrificing. She supported the family. A shrewish, nagging woman, prejudiced, emotional, and ridden by psychosomatic complaints, she could not permit her children to attain independence. Because of her philosophy that there need be no necessarily observed law but that of family want, she had but thinly to rationalize her stealing, lying, cheating, and sharp business dealings. She was proud of her own rigid sexual morality but ignored the overt mutual sexual play among her children and the open, barely disguised masturbation of Mr. X. Yetta, seven years his senior, and Stella, three years older than he, were variously neurotic and delinquent. The family worshipped Mordekai, the second-oldest sibling. He was brilliant intellectually, a childhood musical prodigy, and an opportunist whose peccadillos were simply overlooked.

Mordekai became a proficient musician but eventually gave up hopes of being a concert soloist and turned to other fields of endeavor. He became a professor in a psychological field, married a gentile, and was subsequently much less productive than his childhood promise indicated. His preoccupation with obtaining money was a factor which deterred him from greater success in any field.

Mother returned to her employment within a few weeks after my analysand's birth. No one person cared for him steadily at any period of his life. He was a silent, withdrawn, stubborn, grasping child who fought incessantly with Stella and feared that his murderous and sexual advances caused her hysterical convulsions.

So long as his behavior did not impinge on the individual comfort of his parents, he was ignored. He recalled with pleasure no childhood events except those in which he provoked parental anger. If he could not direct their attention to him or if he were left alone, he was frightened and had temper outbursts.

He slept with his brother from early childhood. He seemed to live for nighttime when he could sleep entwined with Mordekai. Until pubertal years, there was little daytime contact between them. After

Mr. X. had learned that his attempts to please father by imitating orthodoxy failed, he refused bar mitzvah. He sought to gain Mordekai's favor by turning to music and literature. The brothers then talked together during the day about composers and authors. Mordekai indoctrinated Mr. X. into stealing books and records. Thenceforth Mr. X. attempted to make accomplices of various people, and when he had achieved his goal, felt he had obtained love.

His attempts to compete with his brother through learning to play musical instruments and write stories failed. He gave up with two rationalizations: (1) he preferred to live in the reflected glory of Mordekai; and (2) Mordekai would be jealous and withdraw love should Mr. X. succeed.

When my patient was 11, Mordekai was diagnosed to suffer from heart disease. One of our subject's most painful memories was that father then prepared bacon for Mordekai, although at that time he still followed kosher thinking and had not yet become an avowed atheist. At 12, Mr. X. was hospitalized for presumptive heart ailment, a false diagnosis. For years thereafter, he did not dare fall asleep at night lest his heart kill him when he was defenseless. Concurrently he developed a fear of intimacy with Mordekai and could no longer bring himself to sleep with his brother.

Lung infection played a role in his development. In infancy he almost died of pneumonia. At 7 and 11 he had severe pulmonary infections. Twice in his 20s he required hospital care for pneumonitis.

He did little schoolwork. Although his intelligence quotient was superior, almost all his papers were cribbed and examinations were passed through cheating. He obtained a graduate degree through hiring a ghost-writer. Throughout his childhood he stole, lied, cheated, and destroyed property, alone and with gangs. He indulged in long periods of daydreaming of sexual relations, largely with mature, bosomy women. He smothered small animals. In the military he was an accomplished loafer and cleverly incited discontent. He could not tolerate spending time in barracks and was frequently absent without leave, seeking "some woman" to use sexually. He impregnated one girl and refused to help her. He was transferred from one outfit to another. He thought he feigned a psychotic episode and was discharged with a psychiatric diagnosis.

Following his military career, he returned to live with his parents, primarily his mother, and to college to obtain a higher degree. He became afflicted with thoughts of omnipotence. He was incredulous when his attempts to will horses to win races and chandeliers to move did not produce the desired and feared results. His inability to get along with superiors, his poor schoolwork, and his rudeness resulted in his being dismissed from two graduate schools. He became frightened by his fantasies of power and attended a psychotherapist who recommended he leave home. He moved several thousand miles and soon found himself living with a woman very similar to his mother, her teenage son and daughter, and her improvident father.

Treatment

The first year of analysis. When he entered analysis, his delinquent behavior, laziness, rudeness, provocativeness, lying, cheating, stealing, and prodigious stinginess were ubiquitous. He wanted to leave Alice, the gentile woman with whom he lived, but was convinced if he did so she would suicide or die "of a broken heart." He was aware she had had husbands and various lovers, and when left by each of them, had soon found other men. He did much of her housework, lest she have migraine like his mother and renew fears of loss through death.

The early months of his analysis found him attempting to relate with me as he had with his brother. He immediately strove to engage me in conversations about art and literature on factual and experiential bases. Although he then concealed the fact from me, his analytic fees were partly paid by what he considered to be stolen funds, namely a pension from the military which he had neglected to mention. During his youth, soon after he had begun to steal phonograph discs and music books to please his brother, he had arranged to be apprehended and had contrived to involve his brother, thereby emerging unpunished. Within a week after he started his analysis, he managed to get caught stealing ham from a store (from which he had previously stolen food for two years without discovery) and escaped without being reported to the police by telling the grocer he was in analysis with me. His fantasies were that he could thereby get me in trouble as he had done with Mordekai. While in college, he had lifted weights with his brother. A fortnight after he first saw me, he resumed this pursuit. Before his puberty he had slept with his brother and experienced sexual excitement. When questioned regarding the reasons for his renewed weightlifting, he revealed conscious awareness of a fear he might be influenced sexually and in thought by his therapist. He intended to develop huge muscles to frighten me and to protect himself through threat of violence. He lay with one foot on the floor for six months, openly stating he expected a homosexual attack at any moment and wanted to be ready to flee immediately. Within a few days after his analysis began, he decided I wanted him to stop sleeping with Alice. Dreams made it clear that she and I were equated. For three years, he made of me various people from his past Monday through Friday and on weekends made of Alice, me.

An inadequate résumé of the first months of his analysis can be subsumed as follows: He presented his intense problems of dependency veiled through denials, projection, and isolation. He sought to prove he had mother's strength to endure physical stress and survive. He felt it necessary to outdo her. For example, he lifted too great weights and sustained a small traumatic inguinal hernia. Rather than seek medical help, he continued hoisting even larger loads, with great pain, and was intensely disappointed when he could not will the pain away. He counterphobically tried to prove he had his father's strength, that of indifference to the needs of others. He strove to be more callous than father, by provoking unhappiness among Alice and her children and then ignoring their pleas. He had vivid fantasies in which he could manipulate the world and balance the planet on his fingertip, if he tried. He revealed intense fears of his own violent tendencies, but they were hidden from him by his sureness that he never felt angry and through projection. He seemed to feel no guilt for his manifold delinquencies. Early came hints that they were ties with reality. Events which transpired during the interviews revealed that when he became aware of feelings of discomfort or depersonalization, he soon tried to provoke me into anger by baiting, entering the office in my absence, refusing to pay bills when scheduled, intense rudeness, and lawbreaking of various sorts, clearly aimed at disturbing me. When he annoyed me or thought he did, he became relaxed and his discomfort disappeared. At times, he was obviously delighted. He had during his childhood erotized his mother's anger; now he erotized his own and the real or fancied anger of the provokee. As he was gradually confronted with increasing evidence that both external and internal reality were for him largely the projections of his own mental images, he became increasingly aware of physical discomfort. Episodes of depersonalization appeared more often, which he sought to remove through provoking anger and increasing delinquent behavior. When he got or thought he got anger, his feelings of unreality and of not knowing who he was, lifted.

For many months we dealt with quickly shifting transference manifestations (such as Searles [1963b] described in his delineation of the psychotic transference). With bewildering rapidity, he reacted as though I were one or another person in his family or a fragmented representation of that person; his and my identities shifted repeatedly. Simultaneously it became clear that although the ostensible subject matter ranged through homosexual to heterosexual incestuous imaginings to blatant oral and anal material, the data could be best approached through dealing with the oral components.

The first year of his analysis was characterized by an intricate imbrication of shifting defenses. Projection, introjection, acting out, transitory partial identifications, intellectualization, denial, reversal, undoing, and isolation were persistently employed. Nonverbal messages often prevailed. Primary-process thinking was predominant. Nevertheless it was possible to conduct his analysis without parameters. For periods lasting from seconds to days at a time, his obsessional thoughts and projections had delusional conviction. Gradually, such periods shortened and their intervals lengthened as transpired tentative incorporation of his analyst's consistency and calm. Patient confrontation with the unrealities of his pronouncements gradually effected improved reality testing and ego splitting diminished.

The second to fourth years of analysis. After a year of analysis during which he had incorporated a good deal of his picture of me, my identity had become largely that of a bisexual mother, fused with the protective side of Mordekai. Concurrently his father rapidly failed and expired from a malignant disease. Mr. X. was apparently scarcely touched, but the theme of death and its mysteries persisted for over a year. When his father died, Mr. X. soon began to dress and act like me. Unfortunately he did not promptly receive the expected financial and status reward of being promoted at work. He became overtly depressed. He resumed slovenly dress and also increased mother's types of delinquency. However, as he stole, lied, and cheated, and as his behavior was demonstrated to mime his mother's, he became fearful he would literally turn into a woman. Thereon, he began again to spend working hours loafing and seeking the company of women. He did not actually have affairs like father because he was not sure that his analyst, in the role of father, had used them sexually and discarded them. During his youth he had repeatedly used his brother's cast-off women for his own sexual purposes. However, in his vivid daydreams, he repeated his father's delinquency with women. He imagined he went out every night, drank, and committed adultery, as he knew his father had done. His stinginess with Alice, whom he partially considered to be his wife, increased. Father had given almost no money to his family. While weightlifting, he began to see his father sitting on his shoulders and at times he was convinced he had revived his father and had added father's muscles to his own. When repeated confrontations over a period of weeks finally indicated to him that despite his conviction he had fused with his father, he was not in fact more muscular, stronger, or more potent sexually, he felt profoundly empty. Stealing, rule breaking, and lying again flared, and fantasies of strength through indifference and daydreams of promiscuity lessened. His actions returned to miming mother.

Following a vacation period, he had withdrawn from me. He became a more exaggerated caricature of his mother. But when the similarities of his behavior to mother's were repeatedly demonstrated, he began to fear he was female, and to protect himself against becoming mother, he called on visualizations of father and reverted to an attempt to fuse with father. He revealed many fears of fusion through physical or emotional closeness and had to maintain distance through withdrawal and lack of feeling. As he became reacquainted with his analyst during the five months following vacation, he again became more like his picture of me. Following a Christmas depression (Chapter 11, this volume), a flurry of stealing reoccurred. Its meaning was that he thus attempted to counterphobically prove he was stronger than the incorporated conscience of the analyst and that he retained blood ties with his delinquent family. He openly stated his fear of actually becoming his analyst.

During all this time, he had been quite unable to define what emotions he felt or bodily sensations he experienced during any interview, despite patient repetitious inquiries. He spoke with a double language (F. Deutsch and Murphy 1955). For some months I had indicated to him that at certain times he cleared his throat, lifted his head, tensed certain muscles, or made various movements. During one interview, when I had several times called attention to periodic touching of the face, a phenomenon one meaning of which we had determined to mean that he was reassuring himself he was alive, he began to talk of Kafka's *Metamorphosis*.[1] Just as he related that the hero's sister

[1]Martin (1959) stated, "The identification with a cockroach is a feeling of being weak, small, inferior, repulsive and unloved. It is related to an inability of the individual to differentiate his worth from his parents' sick attitudes. It occurs in individuals who are extremely sensitive to others and who cannot individuate. These feelings are made permanent by overwhelming incapacitating physical symptoms accompanying their anxiety" (p. 70).

had become disgusted with him after his change into an insect, Mr. X. suddenly pictured himself as a fly, crawling about the ceiling and walls of the office, eluding attack, and in a position to watch his analyst. With this experience, he became acutely aware that he felt unreal, that he believed a part of him was floating about the room in the form of the fly, but his body was lifeless as his hands clung in desperation to the couch. As on numerous subsequent occasions, his recovery of a feeling of personal integration was dramatically illustrated in the interview proper. In the midst of loss of identity, when he was the fly, he defecated on the ceiling and wall and finally on the analyst. When I struck at the fly and barely brushed it, Mr. X. touched his face and felt real.[2]

Uses of Delinquent Behavior

Maintenance of a sense of reality. The preceding material can be interpreted to indicate two principal utilizations of delinquent behavior as attempts to maintain a sense of reality. His self-image was fragmented, the result of partial identifications with family members, particularly his parents. Throughout the portion of the analysis described in this chapter, there was striking evidence that the maternal and paternal introjects were at war, as had been his parents. When he became a caricature of mother, he projected father's role, that of indifference and sexual promiscuity. Similarly, when he closely mimed father, maternal delinquent characteristics were projected. Both internalized parental figures were necessary for him to feel whole, to have self-knowledge. Consequently, when he acted too much like one or the other, he feared he was losing the introject which was not in ascendancy, became confused about his identity, and shifted his behavior to prove to himself that he retained both figures and was whole. Thus the delinquencies of his parents were used to help him hold on to a feeling of entirety, of reality. The second major way in which asocial behavior was used as a tie with reality radiated from the core that if he did not personally inconvenience his parents, they were withdrawn from him. When his delinquent actions troubled them, both became consistently angry. Other types of behavior brought inconsistent responses or none at all, leaving him bewildered. Because of poor ego boundaries and a

[2]Although the anal components of this remarkable fantasy and experience are stark, it has not been possible to evaluate the role of anal roots in his development of reality testing.

persistent symbiotic psychological relationship, when he was confused, he felt unreal and had no clear picture of who he was or what he should do.

To summate the previous material from the standpoint of his utilization of delinquent behavior as a link with reality: In his special familial group, delinquent behavior appeared to have been accepted without strong conflict. A sadomasochistic relationship between the parents and this man when he was a child resulted in his need to anger to receive a semblance of affection. Other forms of object love were lacking, and his pathologically intense need for parental affection on an infantile level took hostility as a substitute gratification. Mr. X.'s fragmented identifications with his schizoid parents included those in the spheres of their individual types of delinquency. Depersonalization was warded off during the period of his psychoanalysis through a combination of inciting anger in a family member surrogate and living out, primarily at first in action and later in fantasy, the delinquent behavior of one or another parental introject. Since these forms of delinquency varied, primitive defensive mechanisms had to be utilized which would enable him to feel he knew his identity at times when he was reenacting the roles of mother or father and was unsure whether he were indeed mother or father, that is, man or woman.

Sadomasochism. It is beyond the scope of this chapter to fully develop the sadomasochistic theme. The reader is referred to Loewenstein's paper (1957) and to his bibliography for a résumé of psychoanalytic theory.

Mr. X. had no actual sexual perversions. In him was an intense degree of passivity, the prerequisite for masochism, and his passivity was employed in obviously aggressive manners at times. Expressed in his fantasies, he visualized himself as dead, a state of great power, since when one is dead, one cannot be forced to do anything at all. Whatever one wishes to do with the dead person, the wisher must himself do. His passivity was at times aimed at appealing to the mercy of a threatening and protective parental figure (Horney 1935). For example, soon after he bought his first automobile, the car developed a puncture. Intellectually he knew how to go about changing the tire. However, because in part of his equation of automobile with penis and independence, and because at that time he feared Mordekai's retribution for sexual fantasies he was having regarding his brother's daughter, Mr. X. became utterly helpless. He telephoned to Mordekai who came a long distance to push the automobile to a service station, although Mr. X. had a national automobile club card. When his brother took pity on him and helped him, Mr. X. felt less guilty about his sexual fantasies. He could not bring himself to make actual sexual overtures to Alice for many months after his analysis began. In order for him to maintain an erection, it was necessary that she either ridicule him or that he have fantasies in which some woman belittled him, and for Alice to make the actual sexual moves. By this means, he could disclaim responsibility for the sexual acts. Thus suffering was a prerequisite for sexual feelings, a price which had to be paid to alleviate his fears and wishes that he would destroy her with his penis. So long as she was responsible for his erection, his own self-castration to avoid actual castration was nullified (Rado 1933, W. Reich 1933). He imagined scenes of punishment which he himself devised, to avoid the chance he might be tortured in some unexpected way (Eidelberg 1933a,b, 1934; Fenichel 1945; Freud 1926; Laforgue 1930). For example, when he expected a punishment from me, he would come to the interview planning to provoke me into some specific sort of angry behavior; when he succeeded or imagined he had succeeded to anger me, he felt unmistakable sexual pleasure at times. On several occasions, he experienced partial erection. Watching prizefights in which he identified with either the winner or the loser excited him, akin to Freud's stating (1905) that mystery plays and gruesome fairy tales can be used to gratify the same need. At the same time that he actively feared during the early phases of his analysis that I would assault him sexually, he had fantasies in which I did so. This had the effect of giving him fear akin to the make-believe (Fenichel 1945, Loewenstein 1940). He had a vivid memory of a childhood game with his father: Father would flex his biceps, i.e., "make a muscle." Mr. X. would touch the muscle in awe and with conscious wishes that he could remove it and own it; at the same time he feared his father would use the mighty muscle to destroy him for misbehavior. It will be recalled that following his father's death, he became convinced he had taken over his father's muscles and thereby acquired the strength of the dead. Those muscles were to be used for overpowering women and protecting himself from men. But since father's strength was to be employed and father was dead, no one could be held responsible. Mr. X. regularly turned sadism into masochism. When he was angry with Alice, for example, and had to check on her breathing to make sure his anger had not killed her, he could scarcely sleep at night for fear she would enter his room and smother him or stab him in the heart (Freud 1919). There is ample evidence in the above examples and the preceding case material to show the sadism of his superego and the masochism of his ego.

From the beginning of his therapy could be observed his utilization of delinquent behavior in the service of sadomasochism. From childhood he had felt the need to provoke his parents with petty misbehaviorisms to gain their attention. When he felt his parents did not give him praise for his early schoolwork, in his anger at them he created scenes at school, played truant, and arranged to be caught cheating. Eventually, his teachers, despairing of his ever being obedient, insisted that one of his parents come. On one occasion, which was recalled with some vividness, his mother finally acceded to a teacher's demand and forewent her ironclad rule never to be late to work. She went to school, accompanied by Mr. X. He silently gloated in her humiliation and simultaneously felt pleasure in anxious anticipation of retribution from her or father. When he was not punished, he was disappointed. Comments have been made previously regarding his involving his brother in the record stealing, and his subsequent arrangement to be caught stealing ham and his implication of me. At that time, he felt pleasure as he imagined both my destruction through newspaper comment and scenes in which I punished him for his behavior. One time he left a book in my office and returned after my office hours. The janitor had left the door unlocked. Mr. X. entered the office and retrieved his book; simultaneously he took the opportunity to examine my room, although rather briefly. Analysis revealed again pleasure to have accompanied his fantasies of retribution by me. As he stole newspapers from outdoor racks, he felt twinges of pleasure, never overtly genital, with his thoughts of the vendors' frustrations and potential sufferings, and again with his visualized apprehension and incarceration.

A specific method he employed was that of seduction of the aggressor (Loewenstein 1957). Early in his life, a model for this manner of action was his game with father. At times when his father was reading, Mr. X. would sneak up and pinch his father's arm. The father would glower and Mr. X. would become apprehensive. After some time, during which the flexing took place, father would smile and Mr. X. would feel relieved and pleased. During many interviews, the same sort of behavior would be repeated. Mr. X. would enter the room in a playful mood. His teasing would be rude and fearful. He would report some cheating, stealing, or lying episode and await my reaction. Confronted with silence, gradually tension set in and then fantasies of my stern face. After a time he would visualize me to have smiled. The ostensible stimulus for his relieving fantasy might be a shifting of my foot or even a noise from outside the office.

An interesting facet of this man's delinquency is its minor quality. He never committed a crime without expecting the punishment to be light; he seldom did anything for which he could realistically have been severely punished. It is true that he had carried a lead pipe around in his sleeve for some weeks after he left the army to protect himself from a fantasied attack, but he never used it. The one time he nearly committed a major crime was when he felt that a woman had led him on and then refused intercourse. He nearly strangled her but regained self-control before she was more than bruised. At that time, too, he had judged his victim accurately: no complaint was made to the police. In other words, there was a playful make-believe quality to his delinquent behavior, as there was with so many other of his actions.

Substantiation for An Hypothesis

At this point I shall turn to material which suggests that psychosexual development was retarded by cardiorespiratory experiences during his infancy. Before the case presentation is continued, some preparatory remarks of a theoretical nature are indicated.

We can assume that in the infant as well as the adult, the heart and lungs are the organs most definitely productive of actual sensations peculiar to anxiety (Freud 1926, Schneider 1954). While the first mental representations are forming, the image of the experience of the cardiorespiratory systems must be taken from physiological imprints on the growing psyche (Greenacre 1945). The infant no doubt perceives an awareness that with physical discomfort and its successor anxiety, there are changed heart and lung activities.

Mr. X. had a mother who left him to haphazard care within a few weeks after his birth. We hypothesize the angry frustration of the dissatisfied baby and of the need for the presence of a stable, considerate love object for the neutralization of energies. In the case of the analysand, who received inconsistent and often hostile care, if the psychoanalytic theories of object relations and energy neutralization are accurate, there can be little doubt that neither delibidinization nor deaggressivization was abetted. It may be that his infantile pneumonia, occurring as it did at between 6 and 9 months of age, was perceived by him to be a retaliation for murderous wishes and that this additional trauma fixated primarily aggressive energy to the mental image of the physiological experience of severe pulmonary disease with its accompanying changed heart and lung activity and threatened smothering. Perhaps during subsequent periods of intense regression he could, therefore, return to the period of infantile fixation when the pneumonia and extreme frustration tied energies to mental representations (A. Reich 1956). It may be that in this borderline case we can more clearly than in others partly determine the earliest origins of susceptibility to the sadomasochistic intrafamilial relationship which was to follow. It seems likely, too, that the experience of pneumonia contributed strongly to his later choice of heart disease as an identification focus.

His hospitalization was a shock to him. It caused his removal from the family into a foreign area. Without Mordekai to cling to in bed, nights were terrifying. He could no longer establish continuity through physical touching. In childhood, while his arms and legs were interwrapped with Mordekai's, he imagined he took part of his brother into himself and shared his successes through a physical osmosis. In the hospital, he clung to his penis. Dreams related to this period indicated he equated Mordekai with his penis. Holding the generative organ reassured him he still had Mordekai's strength. While in the hospital, he did not have Yetta to tell him what to think and to share responsibility for his sexual fantasies. Stella was not there to fight with, to prove that physical aggression either in the service of love or hate did not kill. He could not see mother and be reassured that his picture of her sphincter morality was accurate. Father's strength through indifference and greed were ethereal when he could not see father. He felt lost and unreal. He was troublemaker par excellence. He cursed, disobeyed all rules, openly masturbated, and generally incurred hostility. He thus gained fairly consistent anger, which served to relieve his tension, and was sent home as incorrigible.

Once home, he had fear his heart would destroy him from within should he sleep and not guard himself from internal sensations by defensive mechanisms he could employ when he was aware, such as sitting erect and refusing to shut his eyes. During the course of analysis we discovered that the danger produced by feelings, whether of love or hate, and even physical sensations, was partly in the potential effect of emotions on the heart. The very heart of which he was so proud because it was strong enough to kill him was so weak that an emotion could force it to beat too hard and perhaps explode. On the other hand, the heart itself was animated and could eat from within were it made angry by the irritations of his emotions. If the effects of the heart were only partial killing, he might become lightheaded and have a convulsion, and thus lose his identity through having become Stella.

For many years he had used earplugs at night to obviate noises which might disturb his sleep. We found that the noises meant some man would attack him from the back, stab him in the heart as he was unaware. At the same time the noisy disturbance itself might anger him and cause a heart attack from within. Following his hospitalization for heart disease, he developed a severe compulsion to check gas jets before sleeping, lest escaping fumes asphyxiate him or others. His explanation for his fear of death through asphyxiation was mechanistic. Loss of oxygen results in faulty supply to the brain and heart. Lightheadedness and feelings of unreality ensue. A weakened heart makes a weak man. If noxious gases and lack of oxygen made him weak, he'd want to cling to someone. But then he'd run the risk of losing his identity through too great closeness.

All through his analysis, a clear connection was seen between the cardiorespiratory apparatus and especially his aggression. As a child, angry with his parents, he had to listen at the door of their bedroom at night to make sure they breathed. During his fights with Stella, he sought to knock out her breath and to choke her. In adulthood, when a woman refused him intercourse, he almost murdered her through throttling. Angry with Alice, he checked on her breathing and listened to her heart. He wore earplugs and checked the gas jets, lest his projected hostility kill him through heart attack. During periods of his analyst's silence, he became panicky if he could not hear breathing.

Let us now turn our attention to what we know of the role of repetition of early events. It is our daily experience to observe repetition in the transference "as an archaic form of remembrance due to a displacement onto the analyst of unconscious strivings" (Loewenstein 1957, p. 206). The repetition compulsion exists as a method of overcoming or mastering painful, past traumatic events (Freud 1920a). Loewenstein (1940) indicated that a slightly modified form of repetition of formerly gratifying situations or fantasies exists, sometimes, as a form of self-punishment for wishes underlying them.

In the case of Mr. X., the seeds for the development of a sadomasochistic personality were to be widely found in his family and societal situation (Berliner 1940, 1947). However, the external manifestations of sadomasochism in him included a specific group of phenomena which cannot be accounted for on the basis of the broader application of clinical and theoretical data which we employ to understand sadomasochism. I refer to the pervading tendency throughout his life to utilize fantasies and actions which appear to be determined by anxieties attached to cardiorespiratory functions. His earliest memories include punching his sister in the abdomen to knock her breath out, choking her, and listening to breathing of his parents to determine whether his hostility had killed them. Later he smothered small animals, feared sexual activities might damage his or another's heart, almost throttled a woman, and checked gas jets and wore earplugs for reasons which have already been outlined.[3]

It seems highly probable that such continual preoccupation with breathing and heart functions indicates an early fixation on these subjects and that with our knowledge of the repetition compulsion and its uses we can conclude that this man's infantile pneumonia, occuring as it did at just the period when the infant develops the capacity for true object relations, formed mental representations in which were linked relationships between experiences of anxiety as reflected in breathing and heart activities and interactions between people. It is clear that the moribund infant could not have survived had he not had special attention when his pneumonia occurred. The nature of the attention may be indicated from an experience which occurred in his 8th and 12th years. At 7, he again had pneumonia. His mother had, so far as he (or siblings with whom he checked) could recall, never remained home a day for an illness of hers or anyone else's before that time. However, on that occasion, she obtained a private room for him in a hospital and nursed him 24 hours a day. Her ministrations were tender and worried. At 11, he had appendicitis. His anxious mother forced her way into his room while he was yet semiconscious following his operation and enfolded him in her arms. For a few seconds he clung to her and cried. As soon as it was clear to him who was holding him, he became frightened and ashamed and thrust her away.

Changes During Analysis

Mr. X. was a man with varying levels of personality maturity. With all his delinquency, he was never discharged from a position he held. To be sure, he failed to get two advanced graduate degrees, in education and psychology. He did not live out his fantasy of becoming professor of a school of music or a concert pianist. But he did achieve a graduate degree in social work and held positions, regardless of his

[3]The omission of other meanings of these behaviorisms is intentional.

lack of promotions. There seems to be little evidence he was able to establish stable subliminations. The dissocial behavior never led to his being apprehended and convicted by civil or military law. He never engaged in major crimes.

While his parents had schizoid tendencies, and while his siblings' psychosexual development was retarded in various areas, at only one time was there evidence of a clinical psychotic break in a family member. Stella bore an hydrocephalic child whom she made the center of her life. When he died, she suffered from a depression which was treated with electroshock therapy. We have examined certain of Mr. X.'s identification fragments. It seems reasonable to assume that there were many others and that some included the taking in of healthier incorporates of family members. In addition, it would be absurd to speak of any personality as comprising only introjects.

By the end of the first 600 hours of his analysis, certain changes had taken place in his behavior and reactions. Although initially his delinquent behavior appeared alloplastic, the actions were soon recognized as autoplastic. They were impulsive and delay was at times scarcely conceivable, but they proved to be predominantly livings out of reminiscences. With his expanding ego and altered superego development, he had become largely a latent delinquent (Aichhorn 1925). At the same time, he was much better able to postpone id and superego gratifications, despite the fact that as yet conscious application of insights was frequently required. Discharge in fantasy, combined with growing ego control over the id and superego and reduction of multiple identifications, made action less necessary. He had gradually come to be preoccupied progressively less with danger of loss of the object than with the loss of the object's love. Castration anxiety, per se, had been scarcely examined. Material which verbally appeared to be anal, phallic, and genital in nature was produced and used for the analysis of orality. During the next 100 hours, there had been a sharp reduction in need for analysis of orality, and an obvious homosexual struggle, then more clearly based on castration anxiety, had become the central theme. Of course, its understanding in terms meaningful to him necessitated a thorough examination of his emotional relationship with Mordekai. There was a growing fear of disapproval by the enriched superego which was replacing the multiform, exceedingly sadistic superego precipitates of his parents with their transmitted lacunae and inconsistencies (A. M. Johnson 1953, Szurek 1955b). The nature of punishment had altered. Earlier, death was the retribution. Now, it was loss of love. No longer were such rituals as wearing earplugs and checking gas jets needed. He still retained his pension, lived unwed with Alice, and carefully checked change made by clerks and bills toted by waiters in order that he could protest if a mistake had been made in the favor of the seller and that he would know when he had been mistakenly given more money than he had coming. He still refused to assume a role of responsibility in his home, and his work relationships, while considerably improved, left much to be desired. However, he slept better, very seldom attached magical significances to his weightlifting activities, which had become less compulsive, was less stingy, dressed neatly as a rule, and brought himself to the point where he could buy his first automobile.

Mr. X. continued his analysis another 250 hours. Material abstracted from those further hours will be employed in an attempt to answer some of the questions raised below.

Discussion

We have in this case a rather unusual opportunity to examine in the psychoanalytic situation the psychodynamics of a man whose life activity was largely pervaded by delinquent behavior. It appears that such behavior had rather specific meanings to him and that its utilization made possible for him a feeling of self-identity.

Jacobson (1954b) stated that in schizophrenics "the struggle between ego and superego is retransformed into conflicts between magic self- and object-images within the deteriorating ego, whereby the self-images and the object images may alternately dissolve and absorb each other" (p. 107). P. Blos (personal communication 1956) suggested that in this man "fixation on the oral incorporative mode represents the larger matrix of ego deformation on which subsequent, fragmented identifications are erected." There seems to be no doubt that he hovered on the borderline of psychosis during much of the earlier period of analysis described here and that the nature of his psychosis was schizophrenic.

It should be remembered that underlying whatever other influencing agents which transpired during his psychical development is the sadomasochistic relationship between the parents and child, and making the parents angry was his way to get a semblance of affection. As Berliner (1956) said, "Other forms of object love were lacking. Secondarily there is a pathologically intense need for parental affection on an infantile level . . . which takes hostility as a substitute gratification. The deficiency of sublimation or neutralization of instinctual energies is characteristic of introjective infantile fixations. The introject, however, is nothing static. It undergoes a process of digestion and assimilation into the ego that manifests itself in an apparently ego-syntonic acting out." In Mr. X. it seems possible to trace some of the earliest sources of his psychical difficulties—those stemming from a period antedating the incorporation of whole objects into the ego. We can assume that in the infant as well as the adult, the heart and lungs are the organs most definitely productive of actual sensations peculiar to anxiety (Freud 1926, Hoedemaker 1956, Schneider 1954).

We know that children unconsciously act out the impulses of their parents (A. M. Johnson 1953, Szurek 1955b). In this case the conviction of obligation to live out delinquent wishes of the parents was at times preconscious. In identification with mother and with the authorization of the introject of mother, he acted like her in two ways: "toward the outside world in being delinquent and toward himself by making himself the person which mother might want to see in him, who would find her approval and also justify her anger which the patient then lovingly absorbs into his narcissism. . . . This aspect explains two features of the case: (1) why there is so little feeling of guilt; and (2) why the patient was not caught and put in jail . . . while delinquency was his obedience to parental authority, he carried in his protecting superego the readily available patterns for justifying himself and getting away" (Berliner 1956). His mother was never overtly punished for her various delinquencies. "The absence of feeling of guilt seems equally explainable from the specific superego function. He may have the feeling that when he steals, he is a good boy and deserves mother's love, the sort of love which made him welcome mother's scoldings and made it possible for him to project his hostility onto the other person and clear himself of guilt, a guilt which he may also have felt when he could possibly be better than his parents" (Berliner 1956).

We can assume that his particular relationship with his mother was a primary source of his retarded psychosexual development. Possibly the pneumonia served as an additional retarding and fixating effector. His psychic growth was handicapped so that the later incongruities between the intrafamilial environment of his school days and subsequent extrafamilial relationships proved too great to reconcile in his mind. The extracorporeal realities with which he had to identify during his childhood were sharply different from those of the general American population (if there be one) in two ways: (1) His family was most unusual. Schizoid parents who were delinquent made for him a weird pattern after which to model his already sick ego. Lying, erotized aggression driven by unneutralized energy, cheating, and lawbreaking in general were models for identification and were ego-syntonic; (2) His childhood area of development was that of a ghetto slum. The neighbors were almost entirely immigrant Jews. His few playmates were first-generation offspring of parents who had trouble integrating with average American culture.

Later, in high school, he made contact with some non-Jews. However, his new associates were of two classes, the first again first-generation children of Jewish immigrants and the second the children of native Americans who were failures, slum denizens. Nondelinquent behavior was largely scorned in his environment. Through high school his models for any but asocial behavior were limited to certain *schul* members and schoolteachers. Unfortunately, part of his safety valve to protect psychical fusion with father included rebellion against acceptance of Jewish tradition in the larger sense. His mother had little interest in Jewish ritual and lore. Schoolteachers were not models to imitate but figures about whom to have sexual daydreams, as mother surrogates.

With the broadening exposure to milieux other than that of his childhood concurrent with university attendance, being a soldier, and later working professionally, the discrepancies between his and his family's standards of behavior and those of outsiders bewildered him and made him more aware of differences between himself and people in general.[4]

I would hypothesize that he became alternately dimly and more consciously aware that for him there were at least three categories of reality: (1) that of his body, its functions and experiences; (2) the reality of his intimate and extended family model; and (3) that of the extrafamilial and extrachildhood environmental world. If this conjecture is accurate, certain difficulties experienced in understanding the progression of therapy become less confusing. In addition to his involving his analyst as a fragmented figure because of the complexities we know in the treatment of borderline and psychotic patients, the actual person of the analyst was for him of greater importance than is usual, as a model of the extrafamilial world. The technical implication would appear to be that a favorable result in this case would hinge on the possibility that, using the incorporative and extrajecting propensities so strong within him, he could introject characteristics of the analyst and

[4]J. S. Slotkin (personal communication 1956) stated, "In this study I came across no anthropological errors."

eliminate undesirable aspects of his former introjects. This achievement would help him feel more average and real.

If he were to more nearly match people he meets in his present day existence, he would be able to carry out interpersonal relationships without the need for provocative and delinquent actions. Naturally, before his utilization of introjection-extrajection mechanisms could be employed in such a manner as to enable him to take over and effectively identify with a more stable figure, repeated confrontation with the unrealities of his fantasies and the unconscious meanings of his symptoms and character deviations must be combined with a sound model for the development of object relations before neutralized energy could be integrated into the ego and superego structures (Hartmann et al. 1949).

In his discussion of this chapter, Spiegel (1956) voiced a question which bears seriously on the therapy of such patients. He compared the psychology of Mr. X. to that of the Wolf-Man (Freud 1918) and found numerous points of similarity. Each man appears to belong to the groups whom W. Reich (1933) designated *Triebhafte Charakter:* the conflict common to each lies more between instinct and narcissism than instinct and superego. Spiegel traced much of the case material presented regarding Mr. X. and found that it could be interpreted to mean that he had regressed to orality and that his depersonalization represented a defense against a conflict related to passive homosexual wishes and a desire to be castrated by his brother and, in the transference, his analyst, to live out a fantasy that he was his brother's penis. (It will be remembered that the analysand equated his penis with his brother during his hospitalization.) On the other hand, Spiegel found evidence which seemed to indicate that Mr. X.'s problem was one of failure of development, rather than regression from an oedipal conflict. Clearly, a nuclear problem is here indicated, namely, to what extent his adulthood illness was the result of regression from oedipal conflicts to earlier points of fixation and to what degree it represented a failure of initial development. Even the material provided by the last 250 interviews does not provide information which can be employed to answer the question with certainty. A partial working through of his homosexual conflict which utilized Mordekai as the object for whom Mr. X. chose to play the role of the suffering woman, in his negative resolution, made it possible for him to gradually assume a more masculine role at home and at work. Preoedipal jealousies waned and enabled him to experiment with being a father rather than a brother to Alice's teenage children. He finally was able to pass competitive examinations in his professional field and to earn a promotion to a position of added responsibility, which he handled much better than he had previously been able to do with jobs of lesser pay and status. At the time of this writing, he was working through oedipal material and recovering memories of experiences related to primal-scene activities of his parents. He had as yet been unable to marry, although indications were present that he would actually legalize his relationship with Alice in the future. Similarly, he had come to understand more and more the guilt he felt at retaining his pension and the means of self-destruction he used to rid himself of the guilt. But these further data do not answer our question with certainty.

From our knowledge about patients whose personalities are categorized among the borderline group, we realize that they often come for analysis with the desire to have their primitive narcissistic fantasies realized. Mr. X. was such a man. He appeared to lack superego functions which could help in establishing a framework to accomplish analysis of the usual sort. It was necessary that he be patiently taught inherent trust to obviate the blows of the interpretations to his narcissism—interpretations, each of which would mean a frustration, a repetition of what had brought him into analysis.

In his discussion of this chapter, Hoedemaker (1956) touched on the problem of handling the patient's narcissistic needs while frustrating him through interpretations. He said:

> What is the meaning of the behavior of the patient and is there an underlying purpose to this behavior? Dr. Boyer . . . recognizes the curative role which he has played with this patient by becoming a silent, observant, respectful, truly interpretive person while this patient paraded before Dr. Boyer all the details of the sick identifications with which he was stuffed. He had paraded before Dr. Boyer also how his nuclear ego structure has literally been captured by these identifications, rendering him helpless to cope with himself and the world about him on anything resembling a realistic basis. . . . He has needed a contact with another person who is sufficiently realistic to remain an observer unentangled by the cross currents which hold this man's ego at their mercy. . . . Returning them to the purpose of the patient's behavior, why cannot this patient's contact with Dr. Boyer be the end of a pilgrimage in which he has sought help? If this is so, the beginning with his identifications with his parents, leading to the interactions with other

people in the environment, finally culminating with his relationship with Dr. Boyer, do not all of these adventures have a common causative factor which unites them?

It seems probable that his *modus vivendi* of dealing with external objects as projections of himself and as potential sources of identifications combined with his expectation of magical fulfillment of narcissistic needs were the phenomena which enabled him to tolerate analysis without parameters.

But to return more directly to the question Spiegel voiced: there can be no doubt that his psychosexual growth was hampered severely by his earliest relationships with his mother and her substitutes, and subsequently that the soil in which he was to grow was poisoned by unhealthy personalities with which to identify.

During the first phase of his analysis, as I think of the arbitrarily chosen initial 600 hours, it was necessary to test phases of reality and repeatedly correct even physical misperceptions, in order that he even see, hear, and feel the externum more nearly as it existed. When I greeted him with a warmly felt smile, he as often as not perceived me to be scowling. When I heard the tone with which someone outside the office spoke to him and later learned of Mr. X.'s misconception of the character of the tone, I found it necessary to indicate to him how the outsider had sounded to me. On very hot summer days or quite cold winter ones, during a period when the office ventilating system was improperly functioning, Mr. X. seemed incapable of knowing what the temperature was. Sometime later, after such things were mentioned and misperceptions rectified, he came to be able to dress in accordance with the weather. (I am not here suggesting that there were physiological defects in his perceptual systems.)

During the second phase of his treatment, he proceeded to work through, although as yet incompletely, his negative oedipal resolution.

But do we find the answer to our question in such data? I think not. The mutual influences of regression and failure of maturation are too complex to be evaluated, I feel, by the means we now possess. He has largely worked through his homosexual problems. But does this mean that his psychosexual development as it appeared when he entered analysis was the result of regression to an earlier period of fixation? Does it mean that he has grown sufficiently in his analysis as the result of continuous contact with a more mature representative of adulthood to seriously touch genitality for the first time? I believe that the most we can do with this serious problem at the present stage of development of our knowledge and tools is to state that we know that some portion of his psychosexual level was the result of failure of maturation and that some part was defensive and regressively determined. I am inclined to agree with Kubie (1956) who tells us that new techniques for evaluation through experimentation and indeed even new ways of postulating the questions to be asked will have to be developed before our crude capacities to estimate quantities can be improved.

Summary

A borderline schizophrenic, Mr. X. was the product of schizoid parents whose behavior included varying sorts of delinquent behavior. His mother cheated, lied, dealt sharply in business, shoplifted, and indulged in other kinds of stealing. His father contributed almost nothing financially to his family but spent his earnings on solitary pleasures, including visits to houses of prostitution. The family relationships were cemented largely with sadomasochism and a pervading atmosphere of psychological fusion between mother and children. Mr. X. felt he was ignored or handled inconsistently except when he inconvenienced his parents by naughtiness, when he received fairly uniform hostility from his parents, hostility which at least was dependable and designated a meaningful, secure response. He felt his mother praised him by implication when he performed delinquent acts which coincided with her ego-syntonic immoralities and inconsiderations. However, his identity was sufficiently insecure that he feared actual psychical fusion and complete loss of a sense of personal identity when he mimed her too closely. At times when such a fear was roused, he changed his behavior to coincide with his father's delinquent (and other) acts. Such a solution of his fear of loss of personal identity was unsuccessful, nevertheless, because of his mutual identification with his parents and the sense of personal loss when the loss of one or the other introject was threatened.

The first year of his analysis was marked by evidence of psychosis although it was possible to continue his therapy without the use of parameters. His analyst was scarcely viewed rationally at any time but was instead seen to be composed of projected introjects. However, patient confrontations and calm resulted in a gradual beginning identification with the therapist. The reduction of unneutralized energy which coincided with the slow development of a true object relationship in addition to monotonously repetitious interpretations of the meanings of his various delinquent acts in terms of identifications with his parents resulted in a gradual abatement of their performance so that by the end of three years of analysis, delinquent behavior largely transpired in fantasy. With expanding ego strength and reduction of superego sadism and lacunae, he became much better able to attain improved social and work relationships.

Mr. X. had somatized much of his anxiety, and slow analysis of the meanings of muscular tensions and symbolic gestures was necessary before some conflicts could be freed for examination. Such loosed material enabled deeper analysis of the uses of delinquent behavior in the service of sadomasochism.

During infancy he had suffered severe cardiorespiratory distress. Throughout his life, many actions, neurotic symptoms, and delusions contained elements pertaining to suffering or death through cardiac or respiratory affectation. Tracing their meanings enabled me to hypothesize that unneutralized energies had been tied to the psychical representations of those early experiences and thus made unavailable for use in psychosexual development.

This chapter was written after he had completed four and a half years of an analysis which lasted almost two more years. At this time, he maintained two overt delinquencies: (1) he lived unmarried with the woman he feared leaving and largely refused to take responsibilities in the household; (2) he continued to accept a government pension and falsify his condition when Veterans Administration examinations occurred. Subsequently, when his continuation of those behaviors was interpreted in terms of his using them to maintain ties with me, he renounced the pension. However, when he sought to get married, his sincere offer was refused. Subsequently, he provoked her to leave him and established relationships with another woman which were much less tinged with sadomasochistic elements. When this chapter was written, he continued to be afraid that the retention of his new introject would be imperiled and that he might revert to the chaotic, fragmented earlier identifications and return to the borderline state from which he had largely recovered. When his treatment was terminated, his improvements had become stable.

This chapter demonstrates meanings of delinquent behavior in a borderline schizophrenic and indicates that interpretation of its meanings in the atmosphere of growing object relations and recovery from his former psychopathological status enabled him to give up the delinquency, although asocial fantasies continued to serve him defensively when he was anxious.

3

Time of Appearance of the Dream Screen

I have observed unmistakable manifest dream screen experiences only rarely in my psychoanalytic practice. Each analysand who presented the phenomenon was schizophrenic or suffered from a borderline state. Uniformly, the patient had reached the state of development in therapy when narcissistic identification was giving way to true object relationships via the transference and the dream screen episode immediately followed a threat of loss of the new object, which was intensified by a repetition in the environment of an experience reminiscent of a severe traumatic event from childhood.

Lewin (1946) introduced the concept of the dream screen in a study in which he elaborated the idea that sleep "repeats an orally determined infantile situation, and is consciously or unconsciously associated with the idea of being a satiated nursling" (p. 433). A young woman reported: "I had my dream all ready for you; but while I was lying there looking at it, it turned over away from me, rolled up, and rolled away from me—over and over like two tumblers" (p. 420). From the analysis of this dream, Lewin was able to introduce the new term, *dream screen*, which he defined as "the surface on to which a dream appears to be projected. It is the blank background, present in the dream though not necessarily seen, and the visually perceived action in ordinary manifest dream contents takes place on it or before it" (p. 420).

Lewin (1948) further commented about the dream screen: "[It] represents the idea of 'sleep'; it is the element of the dream that betokens the fulfilment of the cardinal wish to sleep . . . it represents the maternal breast usually flattened out,[1] as the infant might perceive it while falling asleep. It appears to be the equivalent or the continuation, in sleep, of the breast hallucinated in certain predormescent states, occasionally observed in adults (Isakower 1938)" (p. 224). Following Eisler's view (1922), in which each falling asleep psychologically repeats the events that take place in the baby when it falls asleep after nursing, Lewin (1948) went on: "The blank dream screen would approximate the baby's state of mind in sleep. The prototypic dream would be blank; it would consist only of the dream screen . . . plus whatever elementary disturbing sensations might enter from other external or internal fields of perception" (p. 224).

Rycroft (1951) sought to answer two questions regarding the dream screen: (1) At what stage in analysis are such dreams apt to occur? (2) What is the dynamic process they represent?

Rycroft's patient (personal communication 1959) "was in a state of 'narcissistic identification' since (1) he had withdrawn interest from external objects, (2) he was preoccupied with an introject, and (3) he identified himself with this introject." The analysand presented dream screen phenomena at a time when an object relationship was developing. Rycroft considered the most significant aspect of the appearance of the screen phenomenon to be that it marked a shift from narcissistic identification[2] with the internal object to turning toward an external object. He concluded that the phenomenon of the dream screen represents, in addition to the fulfillment of the wish to sleep at the mother's breast, an attempt in the course of the analysis to reestablish an object relationship with the mother via the transference.[3]

Case Material

Fragments of two case histories, typical of the seven available, are employed to offer evidence for the tentative hypothesis which is proposed in this chapter.[4]

[1]The fact that infants watch their mothers' faces while nursing (Spitz 1946, 1950) and that psychotics study their therapists' faces while reliving nursing fantasies (Chapter 1, this volume) does not obviate the essential validity of Lewin's conclusions, inasmuch as the concept of breast might easily become fused with the concept of face, as the author has observed in the treatment of psychotics.

[2]"Narcissistic identification," as used by Rycroft and myself, follows Fenichel (1945) and Freud (1917b).

A Schizophrenic Woman

History. Mrs. K., a married woman in her 30s, began psychoanalysis within a few weeks after her second hospitalization and reception of electroconvulsive therapy, following a severe schizophrenic episode which had become patent during a pregnancy. She had been an "as if" person (H. Deutsch 1942). She had split her parent images and visualized her overtly cyclothymic, intellectual, delinquent, promiscuous, exhibitionistic mother as only intellectual and her sensitive, crass, bawdy, sharp business dealing father as solely sexual. Throughout her years at home she had lived in fear of the repetitious manic and depressive episodes which removed her mother physically and/or emotionally from the family. Her memories of home life were primarily centered about arguments, shrill accusations and counteraccusations, and a pattern in which her two sisters, her brother, and she played one another off against the individual parents and the father and mother off against each other, while the parents sought to turn each child against the other parent. She identified herself primarily with two introjects, the first the distorted shadow of the mother, the second that of the father. Her self-image consisted of sexual and intellectual facets which appeared to her an irreconcilable duo. She had lived her life as a caricature of her mother. She had continually sought new introjects and assumed attitudes and gestures of her various lovers, male and female. In her choice of sexual partners, she vacillated between those whom she classified as physical and those she viewed as artistic-intellectual.

Treatment. The transference situation was confused and stormy from the beginning. In the initial interview she claimed that her illness sprang from having at 4 years observed her mother and a maternal uncle as they had sexual relations. Numerous themes radiated from this central hub from time to time during the course of her therapy. During the early months of her treatment her behavior and associations indicated that she was for minutes or hours performing the role of one entire or fragmented introject, and I was reacted to as though I were a projection of another. At the same time, I was perceived for over a year as a glorified and a sexual maternal figure, endowed with highly

---

[3]See also R. Fliess (1951), Garma (1955), Heilbrunn (1953), Kanzer (1954), Kepecs (1952), and Spitz (1955b, 1957).

[4]I am indebted to Dr. José Remus Araico for one case history, that of a borderline patient (personal communication 1957).

unrealistic, charismatic attributes. An almost unbelievably intense hatred existed for a previous therapist who seemed to her to be the image of her despised father. The therapy consisted for many months of confrontations with reality, interspersed with very careful rectifications of her own id interpretations. She had to feel that she conducted her own analysis and perceived each interpretation which varied from her planned comments as a personal loss.

Almost from the beginning she gradually identified with my calm, and progressively she assumed more of my attitude of observation. Her manifold delinquencies were called by their accurate, common names, and she was not permitted to hide behind prettied-up explanations of her cheating, stealing, and obvious hypocrisies. With her growing assumption of my attitudes and calm in the interviews, her gross actings out diminished externally, although with a temporal lag. The fragmentation of introjects and extrajects diminished, as did reality-testing deficiencies in general.

Toward the end of the first year, when oral-masochistic techniques which she felt had bound mother to her in a sort of psychological syncytium failed to involve me, she began to view me as supremely sexual and yet unrealistically intellectual. A highly erotized transference developed during the ensuing 12 months, in which she paraded all the techniques with which she had tried, generally without success, to woo her father. Although the transference had the appearance of an oedipal relationship, I yet existed partly as a projection of her internalized parental images, with the paternal introject more highly colored. She began to develop the capacity for true ambivalence so far as I was concerned, although preambivalent relations largely persisted with other objects. Thus, during this period her identification with internal objects was giving way to the development of a true object relationship with me. Gradually, as she began to be convinced that her reactions to others were largely based on her seeing in them projected parts of herself, she began to gain more than intellectual insight into the motivation for her quest of a penis, the acquisition of which was supposed to enable her to gratify her mother sexually, in return for the privilege of fusing with mother's breast and living in ecstasy (Boyer 1955, Lewinsky 1956).

At the time of the episode to be discussed, Mrs. K. had for some months been begging for intercourse. She had used all her wiles to tempt me to engage in the mutual acting out. A few weeks before the period to be described in detail, she had taken to lying on the couch with her legs spread apart, her breasts thrust upwards, and making caressing movements of her body and legs with her hands, as she sensuously shifted her position. During the interviews she had strong sexual reactions. Her dreams were laden with experiences in which she openly involved me in sexual relations, primarily of an oral-genital nature. Her picture of orgasm was a state in which sexual partners fused, and upon separation each had taken on qualities of the other. Although she consciously wished to abandon her behavior during the interviews, she could not, and was frequently amazed when the analyst pointed out her sexual actions. While she was going through this phase, vacation dates were set for the summer. She seemed undisturbed.

The night of the interview when the period of absence was named, her husband forced cunnilingus upon her. During the following session she returned for the first time in many weeks to her early observation, fantasied or actual, of mother and uncle engaged in sexual activity. She decided that her previous conviction that she had viewed intercourse was fallacious. She claimed that she recalled with great emotion and clarity standing in the bathroom door and watching either cunnilingus or cunnilingus and fellatio. She stated that she had urinated and probably simultaneously masturbated. She had wanted to experience the sensations of each partner, obtain their fluids, and become fused male-female, totally satisfied and oblivious. While on the couch she had genital sensations which she described in such a way that there could be no doubt she imagined her vulva and clitoris as fused and elongated. She burst into tears with the thought that her tears were like a male orgasm. Then she felt relieved.[5]

During that interview she presented a dream in which she abandoned me for a female therapist, my imagined wife, whose words might be more palatable "to drink." The next day, a Friday, she ranted about men's perversions with their daughters. When she was confronted with slightly obscured sexual activities which she performed on her young son, she equated him with her younger sister, with whom she had been actively incestuous, and proceeded to relate with real feeling details concerning homosexual activities of adolescence. When it was demonstrated that her reasons for believing she had then possessed a retractable penis were fallacious, she became utterly furious.

[5]B. D. Lewin (personal communication 1960) stressed that in this remarkable hour, Mrs. K. was struggling between an oral and a genital position and was attempting to compromise by the body-phallus equation (1933).

On Friday night she fortuitously met a known homosexual woman and was strongly attracted. She vividly imagined herself sitting astride the woman, with her vulva and clitoris fused into a penis which brought herself and the partner to orgasm in which each participant melted into the other.

On Monday she reported a weekend marked by elation. She no longer needed analysis and was a "complete woman." She had been intensely narcissistic and had unwittingly provoked her husband into nearly beating her.[6] On Sunday night she had visited the movie *Baby Doll.* During the interview she said that she had been unaffected by the cinema. Sleep had come easily, but during the night she awoke experiencing intense orgasm. She felt she had experienced a dream without visual content.[7] She had found her hand pressed on her genitalia when she awoke. Questioning revealed her conviction that a penis had grown there. When she was confronted anew with the fact that no penis was present, she became very angry, cried, and complained of feeling raw between the legs and of having lost something thence. She became intensely excited and begged for sexual relations. Then she recalled that during the movie she had sat with her legs drawn up in her "sleeping position," with her hands pressed against her genitals. Suddenly she had the vivid fantasy that I had an erection. She wanted to suck and plunge her head up and down until ejaculation occurred and then to swallow the semen. This was a newly conscious desire. She had often performed fellatio but spat out the semen lest it choke or poison her. Now she would swallow the semen and all the rest of me. Then she would sleep. She would be my baby, but I would be in her body. She said:

> So you're not a man at all. You're a breast with a nipple. When I was psychotic, I was anxious with amorphous fears. I couldn't put my finger on my insomnia. I was afraid to sleep. I was afraid I would die. Never wake up again because of amorphous guilt. Mostly about the aborted babies. I literally feared God would strike me dead with sleep. I'd go to Hell. I had recurrent fantasies [hallucinations] I was in a boat crossing the River Styx. Charon was there. I'd never get to the shore of Hell. I'd be forever on the water. My mother's urine and my urine. The stream of my hostility for not being granted babyhood forever. I've thought of myself as a pretty baby doll. I've wanted to kill all the others so I'd be the only one.

[6]H. Deutsch (1933) portrayed a hypomanic woman whose principal denial was the absence of a penis. See also Lewin (1950).

[7]Kanzer (1954) suggested that the blank dream could hide the phenomenon of feminine castration.

On Tuesday she brought a dream:

It was terrifying. I was in a café with open booths. My husband had left me. He, Marilyn[a mother surrogate], and I were sitting with others. He went to Marilyn. I lay on the floor or a low bed. He placed her on a bigger bed across the room and mounted her, sitting with his legs astride her and his penis in her, and rocked back and forth. I watched and whimpered. They looked as if they had pleasure. His look was of sadistic triumph. He was oblivious of me and without concern for her. She looked as if she enjoyed it. Her mouth was slightly open and there was hard breathing. Excitement. The blankets were strewn around on the bed. She raised her hips. They were both clothed but she had no pants on. I didn't feel they had orgasm. He got up and reached for my younger sister. Then I stopped watching him and don't know what he did to her. He came to me and we danced. I asked if he had done that with Marilyn to make me cry, but he said nothing in the whole dream. It was a slow dance without music. Then he changed into a Texan I used to know.

She interrupted her recitation to talk about the Texan. He had chosen another woman. Mrs. K. had been angry, not at losing the man, but, because he would have access to the breasts of the Jewish woman who closely resembled Mrs. K.'s mother.

She returned to the dream:

Then the Texan and I had intercourse. On a bed, I think. As I was having it, I began to see it on a film. Then the picture melted down and we melted together and the film was blank. I could still see the film. It seemed I was surrounded by square objects. A house of cards. I felt myself funneled down some place and I was insane. I had a sense of sinking, a loss of identity. His identity was lost, too. We had become a fluid together. He was in me, after the house collapsed.

Recalling the Isakower phenomenon (1938), I inquired whether she had experienced or was feeling sensations in her mouth. This she denied, but stated she felt pain in her right arm, a sensation she associated with self-punishment for childhood masturbation.

I had the pain then, too. I stood and screamed and screamed. I wrenched myself out of the horror with my arm hurting and my body quivering. The reality of the dream enveloped me. I lay on my left side with my knees up in my sleeping position and my right hand over my vagina. In the terror I thought of my need for you.

At this point she moaned and sobbed. Crying had been very rare during her analysis.

I wanted to call you then, at two o'clock in the morning [nursing time]. But then I remembered that I was in analysis and I had to relive these experiences to get well.

At the end of the interview, she added as an aside, and for the first time, that on the preceding Friday night a homosexual woman had seemed repulsive to her.

During the next week, material continued to emerge regarding her intense desire for a penis and the magic she ascribed to the possession of such an organ, combined with recollections regarding homosexual experiences and particularly her strongly felt attraction to the woman she had met on Friday, and her defensive reaction of repulsion.

Associations obtained subsequent to the data presented above revealed that her reaction to the threatened leaving was the loss of the mother's breast, equated with body and penis. The forced cunnilingus was frightening because it reminded her not only of the experience at age 4, but because her husband might devour her supposed phallus. She reacted with the body-phallus compromise and the renewed strong denial that she had no penis. The elation of the weekend seemed to serve the purpose of denying her incapacity to satisfy the homosexual woman, that is, recombine with a woman in a fusion state, through use of a penis constructed of her joined vulva and clitoris. When she saw the movie *Baby Doll*, in which the heroine so sharply resembled Mrs. K. in certain aspects, her genital pressing coincided with Baby Doll's thumb-sucking while, as Mrs. K. viewed the scene, blissfully fantasizing fellatio. The blank dream with orgasm ensued, followed by further denials of castration. The restitution attempt took the form of fusing with the analyst through fellatio. The dream screen experience, combined with the associations of the preceding interview, may well present the repressed content of the earlier blank dream.

The interruption of the manifest dream relation with the reminiscence about the Texan and the big-breasted Jewess likewise affirmed the homosexual nature of the dream material, as the presence of Marilyn had done in the manifest content.[8] Apparently as intercourse neared climax, fusion melted the mother and child together. The dream content disappeared except for the screen. However, the sleep which resulted was by no means untroubled. Perhaps the retention of the breast-sleep-image, the screen, revealed the significant difference between early infantile sleep and mania, namely, the partial uncon-

[8]This woman's blank dream and elation employment seem to be closely related to that of Lewin's hypomanic patient (1932).

scious awareness that the fusion is only an impossible dream. This would be consistent with the fact that a hungry child's dream of eating does not keep him asleep indefinitely.

An additional factor merits mention. When she was in her parents' bedroom, she lay on a pallet lower than the bed. When she stood in the bathroom and watched her mother and uncle at 4, the bed was on the other side of the room.[9] She probably urinated. She had been constipated for some days before sitting beside the homosexual woman. In the manifest content of the dream, she lay on the floor or a low bed in the position in which mother administered her enemas. This phenomenon could be viewed as indicating that her fantasies of sitting astride a woman were also examples of identification with the aggressor. In the dream, the action was executed on mother and younger sister. She had watched the latter receive enemas in the same position, with flushed excitement and pain. When Mrs. K. had been exposed to enemas, she had gladly submitted. Her constipation stopped after the dream screen experience.

Further speculations could be made regarding the role of Hell, reached by crossing a river of urine produced by hostility and excitement. Whether this would be a hell in which one could forever play with feces or no, it appears that the death would be a prolonged sleep, an everlasting union with mother, achieved through urogenital routes, routes she sought to use after physical sucking on mother had to be renounced. It cannot be without significance that her mother used to talk of the application of urine for relief of pain, a custom of her homeland, or that Mrs. K. thought she recalled mother's applying urine to her brow for the treatment of headaches.

A Schizophrenic Man

History. Mr. M. was a moral masochist, an impulse-ridden person, and grossly dependent. His symptoms defended against guilt and hostility, fundamentally against his mother who suffered from a cyclic disorder. When he was 22 months old, a brother was born. For about two years Mr. M.'s jealousy was nearly uncontrollable, and he tried on various occasions to murder his rival. From about the age of 4, his hostility was defended against by insecure reaction formation. He became his brother's keeper, a watchful, careful guardian who gave the younger one belongings and services and protected him against the

[9]Whether this experience was real or imaginary, the mental content is significant.

attacks of other children, which Mr. M. frequently provoked. When he was 8, his mother died delivering a baby girl. The stepmother demanded strict obedience within the home and encouraged delinquency without. The father was overbearing, intolerant, and demanding. His principal treatment of his sons consisted of ridicule and teasing; his daughter he abandoned. Mr. M. went through life guilt-ridden and seeking physical and mental pain.

He developed a life philosophy of helping others. He became a schoolteacher and an athletic coach, after a career of strenuous sports competitiveness. When his third child had died soon after birth and his wife, on whom he was deeply dependent, nearly lost her life, he became somewhat withdrawn and turned to religion. He decided that his help for others was insufficient and that he would become a psychological counselor to carry on the work of Christ. Although he was academically and financially secure, he reentered a university to obtain a higher graduate degree. While reading psychological literature he was repeatedly confronted with phenomena surrounding reaction formation and became obsessed with fears lest he should go insane and murder, particularly women and small children. He sought psychiatric assistance, but rapidly deteriorated into a man who could not leave his house, room, and eventually bed, lest he go berserk and murder. He became hallucinated and deluded, was hospitalized and given electroconvulsive therapy. In his posttreatment elation he undertook considerable activity. So far as he was concerned, he was well. He had not been actually ill, but tried by God, in order that his experience of pseudoinsanity would give him more counseling understanding. His former state gradually recurred. Severely phobic and terrified, he appeared for therapy.

Treatment. The first nine months of his analysis found his identification with introjects abating and a true object relationship budding. In the transference situation, I, having earlier been endowed with the qualities of projected introjects, became fairly consistently treated as the mother, particularly as a preoedipal figure. During the period of the shift from narcissistic to object identification, vacation dates were set. The following interview, on a Friday, he was silent, a reaction which was new, before a threatened period of absence. On Monday he reported a weekend of elation. He was jocular and teasing. His verbal content was laden with sarcasm, ridicule, and denials. He spent the first 40 minutes of a 50-minute period in an increasingly desperate attempt to provoke me into anger. My silence became unbearable to him. He writhed and hurled cursing insults. Similar behavior had been observed previously and had meant that when I was silent, Mr. M. feared he had murdered me. Finally I inquired whether some event had disturbed him over the weekend. He ignored the question for five minutes and then shouted:

I'll not satisfy your fucking-arsed Freud theory by being angry with my wife.

He suddenly stopped and reported a dream of Friday night:

I carried sick children or guinea pigs in the back of my station wagon, to help them. But they got germs in my back end.

He then recalled that he had had to assist in the burial of a guinea pig on Saturday, saying:

My daughter's guinea pig died. I tried like hell to save it. I was scared. I'm scared as *shit* of death. One time we had a cat that died and I couldn't touch it. I had to have my wife carry it out to the grave. Maybe I'm mad at God for letting things die. God's doing wrong. He shouldn't *kill* things. He's unfair. I don't believe in Heaven. Hell, no wonder I fear death.

On Tuesday he appeared calm and thoughtful. He said:

It became evident that I hate God with a passion. I had a dream last night. I couldn't see anything but a hazy, gray cloud. I thought the words, "The most horrible hate is the core hate, the anal hate." Anality is parsimony. The root core part of my problem is my hate for God. If I can get the roots tranquilized, the trunk and the branches and leaves won't be poison.

He returned to the material of the previous interview. He had heard the pig squealing. The pig lay on its side, paralyzed and quivering. His first impulse was to feed it; to hold it to his chest.

But I saw it was paralyzed. I was afraid to touch it. Germs. Poison. Shitty sick, vile, weak. I'd get it from touching the fur. Finally I gutted up and touched it. I was afraid to look at it. It might die. I'd have to bury it in the cold ground. Oh, Jesus, now I remember. After my mother died, I used to dream my mother had been buried alive and was screaming and clawing to get out. Then I heard that dead people's hair goes on growing and I dreamed she was all hairy.

He cried. He opined that if his mother had not died, he would not have become sick. He castigated his stepmother and continued:

I buried the pig under a tree. By the roots. To fertilize the tree. I want my ashes thrown on a flower bed. In the dream, the animals were sick. In the back. In my anus and colon. I wanted to push them out. Poison and bad. But I had to hold them in and help.

I inquired why the pigs had been in the back of the car.

Hell, I ate them.

I asked whether he feared he might eat the dead animal.

Christ, yes. That's *why*. Did I really want to feed on my dead mother and keep her in me? Shit, yes.

At this point in the interview he felt physically helpless. The couch seemed to him to have spread out.

I feel like I was on the operating table. With my penis exposed. Nekkid. I feel so damned cheap like I was a damned sham. I feel *sick*. I don't want to die. My mother's in Heaven. I've not been a gentleman. I've been a wild animal. She'd be there and she'd be ashamed of me. The dream was just haze. Like looking at a cloud. I see it now. It's white. Now I see a pug nose on it. A lit red light bulb. A baby's head? A darning egg, to hold in the hand? Now it has become a rain cloud. It's angry and raining, now. The nose has gone. Lightning and rain come out of it. I see the tree. My tree. It's not a successful feeding. An angry one. A bad old deal. The storm might kill the tree. Then it would be dead, decayed wood. Worms would eat it like they ate my mother. Now the storm is leaving and the sun's coming through. God. If I were well, I'd have nothing to work on. No aggressive need. I'd be so satiated. I'd end up a damned peeper. Just watch people's faces and reactions. The ball game would be over. I don't want to get well and have to leave you. I'd be unable to see you any more.

A brief summary of the fragment concerning the dream screen experience is in order. He reacted to what he perceived to be a threat of desertion by withdrawal. The guinea pig became ill and Mr. M.'s impulse was to nurse it to prevent its death. The dream of the children in his colon revealed his regressive, cannibalistic method of preventing loss. An elation reaction ensued and seemed to serve both as a denial of the devouring and of the threat of retaliation for ingestion and anger at God. God, as his analyst, was consciously equated with father but unconsciously with mother as indicated by ample prior and subsequent material. During his acute psychosis he was sure his insane (shitty-dirty) thoughts would transmit psychosis to his therapists. His fears that he had murdered his mother were evident from associative material previously produced. It was at this point, then, that the dream screen phenomenon appeared. It will be recalled that his first associations were "Anality is parsimony. The root, core part of my problem is my hate for God. If I can get the roots tranquilized, the trunk and the branches and leaves won't be poison [to my eaters]." The overdetermination of the following statements is obvious enough: the equation of vagina and anus, the fear of massive homosexual desires, the denial of feminine castration, the taking in by eating and retention to prevent loss, the transformation of the eaten through hostility into poison, the murder of the woman by the penis, and the retributive wish to kill through feeding poison via defecation all seem clear. Then in the interview appeared a state somewhere between depersonalization (Blank 1954) and hypnagogia (Isakower 1938).[10]

The symbolism of the associations which appeared during his dreamy state is sufficiently lucid. In addition, following interviews revealed that the meanings of the symbols were preconsciously known to him. The cloud-screen became a breast with a big, attractive nipple which was simultaneously a baby's nose, as was the nipple-breast at the same time a baby's head, to be nursed and held in the hand. Threatened removal of the breast produced fury in the baby whose anger was projected onto the breast which angrily fed the baby-tree and resulted in its death, which then, through reaction formation, did not kill children-flowers but instead nourished them. To reverse the reaction formation, the babies were killed by the hostility-poison which was defecated on them. Mr. M.'s associations to these phenomena led to emotional speculations regarding his reactions to the birth of his sister and the revived fury against the baby which killed the mother, if his own anger did not.

The wishes to eat and to be eaten are clear enough in this material. Then was stated the wish to sleep: "If I were well [that is, reunited with my mother's breast in an objectless state without hostility] I'd have nothing to work on [that is, to grab on to and bite], I'd have no aggressive need. I'd be so satiated." Then came an interesting statement reminiscent of the observations of Spitz (1946, 1950) and Boyer (Chapter 1, this volume) that babies and psychotics watch their mothers' faces and reactions while feeding: "I'd end up a damned peeper [damned because of later scoptophilic tendencies]. Just watch other people's faces and their reactions. The ball game would be over [that is, athletic struggle for the ball and the goal, the breast and reunion]."

Discussion

The case fragments contained in this chapter present common denominators applicable with but slight differences in detail to the six histories from my practice and that provided by Dr. Remus.

[10]See also O. Sperling (1957) and his references.

The mothers of Mrs. K. and Mr. M. had been cyclothymic, and both patients had suffered overt schizophrenic episodes. Although they had begun treatment while actively psychotic, each had been able to tolerate psychoanalysis without alterations in the basic technique. Each had been interviewed four or five times per week in the usual couch situation, and the therapist had maintained his role strictly as clarifier and interpreter. Each had made a definite shift from dealing with the therapist as projections of introjects to a tenuous but clear object relationship, having made of him a generally consistent transference figure while simultaneously identifying with certain of his realistically evaluated ego and superego attitudes. Both analysands had been confronted on previous occasions with separations from the analyst, after the shift from narcissistic to object identification had begun, but neither elation nor dream screen had followed. The earlier separations had been assumed by the analysands to have been for business purposes and had lasted but for a few days. The vacation period had been announced as such and each patient subsequently revealed sharp jealousy and fear of loss of the analyst's love. In addition to the holiday threat was an event in the environment which stirred memories of severe past traumata, each having to do with the loss of the mother. Regression to an elated or hypomanic state occurred, the analysis of which confirmed Lewin's explanations (1950).

How can the appearance of the elations and the dream screens be explained? Each patient had been able to form tenuous object relations in early childhood. However, the mental states of the mothers had left them periodically bereft, probably partly inasmuch as neither possessed a father capable of becoming a satisfactory mother surrogate. During their lives, each patient had turned to various figures in a frantic attempt to regain the earlier relationship with the mother; the sex of the tentative love object was unimportant. When relations with such mother substitutes reached the bedroom phase, each had withdrawn into narcissistic states. In the analytic situation, each was markedly fearful of intimacy with the analyst and used withdrawal of various forms to maintain distance. Nevertheless each had begun to develop a basic trust (Erikson 1950) and to learn to accept the analyst more as a real person. With the concatenation of shift from narcissistic to object identification, threat of loss of the new, good mother and the external event which revived memories of childhood trauma, each renounced the new attachment and regressed to a psychologically objectless state, an attempt to fuse with the breast. The superego was largely renounced, with its archaic, maternally determined facets, and then followed the dream screen experiences, the analysis of which confirmed Lewin's hypotheses, that is, they represented a state of fusion with the breast, a renunciation of ego and object relations. The analyses of the experiences enabled recovery within a few days to the prevacation threat state of relationship with the analyst. It could also be said that each patient regressively sought to deny an object relationship which could again prove disappointing and sought to fuse with the new maternal surrogate, to eat and be eaten by, to prevent loss.

Rycroft's (1951) contention that the dream screen represents an attempt in the course of the analysis to reestablish an object relationship with the mother via the transference seems paradoxical, inasmuch as fusion with the breast is a renunciation or denial of an object relationship. However, the paradox may be only apparent, depending on one's viewpoint. In a personal communication (1959), he added the following data which may reconcile his and my standpoints, explaining a modification of his theme and adding further data regarding his presented case. He stated:

> After the dream he [the patient] projected the introject ["ideal breast"] on to the analyst. The resulting relationship I inaccurately, but I think comprehensively, called an external object-relationship, even though, as I put it, "the external object still has the projected imago of the phantasied breast." What I then called an external object-relationship I should now call a projected internal object-relationship, but I would maintain that my patient's outlook was still one of narcissistic identification, but that it differed dynamically from the prior one in that the projection on to a real person, myself, opened up the possibility of a true object-relationship. Another way of putting it would be to say that the dream screen initiated a double cathexis of the analyst, one narcissistic and identificatory, the other an object cathexis, and that this double positive cathexis neutralized his fear and suspicion of me. It is my view that the events leading up to the dream, the quasi-hallucination, etc., were the process of projection *in statu nascendi.* Although the clinical material I presented showed clearly the importance of the threat of the loss of the newly discovered object I failed to take account of it in my theoretical formulation. This I think is the reason why I interpreted the screen dream in a progressive sense in contradistinction to your regressive interpretation. However, if one draws a distinction between the significance of a screen dream occurring and the interpretation of the screen dream, our apparently contra-

dictory interpretations can be reconciled, since these patients, instead of abandoning their new object when threatened by its loss and actually regressing, only have a dream of regressing and by doing so maintain the new object-relationship. When writing the paper I had the idea that one can only have a dream about the breast if one has got further than primary identification with it, that if it can be visualized it cannot be imagined to be in or attached to the mouth. If this idea, which derives, I think, from Lewin and Clifford Scott, is right, then a screen dream represents an advance in the level of regression, a decrease in the depth of regression, to which the patient can regress if he has made the crucial advance from narcissistic to object identification.

Summary

Visual dream screen phenomena were presented by seven analysands, all of whom suffered from borderline states or schizophrenia. From the information available from their analysis, a tentative hypothesis is offered that dream screen experiences appear in therapy when patients reach the state of development when narcissistic identification is giving way to true object relationships via the transference, when there is a threat of loss of the new object, and when an event occurs in the environment which strongly reminds the analysand of a severe childhood trauma interpreted as desertion by the mother or her surrogate.

Acknowledgments

The author is indebted especially to the following colleagues, who, among others, have made valuable criticisms of this paper: Drs. Stanley Goodman, Bertram D. Lewin, Ramón Parres, José Remus Araico, Charles Rycroft, and Emanuel Windholz. Particular thanks are due to Drs. Milton Wexler and Albert A. Rosner for prepared discussions at meetings.

4

Psychoanalysis in the Treatment of Schizophrenia

I have sought to employ psychoanalysis with few parameters in the office treatment of individuals suffering from schizophrenia. The goal of the experiment has been to determine whether the procedure could be utilized effectively for simultaneous and/or tandem alleviation of psychotic and neurotic components. Inasmuch as insufficient time has elapsed to evaluate adequately the efficacy of the method, this chapter must be considered a report of work in progress.

Eissler (1953) introduced the term *parameter of a technique.* His definition was "the deviation, both quantitative and qualitative, from the basic model technique, that is to say, from a technique which requires interpretation as the exclusive tool. In the basic model technique the parameter is, of course, zero throughout the whole treatment. We therefore would say that the parameter of the technique necessary for the treatment of a phobia is zero in the initial phases as well as in the concluding phases; but to the extent that interpretation is replaced by advice or command in the middle phase, there is a parameter which may . . . be considerable, though temporary" (p. 110). Eissler formulated the following criteria of a parameter if it were to fulfill the conditions which are fundamental to psychoanalysis: "(1) A parameter must be introduced only when it is proved that the basic model technique does not suffice; (2) the parameter must never transgress the unavoidable minimum; (3) a parameter is to be used only when it leads to self-elimination; that is to say, the final phase of the treatment must always proceed with a parameter of zero" (p. 110).

Psychoanalysts generally consider schizophrenia to be an emotional and mental disorder resultant from (at least) emotional deprivation experienced during infancy. Implicit in most writings and explicit in some is the viewpoint that such deprivation is usually found to have persisted throughout all psychosexual developmental levels (Jackson 1958, Kanzer 1954a, Modell 1956). In my experience, it is improbable that schizophrenia can develop without such continuous traumata and probable that such injuries are outwardly more often subtle than gross.

The methodological approach employed in this study has been judged untenable in view of such a philosophy regarding the genesis of schizophrenia, inasmuch as classical psychoanalytic technique has been considered to be designed for the development of projections rather than introjections (Wexler 1957).[1] The procedure was undertaken as an experiment. I, in company with many colleagues, have been confused by bewildering contradictions both in literature and teachings regarding indications for psychoanalysis and psychotherapy. It seemed that some authorities advocated psychotherapy for psychoses and borderline conditions, but while paying lip service to such a stand, appeared to employ psychoanalysis with few if any parameters in the treatment of certain cases of borderline and psychotic conditions. I determined to learn what analysis (in my hands) did with patients of all categories.

Kolb (1956) summarized the "essential" deviations from classical technique in treatment of schizophrenia. He indicated that the initial transference situation demanded patience, tolerance, and ready availability of the analyst, who must have a personality different from that of the child's parents; communication must be established on the basis of the patient's private symbolizations, which are to be interpreted in relation to reality, and the analyst must be an active participant, free to disclose his feelings and the meanings of his actions. Kolb felt that full resolution of the "schizophrenic process" had so far never been achieved, and advised against such a goal because of possible undesirable effects.

Not all analysts have agreed that the modifications indicated as essential by Kolb are required for therapy with psychotics and borderline states. Among American analysts, for example, M. Sperling (1946, 1955, 1957) successfully employed classical technique in the treatment of psychosomatic patients who suffered from such disorders. Jacobson (1943, 1954a,c) and Lewin (1950) indicated no change of technique

[1]Wexler (personal communication 1956) stated, "Introjective processes also occur, but I believe the projective elements in the situation create overwhelming difficulties."

during periods in which their patients were overtly psychotic. Brunswick (1928, Jones 1955), it will be recalled, successfully analyzed the Wolf-Man, relieving him from paranoic psychosis. Brenner (personal communication 1959) successfully analyzed a patient who had been hospitalized for a psychotic episode.

Of particular interest from the standpoint of this study are the observations of Wexler (1951a), who concluded that: (1) in the treatment of schizophrenics the primary task is the restoration of the reasonable ego; (2) between the therapist and the ego rages a battle in which instinctual impulses of all varieties threaten to erupt even in the face of a devastatingly punitive superego which plays an important role, along with urgent instinctual demands, in producing schizophrenic disorganization; and (3) the schizophrenic ego can be strengthened by the therapist's determined active assumption of superego roles. He (1951b) added further: "the suggestion that it is with internal objects that schizophrenics are preoccupied. In the schizophrenic the internal objects are cold and unloving, the paradigm of the unloving mother. The contact originally established through the superego . . . aims at getting the patient to acquire a new internal object, the therapist, who, as an internalized, constant figure helps restore intrapsychic stability and thus facilitates a return of the patient's interest in outside reality." Wexler (personal communication 1956) further stated: "The id-superego struggle represents the conditions which make internalization and therefore stabilization impossible. Id-superego struggles lead to and are consequent on a psychosis. They are not the psychosis itself."

Method

During the years thus far devoted to this experiment, all psychotic patients who have applied for psychiatric care have been accepted in psychoanalysis except for those for whom there was no time, those who could not pay minimal fees, and those few who suffered from involutional psychoses. An additional eighteen schizophrenics have been seen in psychoanalytically oriented psychotherapy. Sixteen of them had insufficient funds or time limitations which made psychoanalysis impossible. In two cases, family interference precluded prolonged contact. They are excluded from this chapter.

As soon as it was determined that the prospective analysand could be reasonably expected to have an unlimited length of time to devote to his treatment, he was informed that the object of the proposed therapy was to make him comfortable with himself; therapy was to be of an experimental nature, without guarantee of complete success, but with some expectation of improvement, and an indefinite period might be spent. He was further told (1) he would lie on the couch unless he felt too great anxiety at some time: then his impulses to sit would be discussed and if immoderate anxiety persisted, he could sit; (2) he was to attempt to say whatever came into his mind during the course of the interviews and to report emotions and physical sensations; (3) the analyst would not accept cancelations for any reason;[2] (4) the analyst would be absent on certain set federal holidays and for short periods in addition to a summer vacation period; the analysand could omit other federal holidays without payment provided he let the analyst know of his intention two weeks before the planned absence; (5) the analyst usually asked his analysands their vacation preferences during the summer months, took a consensus, and adjusted his time to conform with the majority choice; the analysand was permitted to take the time he must without payment, but if he chose some other time, he would be charged; (6) no bills were sent out: he was to pay on scheduled dates and the fees were to cover specific times; (7) analysis would not be undertaken without an agreement that he would act on no potentially irreversible decisions without his and the analyst's understanding the implications of his proposed act; (8) the analyst conceived his role not to be one of giving advice but of learning everything possible about the analysand and reporting the knowledge to the patient when he considered him ready to hear it; (9) he could expect to have many emotional reactions to the analyst and the analytic situation: some would seem mysterious to him: he would perhaps become discouraged periodically and all his reactions would be subject to analysis; (10) the analyst expected psychological tests to be taken at the beginning of treatment and every six months thereafter during the analysis; (11) there would be a trial period lasting no longer than one month during which either analysand or analyst could alter or terminate the therapeutic relationship; and (12) whatever transpired between analyst and patient would be considered to be confidential, although the analyst reserved the right to communicate material to people concerned when

[2]Haak (1957) listed nine reasons for dealing strictly with the matter of fees. His fifth point was: "The analysis must involve a sacrifice." Haak meant financial sacrifice. Every analysis involves sacrifices. In my opinion, financial sacrifice is of less importance in interfering with successful analysis than accumulation of guilt within the patient and hostility within the analyst.

he considered such a move to be essential, after informing the patient of his decision.[3]

With some prospective analysands, all the abovegiven statements are made within the period of one interview. With others, they are made over a period of several. Among the group included in this chapter, the couch position was assumed after a delay no longer than two weeks. In most cases, the agreement to begin the experiment was made within a maximum of two or three sessions. Such a procedure would seem to indicate the presence of an unusually large capacity for rational ego operation on the part of the subjects. The data which follow may clarify this issue somewhat.

Extensive notes were written during each interview. In my opinion, this procedure has abetted rather than hindered therapy. It is often initially interpreted by the analysand as proving the worth to the analyst of the patient's productions. My impression, however, is that a scientific model is furnished as a substratum and that it encourages the maintenance of distance between analysand and analyst and between the observing ego of the patient and produced data. More will be said about the subject of the advisability of distance-maintenance below.

In only four cases was it necessary to speak to a relative about anything at all; on occasions the brief conversations were unscheduled. Hours were regularly scheduled four times weekly; occasionally the interviews were increased to five, and in one case, six. Telephone conversations with patients were very rare. Of the two cases which might be judged as outright failures, one telephoned frequently during the first weeks of her therapy; the other was the only one seen six times weekly.

As is clear, the beginning atmosphere of the situation was one in which the potential analysand was told that treatment was to be experimental in nature, but at the same time he was inferentially informed that the analyst was unafraid of the subject's anxiety, love, or anger and that he could expect some degree of setting of behavior limits. Some analysts who have reviewed this paper have felt that such inference

[3]Wexler (personal communication 1956) suggested that items (1) and (9) constitute parameters. I am undecided. They may constitute a modification of treatment from the "basic model technique" (Eissler 1953). While items (1) and (9) are to a degree prejudicing preparatory remarks, if they constitute parameters at all, and are not just explanatory, educative preliminary instructions, they must belong to those parameters which are consistent with psychoanalysis in which the basic treatment technique is not modified. I hold with almost every other colleague I know that questions, clarifications, and so forth, do not constitute deviations from basic technique.

constitutes the employment of a parameter. Others have stated it as their opinion that no analysis begins without such inferences. The patient was also told, again indirectly, that he would have ample time to work out his conflicts (Braatøy 1954). I obviously considered defining conditions to be important from the beginning. Such a procedure clarifies as subjects of analysis variations of behavior which might otherwise be less clearly foci of investigation.

No patient to whom the proposal was made refused to enter analysis. Each, with one exception, was referred by a physician, social worker, psychologist, psychiatrist, or psychoanalyst whom he had consulted voluntarily. One woman was dissatisfied with the psychiatrist who was treating her and came to me after one of my former analysands had spoken with her.

All who treat schizophrenics seem to agree that the initial phase of psychotherapeutic work with the schizophrenic involves the *establishment of contact*, so that the physician may form as it were a bridge between the patient and reality (E. B. Brody 1952). Some psychoanalysts have stressed the need to foster a positive transference, at least in the earlier phases of therapy (Alexander 1931, Federn 1952, Nunberg 1921). The analysands whose cases are here reported appeared to have established positive feelings before they ever got to the office. The analyst's approach apparently cemented such feelings and established immediate contact. That the contact remained workably intact will be demonstrated later.

Let us go back a step. What happens before the psychoanalysis is suggested?

The majority of psychotic cases are initially treated essentially as are neurotics. In certain cases special rules are made as conditions of therapy. Such conditions are always in the direction of indicating the patient's responsibilities and of giving ego and superego support. They imply the analyst's awareness that the potential analysand may need assistance in maintaining his obligations. In the present series, there were two instances in which special conditions were set. They will be presented shortly. The initial communications of the analyst's self-confidence and lack of apprehension regarding the patient's fears and anger are nonverbal. At times, potential analysands have attended other psychiatrists and/or psychoanalysts who have overtly or covertly warned them that entering psychoanalysis would be a dangerous undertaking for them. When such data are verbalized, I agree that analysis will be a difficult procedure and state that the analysand can expect periods of regression.

Case Material

Mrs. K.[4] was a 37-year-old housewife who had become severely overtly psychotic during a pregnancy. She was three times hospitalized and twice treated with courses of electroconvulsions. Following her third immurement and second series of shocks she was briefly euphoric, but soon regressed to a terror-stricken, hallucinated, deluded, and depressed state. She became intensely fearful of the (factually present) hostility which she sensed within her psychiatrist onto whom she had transferred her hatred and fear of her father, and she was equally or more afraid of her hostility toward him. Typically, the apprehensions could be traced to fears of being eaten and of destroying through devouring. She met an erstwhile schizophrenic woman whom I had analyzed, apparently successfully. She had read psychological literature extensively and intensively. Despite (and because of) her psychiatrist's warning that her leaving him would irrevocably harm her and that her entering psychoanalysis with me was the worst possible step (because I was a money-grabber and unethical), she appeared, clamoring for psychoanalysis. Nothing else would do. She was still actively delusional and hallucinated. She presented her past and present histories systematically and offered interpretations regarding the development of her illness which later proved to have been largely accurate. She had been a chronic delinquent, promiscuous, overtly homosexual, impulsive and an "as if" person (H. Deutsch 1942). During the first hour she stressed the wealth of her brother and father. In the first three interviews, I indicated uncertainty whether analysis was applicable for her.

During the fourth hour, although no agreement had been reached that she would be accepted in therapy of any form, she began to manipulate me financially. She had learned, she thought, my regular fees, but, of course, she would be able to pay only much less. I asked my first question, other than previous rare requests for amplification: "Why did you emphasize in the first interview the wealth of your brother and father?" She said that had been to assure me of eventual payment. I determined her real financial status and said that if I decided to take her in therapy, I would charge a low and reasonable fee, which would be paid according to my regular schedule. I then inquired how she would feel, paying for her therapy with money taken from her father and/or brother. She replied she wanted to feel in-

[4]See Chapter 3 for further discussion of Mrs. K. and Mr. M. (below).

dependent, whereon she was asked why she had not repaid to her brother from her ample savings money lent her for hospitalization. She replied that it had been a gift of love. She then revealed that she owed previous psychiatrists large sums of money. I told her that she would be taken into analysis for a trial period, only after she had paid them. I also informed her that her fee would be subject to subsequent increase should her financial situation improve or should she take money from a relative. In this case, I actively assumed the role of external superego. It could rightly be stated that the pressure involved is outside analysis.

Mr. M. was a man in his middle 30s. After he had been twice hospitalized and given electroshock for schizophrenia, he turned to taking large doses of tranquilizers, which helped him not at all. Before he was accepted in psychoanalysis, I stated that a condition of treatment was the renunciation of such drugs. In this case, my move was considered to constitute ego support.

The use of parameters, as I understand the term, during the course of analysis has been most sparing. Examples of their employment follow.

During the analysis of Mr. A., a severely obsessional man who had fixed delusions, he settled into a rut of masochistic, stubborn defiance which did not respond to interpretations. After several months of such behavior, I told him to set a date for termination. He decided he would stop 30 years hence. I arbitrarily set as an end date one year (Freud 1918).

Mr. X.[5] became increasingly delinquent in paying his bills. Eventually he was told he would have to pay his bill accurately at the beginning of the session at which it was due or the hour would be terminated and he would be charged for the interview or interviews until the obligation was met.

After three and a half years of analysis, Mrs. C. (Boyer 1956), who suffered from an ambulatory schizophrenic condition with hysterical features, lost her younger sister in a car accident. She had been the middle sister of three whose ages were minimally separated. Both parents had been immature. The mother was cold and engrossed in a continuing symbiotic relationship with her own mother. She had quite literally put her children into a garage during the daytime and forbidden them entrance to the house except at mealtimes. The father was capable of communciation of affection only with infants. The three

[5]See Chapter 2 for further discussion of this patient.

girls found security in their own interaction, and at least the middle one was largely unable to distinguish herself from the others. Her analysis had gone well. No evidence of psychotic thinking had been observed for many months, although some concretization of thought remained. Psychological tests reflected the improvement clinically manifested. The sister was killed on a Friday night. Mrs. C. sought to reach the analyst by telephone, her first attempt. He was out of town. She responded with a brief and seemingly superficial psychotic episode, persisting until the morning of her Monday interview. At the end of that interview, during which she had lapsed into a panic and highly unrealistic thinking, the analyst put his arm round her and told her she need not fear return to insanity. Her response was to repeat over and over, "My doctor, you are my doctor." Her psychotic episode disappeared. She stated she had been consciously trying to go crazy in order to make her sister's death to have been false.

There were a few occasions when it was strongly suggested that an individual cease drinking or face a feared situation, in order that the reasons behind the action might be uncovered. Such parameters were temporary.

The third example cited was the only unusual one employed.

These statements do not imply that other steps which could be labeled as falling outside the realm of classical analysis were not taken. However, such steps were the results of unconscious motivations on my part, countertransferences, plus ordinary stupidity and inexperience. I am not claiming the technique was unvarying for all cases (Glover 1955). As Anna Freud (1959b) said, each patient makes of the therapeutic process a special mixture. His relationship is with a therapist whose personality is of signal importance and constitutes a new experience, partly educational. The kinds and degrees of externalizations and the development of the transference depend on the patient's personality structure, the variable components of hysteria, obsessive character traits, sadism, masochism, and so forth, as they interact with the new object as well as the mental representation of the new object.

My practice is conducted almost entirely in the office. Only one of the patients whose data are included in this report was at any time hospitalized while under my care. My experience has been that hospitalization for psychotic episodes is usually unnecessary. Of course, this opinion is partly determined by the natures of patients who have been referred to me. However, my experience is affirmed by the treatment of psychotics in various groups who do not choose to hospitalize them (Eaton and Weil 1955).

To define stages of the analysis of schizophrenics is difficult. Treatment might be divided ideally into two phases: (1) the establishment within the analysand of reasonably stable ego and superego introjects, a phase which would roughly coincide with removal of psychotic thinking mechanisms or at least marked diminution of their cathexes, and with the development of true transference rather than the continued employment of transferences; and (2) analysis of the neurosis.

It is apparent that an entire person applies for help. He is not only psychotic. "Not all modalities of the ego undergo regression in the same patient, and the various ego functions are differently affected from patient to patient" (Arlow 1952, p. 114). He has lived through all the periods of psychosexual development, although because of varying degrees of ego-stunting and environmental vicissitudes, later conflictual stages have left in him neurotic compromises which are distorted in degrees of grossness.[6] In his treatment, psychotic and neurotic material may emerge simultaneously. While the analyst is obliged initially—and initially here refers to a period which may cover some years—to aim at providing new ego and superego models, there are many times when the products of neurotic conflicts appear and toward which the analyst's attention is turned to such an extent he cannot ignore them. Nevertheless, during the first phase of the treatment the primary goal is kept uppermost in the therapist's mind. This requires a substratum of directed awareness. Thus analysis begins with a consistent pattern of confrontations with distortions, contradictions, and other abandonments of contact with reality, coincident with interpretations (as a rule) regarding the defensive meanings of hallucinations, delusions, etcetera. While I would not go so far as to follow Wexler's experimental procedure of very active assumption of superego role (1951b), I do offer superego support as illustrated by the above examples and in other less gross ways, as through choosing to stress the analysand's anxiety when he has transgressed morality and by calling asocial and antisocial actions by their accurate names. Within the framework of the therapeutic situation, such support is not limited to the prohibitive functions alone.

[6]The long-standing debate on whether psychotics do or do not achieve genital primacy is as yet unresolved. My experience with native neurotic males as contrasted with those who were reared in or whose parents were reared in Austria and Germany has led me to believe that but few American males achieve genital primacy. It has been my impression that there are psychotics who have reached as great a degree of genital primacy as is to be found in the "average" American male neurotic. However, my figures would not bear statistical scrutiny.

As Kolb (1956) stated, initial communication must be established on the basis of the patient's private symbolizations, and they are to be interpreted as a rule in terms of objective reality. But here a great difficulty arises. The question of what is at any moment subjective and what is objective reality is scarcely subject to review here. However, one must keep in mind the segment of reality one strives to communicate, at any particular time. Three vignettes may illustrate this point.

When, after several years during which she had not been in psychoanalysis, Mrs. L. returned in a schizoaffective (largely manic) state, she imitated animals in gesture and voice. Her contact with reality was very tenuous. Because of my memory of the meanings of her symbolizations during her previous period of analysis, I understood her to be expressing her conflicts in the storybook manner of children. However, I told her that it seemed to me that she was behaving and speaking as she was to impress me that she was very frightened and needed help immediately, although she assumed I would not have immediate time for her. Her mimicry of animals abruptly ceased and she was able to express herself in near rational terms for several minutes. The animal caricatures did not recur.

When Mrs. D. first reclined, she saw knobs of cabinets at the foot of the couch as eyes which were looking at her; she made of the grain of the wood other facial features. She strove to, but could not, compose them into a single face and was frightened because her perceptions indicated to her, as did similar illusions elsewhere, that she was being spied on. I responded that she had entered treatment with an awareness that her innermost secrets would have to be shared with me so that she and I might be enabled to learn together wherein lay distortions and urges which were not useful in terms of adult existence. At a later time when she saw the same features and was indicating their similarities to the facial features of various members of her family, I suggested she was striving to identify her split ego parts and to find herself as a separate entity.[7]

From these comments, however, one should not derive the idea that it is my belief that interpretation of content is initially of *primary* importance. More significant appears to be an attitude of calm optimism and lack of aggression on the analyst's part, tempered by the early warning that success is not guaranteed. As Fromm-Reichmann (1952) said: "With the schizophrenic, unqualified thriftiness in content interpretation is indicated . . . [the schizophrenic] is many times aware himself of the content meaning of his communications . . . and [he]

[7]This interpretation I owe to Dr. José Remus-Araico.

needs help in understanding the genetics and dynamics. . . ." (p. 96) To quote Arlow (1952): "An interpretation regarding content arouses in the patient feelings of guilt concerning what he considers . . . dangerous impulses. An interpretation regarding defense, on the other hand, makes the patient feel that the analyst appreciates how he is struggling against the impulse. If the analyst is not a superego figure, he is certainly, at such moments, a witness in the struggle between the impulse and the patient's own superego. An interpretation regarding defense, therefore, serves to restore somewhat the patient's damaged self-esteem, and it confirms that small portion of his mature ego in its trust of the analyst and of the therapeutic procedure. In this way, a relationship to a real external object, the analyst, is strengthened" (p. 114). Thus, during the first phase of therapy, and particularly at its beginning, while attention is called to distortions and contradictions, isolations and denials, etcetera, concurrently the usual emphasis of content interpretations is toward their defensive nature.

As was stated before, no patient to whom psychoanalysis was offered with the approach delineated has refused therapy. Thus we assume from the beginning the presence of a tentative positive transference situation among the patients here reported. It is well known that the transference relationship of the schizophrenic is volatile and in the nature of a testing experience. Fromm-Reichmann (1950) emphasized the hindrance resulting from incorrect interpretations and pretense of understanding. With these observations I am in complete agreement. The initial doubting trust accorded the analyst is tenuous. However, I cannot hold with Federn's advocacy of maintenance of the positive transference with whatever maneuvers seem indicated to support it (1952). The patient's lack of confidence in his environment is accompanied by similar judgment of his own defenses against anxiety. It reflects "the inconsistent and contradictory nature of early object relationship with his parents" (Arlow 1952). The maintenance of a positive transference, then, indirectly (at least) confirms the patient's fears of the power of his anger and his projected anger. No analyst can pretend with success to be someone he is not, and schizophrenics above all patients can sense his anxieties and hypocrisies. Kolb's warning (1956) that the analyst must be different from the analysand's parents seems superfluous. "Consistency in the therapist's attitude and consistency in the interpretive effort create the atmosphere which makes therapy possible. They constitute for the patient a salutary experience, making possible a piecemeal introjection of the warm and reasonable approach of the analyst as a superego figure" (Arlow 1950, p. 114). Part of this consistency, which is perhaps not sufficiently underlined in many writings, is repetitious reminding of the patient of the tentative nature of interpretations and regular encouragement of his active cooperation in modifying answers to enigmas, a step which assists him in reducing the severity of his superego by permitting him to view his new parent model as fallible.

It is to be remembered that with inadequate differentiation of ego and id, tensions are often fixated to physical phenomena. The most primitive psychological organization, that which exists before object and ego remain fused, is characterized by decreases and increases of inner tensions. At that stage of development, the psyche can neither register its needs or experience them as wishes, nor provide for their relief. The tensions, not yet structuralized, remain on the physical level without psychological elaboration (Braatøy 1954). It is a common experience when one deals with psychotic or borderline patients to find tensions tied to physical levels, whether these be in the nature of the phenomena usually labeled psychosomatic (M. Sperling 1957), postural states (Braatøy 1954), or so-called organ neuroses. Their use of a double language (F. Deutsch and Murphy 1955) is common and its analysis is mandatory. In a previous report (Chapter 2, this volume) I have reported a fragment of the history of a schizophrenic whose analysis was given tremendous impetus through repetitious direction of his attention to physical tension and movements.

> For some months I had indicated to him that at certain times he cleared his throat, lifted his head, tensed certain muscles, or made various movements. During one interview, when I had several times called attention to his repeatedly touching his face, a phenomenon one meaning of which we had determined to signify he was reassuring himself he was alive, he began to talk of Kafka's *Metamorphosis*. Just as he related that the hero's sister had become disgusted with him after his change into an insect, Mr. J. suddenly pictured himself as a fly, crawling about the ceiling and walls of the office, eluding attack and in a position to watch his analyst. With this experience, he became acutely aware that he felt unreal, that he believed a part of him was floating about the room in the form of the fly but his body was lifeless as his hands clung in desperation to the couch. As upon numerous subsequent occasions, his recovery of a feeling of personal integration was dramatically illustrated in the interview proper. In the midst of his loss of identity, when he was the fly, he defecated on the ceiling and wall and finally on the analyst. When the therapist struck at the fly and barely brushed it, Mr. J. touched his face and felt real.

Such dramatic episodes serve to call the attention of patients, sometimes at long last, to the fixation of physical phenomena of tensions, whether these are in greater part neurotically determined or are the result of lack of differentiation of ego and id. Such occurrences, however, are not commonplace. More frequently when only clarifying and interpretive techniques are used, rather than cathartic techniques such as advocated by Braatøy (1954), we see in the severely obsessional personality who has employed muscular control to avoid awareness of tensions, the appearance of annoyance which becomes anger. Such responses are usually called release phenomena.

Results

Thirteen schizophrenic cases supply the data for this study. Twelve[8] had seen other psychoanalysts or psychiatrists who confirmed the diagnoses and recommended supportive or physical therapies or commitment.

In the ensuing résumé of their progress in analysis, Rorschach tests confirmed clinical judgment except where otherwise noted.

Mr. A. was a rigidly obsessive and compulsive man of 44. He had been deluded for 30-odd years. His analysis lasted six years, 1,200 hours. There was no evidence of psychosis after two years; there was no regression during the next seven years. Obsessions and compulsions persisted but were much less troublesome. His character structure was modified, and he achieved good social functioning.

[8]Mr. A. had been treated supportively for some ten years by three psychiatrists. He had also been interviewed by two psychoanalysts who diagnosed paranoia and advised against analysis. Mrs. K. had been treated with electroconvulsive therapy by two psychiatrists and supportively by a psychoanalyst. Mr. X. had been treated supportively for over a year by a psychoanalyst. He had been discharged from military service as schizophrenic. Mr. M. had been twice hospitalized and received ECT. He had also been treated supportively by three psychiatrists. Mr. P. had been treated supportively for over a year by a training analyst and diagnosed by two other psychiatrists. Mr. R. was interviewed by a psychiatrist who confirmed the diagnosis. A psychoanalyst refused to take him in therapy of any kind on the ground that it would be "too dangerous." Mrs. Y. was treated with ECT on two occasions; a staff conference of psychiatrists and psychoanalysts diagnosed her malady. Mrs. T. underwent two years of analysis after her therapy with the author had failed. The second analyst confirmed the diagnosis. Mrs. O. was treated by two psychiatrists supportively. Miss Q. was interviewed by a number of psychiatrists and psychoanalysts, all of whom recommended physical therapies or commitment. Mrs. S. was treated supportively by a psychiatrist. Mrs. U. was treated supportively by a psychiatrist for several years. Two psychoanalysts diagnosed schizophrenia.

Mrs. K. (Chapter 3, this volume) suffered an hysterical character disorder. She was 39. An acute psychotic episode had resulted in hospitalization and the administration of electroconvulsive therapy. Analysis lasted two and a half years, 500 hours. She abruptly stopped treatment in the heat of acting out. There was no psychotic thinking discernible after one and a half years; no regression had occurred during the next three and a half years, despite severe marital conflicts. Emotional lability persisted, though with greatly reduced intensity. She returned for further analysis of dependency and moral masochism; her treatment lasted three more years and was terminated after significant structuralization had been achieved. Some 20 years later, in a situation of great external stress, she suffered her only subsequent psychotic relapse and killed herself, using drugs.

Mr. X. (Chapter 2, this volume) was a rigidly obsessive and compulsive man of 33. Delusions and hallucinations could be traced for fifteen years. Analysis lasted almost six years, 1,000 hours. No psychotic thinking persisted after four years; there was no regression during the next four years. There remained obsessive thinking and compulsive behavior of greatly reduced intensity. Chronic delinquency was abandoned. He made a good social adjustment.

Mr. M. (Chapter 3, this volume) was a man of 35 who suffered from an hysterical personality disorder. He had experienced gradual withdrawal for three years, culminating in an acute psychotic flare-up which was treated intramurally by electroconvulsive therapy. Analysis lasted three years, 450 hours. He retained unusual contact with his unconscious during the entire analysis, but there was no evidence of psychosis after two years. During the ensuing two and a half years his neurosis continued to improve. He developed a remarkably acute sense of humor and no symptoms remained except for occasional tension headaches.

Mrs. Y. (Chapter 11, this volume) was a 32-year-old woman who had an hysterical personality disorder. She underwent two acute catatonic episodes during the course of less than a year, each of which was treated intramurally with electroconvulsive therapy. Analysis lasted four years, 750 hours, and was terminated largely because of the hostility of her husband. No clinical evidence of psychosis existed after one year, although Rorschach tests revealed traces of schizophrenic thinking throughout the analysis. Sexual maladjustment persisted at termination. Four years later Mrs. Y. suffered an acute hypomanic psychosis and resumed psychoanalysis, the first two weeks of which were conducted intramurally. Severe depression followed the excited phase of her illness. No clinical or psychological evidence of psychosis existed after six months. Analysis lasted thirteen months, 225 hours. At termination she was free of neurotic symptomatology. There has been no regression during the ensuing two years.

Mrs. M. was a very girlish woman of 26 who had suffered from pseudoneurotic schizophrenia for eight years. Hysterical symptoms predominated. Analysis with me lasted four years, 750 hours, and was ended because I interrupted my practice. She retained unusual contact with her unconscious, but after two and a half years did not give clinical evidence of psychosis beyond some concretization of thought, with the exception of the episode described above (p. 71). She was transferred for further analysis which has lasted one and a half years, 300 hours, and is being terminated as "successful." There has been no further psychotic regression.

Mrs. O. was a 29-year-old woman who had suffered from pseudoneurotic schizophrenia for 15 years. Hysterical symptoms predominated. She was seen in psychotherapy for a year and a half, 150 interviews, and made a borderline social adjustment but had improved little. Three years later she underwent an acute psychotic episode while pregnant and was treated by eight months of analysis, 150 hours. Termination was consequent on financial difficulties. No evidence of psychosis persisted after about six months, and there has been no regression in three and a half more years although she has borne another child. Frigidity and phobias remain.

Mr. P. was a 50-year-old man who had suffered from pseudoneurotic schizophrenia for 35 years. He had undergone previous psychotherapy because of hysterical and obsessive symptoms and overt homosexual activities with a son. Analysis lasted two and a half years, 450 interviews. Psychotic thinking persisted for a year and a half; there has been no regression in six subsequent years. Neurotic sexual symptoms and obsessional handling of money persist.

Miss Q. was 27. She had suffered from schizophrenia for twelve years. Analysis lasted three and a half years, 800 hours. There was little discernible change. During nine subsequent years she has been treated supportively by various therapists. It is unlikely that she would have been able to be maintained extramurally were it not for independent means.

Mr. R. was 29, an overt homosexual, a pseudoneurotic schizophrenic. Analysis lasted one year, 200 hours, and was terminated because of his having to move to a distant area. Psychotic thinking remained, but he was in better control of his impulses and functioned socially in an improved manner. He was refused analysis elsewhere because, in the words of the analyst he consulted, "of the danger of regression." In correspondence, Mr. R. stated he had continued to improve over the next seven years. Inversion persisted, but did not again interfere with his professional life.

Mrs. S. was 25, a pseudoneurotic schizophrenic. Analysis was abruptly terminated after four months, 60 hours, for external reasons. Confusion had abated and she had begun to accept responsibility. During the first year after cessation of analysis, sexual acting out was rampant. She then stabilized. During four subsequent years follow-up interviews revealed no indications of psychosis, although Rorschach tests continued to reveal "traces of psychotic thinking." Her neurotic symptoms have diminished in intensity.

Mrs. T. was a 37-year-old woman whose hysterical symptoms and chronic alcoholism had masked schizophrenia for at least ten years. Analysis lasted two and a half years, 500 hours. Psychotic behavior and thinking and severe mood swings ceased after one and a half years. She became a neurotic drinker and her violent acting out largely abated although analysis was abruptly terminated by mutual acting out on the parts of her husband and Mrs. T. A year later she had reverted to her former state. Two further years of analysis with another therapist were fruitless. During the ensuing six years she has lived marginally and has been periodically hospitalized.

Mrs. U. was 35. Severe hysterical symptoms had masked schizophrenia for about 20 years. She had undergone three years of psychotherapy without improvement, elsewhere. Analysis continued for seven years, 1,000 hours. After four years there was no clinical evidence of psychosis; after six, Rorschach tests were interpreted as normal. During the six years since the termination of her analysis there has been no psychotic regression, although she retains a phobia which prevents her driving a car. Recently she reentered analysis for removal of her phobia. In five months there has been but slow progress.

Discussion

A number of important symposia have considered the essential nature of psychoanalysis and its applicability to conditions other than fairly standard transference neuroses.[9] The consensus of opinion on the

[9]A Symposium on the Theory of the Therapeutic Results of Psycho-analysis, Marienbad 1936; The Traditional Psycho-analytic Technique and Its Variations, New York 1952; The Widening Scope of Indications for Psycho-analysis, Harrison, N. Y., 1954; Psychoanalysis and Dynamic Psychotherapy, Los Angeles 1955.

part of participants has been that the employment of parameters is necessary when analysts deal with such conditions. It is here held that the technique described in this paper more nearly approaches classical psychoanalysis than the literature indicates to be advisable or possible. There are a number of areas, however, in which the efficacy of the experimental technique here employed for the treatment of schizophrenics is as yet questionable. It may be that the surprisingly good results indicated are the consequence of something in my personality and are not to be considered proof of the applicability of the method. Then the persons dealt with here had sufficient ego strength to permit them to live extramurally and to be seen in the office. Again, the series of analysands is too small and the time elapsed too short to validate the method—and there is the possibility that it could be validated only by an analyst whose personality is similar to mine. If the technique be applicable to schizophrenics such as the range included in this group, the results still cannot be used to advocate generalization to all schizophrenics. No claim is made that any patient has been permanently relieved of his psychosis or that the alteration in character structure or neurosis is not subject to future change. As Wexler (personal communication 1956) indicated, the alteration of neurotic elements at times suppresses psychotic features, although this generally happens during the acute phase.

Nevertheless, there appears to be a demonstrated tendency in the progression of therapy in this group of schizophrenics which indicates that they achieve ego growth and modification of their superego structures and become capable of the development and resolution of true transference neuroses.

There is an apparent discrepancy between the indicated and as yet unproven results of the experiment and the theoretical prognostication voiced by Wexler and others. It seems unlikely that the discrepancy can be resolved by assuming that the individuals treated were misdiagnosed. It is true that no patient who had required lengthy hospitalization was seen. In addition, there was no instance of a deteriorated schizophrenic. All analysands were ambulatory, and most had a fairly sizable "reasonable ego" to start with. Nevertheless, with one exception, all had been adjudged psychotic by other psychiatrists and/or psychoanalysts, each of whom had recommended treatments other than psychoanalysis. There is no doubt that some of these cases would have been hospitalized for treatment with other therapists.

It would appear that the discrepancy may be resolved by considering two factors: (1) what transpires during the first phase of treatment, and (2) personal attributes of the therapist.

The First Phase of the Analysis

The atmosphere of the beginning of analysis was one in which there was an appeal to the ego of the patient. He was invited to participate in a mutually conducted experimental process. At the same time, there was a clear setting of rules and at times a more direct appeal to the controlling aspects of the superego. He was directly told of his responsibilities in the proposed analysis. One potential analysand was required to take a moral step as a condition of analysis. At the same time, there was implied reassurance of available unlimited time, of expected regression, and of lack of anxiety on the analyst's part. There was an implied but clear statement that the analyst chose to deal only with the analysand, one which inferred he was the patient's ally alone. The analyst inferred his determination to maintain an observing distance. He then undertook therapy in an atmosphere which made it obvious he was on the side of the ego (reality) and one aspect of the superego (morality) but he was unafraid of eruptions from the id, either the analysand's or his own.

When an analysand assumes the couch position, his contacts with the analyst are immediately diminished. Except for the entrance and exit of each interview, he maintains contact almost exclusively by hearing. When a neurotic patient lies on the couch, he is invited to regress. Stone (1954) said: "Most important in the ultimate dynamic meaning of this [analytic] ensemble is the relative emotional vacuum which the analysand must fill with transference impulses and fantasies, and the parallel reduction of reality-testing opportunity which facilitates the same process" (p. 571). When a psychotic patient takes the couch position his state is already more regressed. His impulses and fantasies are often rife. He appears to be reaching for new objects, partial or whole, to replace the old ones within his ego and superego to which he ambivalently clings. In his hunger for introjects which will be emphasized because of the regression-inducing analytic ensemble, he will of necessity use primarily his hearing. Thus the words, voice tones, and sounds of the analyst will be of great importance.

The severely regressed patient is intensely dependent on the observing, interacting, and educating analyst (Balint 1959). Like the baby, his means of communication are often preverbal. With the analysands described in this chapter, there was no uniform regression. The content of verbal messages was important. But of importance also were the voice tones and emphases; the analyst's heard movements were at times of tangible significance. The only patient in this group who could tolerate hours of silence on the part of the analyst during the first few months of therapy was Mr. A. The analyst was more noisy than is usual with the analyses of neurotics, in every other case. Frequently, however, his communications were in the form of grunts, hm's, yes's, and so forth. Open verbal reassurances were rare, although the third illustration of communication of reality (page 73) is an example of a type of procedure sometimes initially employed which is simultaneously reassuring and educative. Remarks never intentionally and rarely unintentionally went beyond confrontation, clarification, questioning for amplification, and interpretation. Reconstruction was regularly employed where indicated. In a previous paper (Chapter 1, this volume) I have postulated that auditory overstimulation can be traumatic to the formation of the ego, and in Wangh's discussion of the same paper (1955) he suggested that a common path of orality and the auditory sensation might be operative in the patient described. There was no doubt that in that instance the voice of the mother, quite apart from its contents, became a bad introject and the voice of the therapist a good one. However, I very rarely intentionally alter my voice. I never knowingly play an artificial role. At times when a patient is long silent, after interpretations have failed to induce verbal communication, I gently cajole or indicate monetary economy. At rare times, I will compare the patient's behavior to that of a sulky child or tell a pointed brief story, the content of which is relevant to the important subject matter of the moment. With psychotics, while I make more noise during the initial phase, that noise, I believe, does not transcend standard analytic preparatory technique, and does not constitute a parameter.

In the case of Mrs. P. (Chapter 1, this volume), no psychoanalysis was undertaken, although such a procedure would have been attempted had family attitude and finances permitted. With the exceptions that she was seen face to face and hospitalized and that a gift was given, my usual technique was employed as it is with severely regressed schizophrenic patients during the initial phase of therapy. I refer here to her comments regarding the voice: "My husband is trying to make me ill now." "He tries to provoke me with his voice and his words. . . . That voice scares me. It leaves me completely alone. . . . It takes him out of me in every way possible. . . . I feel emptied out with that voice." I had given the patient at one time some candy. "My husband said I said the candy made me well. It was your voice. Even when you said the wrong things. Your sweet, purring voice, like a cat. It babies me in my mind. It says 'You're a nice girl. You've got a nice figure.' You like me and that makes me feel well. You want to help me just for myself. You don't try to make me do things for you." "Now I don't let my mother's voice go inside of me. It's not my husband made me sick. It's my parents' voices. I want to be empty of them" (p. 15).

It is my conviction that the introjections which take place during the initial phase of the analysis, while numerous and at times vague, are the result of taking in preverbal as well as verbal communications. Mrs. P. introjected her concept of my evaluation of her. She was correct when she said I liked her. I do not believe an analyst can remain completely objective about an analysand. Perhaps my positive feelings for her made it possible for her to begin to like herself. Her statement that I made her, by my voice, feel as though she had a nice figure was a distortion. She did not in fact have a nice figure. Many other psychotics have made the same statements: that the analyst liked them and wanted to help them for themselves. Despite the fact that I sometimes became annoyed, I did in truth like all these analysands. And I did want to help them to get well for themselves. But I also had a personal investment in their improvement. A second and perhaps even more important introjection has been that of my calm, expectant, hopeful attitude with its constant implication that gratifications can be postponed with benefit to the recipient. Two elements combined to produce the analysand's evaluation of the therapist's feelings toward them: their own need for love and his consistent, sympathetic listening combined with a patient, accepting, but simultaneously guiding attitude. I did not *tell* them in so many words that I liked them. The third parameter, in which I put my arm around the distressed woman, was the gross exception. That parameter, as were the other two, were subsequently "fully" analyzed, but the communication effects obviously remained.

As was illustrated above, under the heading *Method*, preverbal communications are of signal importance with many, if not all, regressed patients. The analyst's understanding of them and communication of their meanings enables patients not only to break through resistances and to help them to learn about realities but to restore body-ego deficiencies and to separate self from nonself. In addition, their interpretation helps analysands to progress in ego growth to where they can accurately communicate in *words*. It is not unusual, as we all know from clinical experience, that the words being *said* may have little importance as messages in themselves, but constitute the contributions of a decathected part of the self, while the meaningful cathexis is invested in the posture and movements of the moment.

A number of analysts have stressed the role of the superego in schizophrenia, as, for example, Pious (1949) and Wexler (1951b). There can be no doubt that mitigation of the archaic severity of the superego is essential for lasting benefit. Throughout the first phase of the analysis, I stress my awareness of the patient's superego struggles and patiently, although indirectly, educate him in regard to a more realistic evaluation of a perhaps more appropriate degree of guilt for actions and thoughts. In general, my philosophy in this regard is that guilt is appropriate when one's behavior, without just cause, jeopardizes the rights and happiness of others.

There is an inherent potential danger in such a technique of therapy, that of making the analyst too much what Balint (1959) referred to as an ocnophilic object, that is, that too much of the analyst is introjected in the replacement process and the patient's need to cling and touch the new introjects will prevent his freedom of individual development. It is not clear to what degree such a potential hazard could be avoided. All I can state regarding this is that during the subsequent analysis of the neurosis, it is my impression my analysands are largely able to alter those introjections in manners suitable to their growth as individuals.

An element of the first phase of therapy which warrants underlining is the maintenance of distance. There can be no question that permission for great intimacy is necessary at times. However, all schizophrenics appear to have a fundamental fear that their incorporation of the analyst or his parts will result in his destruction. At times, the fear is that his destruction will result from his being emptied out. At others, there is a conviction that he will become insane or dead because of an exchange of introjects. I have found that my writing during the interviews has been regarded by my analysands generally as establishing a needed distance. The rate of writing and the pressure of the pen lessen the patient's feeling of being in a vacuum during the early phases. He can compare his evaluations of the analyst's mood with the emotion expressed in his writing and feel less unreal at times when such feelings frighten him.

Personal Attributes of the Analyst[10]

During my psychoanalytic training my supervisors often said that I had an unusual understanding of unconscious products. For the greater part of my psychiatric and psychoanalytic practice I have usually felt

[10]It has been considered that the disagreeable exposition of self is here necessary, because of my conviction that the personal qualities of the therapist are of considerable importance in the analysis of schizophrenics.

at ease when faced with them and largely understood their meanings. In earlier years I had pressing need to understand in rational terms the actions and verbalizations of the most significant individual in the formation of my character, who suffered from a borderline psychotic personality disorder and experienced transient overt psychotic episodes.

Coworkers of John Rosen have said he did not feel an unusual facility in comprehending psychotic productions constitutes a deciding factor in a therapist's successful handling of schizophrenics. I feel in no position to judge. If others attempt the method I have here outlined, a comparison of their results with my own may serve to supply empirical data on the basis of which comparison can be made.

I early developed a great skepticism. It was necessary for me to doubt teachings. A learning defect resulted, revealed in an inability to synthesize taught material. I had to investigate for myself. I hope that these qualities have been sublimated into a useful bent for a scientific approach. It is possible that the combination of the abovementioned traits enables me to maintain a distance while simultaneously interacting with psychotic patients. This, if true, perhaps contains an explanation for the apparent fact that psychotics remain largely at ease with me and are able to work through their fears of eating and being eaten.[11]

Wexler's Suggestion that the Therapist's Active Assumption of Superego Roles Strengthens the Schizophrenic's Ego

In schizophrenia, as Wexler (1951) said, the separation is from the reasonable ego, and the task of therapy is to resurrect that structure. One ego-sector of the schizophrenic, however, the superego, is archaic and devastatingly punitive. Its effects, combined with instinctual demands which are urgent because of the malformed ego and the failure of development of stable countercathexes (Hartmann 1953), produce psychotic disorganization. Wexler found that the therapist's active assumption of superego roles strengthened the ego.

Not only with schizophrenics do we observe the ascription to the analyst of, or the desire that he act in, the role of the prohibiting superego. Theoretically we should expect individuals whose stability appears to depend on a life pattern of seeking instructions to direct conforming behavior to ascribe to the analyst the role of policeman. Patients whose psychosexual development has been stunted to the

[11]Compare with the remarks of Strupp (1958) regarding the contribution of the psychotherapist to the treatment process.

degree that they express themselves through acting out, view the therapist as the superego. In my experience, such attribution is the greater, the less mature the development of the analysand. Thus we might suspect deliberate assumption of superego roles to be unnecessary.[12] What he might do instead is to postpone analysis of those projections until such a time as the analysand's ego has been strengthened adequately via the simultaneous processes of identification and removal through analysis of irrationalities.

Wexler (personal communication 1956) found the above argument illogical. He said: "The ascription is certainly greater—and what if then the analyst behaves not as superego but seducer-permitter? Bang!" His summary is most graphic. It may be that semantics are to some degree at the basis of the apparent difference between us. There is a vast difference between the experimental procedure he described in 1951, in which he assumed a *very* active superego role, and the technique employed and described above. That I acted as a superego model is quite clear. However, my method, aside from the special rule set for Mrs. K. and the parameter employed in the case of Mr. X., was relatively subtle. I never spoke of what the analysand should do or gave similar admonitions. Rather, I was indirect in my superego support, aside from making the prospective analysand's obligations quite clear before analysis was undertaken. I cannot conceive of an analysis in which the analyst does not make selective interpretations. My preparatory remarks and questions are frequently selective and lead to effective interpretations.

The outlining to the prospective analysand of the procedure described above is one which makes easy the projection onto the analyst of superego facets as well as the establishment of a sense of confidence in the therapist's lack of apprehension regarding his role and demands. At the same time, it is an invitation for ego participation in the battle against both id and superego clamorings, although not all patients at all times would so interpret the invitation.

A specific method of superego support which is carried on throughout the first phase consists of labeling delinquent urges and acts by their gross names. Bribery, stealing, cheating, etcetera, are so called. Analysands regularly interpret a consistent open naming of such tendencies as admonitions to stop them. Such a position is indirectly supported by the analyst's selection of the tendencies to mention and his indication of the patient's relief of anxiety when he has successfully

[12]The controversy about role assumption has been extensively aired in various discussions of the work of Alexander.

withstood an impulse to act upon an urge which would have been inconsiderate of the welfare of others. Such actions on the part of the analyst, obviously, are conjoint with interpretations regarding the defensive nature (and later the id strivings) of the drive derivatives.

Countertransference

Savage (1958) defined countertransference as "the analyst's unconscious reactions to the patient's." He judged countertransference to be an integral and perhaps the most important part of the treatment of schizophrenics. He contended, with Rosenfeld (1952a), that the recognition and analysis of countertransference constitutes "our most valuable asset" for their therapy.

In this chapter, countertransference designates "Repressed elements, hitherto unanalysed, in the analyst himself which attach to the patient in the same way as the patient 'transfers' to his analyst affects, etc., belonging to his parents or to the objects of his childhood; i.e. the analyst regards the patient (temporarily and varyingly) as he regarded his own parents" (M. Little 1957).

The greatest single difficulty in the treatment of psychotics, judged by my experience, lies in unresolved countertransference. Among the cases here reported, countertransference interferences of magnitude arose in the analyses of Miss Q., Mrs. T., and Mr. X. In each case, the essential problem was the same. I was only partly aware, despite my training analysis, that I had entered psychiatry for the fundamental purpose of curing the important person of my childhood, who had suffered. Miss Q. and Mrs. T. were two of the first patients with whom the technique was employed. Qualities within them literally struck too close to home. The analysis of Mr. X. went well until a similar situation arose. Progress reached a plateau. Because Mr. X. was a control case, it was possible for the supervising analyst to indicate that the cessation of progress was due to my own problems. A new period of formal analysis quickly made salvage of the treatment possible. The analyses of Miss Q. and Mrs. T. had been terminated earlier.

Summary

In this chapter are reported the results of a 13-year-long experiment in which schizophrenic patients were treated with psychoanalysis with but few parameters. The empirical data seem to indicate that such an approach is not only feasible but beneficial when used with patients such as those included here. Through its employment, the psychosis appears to be removed and a transference neurosis develops which is amenable to continued analysis with the same therapist.

Before the analyses were undertaken their experimental nature was stated and rules of expected behavior of analyst and analysand were made explicit.

The analyses were roughly divided into two phases. In the first, efforts were largely directed toward defense interpretations, reality testing improvement, and indirect superego support. Preverbal communications were consistently utilized. Under conditions considered as designed for the development of projections, it was found that effective replacement of cold, unloving introjects was accomplished. It is hypothesized that such introjection took place largely through a common oral-auditory pathway. It may be that successful introjection under such conditions depends not only on the method but on special qualifications of the therapist.

Countertransference problems may constitute the principal obstacle to successful analysis of schizophrenic patients of the types mentioned in this chapter.

Acknowledgments

I am indebted to Drs. Edward C. Adams, Charles Brenner, Kurt R. Eissler, Avelino Gonzales, José Luis Gonzales-Chavez, Bertram D. Lewin, Ramón Parres, José Remus-Araico, Santiago Ramirez, Martin Wangh, and Milton Wexler for constructive criticisms. I am, however, solely responsible for the content and hypotheses here presented.

5

Technique in the Treatment of Characterological and Schizophrenic Disorders

In this chapter a case fragment is used to delineate a technique in the treatment of certain characterological and schizophrenic disorders. It has evolved as a result of my use of psychoanalysis within the framework of the structural theory in the treatment of such conditions, without essential modification of procedures employed customarily with neurotics. I have avoided role-playing and resisted consistently patients' attempts to make me change my analytic stance. I have interpreted the psychotic and neurotic transference in their positive and negative aspects without the use of reassuring or formal educative techniques, never attempting to foster the so-called positive transference.

The case study abstracted here was chosen for two reasons. First, its course was smooth and the technique used demonstrates the most recent of an ever developing series of modifications. In a sense this study is misleading because the progress of the patient was unusually even and the apparently successful result followed unusually quickly, the psychoanalysis having occupied just less than three years. When this chapter was written, no claim of cure could have been made. However, the patient returned for help with a neurotic problem two years later; that period of psychoanalysis lasted a few months. During the subsequent eight or nine years, she has remained well. Second, the patient presented an uncommon symptom complex, a variant of that described by Greenacre (1947) under the rubric "vision, headache and the halo," which served the same defensive and adaptive purposes, the analysis of which was crucial to the therapeutic outcome.

Case Material

The principal although not initial complaint of an attractive, highly intelligent 25-year-old woman was terrifying black sensations in her head, which had begun during her puberty. She had kept the symptom secret, fearing its discovery would lead to her being hospitalized as mad. The sensations did not make her dizzy, but she always lay down while experiencing them, being apprehensive she might otherwise become lightheaded, fall, scream, babble, lose excretory control, and reach a state of helplessness, requiring permanent care as if she were an infant. Although they were not mentioned during the first months of her analysis, she also had a number of phobias, some of which are noted below.

History

She had gone through life smitten with guilt for infractions of an exceedingly high internal moral code and aspiring to be angelic in thought and deed. She had placed various people on pedestals, inevitably choosing individuals who disappointed her by being morally less than perfect, and had from her earliest memory felt unwanted and unloved and despised her parents, ostensibly because they argued, drank, and lacked respect for one another.

During her high-school years she had considered herself to be fat and ugly and avoided opportunities for dates. She left her parents' home at 19 for the first time to attend a university. While there, she could not concentrate on her studies. During her first term she became progressively withdrawn. She made no friends and felt the world to be unreal. She attended a few classes but became inexplicably frightened and soon found herself spending her days in women's rest rooms. There she would lie on sofas in a thoughtless trancelike state until other girls entered; then she would sit on a toilet seat cover until she was again alone. She was afraid that if she were seen lying on the sofas, she would be reported and hospitalized as insane.

She failed a term and was placed on probation. During the next semester, a man who strongly resembled her father asked her to go on an automobile ride and she accepted her first date. She passively submitted to a kiss but was frightened when he sought to be more intimate. He became angry and excited and masturbated before her. She experienced the black sensation in her head and felt guilty because she had not permitted intercourse. She readily accepted a second date on which she refused intercourse but performed fellatio, being careful to remove her mouth before ejaculation. She experienced disgust and gagged. Soon thereafter she permitted intercourse and became pregnant. The gestation was greeted ambivalently. Her mother had expected her to become a schoolteacher, a career toward which she had sharply mixed feelings. She now had an excuse to marry and avoid further pursuit of that profession. At the same time, she feared her mother's wrath and abandonment. Once married, she studied subjects she enjoyed and was able to complete her college work with excellent grades, despite many hardships.

She found all sexual contact repugnant. Although before the marriage she found fellatio less disgusting than intercourse, now she could not tolerate oral-genital activities and usually refused intercourse. She was grossly but unwittingly exhibitionistic and seductive, but when her husband sought sexual relations she taunted him until he either raped or slapped her. Most frequently he responded to her provocation by masturbating before her; her observations of his manipulations produced the terrifying blackness in her head. She gradually slept less often with her husband and, although she was tall and their bathtub was short, chose to sleep in the tub, holding her arms about her as she was curled in a near fetal position. When she held herself so, she entered a trancelike, thoughtless state and drifted to sleep.

It was later learned that her provocations of fights before sexual relations imitated what she either assumed or observed to be frequent actions of her parents when she was 4 to 13 years of age. During that period, her father often came home late at night intoxicated. Her mother responded by provoking a fight which the patient thought to have been followed by sexual relations during which her mother complained that she was disgusted.

When the patient's son was born, she transiently believed his birth to have been the result of parthenogenesis. Although the marriage pattern did not change, she felt she could not divorce "for religious reasons." Two years later, three events coincided. Her father died. His death came after a long illness and she felt nothing concerning his demise. During the course of her analysis, she maintained he had died for her years before and consistently denied grieving when he factually became deceased. A daughter was born and she once again briefly believed the birth to have been parthenogenetic. Soon thereafter, marital life became so miserable that her husband left the home and went to a different state to continue his education. Although she was relieved, she soon became depressed and, although she was a devoted mother, was sure she was neglecting her children. Concurrently appeared nightmares in which she was beaten or raped by her husband, a black man, or some middle-aged white man; they were followed by the black sensations. She progressively provoked strife with her mother-in-law, based on a conviction that the mother surrogate would take her children from her. Fearful she would go insane and harm her children psychologically, she sought treatment. Although the mother-in-law was paying for the analysis, she could not believe such largesse was evidence of good will toward her, preferring to think it was a gift to her children. She considered herself to be schizophrenic and had heard that during treatment for that disorder, patients sometimes regressed. She reasoned that her mother-in-law thought she would become hopelessly insane during her treatment and then have reason to take the children.

Treatment

The patient was referred for analysis by a colleague who had diagnosed her to be schizophrenic. She had seen him for marital counseling, complaining that her husband was brutal and preferred masturbation to intercourse. That analyst suggested that she might have provoked some of her husband's behavior, and she had responded with righteous indignation, needing to believe that she had been an innocent victim of his psychopathology. Yet when leaving that therapist's care in an apparent rage, she had requested analysis by me, having been told by a former patient that I treated schizophrenics and was "tough." I understood from this information that she feared she was insane, feared her capacity to act unwisely or impulsively, and craved a strong superego and ego surrogate who would care enough for her to insist that she behave.

In the first interview, she spoke under pressure and her sentences were so disconnected that I understood much of what she meant only because of my knowledge of the products of primary-process thinking. She complained that she had been wronged by her husband and former therapist. Before I speak of my response to her, I shall present some of my ideas concerning what must be accomplished in the initial stages of dealing with such patients and the techniques I have developed to accomplish those goals.

In previous publications I have suggested that the primary task in treatment is to restore and/or develop within the patient a reasonable ego and superego, and that this can be accomplished by modifying or replacing cold, unloving, and archaic introjects (Boyer 1966; Boyer and

Giovacchini 1967, chap. 4; Chapter 4, this volume). I have expressed the opinion that therapy must be directed toward the growth of intrapsychic and interpersonal communication techniques. I have come to believe that the most important initial step is the presentation to the analysand of a calm, patient, objective, implicitly optimistic attitude with which to identify, that of a person who does not respond with anxiety to reactions of panic or attempts at manipulation but who treats each production of the patient, whether verbal or otherwise, as though it is important enough to heed, and who does not believe that the immediate satisfaction of urges is necessary. Although it is my viewpoint that the role of interpretation in the structuralizing of the ego (Boyer and Giovacchini 1967, chap. 6; Giovacchini 1969) is the most important contribution psychoanalysis has to make in the treatment of these conditions, I do not think that interpretation can be optimally effective until the cathexis of maladaptive introjects has lessened and healthier ones have begun to replace them.

Loewenstein (1956) differentiated among three functions of speech: the cognitive, the expressive, and the appeal functions. In the psychotic the second two functions predominate, and it is the task of the analyst to respond to the appeal function only by interpretation, to transform the appeal function to the expressive function, by demonstrating to the patient that he expresses something about himself when he speaks of other persons or things. The analyst attempts to exclude both the functions of expression and appeal from his own speech. In my experience this effort on the part of the analyst should begin immediately, and his using the cognitive mode which appeals to the patient's ego rather than his id reduces immediately the tenuousness of contact between analyst and analysand. Technically, I thus make contact through interpretation and direct my interpretative efforts to the surface, stressing the defensive nature of the patient's productions.

Believing that the patient craved control and feared herself to be insane, I appealed to her rationality by responding in the cognitive mode. Having understood her complaint that she was wronged by her husband and previous analyst to mean she feared she had provoked their behavior, I told her that it seemed she was worried that she had a problem related to provocativeness for which she feared she should feel guilty. She was indignant and threatened not to return. I ignored this irrationality and again appealed to her ego, saying we could begin regular interviews the next day.

My instructions concerning the conditions of her treatment were that I would expect her to make a sincere effort to tell me whatever came to her mind and to keep me informed about emotional and physical experiences which occurred during the interviews, that I did not send statements but expected to be paid accurately during a specific interview of the month, that she would be charged for any cancellations unless her time were filled by another patient, and that I was generally absent several times yearly for short periods and once for an extended time. I have found with such patients that specific conditions offer needed ego and superego support.

In the second interview she was obviously calmer and reassured. She said she should talk about her sexual problem, a problem previously unmentioned, but she could not do so. Therefore she would tell me about her past. During the next five interviews she recounted many dreams and events from early childhood and complained bitterly that she had never been loved. Her sentences were fragmented and frequently involved a series of loosely related subjects. There was a tendency toward clang associations. The material was laden with massive denials and contradictions. When she was confronted gently with obvious contradictions, she acknowledged them briefly and proceeded as though I had made no intervention. Highly cathected black-and-white oversimplifications were rife. The dreams all involved the themes of falling or flying, and her associations were regularly of being abandoned. At the same time she said she had hated her parents. She complained that she had never been held, even as an infant, and simultaneously said she could never tolerate being touched by either parent. She claimed that her mother and father had always drunk immoderately but also talked of her father's having been a successful businessman except for a short time and of her mother's puritanism. She claimed her parents had always argued loudly but remembered with scorn her mother's enjoyment in doing things for father. She averred she had feared that one parent would murder the other, although there were no physical fights, and yet had hoped for the death of either to spare her the terror she experienced while hearing their arguments. She maintained that her parents had no love for each other or any of their six children. She was the second, preceded by a brother two years older and succeeded by a sister one year younger and brothers three, five, and seven years her junior. She complained that her sister and youngest brother had been parental favorites. Early memories also included scenes in which her elder brothers were beaten by the father for disobedience and one in which mother whipped her when she was about 5 years old because of exhibitionistic and voyeuristic play with the eldest brother.

In the sixth interview she said she would never lie on the couch, which had not been mentioned previously. Since she had presented so much material negatively, I understood this communication to mean she now felt sufficiently secure that she meant to lie on the couch. During those interviews I had been generally passive. Sometimes when she became very tense and was silent for some minutes, I suggested that she might be feeling embarassment because of her awareness that some of her denials and gross contradictions were logically inconsistent. On three occasions, after I had made some simple, clear remarks, she asked me to repeat what I had said. I understood this to mean in part that she was testing to see whether I would humiliate her by responding as though she were truly incompetent, and I answered that she seemed to feel the need to view me as someone who didn't believe she could remember and make use of her memory (Hoedemaker 1967). Each time she was obviously relieved, demonstrated she knew very well what I had said, and temporarily relinquished speaking confusedly.

In the seventh interview she lay on the couch. She was frightened, blushed, alternately pressed her thighs tightly together and spread her legs slightly, and manipulated the buttons and zippers on her modest dresses. She was frightened and complained for the first time of the black sensations in her head. It was obvious that she was having fantasies, whether conscious or unconscious, of sexual attack and seemed probable that the black sensations were associated with fantasies of seeing an erection. However, I chose to ignore the phallic or genital fantasies, merely asking for elaboration of her experience of the black sensations and obtaining some factual historical data pertaining to them.

Over the years I have come to the conclusion that to deal early with genital sexual material in psychoanalysis of such patients is contraindicated. With Rosenfeld (1966a), I do not interpret apparently oedipal material on a libidinal level. Such a procedure is usually understood by the patient to be a seductive invitation from the analyst and stirs up acute psychotic excitement. The patient's anxiety increases regularly and frequently results in defensive regressive maneuvers whenever he believes he has forced the therapist out of his analytic role. If I refer to such material, I do so from the standpoint of its aggressive and manipulative aspects, or interpret upward, using a technique learned from Loewenstein in a seminar he conducted for candidates of the San Francisco Psychoanalytic Institute (1952). Thus, as an example, if the patient relates that he has open fantasies of intercourse with his mother, I respond that he must love her very much. I believe the patient who suffers from a severe characterological or schizophrenic disorder has massive fears of vicissitudes of his aggressive impulses and that analysis proceeds smoothest when attention is directed gently but consistently toward the analysis of the protective maneuvers he employs to defend against his fear that his hostility will result in the analyst's death or his own.

Thus after the patient lay down and manifested such fears of sexual involvement with the analyst as a parent surrogate, I made no comment relating to this theme. When she remained silent for long periods and challenged me to prove that my silence did not mean I hated her, my remarks pointed at the projective aspects of her own hostility as manifested by her self-devaluation.

After the first few weeks, she no longer spoke of her past. Long periods of shivering silence were broken by highly emotional accounts of her present interpersonal difficulties, all of which she attributed to the ill will of whichever adults she contacted. She assumed that the alleged hostile treatment afforded her was due to her physical ugliness. She admitted no positive feelings toward anyone but her children and was sure they preferred their paternal grandmother to her. At the same time, preparing for possible future divorce, she quickly learned the necessary skills and found a job as a private secretary in an office where it appeared to the analyst that she was treated with deference and trust but in which she felt she was slighted and scorned. It was impossible to obtain coherent information from her concerning any current event. A combination of causes contributed to the distorted reporting. She was apparently unaware of her provocativeness, misinterpreted others' gestures and expressions to indicate adverse opinions toward her, and was terrified of reporting fantasies directly. Of course, she also was simultaneously convinced that the analyst read her mind and that his silence indicated his disgust with her; yet she consciously withheld information. It became apparent that she generally believed herself to be reporting actual occurrences accurately but that her perceptions of external events were grossly distorted because she projected unconscious sadomasochistic, voyeuristic, and exhibitionistic wishes onto others. Before I speak of the technical procedure I chose to use at this time, I shall summarize its rationale.

By this time, although still frightened, the patient had begun to introject some degree of the analyst's attitude of calm and patient optimism and to feel that she might be worth saving. Whereas she had spoken previously only of despair concerning her future, she now uttered occasional words of hope. Earlier, she had felt panicked by frustration either within or outside the consultation room, but now she queried herself with the analyst's words, "What do you fear might happen if you do not get immediately what you want?", and was able to avoid a temper tantrum or withdrawal into a state of apparently thoughtless inactivity. Yet she still sought to have the analyst do all of her thinking, and it was obvious she ascribed omniscience and omnipotence to him. The major problem which seemed to confront her analysis was the need to reach a therapeutic alliance. The development of such an alliance requires the patient to develop some distance from his problems and emotions so that he can think about them as well as experience them. This woman was engaged in three principal kinds of behavior which she did not understand. She massively projected parts of her own identity onto others, she grossly misperceived external as well as intrapsychic events, and she provoked hostility on the part of others which she could then use to rationalize her own anger. It was obvious that she was reenacting childhood behavior, both living out and acting out. I use the words living out to mean repetitions of earlier behavior which are not connected directly with the analytic situation and acting out to mean behavior which attempts to solve transference problems through action. Rosenfeld (1966b) discussed the relationship between acting out and the aggressive drive.

As stated above, I have concluded that in dealing with such patients interpretations should be directed toward aggressive drive derivatives during the early stages of treatment and that oedipal libidinal interpretations are generally useless if not actually damaging to treatment. I have also learned that gentle, consistent confrontations of the patient with his inconsistencies and misperceptions make him curious about the meanings of his behavior and thinking. On reviewing the case histories of my patients of recent years, I find I have been confronting them more and more with their misperceptions, inconsistencies, and distortions of events in the consultation room and less with external events (Boyer 1967a). Where the events are known to the analyst who can then remind the patient of what actually transpired, it is more difficult for the analysand to maintain the validity of his altered presentations. Simultaneously, the patient is in general eager to use the psychoanalyst as an ego and superego model. However, in this case, there was a special situation which made it seem optimal to direct the analysis toward the understanding of her defenses against aggressive impulses, without focusing on her hostility toward the analyst.

From the outset there had been a split transference of grand proportions. She had almost no awareness of hostility toward me, and the principal focus of her anger was her mother-in-law, so clearly a substitute for her mother. Lesser and more diffuse aggression was directed to other relatives and work colleagues. As stated previously, in general I believe interpretations to be most effective when they are directed toward the surface, i.e., toward what is closest to the patient's consciousness, in direct opposition to the viewpoint of many members of the Kleinian school (Avenburg 1962, Segal 1967). Ordinarily in my treatment of such cases, I focus from the beginning on the defensive aspects of aggressive drive behavior which manifest themselves in the transference situation, by directing attention primarily to what transpires in the consultation room. In the present case, too, initially I thus focused my remarks. However, they were met with little more than ridicule and the patient's responses were usually directed toward the hostility of her mother-in-law. The bulk of that hostility, as I understood the situation, was projected from the patient, although some resulted as well from her provocative behavior toward that rather unusually kindly woman. I decided to follow her lead and exploit the split transference.

For the development of a therapeutic alliance, the patient must develop curiosity about himself. This woman seemed for some time to have very little. She maintained that she was and had been mistreated because of the innate hostility of others, their greed and desires to use her, and her imagined physical ugliness. I decided to direct our attention simultaneously in two directions. I mentioned her slips of the tongue, gestures, leaving the door ajar, periodic muscular tensions, and manipulations of her clothes. Initially she was infuriated that I should call attention to such apparent trivia but then became interested in possible meanings of such phenomena and was pleased with herself when she could analyze them. Yet she did not extrapolate from her experience inside the consultation room to events outside. Thus I began to reconstruct aloud what I guessed might actually have occurred and then been misperceived in her encounters with relatives, work colleagues, and especially her mother-in-law. She was at first outraged and panicked when I suggested that external events occurred in manners other than she had reported. Then, however, she checked my guesses and was amazed to find them to have been generally accurate. At the same time, she was relieved to discover that I could make errors. She thus began to view me as fallible and to know that her active cooperation was requried for developing self-understanding. I also used another technical maneuver I have found to be of value.

A task of the treatment of such cases is to assist the patient in improving intrapsychic and interpersonal communication. In any psychoanalysis, betterment of intrapsychic communication is implicit. Not infrequently, with these patients, there is a lag in the improvement of the understanding of interpersonal messages. When a patient presents data in a manner which is influenced heavily by the primary process, in general I understand a large part of his message. Even when I think I comprehend all of what he has told me, I tell him I think I understand what he has sought to convey but ask him to tell me more about it in different words. He is simultaneously reassured that I have gleaned some of his meaning and frightened by my implicit statement that his message is obscure. He presents the material in a somewhat more logical manner. After some time, he begins to test his new manner of communication with people outside the office and is pleased to observe that he is better understood and has fewer interpersonal difficulties.

To return to the present case: subsequently, during a period of a few months, I reconstructed past events from her current actions both in the consultation room and in her interactions with others. She then began to consider the possibility that her past perceptions also had been awry and began to admit that she might have been treated less badly than she remembered. Thereon her provocative livings out and actings out diminished and a solid working alliance was established. From the end of the first year, she actively conducted her treatment. One example of the correction of an ongoing interaction follows.

As noted earlier, during the first few months she was convinced that her mother-in-law was trying to take her children from her and that they preferred their paternal grandmother to her. When I guessed that she had been unwittingly provocative and then misinterpreted the mother-in-law's contributions to the strife between them, she gradually validated my notions positively. As she did so, she remembered how as a child of 7 or 8 she played secretly with her youngest brother, trying to nurse him on her body and investigating his genitals. With her typical use of denial and reversal, she recalled she had believed a brother to have been her own child whom her mother had stolen. With the recollection of these memories, she gradually shifted her attitude toward her mother-in-law. They became friendly and cooperative. Simultaneously her fear that her children preferred their grandmother disappeared. As she renounced the previous attitude toward the older woman, she also repressed once again the memories of her activities with her youngest brother.

As the hostile components of her relationship with her mother-in-law were analyzed, she was able gradually to focus on some hateful aspects of her behavior toward me and the split transference disappeared, both positive and negative aspects being centered on me.

Let us turn to the vicissitudes of the black sensations in her head. When she first lay on the couch she behaved like a frightened girl who expected sexual attack. Although the temperature of the consultation room was fairly constant, she frequently became suddenly cold and complained bitterly that the analyst was secretly manipulating the heater and the air conditioner in such a way as to cause her physical sensations. A blanket was on the couch but she avoided touching it. I always worked in my shirt-sleeves. She was incredulous that I was not uncomfortable when she perceived the room to have become insufferably cold. When she entered the office, she looked only at my face and on many occasions it became obvious that while she knew in detail the contents of the room which she could see while lying down, she was consciously unaware of items in what she termed my half of the office. Her dreams provided information that she had registered unconsciously details of my dress and all of the office accoutrements. On various occasions, when she felt suddenly cold, she also experienced the black sensations. Interpretations indicating her to have romantic thoughts concerning the analyst were dismissed with indignation. Then the black sensations and experiences of sudden changes of temperature stopped. Because her symptoms had ceased without their having been understood I assumed she was engaging in some unreported acting out. Therefore I asked whether she was withholding information concerning her behavior outside the office, and she reported that she was having an affair but she could not bring herself to supply detailed information. She vigorously denied that she was attempting to protect herself from disturbing thoughts concerning the analyst but ceased the affair and had no further social engagements with men. She then became consciously aware of the contents of my half of the office. For some months there was no recurrence of the black sensations or the perceived temperature changes. During this period she rarely mentioned her husband except to complain when he was tardy in sending child support money. After she renounced her affair she said she had decided on divorce, but then she did not mention further relations with her husband or whatever actions she might be taking pertaining to legal separation or divorce. Just before the cessation of the black sensations, she described them visually, saying the sensation was "like a ball of collected black strings, with the ends sticking out everywhere." Later she would say that each of the strings was the surface manifestation of a fantasy which had to be unraveled. From this time forward, she made the black sensations and their visualization a conscious focus of her analysis, attempting to relate most major associations to them.

During the first half of the second year of analysis she had a consistent pattern of activities preceding sleep. She lay on her side, knees drawn up, and hugged herself. Then she rocked herself, while visualizing being held and rocked in the analyst's arms like a baby. She felt blissful at such times and denied awareness of any sexual sensations or thoughts. The trancelike state formerly experienced without conscious thought or feeling in the bathtub of the marital home was relived, but now with satisfying thought content and intense physical sensations of warmth and comfort in the upper half of her body. Gradually she began to have fantasies of nursing on the analyst's penis and she savored the sensations of fullness in her mouth and the milk she sensed drinking from his penis. With no suggestion from the analyst, she consciously equated the penis with her mother's breast. She said she should be experiencing jealousy of her younger sibs, but that she could not recall them as nursing babies nor could she remember having ever seen her mother's breasts except in adult years, when they were flat and sagging. She said she thought she should also be experiencing some sexual feelings while visualizing sucking on the analyst's penis, but that she did not and she voluntarily steadfastly denied sexual desires directed at father, mother, or analyst. She was happy and contented and the former feelings of having been discriminated against at work and elsewhere outside the consultation room, while conscious at times, were but superficially cathected. She often withheld information and recognized her behavior as illogical but said it was her intention to prolong the analysis as long as she could, because she was happy for the first time in her life. She volunteered the information that the money she got from her mother-in-law to pay for her coming to see me was also equated with mother's milk and permission to be held by father but said she needed to have the experience of being loved and prized, even though she was aware that the fantasies and actions were entirely unreal in terms of actual expectations from the analyst or any other persons in her adult life. During this approximately six-month period the analyst waited and was almost totally silent, beyond responding to her greetings at the beginnings and ends of hours. Then came a change. However, before that alteration in behavior and content is reported, I shall explain my rationale for remaining passive during the six-month period.

Hartmann (1939a) stressed the need of the presence of an average expectable environment for the unfolding of innate maturational tendencies and the differentiation of id and ego. We are accustomed to think of the serial development of the oral, anal, phallic, and genital phases of psychosexual and psychosocial development.

The patients suffering from severe characterological or schizophrenic disorders whom I have analyzed or am analyzing number 30. All had undergone obvious regressions, usually phenomenologically psychotic, at puberty or subsequent periods when unresolved oedipal conflicts had been reawakened. Thus they had had environments which were sufficiently favorable to have permitted unfolding of the innate maturational phases. The predominant symptomatology reflected strong fixations, perhaps combined with developmental failures. In the analytic situation identificatory processes and the structuralizing effects of interpretations had resulted in the replacement of unhealthy introjects by more mature ones in the large majority of these patients. When pregenital problems had been more or less satisfactorily resolved, they were able to analyze phallic and genital conflicts with at least moderate success. These data suggest the optimistic but unproven supposition that such patients may in the therapeutic situation achieve a controlled and adaptive regression (Hartmann 1939b, Lindon 1967, Winnicott 1955) to a period which has attributes of a more optimal mother-infant relationship than existed when the patient was an infant; when such a relationship has developed, innate maturational tendencies can continue to unfold accompanied by alterations of the far-reaching effects of early learning, provided ill-timed actions of the psychoanalyst do not interfere. I hesitate to suggest that the same may be true with patients who have remained autistic from infancy or had childhood psychoses which can be traced to failure of separation-individuation (Mahler 1963; Mahler and Furer 1960, 1963; Mahler and La Perriere 1965; Mahler and Settlage 1959). I have no clinical material from which to draw conclusions.

The patient whose analysis provides the data for this chapter appeared to have established a therapeutic alliance. She had the capacity to simultaneously regress and to observe and was curious to learn about herself. Her regressive behavior was limited largely to her presleep activities and the analytic room. Interpersonal relationships were steadily improving, and she was handling family problems more realistically. She was being promoted rapidly in her work and had achieved a responsible position. I was comfortable with her continuous period of regression and thought it to be advisable for her to have time to experience the sense of well-being she seemed to need, inasmuch as there was continuous evidence of improvement.

Although during the analysis until this time she had avoided touching the blanket which lay on the couch at her side, she now began to contemplate covering herself to experience in the office the presleep experiences she had so repetitiously described. As she did so, the black sensations recurred, but with diminished intensity and scant fright. Rather, they were viewed as interesting and to be investigated. She finally braved covering herself with the blanket and for a period relished the comfort of lying on the couch, visualizing being held by the analyst and sucking on his penis, which for the first time she pictured clearly as erect and circumcized as had been her brothers' and her husband's. She recognized the absurdity of her fantasy, since it involved her lying on the analyst's lap and she was but a little shorter than he. Then she began to feel sensations of bladder fullness, whether covered by the blanket or not. This was confusing to her. She had always urinated at home just before coming to the office, and now she began also to use the toilet provided for patients. Then occurred episodes of watery diarrhea, for which no medical explanation was found, when she checked her fantasy that she had belated symptoms of amoebic dysentery from childhood trips to the tropics with her parents. She had always been mildly curious about the analyst's other female patients, but now she became moderately interested in both male and female sibling surrogates. Then she became aware that while she had either sensations of urinary or fecal urgency while on the couch she was also sexually excited.

It will be recalled that previously, when she had the presleep experiences in her home, she had felt warmth only in the upper half of her body. Genital sensations remained repressed. Apparently the experiencing and analysis of her period of regression had served the purpose of removing repressions and structuralizing some needs. Whereas bladder, anal, and vaginal sensations had previously remained at least in part fused, now she was able to separate them.

There had been no conscious sexual excitation for many months. She now revealed that she had never knowingly touched herself between her legs from the age of 5 or 6 years except to cleanse herself or care for menstrual discharge. Before analysis she had suffered from dysmenorrhea and profuse flow, but while she was living out the fantasy of being held and nursed she had felt no menstrual discomfort and excessive flow had been rare. Now the menstrual symptoms recurred. She found herself tempted to explore her genitals with her hands. In contrast to her previous blissful serenity while in the analyst's presence, she became fearful that he disliked her and would abandon her were she to touch her genitals. For months she had not reported dreams. Now recurred nightmares in which there were violent attacks performed on her by men, with mutilation and bleeding. The manifest content gradually changed so that genital mutilation took place, at first caused by knives and then by the insertion of huge instruments. She thought that as a child she must have feared sexual assault by her eldest brother, but she could remember only their handling each other and exhibiting themselves. Eventually she decided that she should explore her genitals. She said: "The ends of the strings are sticking out and I want to see whether I can unravel them."

She began to explore her genitals and rectum with her fingers. She found herself putting all of the fingers of both hands into either orifice and stretching it. She remembered in detail much sexual play during her third to sixth years, principally actions which took place while she was alone in the bathtub. She was convinced that she had then stretched both the vagina and rectum and inserted various objects, including the nursing bottle of her younger brother, a cream bottle, a lipstick, and a tube of toothpaste, the contents of which she alternately squeezed into her vagina or rectum or ate. Always aware of hatred and envy for her younger sister, whom she felt to be favored by both parents, now, via highly cathected fantasies of the analyst's sexual involvement with his other female patients, she remembered intense childhood jealousy and an attempt at murdering her rival.

One of the phobias with which she had come to analysis was that of going into dark places either while alone or with a man. During the early weeks of analysis she had recalled that at the age of 6 her father had been angry with her because she was afraid to go to the basement to get food for her mother and had dragged her into the cellar over her screaming protests, presumably to show her there was nothing to fear. In the version then presented, father had been drunk and mother had stood by while he buffeted the child. This memory now recurred but in a different light. She recalled that prior to that time she had eagerly gone to the basement and had enjoyed sitting on the washing machine while it was hot and vibrating. On one occasion she had taken with her a lipstick, painted her genital area, and then been spanked by her mother. In her reconstruction of what might have led to this behavior, she supposed that she had used the lipstick to make her genitals more attractive to father, equating mouth and vagina, and that the red coloring had also been a substitute for blood which she had supposed was the result of some activity between her parents. After she presented these data which preceded her father's taking her to the basement, she remembered that her father had been listening to a romantic opera, one of his favorites, and she had disturbed him to request that he help her look for a toy she thought she had left in the basement. He had reluctantly agreed, whereon she became panicky he would beat or sexually attack her. Because he was angry that she had interrupted him, he insisted she go with him.

She could not recall having ever seen her mother naked or pregnant, or evidence of menstruation. Her father had been a successful businessman during her early years and apparently respected by mother. However, when she was 4 or 5, he became an inveterate drinker for some years. Mother during that period had been the efficient member of the household. The patient now hypothesized, but did not remember, that she had equated mother's efficiency with the acquisition of father's penis and had thought babies to have been transformations of the stolen penis, which could emerge either in the form of fecal sticks or infants. She finally wondered whether she had ever seen either of her parents naked.

During the next few interviews black sensations recurred frequently but were accompanied by little anxiety. At times the black strings were visualized as the heads of snakes which could bite and swallow. She then recalled with embarrassment having at 3 or 4 years of age tried to nurse on a bitch, shoving the puppies aside, and got black hair in her mouth. Thereon she spoke for the first time of lifelong fears of snakes and spiders in terms of oral-genital fantasies in which she equated pubic hair and penises which could bite. She said those fears were gone and I never heard of them again. Then, while she was visualizing the black mass in her head, it began to jump up and down and assumed the form of a huge black phallus.

She had mentioned rarely that there had been a black maid in the family all during her childhood. Now she said she had wondered whether that woman were her true mother and remembered having seen the maid's pubic hair while she was urinating and been awestruck. She remembered also that throughout her analysis at various times when she was not in the office she had visualized an erection and experienced the black sensations. She had meant to inform me but had forgotten. Finally she said she thought she recalled walking into her parents' bedroom and seeing her father alone, in profile and naked. She had been 4 years old at the time, and her mother was pregnant with her second youngest brother. The interview which will now be related in detail occurred a week later.

She entered the office looking amused and said she thought she now understood the meaning of the black sensations in her head. She remembered a dream which had surprised her because she'd not thought of her husband for several weeks. Their divorce had become final some months previously. She said:

My husband had a baby, probably literally had a baby. He carried it around as a little girl would a doll she liked. I talked to him or to you as I stood before a mirror. I squeezed blackheads out of my face and each time one came out I'd say: "This is to show you that I'm not afraid of such and such." He carted the baby around. I was somehow in the picture. He also had an enormous penis, at least twice as big as his erection, that is, twice as long.

At this point in the interview she wrapped a facial tissue around her index finger like a bandage.

There were about 20 of me and I remember having intercourse over and over again. No. I just remember the feeling of his penis outside of me while he held me. His penis was white and shining and there were no hairs. It was like Jesus' would be if He had one. I was as surprised and awestruck as those three little girls must have been in Portugal when they saw the Virgin Mary. It was a miracle. I can't remember actually seeing the erection so much as seeing it glow. I was really astonished the first time I saw and felt my husband's erection, it was so long and hard.

She now found herself tearing the tissue to shreds, and continued:

I feel like an animal in a cage. I wish the hour would end so I wouldn't have to use another piece of tissue and make a bandage of it and tear it up, too. I think I'm playing with it instead of masturbating. Now I have to go to the bathroom. I couldn't masturbate here and I dislike even wanting to. Now I want to put my hands in my mouth. It would feel good to make my mouth bigger and take all of that huge penis inside. Now I want to spit. When he shoved his penis in my mouth I gagged and gagged. I was trying to get all of it inside me and swallow it. Maybe I wanted to have a penis after my brother was born, and then believed I'd had my brother all by myself. I'm not confused about my father and his penis any more. I'm confused about my mother. How did I graduate from wanting to suck on a breast to wanting to suck on a penis? My mother was so capable that I thought she must have a penis, too, and that both men and women could have babies all by themselves. I'm glad I no longer believe I *am* a penis and I want to lose the idea I have a penis somewhere. I've always feared my clitoris would grow into a real penis. I was afraid my mother would catch me in the bathtub when I'd rub on it and make it hard. Maybe she'd see it and take it away and then I couldn't have babies all alone.

During the interviews of the next two weeks her productions were limited largely to attempts to understand the dream. She saw the blackheads as representing the black ends which stuck out from the ball of tangled strings. She recalled vividly and with much abreaction her invasion of the parental bedroom. Her father had been alone, standing in the lighted closet of an otherwise darkened room. She was convinced she had seen his erection in profile and was awestruck. As she spoke of the experience she had to urinate and saw light in her head. She was sure she had experienced the sensation of a great light in her head when she had viewed father, had felt dazed and intense urinary urgency. She had groped her way to the toilet and "almost blacked out." She had as an older child seen a brother masturbating. Now she thought that she had then decided unconsciously her father had been masturbating and subsequently tried to provoke men to masturbate before her, hoping that they, as father surrogates, would rape her. When the son with whom mother was pregnant was born, the patient believed the child to be her own. She thought but did not clearly remember that when mother was big with pregnancy, the patient had become seriously constipated and that she finally had a large bowel movement when mother went to the hospital to have the baby. When her own son was born her experience had been that of having a large bowel movement. She had thought that girls were born with penises but that some injury cut the penis off, leaving only an internal stub which might grow into a large penis once again. An alternative hypothesis had been that a woman could obtain the penis during intercourse, by biting it off either with her mouth or her vagina.

During this period she did not mention some ideas she had presented as theoretical during earlier interviews. However, she presented all the recollections from childhood with vividness and conviction. Other data were offered but their presentation here would be redundant. One item perhaps deserves emphasis. During the time when she had been living contentedly in the fantasy of nursing on my penis, there had occurred a series of interviews in which she found herself lying rigidly on the couch. She then had dreams the manifest content of which had been a little girl sitting on her father's lap and gradually standing erect and stiff. She now offered the interpretation, with no hesitation or even wonderment, that she must have imagined that she was father's penis. She thought she recalled that while she lay on the sofas while a freshman in college, she must have been trying to allay her fears that she was displeasing her father through failing at school by imagining she was his erection and therefore his prized possession.

In adolescence she had grown very fast and was quite tall. She had also suffered from acne and was especially ashamed of blackheads. From her early teens she had been convinced a reason she was disliked and mistreated was because she was fat and her skin was ugly. After the acne disappeared, her skin remained a bit oily. While she was analyzing the dream she admitted she had never been overweight. She decided that she had equated being tall with father's erection and had displaced her concern about her height onto being fat, equating obesity and pregnancy. The blackheads were equated with the snake-penises and were also evidence that she was pregnant. After this bit of analysis, she was no longer unduly concerned about her physical appearance.[1]

The recovery of the visual trauma of seeing father's erection was the last major step in this woman's analysis, which lasted only a few months more. There were few and barely cathected recurrences of the black sensations, her self-depreciation disappeared, she increased even further her capacity to perceive correctly events in which she became involved, and she became a happy and confident woman. A last fear was recognized and resolved. As noted earlier, when she began analysis, on entering the consultation room she looked only at the analyst's face and did not consciously record office accoutrements in "his half of the room." Although she gradually became able to see those objects, before the recovery of the visual trauma she remained able to look only at the analyst's face. During the analysis, on various occasions interruptions during her interviews had required the analyst to walk past her and on each occasion she had sat up as he arose to go to the door. When her actions had been questioned, she had responded vaguely. Now another interruption took place and she remained supine. She became consciously aware that she had been avoiding looking at the front of his trousers and then that she had gone through life afraid to satisfy a wish to look for evidence that a man had an erection.

[1]This fantasy of childbirth through the skin in the form of blackheads resembles that of a former patient, who believed his mother bore children through blisters induced by the applications of suction cups in the treatment of pneumonia (Chapter 12, this volume) and that of an author who had babies come from carbuncles (White 1949).

As mentioned before, during one period of her analysis she had had a brief affair with a man of the age of her father when he died and as she thought her analyst to be. Subsequently she had accepted no dates although she had opportunities. After the recovery of the memory of having viewed father naked, she continued to work through her transference neurosis in oedipal terms. Then she established a highly pleasing alliance with a man who was eminently suitable to be her children's foster father. Their sexual relations were very gratifying to her.

Throughout her treatment there had been frequent, usually brief interruptions due to the analyst's absence. In the first two years her anxiety was analyzed in terms of oral-sadistic fears and impulses. Her relationship with the new partner had its beginning two months before another planned absence of the analyst, of two months' duration. Just before the separation, she tried to provoke the lover to leave her, using what seemed to me to have been largely voluntary misperceptions of his communications to her. I suggested she was seeking to get him to leave her because she had wanted me to be jealous and to have punished her through means of my absence. During the separation she got along well with her lover. On my return, we analyzed further the meaning of her behavior. Her use of regression was understood as a defense against the separation and an attempt to deny that some aspects of her love for the analyst were based principally on transference elements.

During the analysis of the transference neurosis in oedipal terms it became clear that the visual trauma at the age of 4 had resulted in an attempt to master the psychic injury through the simultaneous use of a number of maneuvers. Regression, denial, repression, and reversal had been used to defend against hostility pertaining to genital sensations and desires. Simultaneously, that erotized aggression was discharged unsatisfactorily and guiltily through repetitious reenactments of the original trauma with her eldest brother who became her father surrogate. There had been an uneven and precocious development of a sadistic superego. While engaging in much voyeuristic and exhibitionistic behavior, she had provoked punishments from her mother. At the same time she had identified both with the phallus of the father and the pregnancy of the mother. Her fears that the mother had stolen her baby were now understood as a denial and reversal of her wish to steal mother's babies and supplant mother as the wife of father. Scant material emerged which could lead to convincing awareness of a theme which was implicit in much of the data, her wish to supplant her father in his relations with mother.

During the last months of her analysis, yet another vicissitude manifested itself with regard to the black sensations in her head. While resolving the oedipal aspects of her transference neurosis, she spoke of fantasies of having intercourse with the analyst while in fact having sexual relations with her fiancé. Previously her preoccupation with the analyst's penis had been concerned with its use as a substitute breast. Now, while visualizing the analyst as a genital father surrogate, the black sensations recurred, although with scant emotional involvement. Over a period of some weeks she repeatedly saw the skein of black threads and as she divested herself of unwanted ego and superego traits she had introjected from various family members, she saw herself pulling out individual black threads and discarding them. Thus the black threads were seen as introjects.

Her relationship with her fiancé seemed to be solid. She felt secure and had scant impetus to continue her analysis. Marriage arrangements were set and she wanted to enter into the new nuptial state without interference from a continued relationship with her analyst. It seemed fruitless to continue the analysis, although likely that there had been inadequate actual recall of primal-scene and toilet-training experiences, and of her implied prolonged fantasy that she had been the analyst's penis. My reasoning was that she would return for further analysis should further difficulties prove to be particularly troublesome. One phenomenon which evidenced itself led me to be optimistic. She had given evidence that she either had an unusual capacity to analyze consciously, without reporting the steps of her analytic activity, or preconsciously. It will be remembered that she had reported certain fears or phobias only after they had disappeared.

Discussion

The material which has been offered could be discussed from many viewpoints. However, the principal aim of this chapter is to illustrate a technique for treating certain patients who suffer from characterological, schizophrenic, and schizoaffective disorders. A technical approach depends on a theoretical orientation.

The following discussion consists of a statement of my theoretical orientation, an outline of the evolved technique, and remarks touching on subjects which do not pertain directly to these matters but have been of special interest to audiences before whom the material has been presented.

Theoretical Orientation

The structure of the ego and superego is determined in large part by introjects and results from the interaction of inborn and socialization factors. These introjects are potentially subject to modification. The roots of severe characterological and functional psychotic disorders can be traced to qualities of the symbiotic and separation-individuation phases described by Mahler and her coworkers. Infantile deprivation or overstimulation (Bergman and Escalona 1949; Chapter 1, this volume) in infancy, whether due predominantly to hereditary and/or constitutional defects within the baby or psychological defects within the mothering figures, does not produce all of the pathological attributes of patients who suffer from such disorders. They have traversed to some degree all phases of psychosexual and psychosocial development, have manifold areas of developmental failure and fixations, and uneven levels of ego and superego development, and the various ego functions are affected differently from patient to patient. In borderline and schizophrenic patients, defensive regression typically transpires in response to adolescent or postadolescent stresses which reawaken unresolved oedipal conflicts (Arlow and Brenner 1964, Glover 1955).

In what follows I shall speak of data obtained from certain investigations into the genesis of schizophrenia. I shall assume that their implications hold as well for patients who have characterological disorders.

Investigations into the environmental influences on the development of schizophrenia has led to many studies of schizophrenic patients and their families (Boyer and Giovacchini 1967, chap. 3). It has been shown that schizophrenic behavior serves various functions in particular kinds of family organizations and cultural groups and that serious impairment of ego functioning may be related to the failure of parents to transmit properly the usual communicational tools of the larger society. The families of schizophrenic patients have discouraged the learning of methods of communication which are based predominantly on secondary-process logic and include generally understood, rather than idiosyncratic, symbolic connotations. Individuals who have been reared in such infavorable milieus do not learn to exchange information well in extrafamilial or cross-cultural situations. It seems probable that they regress defensively when confrontation with their message-sending and -receiving difficulties is superimposed on already existent intrapsychic conflicts.

Consistent with this theoretical orientation regarding the origins of schizophrenia is the notion that the primary therapeutic task is to restore and/or develop a reasonable ego and superego. Theoretically this can be accomplished by modifying or replacing unloving and archaic introjects.

The development of a reasonable ego and superego is accomplished through the diminution of primary-process attributes and influence, and the enhancement of those of the secondary process. In psychoanalysis, the effects of two phenomena are crucial to such id-ego differentiation: identification and the educative and structuralizing effects of interpretation. It is inherent in id-ego differentiation that intrapsychic and interpersonal communication will be improved, but at times technical maneuvers can be employed to speed the development of the latter.

It is generally accepted that the psychological treatment of the disorders which lie nearer the psychotic end of the continuum of conditions which reach between the transference and narcissistic neuroses is especially difficult because of two principal problems, the nature of the transference relationships and the intense fear of the patient of the vicissitudes of his aggressive impulses.

Technique

What follows is a brief and oversimplified statement of the technique which has evolved. Most of its elements have been demonstrated in the case presentation.

The first task of treatment is to encourage id-ego differentiation and reduction of the archaic and sadistic qualities of the superego. Such differentiation results from the incorporation of new introjects and the structuralizing effects of interpretation which is done within the framework of the transference relationships.

Presentation to the patient of a calm, accepting, objective, incorruptible, and intrinsically optimistic analyst offers him an attitudinal model with which to identify. The patient has two main fears which constitute severe hindrances to treatment, that of the magical powers of his aggressive drive derivatives and that of the loss of ego controls. The analyst's communications to the patient during the period when his transference manifestations are predominantly the result of his projection of part objects should be directed toward the patient's ego strengths and his aggressive drive derivatives. The analysis of pregenital drive derivatives will have two phases. In the first, analysis will be directed toward understanding the part-object projections and later, coincident with the development of a stable transference neurosis, the whole-object projections. Analysis of oedipal conflicts will follow that of pregenital conflicts.

Interpretations will be made from the side of the ego whenever possible, and the defensive nature of the patients' productions will be stressed, predominantly from the side of object relations rather than that of content. They will be directed toward the surface, although with such patients, the surface is at times more difficult to determine than with neurotics (Giovacchini 1969). Verbalization of all communications will be encouraged. It will be demonstrated to the patient that awareness of unconscious fantasies strengthens rather than weakens ego boundaries. It is generally accepted by psychoanalysts that interpretations which include genetic aspects are more convincing and structuralizing. Therefore the recovery of actual memories is consistently encouraged. Such memories are more easily recovered when the patient is kept aware of what he is experiencing in the analytic situation and his attention is directed toward prior situations when he felt similar emotional and physical sensations. With most patients, analysis of posture, gestures, and physical tensions facilitates such memory recovery.

The analyst will not be overtly reassuring or formally educative. He will use reconstructions appropriately. One function of this step is to demonstrate to the patient the need of his activity as a participant observer by revealing the analyst's fallibility. The development of a therapeutic alliance is mandatory. An element of that alliance is the patient's curiosity about the dynamic and genetic reasons for his special uses of defensive maneuvers. His controlled regression will be encouraged. He will be allowed time to develop from earlier levels of integration and for working through.

Superego support will be given indirectly. The analytic framework will be of such a nature that what is expected and allowable on the part of the patient are made clear from the beginning (Chapter 4, this volume). The analyst will attempt to retain his anonymity and will aim at obtaining the patient's fantasies.

Special attention will be directed to the defensive purposes of regression and acting out. When the patient consistently omits relevant material, the analyst will seek to stimulate him to fill obvious gaps.

Especially when therapeutic plateaus are reached, the analyst will turn his atttention to self-analysis to determine whether his own unconscious problems or attitudes contribute to his lack of understanding of what the patient presents to him and to the lack of therapeutic progress. If such problems exist and self-analysis does not alleviate the therapeutic block, the analyst will seek further personal analysis.

The analysis of superego introjects is as important as that of ego introjects. While the understanding of paranoid elements and their uses is mandatory, depressive elements must not be overlooked. Treatment is perhaps speeded if analysis of depressive elements is stressed whenever possible over that of paranoid elements.

The patient's capacity to think, remember, and analyze for himself will be encouraged. His defensive uses of confusion, forgetfulness, and dependency on the therapist to analyze for him will be interpreted consistently. The analyst will be as passive and make as few interpretations as is consistent with the patient's anxiety. I have the impression that some interpretations given to such patients are aimed more at alleviating the anxiety of the analyst than that of the patient. Others seem to be made *pro forma*. Unnecessary interpretations increase the patient's dependency and interfere with his self-growth. They also rob him of the exhilaration which coincides with successful bits of self-analysis.

The case history and discussion which have been offered thus far, in addition to the section which follows under the title "Vision, Headache, and the Halo," have been presented before a number of audiences which have included at least 500 psychoanalysts. They have been discussed extensively and intensively. The principal questions which arose pertaining to the present material had to do with diagnosis, the transference relationships which developed, and the efficacy of the outlined procedure. A specific query concerning the transference had to do with the reasons why this patient did not develop a clear transference psychosis during her analysis.

Diagnosis

The difficulties encountered in establishing a diagnosis stated in usual psychiatric terms of patients whose disturbances lie in the continuum extending between the transference and narcissistic neuroses is well known and will not be repeated here (Boyer and Giovacchini 1967). The analysts who voiced their opinions about the diagnosis of this case were divided. Those whose viewpoint is influenced heavily by Kleinian psychology were inclined almost uniformly to consider the patient to have been schizophrenic, whereas those oriented more to the structural theory preferred the label borderline syndrome[2] or psychotic character (Frosch 1964). My own tendency is to consider her to have had a severe hysterical personality disorder with schizoid trends.

Transference Relationships

The nature of the transference provides data which can be used in establishing a diagnosis (M. Little 1966, Modell 1963).

In my psychoanalytic experience with 30 patients who have suffered from severe characterological disorders or schizophrenic or schizoaffective psychoses, the transference has been divided almost always into two overlapping phases (Boyer 1966; Boyer and Giovacchini 1967, chap. 4; Chapter 4, this volume). The first phase has corresponded to the syndrome generally subsumed under the term transference psychosis, although other names have been used (Fromm-Reichmann 1939, 1950; M. Little 1958; Pichon Rivière 1951; Searles 1963b; Wallerstein 1967). During its analysis, the patient achieves a higher degree of id-ego and id-superego differentiation. The 25 patients who have had, or appear to be on the way to having, a favorable outcome have developed a stable transference neurosis.

The patient whose case fragment supplies the body of this chapter was one of the few in whom the clear development of a transference psychosis was absent. I cannot offer a satisfactory explanation. The special element of the initial intense split transference may have contributed. Psychotic elements were included in her use of the mother-in-law as a mother transference surrogate. A second explanation has occurred to me, but the available data do not support it unequivocably: it seems likely that she had a warm and loving early relationship with her black maid.

Although a detailed review of the patient's history which would include the chronology of development of defenses, adaptive techniques, and symptomatology would be of interest, it will be omitted because of considerations of space.

[2]The status of the concepts borderline state and borderline case has been the subject of many articles, symposia, and reviews; for example, Grinker et al. (1968), Paz (1963), Rangell (1955), and Schmideberg (1959). The consensus has been that for the diagnosis of the individual case, it is necessary to assess the libidinal orientation and to make an inventory of ego functions. Recent reports of studies directed toward that inventory are Bellak and Hurvich (1969), Grinker et al. (1968), and Kernberg (1967).

Efficacy of Treatment

As noted above, 30 patients of the mentioned diagnostic categories have entered psychoanalysis. Seven began their treatment while still floridly psychotic or just after they had been treated with electro-convulsive or insulin shock therapy; all developed obvious transference psychoses. Five subsequently developed transference neuroses. Three subsequently analyzed pregenital and oedipal problems successfully and have had no psychotic regressions during the past ten to 15 years. Two of the three reentered analysis at a later period because of neurotic depression which responded to treatment. Two terminated analysis because of unavoidable circumstances while their transference neuroses were being analyzed. They retain neurotic problems but have not suffered psychotic regressions for five and eight years, respectively. Two patients committed suicide when I was away from my office and their transference psychoses had not been analyzed. One had attempted suicide repeatedly before treatment began. He took his life when his psychotic wife ran off with another man at a time which coincided with my departure.

The 23 patients I have analyzed or am analyzing who were not acutely psychotic when treatment began presented the features of severe disturbances characterized by various proportions of the symptoms of the hysteric, the obsessive, and the impulse neurotic. A number would fit the diagnosis borderline syndrome as outlined by Kernberg (1967). Six of them had been hospitalized once too many times each and treated with shock therapies for schizophrenia or schizo-affective psychosis. A dozen had undergone brief psychotic episodes for which they had not been immured or, as in the case of the present patient, had suffered questionably psychotic reactions. Twenty of these patients developed transference psychoses. Of the 23, 11 worked through pregenital and oedipal problems and none has suffered psychotic regression. Their analyses were terminated two to 15 years ago. Nine others reached less satisfactory results. Eight of them, while obviously improved, still have problems of various degrees of severity, although none has reverted to overt psychosis. One became psychotic anew and refused further analytic treatment; she has been hospitalized for the past five years.

The treatment of three cases resulted in unqualified failure. None had undergone an acute psychotic episode prior to analysis and none developed a transference psychosis although the erotized transference of one reached awesome proportions. In two instances, the failure was probably due to my own unanalyzed problems (Chapter 4, this volume).

Vision, Headache, and the Halo

While studying reactions to stress in the course of superego formation, Greenacre (1947) found patients to have presented material which showed connections between visual shock, headache, and the development of a halo.

> Schematically the sequence is as follows. The child receives a stunning psychic blow, usually an overwhelming visual experience which has the effect of dazing and bewildering it. There is generally the sensation of lights, flashes of lightning, bright colors or some sort of aurora. This may seem to invest the object, or objects seen, or it may be felt as occurring in the subject's own head experienced literally as seeing stars. The initial experience always produces the most intense emotions, whether of fear, rage or horror. There is at first a feeling of unreality, or of confusion. The shocking stimulus arouses an erotized aggression which demands subsequent mastery. Sometimes the little voyeur feels impelled to repeat the experience as though to test its reality. Peeping or fantasies of peeping are accompanied by sensations of tension and strain in the eyes or across the frontal region. Headaches occur later when new situations reactivate the original trauma. Mastery is attempted by successive repetition in fantasy (reality testing), partial regression, or by the development of severely binding superego reaction-formations of goodness which are supplemented by or converted into lofty ideals. As the tense goodness relaxes a little, the headache improves and the ideals are loftier but less exigent. Figuratively, the child develops a halo to which, if it remains too burdensome, he reacts by throwing it defiantly away . . . or by endowing someone else with it. Such children and adults seem to overvalue enormously those whom they love, projecting onto them the extreme ideals and demands they first required of themselves. Quite often the loved one is seen as a saint on a pedestal, worshipped rather than loved, and kept almost inviolate in an overestimation which is in actuality a devaluation. (pp. 132–133)

She added:

> Such strong visual stimulation adds very much to the stress of superego formation at whatever time it occurs, although its effects are much abated during the latency period. (p. 145)

Greenacre found the sight of the genitalia of the adult of the opposite sex to be most likely to produce visual overstimulation. The sight of the female genitals was never invested with the shining light. The pedestal on which these children placed people was determined by the observation of the erect genital of the father. The symptom complex was noted to occur particularly in patients with strong obsessive and compulsive trends and the symptomatology to be strikingly clear in schizophrenic patients.

The similarities between the symptom complex and its genesis in the case of the woman whose case history provides the material for this chapter and that of Greenacre's vision, headache, and the halo are striking, as are the defensive and reliving purposes and the effects on superego development which she described. It is unnecessary to spell out the areas of agreement and the minor variations. There are two obvious differences. The present patient's symptom complex was vision, black sensations in the head, and the halo; she did not reveal a strong anal fixation, resulting in obsessions, compulsions, and the use of displacement as a cardinal defense maneuver. This woman's character structure was more akin to the hysterical personality disorder.

The many discussants of this chapter and its author are unable to explain the reasons for the variant symptomatology. Garma (1968) made an interesting observation. In the present case the patient gradually visualized the blackness in her head more and more concretely. What was originally perceived as a black mass became a tangled skein of strings which subsequently were seen as phalluses with oral-sadistic characteristics. Long (1968) and Simmonds (1968) suggested calling this patient "The Medusa Lady." In earlier studies on headaches Garma (1958) had shown that they sometimes represent negative hallucinations. Schechtmann (1968) has given supportive data. Greenacre (1967) considered the second difference to be perhaps more apparent than real. She noted that the patient had an unusual degree of polymorphous perversity in her psychosexual development and that one manifestation of her erotized aggression, in this instance self-directed, consisted of the patient's anal and genital manipulations with all of the fingers of both hands. Greenacre thought that further analysis of the patient's toilet-training and its effects on her personality development would reveal more obvious evidence of qualities of the obsessive-compulsive neurotic. Similar observations were made independently by Aray (1968) and Teruel (1968). This supposition cannot be validated on the basis of the available material.

The symptoms vision, blackness in the head, and the halo, appear to be unique in the psychoanalytic literature. Abraham (1913) was the first to write of blackness before the eyes as a symptom which expresses an inhibition of scoptophilic tendencies. He wrote of a man who had a pronounced aversion to looking at his mother and sister, even when they were fully clothed. The patient suffered from anxiety lest he should unintentionally impregnate either of them. The libidinal wishes directed toward his mother were transferred to other, mainly older women, but were prevented from showing themselves in their real character, being expressed as a dread of looking at such women. When he looked at mature women, a blackness came before his eyes.

> In this way the patient was prevented from seeing women who were attractive to him. That he should have found a substitute along hallucinatory paths for this imposed privation is in complete agreement with the psychology of dementia praecox. He would, for instance, see lying naked before him a middle-aged woman who, according to his own account, bore a great resemblance to his mother. He furthermore admitted in a way which carried conviction that his avoidance of the sight of female persons was in effect an avoidance of the female, or more correctly, of the maternal, genitals. (p. 188)

There are obvious similarities between Abraham's case and that of the patient of this chapter. Both experienced black sensations when confronted with visual stimuli which reactivated forbidden incestuous wishes, although the man perceived his to be before his eyes and the woman hers within her head; the man had to avoid looking at women who reminded him of his mother and the woman at men's lower halves, lest she see a bulge which would make her think of her father's erection; each hallucinated the object the black sensations were intended to make invisible.[3]

[3]Clinically, patients complain frequently of a triad of symptoms, each of which results neurophysiologically from changes in peripheral blood flow: headaches, sensations of blackness, and dizziness. For elucidation of the meanings of the symptom dizziness, see Giovacchini (1958).

Summary

A technique for the treatment within the framework of the structural theory of certain characterological, schizophrenic, and schizoaffective disorders has been presented through the presentation of a fragment of an analysis in which have been interpolated explanatory remarks. Problems pertaining to diagnosis have been discussed. The analysand had a symptom complex, a visual trauma followed by sensations of blackness in the head and the development of a figurative halo, strongly reminiscent of the syndrome described by Greenacre: vision, headache, and the halo. The symptom complex had similar origins and psychological uses as that of Greenacre's patients. Its analysis was crucial to the apparently satisfactory result which was achieved in an unusually short time.

6

A Bizarre Suicidal Attempt

Early in therapy, Robert, an adolescent, schizophrenic, identical twin, attempted suicide in a bizarre fashion. His effort failed by chance. While a previous publication dealt with the technical aspects of Robert's treatment (Boyer 1972), this chapter will outline the meanings of the suicide attempt which have emerged during the three ensuing years of his ongoing psychoanalysis.

The meanings included those which are commonly reported for suicidal attempts. It was the result of strong, ambivalent dependence on an archaic, sadistic superego and the need to be free of unbearable guilt (Fenichel 1945, Freud 1917b, Garma and Rascovsky 1948, Menninger 1931). Murderous aggression was turned against the self, and the

---

This chapter is reprinted as it was first published. Robert terminated his treatment voluntarily after he had made significant progress. He observed that as he improved, his mother, a chronic, ambulatory schizophrenic, regressed and treated his brothers and father increasingly badly and that at least one of his brothers was responding with transient psychotic episodes. Robert decided to stop his analysis in hopes that an interruption of his own improvement might enable his mother to improve and cause the other family members less emotional trauma. To be sure, his altruistic motivation for termination was also in the service of defense, coming at a time when he was seriously worried about the potentially magical effects of his hostility on me as a bad-mother surrogate. Unfortunately, his self-deprivation served no good purpose. The parents divorced, and all three of his brothers suffered psychotic regressions. Robert never returned for further treatment with me. Some eight years later, I learned that he had become a chronic, simple schizophrenic, living on welfare and in half-way houses. See Chapter 9 for further discussion of this patient.

act was intended to constitute a rebirth and reconciliation with the loved and hated mother (Garma 1943; O'Connor 1948; Rado 1951; Zilboorg 1936, 1937). Other meanings were idiosyncratic. The act was meant also to result in reconciliation and fusion with his "other half," his twin (Burlingham 1952, Maenchen 1968) and was a symbolic self-castration (Lewis 1933, Resnik 1972). At the same time, it was intended to result in the reduction of his father's power and/or his murder. It is thought by many psychoanalysts that schizophrenic breakdowns constitute regressive defenses against revivified unresolved oedipal conflicts (Arlow and Brenner 1964, Glover 1955). The suicidal attempt was a like event.

Case Material

History

When first seen, Robert and his twin, Frank, were 17. There were brothers of 15 and 12. Despite the length of his treatment, meager information exists concerning his early childhood and no clear picture has emerged of his past and present relations with his younger siblings.

The 61-year-old father, a successful and respected physician, suffered from a severe obsessive-compulsive characterological disorder and was a rigid emotional isolate who had been divorced by a previous wife.

The 54-year-old mother, a chronic schizophrenic with paranoid and hysterical traits, was a virgin until she married at 36. Her symptomatology literally ruled the household. Her husband and sons feared that any serious frustration of her wishes, no matter how irrational, would result in their loss of her through permanent insanity.

The boys were reared in an atmosphere devoid of physical affection, with grossly inconsistent treatment in all areas including discipline. Overt expressions of anger and sexual interest were taboo. At 21, the twins are still supposed to have "double dates"; each, being a virgin, is to prevent the other's becoming sexually involved. Yet sadistic teasing and the boys' barely covert masturbation were always tolerated and "nudie girl" magazines occupied the bathroom. The priggish mother was simultaneously overtly exhibitionistic and seductive.

Compared to Robert, Frank was relatively outgoing and successful. Robert was always "cute," a passive follower, and exceptionally well behaved. He felt he had "no personal identity" but was merely an extension of his mother and twin. He could not bear to be alone and spent all of his time tagging after one or the other, agreeably and passively entering into their activities when permitted to do so. Contacts with his father were limited almost entirely to emotionally sterile family dinners. Robert renounced his tenuous hold on a masculine identity after a devastating pubertal experience, but his subsequent feminine identification did not include overt homosexual behavior (Freud 1920). The mother regularly left her bedroom and bathroom doors open and inconsistently shooed the boys out when they entered. When Robert reached puberty at 14 and continued his prior exciting investigations, she repeatedly became angry and hysterically screamed out her conviction that he was about to rape her. That was traumatic in itself, but his own fears that he would act on his rape fantasies were reinforced by his father.

The parents' inconsistent attitudes and treatment of their sons extended also to religion. The mother taught them to read via Bible stories; the father passively acquiesced. At the same time, the parents claimed to be atheists and taught the children that religious beliefs and activities were the results of projective systems. The boys attended many churches with their friends, ostensibly for social reasons.

At 16, Frank induced Robert to attend with him the summer camp of a religious youth movement with a fire-and-brimstone orientation. While there, Robert was intensely stimulated by observations of young couples who were engaged in sexual activities. Seeking assistance in his efforts to be good, he turned to religious leaders who righteously damned such behavior, and he uncritically embraced their teachings. Frank became somewhat involved with a girl and Robert felt deserted. Thereafter, the twins were not close again.

Following their return from camp, Robert became the confidant of a devoutly religious woman, a Mrs. Jones, with whom he spent endless hours. She caressed him and burdened him with her marital problems, which she attributed to the animal desires of her husband. He literally believed her counseling that if he engaged in sexual or hostile thoughts or actions, he would burn in hell forever. Titillated by their contacts, he was terrified by rape fantasies and murderous wishes toward her husband. He consciously equated the woman's seductive and frustrating behavior with that of his mother. To support his efforts to be good, he converted to ultraconservative Christianity. He became so preoccupied with interminable ruminations about good and evil that he withdrew from family and social contacts and his schoolwork suffered severely.

Eventually, he was sent to a child analyst who treated him supportively and with drugs, but his deterioration continued. He desperately turned to deep involvement with Eastern religions and spent most of his time in church activities and ruminations. He hallucinated the voices of God and Satan, who gave him contradictory advice. He became manifestly hebephrenic. Hospitalized, he received electroshock therapy which enabled him to deny his continuing hallucinations and to become craftily evasive rather than merely silly. After his hospital discharge, a further year of similar therapy with his doctor resulted in no changes in his thinking and behavior. Then his father, who had read my publication (Boyer and Giovacchini 1967), asked me to undertake his son's psychoanalysis as a last resort. However, Robert could not bring himself to leave his therapist immediately and I saw him only five times during the next six months, when his doctor was on vacation or hospitalized for an illness.

In those interviews, as later, I dealt with him only interpretively, focusing on the transference. My illustration for him of some of his defensive uses of denial, projection, splitting, regression, and manipulation through passivity enabled him to become aware that his previously unconscious hatred of his therapist had not caused that man's illness and made him hopeful that he might eventually understand himself. With renewed hope, he was able to enter a small, private college. During the fifth interview, I also showed him that he feared both positive and negative feelings and that whenever he began to have feelings of either sort toward me, he immediately switched to religious ruminations. He said he felt vastly relieved and asked to be transferred to my care.

Treatment

During the first interview, I informed him I would be away for two weeks in December (several months hence), to begin to prepare him for the separation and the expected revived conflicts about separation and sibling rivalry which may occur during Christmas reactions (Chapter 12, this volume). However, he seemed oblivious of my message and in subsequent interviews began to deal dramatically with his fears of fusion with me which might result in his or my physical or mental destruction. Following the interview, for the first time in many months, he provoked his mother into terror by walking in on her when she was partly clad. When I reminded him that he had done so previously, when he had been disturbed by wishes for his father's tender concern, he was greatly relieved and said he had been confusing his father and me in his thoughts and during interviews saw his father's face on my body. He suspected that his father feared closeness with him and used his mother as a wall between them. In the next interview he told me that what I said to him seemed so true that he was unsure whether or not he had put his thoughts into my mind. Perhaps the office and I were extensions of his thoughts. He pounded on the desk beside his chair to reassure himself it had physical reality.

The next time we met, he introduced the subject of sex by showing me doodles, which he called penises and testicles, and asked whether physical contact was necessary in psychoanalysis. I asked whether he feared he would have to take the role of a girl to learn to be a man. Vastly relieved, he alluded to a fear of separation. When I asked whether he was worried about my Christmas absence, he claimed he had forgotten about that, but asked for a second weekly interview, which was granted.

After that interview he provoked his father into calling me by repeating his previous actions with his mother. I said he seemed to use his parents as a wall between us and that he feared he would become close with me and then be harmed by separation. I suggested he also feared intimacy which might lead to fusion which could destroy either of us. At the same time, he was afraid that if he became less involved with his parents they might abandon him or be injured by losing emotional sustenance from him. He responded with a veiled allusion to Christmas.

When next seen, he was withdrawn, suspicious, and had recathected his hallucinations of the voices of God and Satan. I spoke of the defensive use of his regression, denial, and projection and he became rational. By the next interview he could tell me that he feared revealing his secrets to me because they might convert me to Christianity and he would be destroyed as a person. I might use Christianity to harm him as had Mrs. Jones after the period in the youth camp. He feared trust might lead to fusion. Therefore, he must stop treatment to protect me as he might turn me into a nonfeeling machine like he was. Another theme which emerged was that of leaving to avoid being left.

October's interviews were occupied with intensely dramatic episodes which were intended to test his fears that he could destroy me with magical thoughts of fusion or murder. Finally, three weeks before Thanksgiving, he said he assumed I would not see him on that day and asked for a substitute appointment.

When we met again, he said Christ was love, but later he'd be able to reach out to people rather than Christ for love. My love for him made him know the voices of God and Satan were projections. Then he became frightened, thinking if he were to love me, I would use him as a woman. His homosexual panic was followed by intense depersonalization, until I said he might have withdrawn to get even with me for not suggesting we meet on Thanksgiving Day. I reminded him he'd not spoken of his brothers during October and asked whether Frank would be home from college on the holiday. He ignored the question, but instead for the first time mentioned masturbation and said he had to make his penis numb to avoid excitement; he agreed when I asked whether when he felt love for me he felt sexually excited. He asked for reassurance that we could meet four times weekly in January.

On Thanksgiving Eve, Robert said he had cried after the last interview because he wanted to smash my face in revenge for my not seeing him on the holiday and for not immediately increasing his interviews to four times weekly.

The information which follows stems from the only interview I have had with his parents, a meeting which took place after the suicidal attempt which will now be described and from subsequent interview material from Robert.

After our Wednesday interview, Robert sought affection from his mother, but she again interpreted his advances to be sexual and was outraged. His interpretation of his behavior was that he wanted to be held, to have her demonstrate that she loved him as much as she did his brothers. During the preceding 25 interviews, his few statements about his brothers concerned envy of them. On Thanksgiving Day, the first time his twin had been with the family in two months, Robert had behaved badly. He was angry because his parents treated all of the brothers alike. He had striven unsuccessfully to have his father control and discipline him.

When the family retired, Robert could not sleep. He prayed to God to advise him as to whether he should kill himself to protect his parents from his anger. He silently left the house. His car had a chassis which could be raised and lowered hydraulically. He drove to a site near his school, parked on the side of the freeway, and decided God had told him to kill himself. He pressed the lever to lower the chassis, leapt from the car, and thrust his head between the descending car and the gravel shoulder. He lay still, listening to the noises of bones breaking as his skull was crushed.

Some hours later, Robert was found by a highway patrolman, still conscious. He was cold and in some pain. He was surprised that he was alive but assumed God had changed His mind.

He was hospitalized for surgical intervention for his depressed fracture. During the three weeks I saw him in the hospital, before leaving for a fortnight, Robert was markedly depersonalized. He considered his suicidal attempt to have been totally rational. Later I learned that during that period he had considered me as merely "an extension of his mind." We were physical and psychological components of one another, and he had told me little because he knew we had the same thoughts.

I shall not comment on his further treatment except to note that on my return he began couch therapy four times weekly. The family were placed in conjoint treatment with another therapist and Robert has continued to receive tranquilizers, now down to minimal doses, prescribed by the psychiatrist who had served as administrator while he was hospitalized. The three courses of treatment have continued.

He has lived at home with his parents and his younger brothers, attending a nearby college where he has done good work in courses which are not designed to prepare him for any future career. He socializes more and has had a few innocent dates. His twin and he are friendly but not very close. He has become decreasingly involved in Eastern religions. During his interviews, transitory psychotic episodes have occurred with decreasing frequency. They have disappeared promptly when their defensive purposes have been interpreted. No overt psychotic episodes have occurred outside the office in a year and a half. I have left him many times, three times for two months each.

During the first eighteen months of his analysis, he continued to be deeply involved in religious activities, working through his need for and fear of fusion with "the Universe," a maternal surrogate. He associated socially only with old women and religious masters of both sexes, whom he used largely for prohibitive superego support. Since then, he has gradually weaned himself from such activities and has begun to seek peer relationships. He increasingly understands his psychological fusion with his twin and his feminine identification. The family have become less secretive, and the boys are less fearful of frustrating their mother. Robert is considering leaving home, despite his awareness that his parents use his illness to keep the marriage intact. Obviously, much remains to be done. Oedipal material is still used in the service of oral needs and anal conflicts have not even arisen.

The Meanings of Robert's Bizarre Suicidal Attempt

It is not easy to separate the meanings of Robert's suicidal attempt into the expressions of drive vicissitudes and defensive maneuvers.

While the attempt constituted the turning inward of aggression, it was also an act of love, intended to protect various people from the effects of his angry and lustful impulses. It was meant additionally to prevent the development of highly desired intimacy with me in my role of maternal surrogate, which might lead to fusion and its dangers.

The fear of intimacy was initially global but eventually became understandable in three ways. The first clearly definable level consisted of a conviction that I was Satan. Satan was equated with psychologists whose entire preoccupation was with corporeal impulses, lustful and cruel. If we became close, he would be imbued with my sinful desires. At the same time, I would become pervaded with his spiritual, Christlike qualities. Then I would be converted to Christianity and become a religious zealot who would misuse him as had Mrs. Jones.

The second level was not accompanied by delusional belief, as had been the first, which had occurred largely during the first month that I began seeing him four times weekly. He fantasized that I was his mother and he was my intrauterine baby. He would control me with passivity and helplessness. At the same time, we were mutually parasitic and nutritive. He also had the capacity to kill the other babies inside my womb. There was a danger that he would eat me up from the inside and also the risk I would abort him.

The third level, which he had mentioned first before the suicidal attempt, reemerged only after the two aforementioned meanings of intimacy. In it, he was a small child, perhaps a girl, and needed to obtain my phallus in order to grow to be a man. To obtain it, he would have to submit to my sexual embrace, during which his oral or anal teeth would bite it off. Hints were dropped concerning two reasons why such an act would be dangerous to him, but neither has been elucidated thoroughly. I might castrate or kill him for his having castrated me, or he might then have to kill his father and service his mother sexually.

The manner in which the remaining reasons, which have so far been ascribed to his suicidal attempt, emerged is almost as interesting as they are. Libidinal vicissitudes predominated.

In late January I canceled a Friday interview. The following Monday his speech was disconnected and evasive. I said he spoke in a manner which he had used when he was angry with his mother and knew would upset her. He responded: "What am I supposed to do? I missed you and was angry with you because you'd gone away with your wife and had fun together, nude." Later, after I said I'd be away for some time in March, he responded by revealing a previously unmentioned fantasy. He said maybe his mother and I could get together and work out our "sexual hang-ups." He recalled that, before he tried to kill himself, he had thought that during the impending Christmas separation his mother and I would be together, producing a Christ-child. As Satan, I would be Joseph, and his mother and I would betray his father, who was God. Before the attempt at self-murder, he had been certain at times that he was Christ, but he had been unable to explain to himself how he had been the product of spiritual love. He had wondered whether his father had been Satan-Joseph and with his mother, the Virgin, had betrayed God.

He then said it was very difficult to accept that he had been so sinful as to have sought to kill himself. He had been trying for about two months to understand how he could have done that, and how he could have viewed the act as moral. He had wanted to know the death experience, but to know it was immoral because "such knowledge was self-glorifying" and the act had been intended to result in rebirth. According to Christianity and Theosophy, to be good means to kill the self, "to kill the mind which is the slayer of the real," which is a solely spiritual experience. To know and not just live on faith is sinful. He said, "On the night I killed myself to be reborn, I wanted to get even with you and mother for what you were going to do at Christmastime." He "had had to kill his mind" and thus had chosen to crush his head, since his mind was in his head. He didn't shoot his brains out because that act could only be interpreted as voluntary suicide and his parents would have been embarrassed and blamed for his death. He'd tried to make the attempt look accidental. When the patrolman had asked him how he came to have his head under the car, he had claimed the chassis fell on him when he was inspecting a tire.

He continued: "Why aren't you afraid of me now? You know I'm trying to get even with you because you'll be away in March. That's why I'm threatening to kill myself again. I can never believe you'll come back when you go away. I always think you'll be with my mother, having fun, nude, and you'll be so happy together there won't be any room for me."

At this point in the interview, he went into a light trance and relived anew his experience while underneath the car. He heard the noise of cracking bones, moaned, and shivered with cold. He thought he'd awaken in Heaven and Jesus would be waiting for him, since God had told Christ, "You should kill yourself to save the world." The crushing of his head was like the crown of thorns. He had tried also to make his wrists and ankles bleed where the nails went into Christ. Then he would be God's favorite son and never again be depressed at Christmastime.

I reminded him that he had both said that he was Christ and that Jesus would be awaiting him. I asked whether this might be related to his being a twin. He was startled into alertness. He then remembered that during the three months before the suicidal attempt he had considered himself to be a troublemaker, doing badly at school to upset his father. His twin, by contrast, had done well scholastically. He recalled that Frank had grown a beard and long hair at that time and "looked just like the pictures of Christ." Robert had wanted to be God's favorite son, but he was only "half a son." He had been separated psychologically from his twin for three years, after the summer camp experience when he was 16, and wanted to be reunited with his brother in love. Thus, Robert strove, via his attempt to kill himself, to achieve fusion not only with his mother, but, as would be expected, with his twin.

Following my two months' summer absence another theme emerged. Soon after I returned, he told me he now remembered that he had read my book before he'd tried to commit suicide. There he had read that a previous patient had committed suicide when I left him. He assumed that the young man had done so because he wanted to destroy my reputation and remove my "potency." Robert said he'd always tried to make his father "impotent" in the eyes of his mother by making a fool of him one way or another and now suspected that when he tried to kill himself, he wanted to reduce my stature in the eyes of the world and more specifically of his mother. Perhaps my loss of status would lead me to such shame that I would kill myself. Ultimately, of course, he would thus have murdered me.

Summary

The therapy of patients who suffer from severe characterological, schizoid, schizophrenic, and schizoaffective psychoses always involve the risk of a suicidal event. This is particularly true with the announcement of a forthcoming absence or during a planned separation.

Robert had developed an archaic, sadistic superego and his sense of personal and sexual identity was insecure. The attempt at suicide was the result of his strong ambivalent dependence on his immature superego and the need to be free of unbearable guilt. As a gesture of love, Robert turned his murderous aggression against himself and defended himself and others from his lustful impulses. Lacking self-esteem and a feeling of inner and outer superego support, he felt himself to be deserted and was desolate. His suicidal act was also intended to constitute a rebirth and a reconciliation with his mother. His being a twin resulted in a variant of that thesis: after his rebirth, he was to become united with his adored and hated brother, his "other half." At the same time, his death was to result in his becoming the favorite son of all mankind at Christmastime, Jesus; that status was to be shared by Frank. His attempt at self-murder, then, can be viewed simultaneously as a call for help and an act of vengeance. The suicidal act constituted an oedipal victory, but at the same time was a regressive defensive action against unsatisfactorily resolved oedipal problems.

A Note on the Language of Psychotic Acting Out

Rudolf Ekstein

In another chapter Dr. Boyer suggests that (1955):

> Case material derived from patients . . . revealed that their Christmas depressions were the result of unresolved sibling rivalries. In them the birth of Christ, a fantasied competitor against whom they were unable successfully to contest, reawakened memories of unsuccessful rivalry with siblings, real or fantasied, in their pasts. . . . There was some indication that they at times identified with Christ in an attempt to deny their own inferiority and to obtain the favoritism which would be His just due. (p. 487)

He wonders then whether the celebration of Christmas could be considered a "culturally integrated, group manicoid, defensive reaction meant to obviate guilt related to murder wishes against siblings." This chapter broadens the issue and suggests that we look as well at a patient's "Christmas psychosis." Boyer asks us, I believe, to differentiate betwen neurotic and psychotic reactions which indicate similar content, but which in the latter case usually invoke lower, more archaic levels of personality organization. An old simile used by W. Reich (1933) when describing the task of character analysis suggests that the analyst through his analysis of the defenses must attack layer after layer of the onion in order to get to the core conflict. This simile, of course, pictures a personality organization which has available a strong and ordered system of defenses which actually makes it possible by means of interpretation to work through transference and resistance manifestations in order to bring about resolution of the core conflict.

Another simile affords perhaps a better glimpse of the problem when we deal with schizophrenic personality organization. The cobra egg, because of its thin and soft shell, permits one to see the outline of the dangerous snake right through the thin membrane, before the cobra hatches. If the shell breaks apart and opens, the baby cobra is ready to strike. We do not need to remove layer after layer, but rather we can see behind the weak and unstable neuroticlike defenses, behind the capacity for some secondary-process thinking, the primary process and the violence of the primitive and disordered defenses. If we peel an onion we might have tears in our eyes before we ever get to the core conflict; if we break the cobra egg we are actually in deadly trouble. I am implying, it is clear, that he who treats neurotics by analytical means has to prepare himself for one set of technical problems, while he who treats schizophrenics, of the kind Boyer has described so vividly, must have much more respect for cobra eggshells and therefore must deal with a different set of technical and theoretical considerations.

The onion metaphor suggests that we slowly penetrate defensive structure after defensive structure and that we cannot expect to know much about the core conflict until and unless we have removed one layer after the other. The secret seems to be deeply hidden behind the defenses although we have learned that the nature of the defense frequently permits a guess as to the nature of the conflict the defense is trying to ward off or keep under repression.

The simile of the cobra egg suggests that we see all layers of the conflict at the same time, that nothing is hidden, and all is operative simultaneously. I am reminded of Freud's (1930) picture of the mind, a fantasy of all the Romes coexisting side by side and visible at the same time, beginning with Roma Quadrata to the modern Rome of today. Freud's picture in which he compared all the Romes of the past and the one of the present with the human mind led him almost against his wish to a special difficulty:

> The assumption that everything is preserved holds good even in mental life only on condition that the organ of the mind has remained intact and that its tissues have not been damaged by

> trauma or inflammation. But destructive influences which can be compared to causes of illness like these are never lacking in the history of a city, even if it has had a less checkered past than Rome. . . . (p. 71)

He suggested that "perhaps we ought to content ourselves with asserting that what is past in mental life may be preserved and is not necessarily destroyed" (p. 71). He may have added that sometimes what is past in mental life has been preserved, but what should be present has never grown, or is not strong enough to allow the resolution of conflict along nonpsychotic lines.

Boyer gives us beautiful clinical material concerning the case of Robert, who seemed to have made a remarkable recovery which permitted him to cope with therapy, cope with his life, withstand long separations from the therapist, and to move toward a more integrated personality.

But what is the nature of the cure in this kind of case?

Content-wise, in terms of dynamics, the Christmas psychosis of Robert is very similar to the neurotic conditions, the conflicts presented, the dynamics entertained, that Boyer described almost 20 years earlier (Chapter 11, this volume).

When we look at the different dynamic explanations we cannot help but agree with the different meanings this patient has given to the bizarre suicide, although we have difficulty finding the dominant aspect, that core conflict for which the onion metaphor suggests we look. Rather, we are impressed with constant fluctuations between borderline states of adjustment, which often resemble neurotic conditions, and powerful, regressive schizophrenic reactions, splitting of self-organization, fusion states, autistic withdrawal, and a breakdown of self- and object constancy.

I have suggested elsewhere (Ekstein and Caruth 1966) that psychotic acting out differs from neurotic acting out inasmuch as the acting out can be understood best in terms of primary-process language.

Neurotic acting out is a substitute for thinking, a trial thought expressed in secondary-process language. Psychotic acting out, however, must be understood as a trial thought expressed in the language of primary thought disorder, much more dreamlike language in which self- and object representations are both projections of the patient's inner life, representing a struggle between unstable introjects and unstable self-representations. The actual objects are represented in their psychotic distortions and the external representations are merely stepping-stones into the patient's dreamworld, his primary-process thought. His return to reality in the form of psychotic acting out is like a nightmare translated into real, often self-destructive activity.

The bizarre suicidal episode of this patient, the meaning of which unravels itself in the consecutive treatment sessions, follows the logic of the dream. The fractured head of the victim has now overdetermined symbolic meaning, stands for Robert and his father, for Robert and/or the sibling, for his broken reasoning powers, and for his damaged genitals, and thus elaborates conflicts which detail the seesaw struggle between individuals and autism on the one hand and loss of self and fusion and symbiotic union with the mother on the other. The Christ in Robert's life represents, then, the twin brother to be destroyed, the annihilated self, the turning away from the mother in order to be united and fused with the father, and the longing for the mother, a replica of the real mother, who may be seen simultaneously as the holy, nurturing Mary and the tempting Magdalena, and who, like Robert's psychotic mother, said: "I don't know how to love him," a phrase from *Jesus Christ, Superstar*, the rock-and-roll dramatization of the Christmas and Easter themes.

Freud's comparison of the human mind with the eternal city of Rome leaves open the question of whether we are to assume that certain destructions in the city or the mind may make total reconstruction impossible; permits us to conjecture whether we are to speak about ego deficits, possible universal destruction; or, whether we are to talk about ego deficits such as the lack of self- and object constancy in terms of basic emotional nurture, basic cognitive stimuli never provided, and now perhaps coming too late, as is said to be true in the case of missed hatching or stimulation phases.

I am returning to the two metaphors: onion, layers, and core conflict; cobra egg, its thin layer behind which can be seen the murderous primary process, the helpless, young, or deadly attacker.

What are the consequences for technique, for interpretation, for the transference situation if we deal with a psychic organization such as that available to Boyer's patient, Robert? The vicissitudes of the psychotic transference are expressed in psychotic rather than neurotic ambivalences. The therapist is split, not between the angry and the kind father, the tempting and the withholding mother, but rather between Almighty God and the seductive, powerful, and deadly Satan on the one hand and the seductive, holy, nurturing mother on the other. But even these deeply split objects cannot be maintained since they fuse with fragments of self-organization; the helpless child and the violent, destructive superego; the murderous brother and the brother fused with his sibling.

Every interpretation under such circumstances is apt to trigger violent acting out, deep depressions, and states of helplessness as Boyer has so aptly documented when he refers to the patient's reactions to the analyst's absences or certain of his interpretations. We are referring to the impaired synthetic and integrating functions of the ego, the triggering of deep regressions, the thin skin of the protective eggshell, and the violent and deadly power of the instinctual drives.

The transference is of a specific nature and does not allow the establishment of the ordinary working alliance of which this patient would be incapable.

We must, therefore, ask questions as to what is available to the therapist in order to create crutches for this necessary working alliance. He uses the hospital, needs a strong support system, uses occasionally an administrative psychiatrist who does the ward management, but also in his therapeutic technique he must allow devices by means of which he can reduce the danger of fusion as well as autistic escape.

Boyer was remarkably successful with his case and I would like to go beyond the dynamics, the meanings of the material, to gain more insight into the nature of his specific techniques by means of which this patient is being helped to strengthen his precarious self- and object constancy and to allow an emotional skin to grow which may safely contain the deadly strikes of the psychotic act; that the psychotic acting out may become the royal road toward the strengthening of reality testing and the secondary process rather than be the primrose path to disaster.

7

Working with a Borderline Patient

I have been engaged in the outpatient care of individuals who suffer from disorders which were long considered untreatable by psychoanalytic therapy. My therapeutic procedures have involved minimal use of parameters (Eissler 1953) and have excluded the use of supportive and nonanalytic procedures such as those advocated by Federn (1952) and Nunberg (1932). It has been my good fortune to have worked with some 30 patients whose diagnoses have ranged from clearly schizophrenic to what are now labeled borderline personality and severe narcissistic personality disorders. I have supervised residents, the majority of whose patients had similar personalities. My work has involved the application of the intermediate position regarding object relations delineated by Kernberg (1976a) which stems especially from such theoreticians as Erickson, Jacobson, and Mahler (within the ego psychological approach) and from the work of Bowlby, Fairbairn, Klein, and Winnicott (within the so-called British schools of psychoanalysis).

Whereas in previous publications I have focused principally on the articulation between theory and technique (Boyer 1976a,b; Chapters 1, 4, and 5, this volume), in this chapter I shall emphasize technique and my own experience while treating a difficult case. It is possible to do this with some degree of accuracy because, like Greenacre (1975), I take notes during each session. I record the general theme of the patient's productions and often note some elements in detail, particu-

---

See Chapter 9 for further discussion of this patient.

larly dreams, fantasies, and nonverbal communications; I note my own emotional reactions and fantasies, whether they remain private or are in some manner communicated to the patient. The fragment of a case history which follows involved culling through some 2000 pages of handwritten notes.

I have found my recording rarely interferes with the patients' communications, and such interferences are generally easily nullified by relevant interpretations. My method is beneficial to patients in two ways: it helps them to believe their communications are valuable and enables them to develop a sense of objectivity about their messages.

A large majority of my patients have benefited from our work. This is confirmed by follow-up information of up to 20 years. Nevertheless, I have found it difficult to assess what in the therapeutic situation has led to successful results.

I grew up suspicious of the words of others and with a deep need to determine realities by personal observation and research. When I reviewed the development of Freud's thinking and that of his followers pertaining to what were called the narcissistic neuroses (Boyer and Giovacchini 1967, 1980), I became certain that the treatment of such disorders within the framework of the structural hypothesis was feasible, and I undertook their treatment on an experimental basis while still a candidate. Initially, I was disheartened by my mentors in my then ultraconservative training institution. They deemed my efforts to be wild analysis and motivated principally by rebelliousness and counterphobic tendencies. Yet what I was doing seemed to me to be logically consistent and to benefit my patients; so I persisted. Given my need for external approval, I was encouraged by the responses of North Americans who were similarly engaged in such searchings, notably Bychowski, Giovacchini, Hoedemaker, Lewin, and Searles, and by Europeans and Latin Americans, especially Eicke, Garma, Rosenfeld, and Rolla, and by the appearance of literature which supported my thinking, such as the contributions of Arlow and Brenner (1964, 1969).

On the basis of my research, I have reached some general conclusions. In agreement with Giovacchini (Giovacchini and Boyer 1975, Giovacchini et al. 1975), Grinberg (1957), Kernberg (1975a), Langs (1975), Racker (1952, 1957), and Searles (1958b), I am convinced (1) that failures in the treatment of such disorders are often iatrogenic, resulting from problems in the countertransference or the therapist's failure to use his emotional responses adequately in his interpretations; (2) that the success of treatment depends on accurate, empathic, and timely confrontations, interventions, and reconstructions which lead to relevant genetic interpretations; and (3) that success also depends on the rectifying emotional and cognitive experience of the patient's development of new object relations with the therapist (Dewald 1976, Garma 1977, Green 1975, Loewald 1960, Viederman 1976). With adequate treatment it is possible for the patient to replace archaic and sadistic ego and superego introjects and identifications with more mature ones, to develop higher level defense mechanisms and adaptations, and to progress from regressed positions and developmental arrests.

I have found with the Ornsteins (1975), Rosenfeld (1966a), and many others that premature oedipal interpretations preclude the re-creation of the preoedipal transferential states. The latter must be worked through before character modifications can proceed. These are the states which Freud deemed unanalyzable (Boyer and Giovacchini 1967).

I find that my handling of transference interpretations is in accord with the principles recently set forward by Kernberg (1975b): (1) the predominantly negative transference is systematically elaborated only in the present without initial efforts directed toward full genetic interpretations; (2) the patients typical defensive constellations are interpreted as they enter the transference; (3) limits are set in order to block acting out of the transference insofar as this is necessary to protect the neutrality of the therapist; (4) the less primitively determined, modulated aspects of the positive transference are not interpreted early since their presence enhances the development of the therapeutic and working alliances (Dickes 1975, Kanzer 1975), although the primitive idealizations that reflect the splitting of "all good" from "all bad" object relations are systematically interpreted as part of the effort to work through these primitive defenses; (5) interpretations are formulated so that the patient's distortions of the therapist's interventions and of present reality, especially the patient's perceptions during the hour, can be systematically clarified; and (6) the highly distorted transference, at times psychotic in nature and reflecting fantastic internal object relations pertaining to early ego disturbances, is worked through first in order to reach the transferences related to actual childhood experiences.

I consider the understanding and pertinent interpretation of the unfolding transference to be of the utmost importance. I have come to contemplate each interview as though it might have been a dream and material from recent interviews as part of the day residue.

Case Material

This report deals with the treatment of a patient whose presenting life pattern and personality included almost all of those elements which are commonly considered to carry a poor prognosis and to contraindicate psychoanalytic treatment, except that there was no evidence of ego-syntonic antisocial behavior. Much of the following history was obtained during the first two vis-á-vis interviews.

History

Fifty-three years old when first seen, Mrs. B. was a twice-divorced Caucasian, friendless, living alone, and almost totally impulse-dominated. She looked and dressed like a teenage boy. She had been a chronic alcoholic for some 20 years and had been hospitalized repeatedly with a diagnosis of schizophrenia. She had been jailed many times and while in the "drunk tank" had masturbated openly, smeared feces, and screamed endlessly. She had lived dangerously, having on various occasions provoked sexual assault by gangs of black men in ghettos. In the last 20 years she had had many forms of psychiatric care (excluding shock therapies), but without effect. She had lived for about a year in a colony designed for faith healing, led by a guru. There appeared to be but two redeeming features when she was first seen: (1) She had concluded that her problems were based on unconscious conflicts and wanted an orthodox analysis. (Various respected analysts had refused her.) (2) Having been told by the most recent therapist of her psychotic son that her interactions with him kept him sick, she wanted very much to stop contributing to his illness.

Her forebears were wealthy aristocrats and included Protestant religious figures. The males all graduated from prestigious universities, and the females, products of noted finishing schools, were patrons of the arts. Her parents treated those who were not their social peers as subhumans. Her bond salesman father's chronic alcoholism resulted in the loss of his and his wife's fortunes during the patient's late childhood. From then on her nuclear family lived on the largesse of relatives.

Her mother was highly self-centered and throughout the patient's childhood and adolescence remained in bed during the daytime for weeks on end, depressed, hypochondriacal, and unapproachable. She vacillated between two ego states. In one, she lay with her aching head covered by cold cloths, moaning and complaining about mistreatment by all, but particularly her husband. In the other, she lay in reveries, reading romantic novels. Much later in treatment the patient remembered that when her mother was in such a dreamy state, she permitted the child to lie with her and perhaps to fondle her mother's genitals, manually and with her face. The mother's withdrawals seemingly could be interrupted only by the temper tantrums of two of the sisters when parties were being planned for social lions or when she was planning to take the grand tour alone. She often left unannounced for her annual European jaunts but sometimes she would confide in the docile Mrs. B. that she was leaving and swear her to secrecy, assigning her the task of tending the other children, who voiced their objections dramatically when they knew of their mother's impending departure.

The patient was the second of four sisters, born three years apart. All were reared by a senile woman who had been the mother's nursemaid. The oldest remains a frequently hospitalized alcoholic spinster. The younger two are vain, childless divorcees who live on generous alimony and who continue to have a succession of young lovers. All five females were contemptuous of the father, whom the mother divorced after the patient was married. Thereafter, the mother gave up her depression, hypochondriasis, and withdrawal and became a spirited woman. She had platonic affairs with young male authors whom she sponsored. The father married a warm woman, became abstinent, and returned to work. After many years, he regressed to serious depression and committed suicide by throwing himself in front of a train. This was one year before the patient first saw me. She had had no contact with him since his remarriage and thought of him only with contempt. When she heard of his death and burial, she felt totally detached. At the beginning of therapy, she indiscriminately idealized her mother and devalued her father.

When she was less than 3 years old, an incident occurred on board an ocean liner. Something happened in a stateroom which frightened the child so that she fled crying to her mother, who was breakfasting with the ship's captain. Her mother ignored her anguish, but a black waiter comforted her, holding her and giving her a cube of sugar. The patient explained to me that she felt the outcome of her treatment hinged on the recall of that memory and on my capacity to accept what she had to tell me without disgust, anger, or anxiety.

Before attending school she was an avid reader of fairy tales, and in her first year she did well. But during her second, she became incapable of learning. She read unwillingly and with great difficulty and was unable to learn the simplest mathematics. She never passed a single test during her grammar or finishing school years. This was unimportant to her parents; they taught her that her obligation to the family was to be charming, to exploit her beauty and wit, and to get a rich doctor as a husband who would support the family.

During the second year of schooling she became sexually involved with a swarthy chauffeur who wore black gloves, but she did not reveal their frightening activities, believing that risking death was somehow in the service of her sister's getting parental love.

During her latency period, she was exceedingly docile and well behaved. She had a severe obsessive-compulsive neurosis and believed that her family's lives depended on her thoughts and actions. She was a religious martyr who projected onto her parents the wish that she die so that her sisters would be the recipients of all her parents' love. In this way the sisters would become less disturbed.

When she was 11 she was sent away from home for the first time to attend a finishing school. She soon lost her previous nighttime terrors of attack by something vague and unvisualized, and gave up her endless nocturnal rituals. While there, she became enamored of a popular girl who seemed perfect, although she knew of her hypocrisies and manipulations. She was content to be one of an adoring coterie of this popular girl so long as the girl's attentions were equally divided among her worshipers. When the patient was 16, however, her idol became enamored of another girl and the patient went into a catatoniclike state. She was sent home from school, and for the next five years she remained passive, felt mechanical, and went through the motions of living.

She never had any boyfriends and was awkward at parties. She wistfully reveled in her mother's attractiveness as a hostess and vaguely wished that she would someday be her mother's social equal.

While she was in her teens, her father, an outcast at home, spent much time boating. The patient, in her role of family protector, willingly went with him, taking the helm while he got drunk in the cabin. She believed her parents wanted her dead and that she should be killed. She went with her father not only to look after him but to make it easy for him to murder her for the good of her sisters.

When her older sister was able to get a rich medical student to propose marriage, the patient was galvanized into activity and got him to choose her instead. Once married, she was sexually passive and anesthetic. On their honeymoon her husband became so infuriated by her sexual passivity that he sought to murder her, being thwarted only by chance. She felt no resentment and never told anyone, thinking his act had been further evidence of the validity of her being destined to be the savior-martyr.

She lived with his parents in one city while he continued medical school in another. He sent her occasional letters in which he depicted his affairs with sensual women. She was vaguely disappointed. His senile father, a retired minister, considered her passivity to be the result of her having been possessed and sought to exorcise her by giving her enemas while she was nude in the bathtub. This was condoned by her mother and her husband. She felt neither anger nor excitement. She wondered at times if he were getting some sexual or sadistic pleasure from his actions and fantasized seducing him or committing suicide in order to humiliate him by exposing him—all for the good of others.

Following his graduation, her husband joined the military and they moved to another part of the country, whence he was shipped abroad. She was utterly without friends or acquaintances. His letters were rare and included accounts of his affairs with uninhibited women. She bore him a defective daughter and could not believe she was a mother. She feared touching the baby, leaving her care to maids. She felt the baby's defect to be her fault, which was somehow associated with her actions with the chauffeur. She began to drink in secret. On leave, her husband impregnated her, and she bore another daughter who again she could not believe was hers and whom she could not touch. She began to frequent bars and to pick up men to whose sexual demands of any nature she would submit, always with total subsequent amnesia. She learned of her actions by having them told to her by the children's nurses. Then she bore a defective son who became an autistic psychotic. She was totally helpless in the face of his unbridled hyperactivity and feces smearing. He was hospitalized after about a year and remained so until his early adolescence, rarely acknowledging her existence in any way. Her husband divorced her, her daughters were sent away to institutions, and she lived alone.

For 12 years and periodically later her life was occupied with bar activities and sexual encounters for which she continued to have amnesia. She would pick up black men and submit to manifold sexual abuses. She passively assented and at times encouraged them to take her money and jewelry. One of her many therapists suggested that she would feel less worthless if she were to prepare herself for some occupation and stop living on what amounted to charity. She managed to complete a practical nursing course and then worked in various psychiatric hospitals where she felt she was of some use because she could understandingly care for psychotic and senile patients. She was fired from a number of such positions for being absent and for appearing on the job while intoxicated or hung over.

In one of the hospitals where she worked, she met a male patient who was her physical counterpart, even to the color of her hair and eyes. They were so alike she wore his clothes. He was addicted to various drugs, including alcohol, and totally dependent on his family and welfare. She soon began to live with him. She adored him as she had her mother and the girlfriend of teenage years. She knew of his many faults but totally idealized him. She felt complete and rapturous with him and at times believed they were psychological and even physical continua. They were married, and the idyllic fusion persisted. Periodically, they bought whiskey and went to bed where they remained for days, engaging in polymorphous sexuality to the point of exhaustion, occasionally lying in their excreta. While she never had an orgasm, she felt complete. Such episodes were especially pleasant to her when she was menstruating and she and her partner were smeared with blood, which she sometimes enjoyed eating. After some nine years of marriage, he divorced her for reasons which she never understood, particularly since she supported him financially. Then she became a mechanical person once again and resumed her pursuit of men in bars.

A year before treatment began, she obtained an undemanding job as a file clerk where her superiors tolerated her lateness and incompetency. She lived on her meager salary and placed no value on material possessions. She believed that she had never had a hostile wish and that throughout her life she had invariably sought to help others.

Treatment

Over the years, I have gradually come to accept for treatment almost solely patients whose activities are apt to influence the lives of others, such as educators, physicians, and professionals who work in the mental health field. Yet it did not occur to me to refuse her request to try psychoanalytic treatment. I found appealing her determination to undergo for predominantly altruistic purposes a procedure which she well knew would be painful. And I felt comfortable with her.

She was seen at what she knew to be reduced rates three times weekly on the couch for about five years, payments being made from a small endowment from a deceased family friend. After a trial six-month interruption she resumed treatment on the couch twice a week for two more years, making a total of over eight hundred interviews in seven and a half years.

Before analysis is undertaken with such patients, I tell them that our work is to be cooperative and of an experimental nature and that we cannot expect to set a time limit; that they are to make a sincere effort to relate aloud whatever comes to their minds during the interviews and to report their emotional states and physical sensations; that I do not send statements and expect to be paid what is owed on the last interview of the month; that they will be charged for cancellations unless their scheduled interviews are filled by another patient; and that I am away frequently for short periods and one long period during the course of each year and will inform them of the expected dates of absence as soon as I know of them. When an occasional patient inquires what is to be expected of me, I state that I shall keep the scheduled interviews and be on time; that I do not give advice unless I deem it necessary; that I see my role as seeking to understand as much as I can about the patients and will tell them what I have learned when I consider them ready. I explain that I expect to be wrong at times and that the final validation will depend on the patient's responses and memories. For these patients I have found that such specific conditions offer needed ego and superego support.

As is common with patients with borderline personality disorders (cf., Gunderson and Singer 1975), during the first two structured vis-á-vis interviews, Mrs. B.'s productions were but slightly tinged with primary-process thinking. However, there was a periodic affective disparity which confused me; I was undecided whether it constituted *la belle indifférence* or schizophrenic dissociation.

During her third interview she eagerly lay on the couch, her speech promptly became heavily influenced by primary-process thinking, and she was at times incoherent. Her verbal productions were highly symbolic, and her language was often unusually vulgar. She made tangential references to fairy tales, fusing elements of *Beauty and the Beast*, *Cinderella*, *Hansel and Gretel*, and *Snow White*, and told a story which involved a good witch who transported children through a magical opening into a paradisiacal world in which the protagonists fused and became perpetually indistinguishable and parasitic, needing no others for their constant bliss. She also alluded to a white elephant and a spider.

She did not seem frightened by her productions or her style of presentation. There was some embarassment about her foul language, but her principal reaction was one of mild curiosity as to why she talked so strangely. My own reaction to her behavior was of bemused surprise at the degree of such prompt regression, of empathy with her embarassment, and of detached intellectual curiosity.

I felt at ease with this patient. As a result of idiosyncratic childhood experiences, I have long comprehended unconscious meanings of primary-process thinking and have been able to use its contents in synthetic manners. I have also devoted many years to the study of folklore (Boyer 1964a, 1975, 1977; Boyer and R. M. Boyer 1967; Chapter 14, this volume) and know most of the psychoanalytic literature dealing with the fairy tales to which she referred, as well as that dealing with the spider (Barchilon 1959; Freud 1913; Graber 1925; Kaplan 1963; R. B. Little 1966, 1967; Lorenz 1931; Mintz 1969–1970; Róheim 1953; Rubenstein 1955). I believe that I understood from her behavior and verbal productions that her conflicts pertained especially to attempts to master early primal-scene traumata and fusions with aspects of various people, oral and anal sadism, and intense sibling rivalry. I thought that the actual, affect-laden recovery of primal-scene memories would be crucial in her treatment and assumed that her vulgarity indicated that they had occurred in connection with the period of cleanliness training or had become attached to experiences that occurred then. I attributed some of her easy regression to a toxic alcoholic brain syndrome and was dubious about the oft-repeated diagnosis of schizophrenia.

I had the uncanny feeling that she talked to me in a distorted childish language as though I were an actual loved figure from her early life. Retrospectively, I regret not having validated my hunch. Had I done so, I might have been aware that she had globally identified me with the only person of her childhood whom she could trust (her maternal grandfather); and my added comprehension would both have made her progress in treatment less mystifying to me and perhaps precluded a near disaster.

In the fourth interview she came to the office drunk, although I had the impression that she was less intoxicated than she seemed. Her lips were painted black and there were white streaks on her face. She was dressed in garish, revealing clothes which exposed filthy underpants. She screamed and cursed and threatened to attack me with outstretched claws. I felt as though I were observing a puppet show. There was an obscure reference to my being a vampire. She threw harmless objects, aimed to narrowly miss me so that I felt unthreatened. She then picked up a heavy stone ashtray and menaced me with it. I felt no anxiety, but sat still and remained silent and observant. When she found me unafraid, she cried and threw herself on the couch, spread her legs apart, and partially bared her tiny breasts. When I remained passive and silent, she sat at my feet, hugged my legs, and eventually touched my penis. She seemed surprised that it was not erect. I then removed her hand and said it was unnecessary for her to express her conflicts physically and advised her to tell me her problems with words. She reacted with rage and tried to claw my face. It was easy to fend her off; I effortlessly held her at arms' length. If she had chosen to do so, she could have easily kicked my genitals as she threatened to do. Her strange behavior and dress seemed to be designated to test the level of my tolerance of what she felt would be anxiety-provoking or disgusting. I viewed her allusion to me as a vampire as indicative of splitting and projective identification.[1]

In the fifth interview, Mrs. B. remembered none of what had happened. When I told her what she had done, she was aghast. She vowed spontaneously not to come drunk to the office again. Most of the interviews of the first year, however, took place with her either mildly intoxicated or hung over.

[1]I have come to understand the operational functions of projective identification in rather simple terms. I agree with Kernberg's view (1976c) that that which is projected remains to a degree unrepressed and that patients maintain some level of continuing to feel what they seek to project onto the analyst, thereby continuing to be preconsciously aware of what they imagine the analyst to experience. Patients' initial aim when they project hostile wishes onto the analyst is to control their potency by defending themselves from the imagined hostility of the analyst and controlling the latter's actions. The analyst is used as a repository for projected internalized objects and attitudes which make patients feel uncomfortable, and they believe they have succeeded in locating them within the analyst. Patients fear that their hostile wishes or thoughts may result in the destruction of the analyst or retributive damage to themselves (Gordon 1965, Grinberg 1965). Once they believe that such hostility is a part of the analyst, they watch the analyst's behavior. Over time, effective interpretations, combined with patients' observations that the projection's alleged presence within the analyst has not proved deleterious, enable the patients to reintroject them gradually in detoxified form and to integrate them into their evolving personalities. Some patients fear that their love is destructive (Searles 1958a) and project it onto the analyst for safekeeping; similarly, with treatment these patients come to view love as not dangerous (Giovacchini 1975b; Chapter 9, this volume).

Discussants have often wondered about my relative lack of fear of attack by psychotic patients. Empirically, I have never been actually attacked, although I have been frightened at times. In my own past, one of my important love objects suffered from a borderline personality disorder and periodically regressed into acute paranoid psychotic episodes. That person was impulsive and violent; and as a young child, I learned to judge the degree of physical danger and to stay away from potential murderous attacks.

For several months many interviews included periods of incoherency which were at times grossly vulgar and talk which was obviously symbolic of early primal-scene observations. Periodically, I inquired whether her interview behavior was designed to test my level of tolerance, to determine whether she could disgust or anger me or make me uncomfortable. Such queries usually resulted in a temporary cessation of her blatant vulgarities and "crazy" talk.

At times she ascribed her speech content or immodest behavior to my will, and from the outset I used such material to help her learn about her splitting mechanisms and projective tendencies and their defensive uses. An example follows.

The physical set-up of my consultation room is such that a shared waiting room has a sliding door which separates it from a tiny hallway that has three other doors, one opening into my office, one into my private lavatory, and one to an exit. Mrs. B. had the first interview of the day, and it occurred at an hour when I had to unlock the office building. I generally arrived early enough for other activities before seeing her. She customarily arrived for her interview just on time, making enough noise so that she could be heard entering the waiting room, although the sliding door was shut. One morning when I emerged from the lavatory some ten minutes before she was expected, I noted that the sliding door was ajar, but I assumed I must have left it so. At the time her appointment was to begin, she buzzed to announce her presence. Since I had not heard her before the buzz, I suspected some acting out had transpired. During the first few minutes of her hour, her talk dealt manifestly with hostility-laden events in her office on the previous day and included the interjection "Oh, shit" and the phrase "He pissed me off." I then assumed that she had been repeating spying activities of her childhood pertaining to adults' uses of the toilet but I did not choose to direct my inquiries to the past. Instead, I asked how long she had been in the waiting room before she buzzed, and I obtained some previously withheld information. It had been her wont to arrive some minutes before I opened the building and to park where she could watch me unseen. On that particular morning, she had noiselessly followed me into the building, entered the waiting room, opened the sliding door, and eventually heard the toilet flush.

Discussion of her behavior and its motivations on that day occupied several interviews and the analysis of some dreams. It developed that she had contradictory views of me. In one, I was a sadistic voyeur who had become a psychoanalyst in order to spy on the "dirty" activities and thoughts of my patients, to titillate myself, and to learn how to frustrate patients by determining precisely what they wanted of me so that I could torture them by refusing to accede to their desires. I "got my jollies" by means of subtly exhibitionistic behavior which excited in my patients those wants that I frustrated. At the same time, I had had a traumatic childhood and had undergone much suffering because of exhibitionistic and frustrating parents and wanted, as a psychoanalyst, to relieve my patients of their misery. It was as if I were two people. I was at times totally hateful, bad, and hurtful and at other times solely loving, good, and helpful, and my alternating personalities determined my totally unpredictable behavior. It was my will that she observe my every act so that she could become exactly like me and arrive at social and professional success, but it was also my will that she should not embarrass me by letting me know that she had read my mind and was following instructions.

When I indicated to her how she had ascribed to me precisely the qualities which she had previously described as her own, she was impressed, and for a time she could more clearly contemplate her self-view as all good or all bad, and her projective tendencies. It was then possible to review the events in the office on the day that preceded her acting out and to delineate ways in which her behavior with me and her ascriptions to me had been in the service of defense against anxiety and guilt over behavior and wishes related to people in her work setting. She had acted toward me as she felt her coworkers had acted toward her. I suggested that she had sought to master a feeling of helplessness through identification with the aggressor, and I postulated that this behavior constituted a lifelong pattern. I did not have sufficient cathected data to make a more specific statement.[2]

At times she was flirtatious in her dress and actions and sought to entertain and amuse me, imitating, as it developed, her mother's party behavior and obeying her parental injunctions about how to "hook" a rich doctor. At the same time she had fused sensations of urinary or fecal urgency and, despite a hysterectomy years before treatment

[2]It will be noted that my inclusion of a genetic interpretation was tentative. While I believe the inclusion of genetic aspects of interpretations is essential from the outset, I hold that genetic interpretations are meaningful to patients only after they have become well acquainted with their uses of various primitive defensive mechanisms and with the current reasons for their appearance. This is in marked contrast to the technical approach of many Kleinians who, from the outset, seek to interpret unconscious motivations in terms of the id rather than of the ego (Boyer and Giovacchini 1967).

began, felt blood on her legs and expressed the wish to smear me with it. Sometimes there was vaginal itching. Occasionally, she spread her legs and began to undress, meantime rubbing her pubis. When I asked her about her thoughts and feelings, it became apparent she was unaware of her actions. On a few occasions, she wondered whether I felt lonely and wanted my face in her crotch. When I commented that she seemed to believe she had put part of herself into me, she recalled what she believed to have been early childhood and latency experiences of lying with her mother and palpating her mother's genitals with her hands and face; she remembered the feeling of pubic hair on her nose and cheeks. In her sober interviews, she was often largely withdrawn and "headachy" or had other somatic complaints, which we came to understand as her imitating one part of her mother's periodic daytime bed behavior. I also focused on her primitive wish to fuse with me as a representative of her mother.

For many months she picked up men at bars and submitted to their sexual demands. When I tried to show her that these men were father figures, she regularly corrected me, making me aware that they represented the phallic and nurturant mother with whom she sought to fuse. However, she gradually became cognizant that her conscious contempt of her father covered rage at him, and with amazement she slowly recovered memories of boating with him. During one session she misinterpreted a noise to mean I was masturbating behind her. I remarked that perhaps there had been a time when she had seen her father masturbate. Over a period of weeks, she recovered the memory of her actions with the chauffeur, which included his placing her hands on his erection, while he wore black gloves. Then she gradually recalled with much embarrassment that during adolescence on the boating excursions with her father, she had watched him masturbate in the cabin; she slowly became aware of her anger that he preferred masturbation to using her sexually.

In the interviews that followed, material continued that involved nighttime dreams and overt or covert themes of mutilations, murder, and desertion. There was obvious blurring of ego boundaries. My interpretations, as always, were transferential and as genetic as I deemed advisable and aimed at reinforcing previous interpretations of the defensive use of splitting. She gradually became aware that she had much anger which she had denied and uncritically projected onto policemen and other establishment figures. Now she began to be more critical of her automatic devaluation of them as paternal representatives. Later she would be able to comprehend a pattern of projection of aggression and reintrojection of aggressively determined self- and object images and the subsequent use of splitting operations.

In this early period, I delayed focusing on the fusion of anal, vaginal, and urethral sensations, judging that data pertaining to this evidence of lack of structuralization of drives would be remembered at a later time when interpretations would be more meaningful. I believed that the content of her primary-process thinking during the third interview had already heralded the fact that primal-scene traumata were partial organizers of her particular ego structure. Periodic interpretations of her wish to fuse with me were gradually understood and elaborated by her. For example, she often responded that she wished to be taken into one or another of my orifices, even including my pores, and to circulate in my blood, lodge in my brain, and govern all my activities, while secretly spying on my actions to learn from them how I handled those elements which she had projected onto me. Only much later, after she had reintrojected detoxified versions of those projections, did she see this fantasy as self-destructive. She then strove to clarify actual differences between us.

About five months after Mrs. B. was first seen, she learned that I had an interest in anthropology and asked to borrow a magazine from the waiting room which included an article on stone-age humans. She had lost her capacity to read easily and with comprehension after the first grade; and I suggested that she wanted permission to learn to read understandingly again and to develop herself as a person rather than to follow the assigned role of dumb-blond doctor-seducer. She promptly enrolled in high school, then college, and slowly developed the capacity to read and write with comprehension. During the following years she received only A's in her extension division college courses.

After she had been in treatment for about six months, I left for a period of six weeks. She had known of my planned absence from the beginning of her sessions, and I had thought her anxiety about the separation had been well understood before I left, since we had dealt extensively with her reactions to her mother's European jaunts. However, immediately after my departure, she attempted suicide by taking an overdose of pills, which I had not known she possessed. She was rescued, so far as could be determined, by chance. It was noted in her hospital chart that she had mentioned her mother's father. During my absence she had no remembered thought about me until the day before her scheduled appointment, and when she appeared for her interview, she seemed surprised that I was alive. She had not died, therefore I must have. When she entered the room, she looked everywhere for something, but when I inquired what she was trying to find, she declined to tell me. Much later, I found out that she had sought a white elephant.

She had hoped that her death would result in my professional destruction. She now viewed her father's drunkenness and affairs as ways of risking death in the hope that he would thereby get even with her mother for her contemptuousness. She also recalled the Oriental custom of committing suicide on the doorstep of the wronging person.

Soon after my return, poignant memories of her early relationship with her mother's father emerged. Apparently, her relationship with that loving man was the only consistently dependable one of her childhood. It formed the basis of the element of basic trust which enabled her to develop psychologically as far as she did. He had held her on his lap, listened to her seriously, and was always considerate of her needs. One time, when she was envious of one of her sisters' having received a soft, stuffed animal as a present, she told her grandfather that she wanted a similar toy which she could care for as though it were a baby. He responded by telling her the story of an orphan baby elephant in India which was adopted by a boy whom it loved and always obeyed, no doubt a variant of Kipling's "Toomai of the Elephants." He promised to get her a white elephant for Christmas. She believed he meant a living animal rather than a toy. In fact, he gave her another white stuffed toy, but she retained the belief that he would eventually give her the living pachyderm. When she was almost 7 years old, he died; but she had the set idea that when she got a white elephant someday, she would also find her grandfather and once again have a dependable, loving relationship with a kindly person who did not misuse her.

She had apparently entered a satisfactory early latency period adjustment, but the death of her grandfather caused her to lose her capacity to learn and to use fantasy constructions in an adaptive manner (Sarnoff 1976). She had not been taken to his funeral where she might have viewed his corpse and thus been confronted with the reality of his demise. Her loss of the capacity to learn had been based on her wish to deny having learned of his death; she would never again learn anything if she had to accept this learning.

I shall now turn to an example of how my coming to understand my emotional response enabled me to change an impasse into a beneficial step. When her son as a young child had come home from the hospital for brief periods, she had taken men home with her and in a drunken state performed fellatio and submitted to sodomy before him.

She had no memory of her actions, but would be informed by the nurses. Sometimes, when she was unwittingly angry with me, she would return to her shameful feelings on being told by the nurses what she had done. I gradually noted that I began to respond to such recitations with irritation and sleepiness, and I found myself being subtly punitive toward her. For some weeks there was a therapeutic stalemate during which her acting out increased and our rapport all but disappeared. I regretted having accepted her for treatment and wondered why I had done so. I fell into a brief trancelike state during an interview with her and when I became fully alert again, had repressed the content of my reverie. That night I had a dream which reminded me of my own past. I had learned in prior periods of personal analysis that I had become an analyst with an unconscious motivation of curing the important but psychologically disordered and dangerous love object to whom I have alluded previously. Analysis of my dream made me aware of another reason: I had sought to protect a younger sibling from the love object. I then knew that I had accepted Mrs. B. in treatment to effect changes not only in her but in her psychotic son. Then I became aware that I had identified myself with her abused child and was expressing my anger by withdrawal and by refusal to recognize her, as she had previously reported her son to have done. Such knowledge permitted me to regain my objectivity. Finally, I could interpret her wish to provoke me to abuse her. She responded by remembering dreams and hypnopompic fantasies in which she was forced to watch women being raped anally or having huge phalluses shoved into their mouths. Three years later I was able to interpret her behavior as an attempt to master her terror and her feelings of dissolution when she had watched the sexual activities of her parents.

Soon she began to experience choking sensations during the interviews. Analysis of dreams showed her use of the body-phallus equation and her wish that I would force her to reintroject both good and bad aspects of herself, which she had projected onto me. Affect-laden memories of her experiences with the chauffeur appeared. Following her grandfather's death, she had turned to that black-gloved man (whom she partly confused with the black man who had comforted her during the shipboard experience) in an effort to regain a loving relationship with a man who would take her on his lap, as her father refused to do. He had forced his phallus into her mouth, causing her to choke. She had concealed their activities, rationalizing that she was supposed to die through choking in her effort to provide her sisters with their parents' finite love. She also now remembered nightly efforts to determine whether her parent were alive by checking to make sure they were breathing while they were asleep. The choking conversion symptom disappeared.

She now recalled with emotion nightly rituals during her latency period. Her family's house was very old. While electrical contrivances had been installed in her third-story bedroom, there remained a gas jet. At night it was permissible to have illumination from the jet, but the lights were not to be used. She was terrified that a vague, never visualized something would attack her from the dark. She feared even more that leaking gas would poison her. She engaged in endless prayers for her own salvation and for the other members of the family. She engaged in counting rituals which were supposed to influence God to save them. She used the rituals to stay awake, believing that she was safe from attack so long as she remained alert. She had a collection of dolls and stuffed animals which covered most of her bed, and she tenderly put them to sleep with caresses and cooings. She endlessly repeated, "Now I lay me down to sleep, I pray the Lord my soul to keep," applying the theme to her dolls and consciously equating being asleep with being dead. While doing so, she sometimes believed she was Christ, grandfather-God's protector of children, and felt her pubis repeatedly to determine whether she had grown a penis. She had to check many times to be sure the window was tightly locked, because if she were to fall asleep with it open, she might throw her babies (dolls) and herself into the snow on the ground below. Her own death would have been acceptable because of its altruistic motives; but to have murdered her babies would have made her a sinner and unsuitable to rejoin her grandfather and have God keep her soul.

Her treatment had begun just before a Christmas separation, and her reactions to my first absence had not been decipherable (Chapter 11, this volume). As our second Christmas separation approached, she returned to thinking of her mother's departures for the grand tour of Europe. Now those memories became cathected with feelings of rage and then with loneliness. She sought to remove the loneliness by joining a singles group and resuming the drunken activities with men she picked up. For the first time, she could remember what she did with her partners. She was exceedingly aggressive, insisting on assuming the superior position. She demanded that the man be passive while she pumped up and down on his erection, at times believeng his penis was hers and was penetrating him. I interpreted this behavior as representing a continuation of her efforts to save me from her anger at me for deserting her like a parent.

The following summer when I left her for another extended period, she went on a prolonged drunk and behaved so crazily that she was jailed. She requested hospitalization and rejoined her second husband whom she knew to be in the hospital. There she entered a fusion state with him. She had no conscious thought of my existence until the week before our scheduled appointment. Then she arranged her release and met me on time.

She explained that in her rage at my leaving her she had wanted to humiliate me by killing herself or getting murdered, but she protected herself by getting hospitalized and joining her husband. Thus she deemed her behavior to have been adaptive and was pleased with herself. She now valued her contacts with me above all else.

Throughout her treatment until this time, there had been rare contacts with her mother, sisters, daughters, and their young children whom she had never been able to touch, fearing she would kill them. When the third Christmas came, she was able to spend more time with her mother and sisters and feel less uneasiness than before. She also had one of her daughters bring her family to visit for the holidays. She found herself infuriated with the excited pleasure and selfishness of the young children. Now she recalled with intensity childhood Christmases which had been immensely frustrating for her, not only because she felt her sisters got more than she, but particularly because she did not turn into a boy or get a penis so she could be Christ, the martyred favorite son of all mankind. She began to realize that her fears of harming her own babies disguised a wish to kill them, as they represented her siblings. Then she became closer to her daughters and enjoyed holding their children. Also her relations with her mother and sisters improved. She invited her son to visit her periodically on leave from a distant psychiatric hospital. Over the next few years during subsequent visits they developed a calmer and mutually affectionate relationship.

She now eschewed alcohol for long periods and only occasionally had sexual relations with men. Her interests were limited to job, school, and analysis. She was gradually promoted at work. There was a growing interest in the lives of her female bosses, and fantasies pertaining to them that I interpreted as displaced fantasies about my life. The previous flirtatiousness with me resumed as did the pattern of coming to the office in altered ego states; the fusion of vaginal, urethral, and anal sensations reappeared. I suggested that her childhood pattern of checking on her parents' breathing was the result of her having been disturbed by noises in their bedroom which she assumed to have occurred during their sexual activities. She then recalled that during preoedipal years, her bedroom was separated from theirs by a bathroom in which her mother's douche tip and bag, which she believed to have been used to give her enemas, hung on the wall and that sometimes mother's bloody menstrual rags were in a bucket of water. Then I guessed that she had repeatedly observed their activities and had experienced excitement which she discharged with urinary and fecal activities during the night. My ideas were accepted with equanimity. She gradually recalled with much feeling repeated childhood observations of their sexual actions which included sodomy, cunnilingus, and fellatio, always accompanied by her mother's groaning protests. She had interpreted their actions in anal-sadistic and oral-fusional terms and had thought that each had a penis like a sword which could kill the other. She had reacted with fused oral, anal, and vaginal excitement and had sought to interrupt her parents by noisy bathroom activities.

In the fifth year of treatment she gradually repressed the primal-scene memories and the observations of father's masturbating on the boat. She did well at work and school, had occasional dates, and developed the capacity to have mild orgasms during nonfrantic intercourse. During my summer absence she briefly reentered a relationship with her second husband, now devoid of its fusional aspects. He was ill, and she cared for him considerately. She began to have vague and emotionally uninvested fantasies about me. Therapy appeared to have reached a plateau in which she was functioning well but retaining a primitive idealization of me, interpretations of which had no effect. She was quite cognizant that I made mistakes and assumed that I had secret faults which she could not verify, but I remained an idol like her mother. I decided to use the parameter of a trial separation in an effort to dislodge the primitive idealization. Accordingly, I recommended that, beginning with my summer absence six months thence, we remain apart for six months and resume treatment just after the following Christmas. She was gratified but apprehensive because she had not recovered the shipboard memories.

She decided to have an earlier trial separation by making a hiking trip with an organized group in the Himalayas and returning to treatment a month before I was to leave for the summer period. During her preparation for the trip, she began to have occasional dates with a black gardener who, she thought, had previously been a chauffeur, her first contact with blacks since she began treatment. She recalled that she had turned to the swarthy chauffeur at the age of 7 after her grandfather's death in an effort to replace him with another sustaining object. Before her trip to India she had passing thoughts about seeking a white elephant and wondered whether she might be seeking a magical reunion with her grandfather. En route to the Himalayas, she went for the first time to the site of her father's suicide and could cry and miss him. She also visited with her mother, sisters, children, and grandchildren and had warm interchanges with them. After her return she said she had seen her family to say farewell, since she expected to have some accident and die while in India, hoping thereby to be reunited with her grandfather.

On the journey, she was very happy. However, she took fragments from shrines and worried that she had desecrated the dead. She bartered with Tibetan women for their jewelry and felt she corrupted them by buying their religious objects, one of which included a white elephant. When she came back to treatment, we discussed her wish to return to the loving relationship with her grandfather, but she experienced little affectual release.

In the last interview before our trial separation, she had a fantasy of using the stone fragments as a memorial stele for my grave. Thus she would have me near her and available for her alone; she would commune with me in time of need.

She did not contact me after six months as we had planned. In January I wrote a note inquiring about her progress. She was intensely gratified and requested further therapy. She had not made the memorial shrine and had again forgotten my existence, being sure that I had died.

Her relationship with the black man had intensified. Over Christmas she had the delusional conviction that her visiting mother and a sister had sought to take him from her. She was furious and tried to hurt them in various ways. When she got my note, she partially decathected her delusion and viewed it as a subject for investigation.

During the next 18 months, the vicissitudes of her jealousy were worked through fairly well. The death of her grandfather and her subsequent seeking to join him in the Himalayas were cathected, but true mourning did not take place; unconsciously, she still did not accept the fact of his death (Wolfenstein 1966, 1969).

She had earlier been unaware of fantasies during masturbation or sexual relationships and had focused solely on the physical seeking for orgasm. Following a reported episode of masturbation, I asked her to visualize what she might have fantasied were she able to shift her attention from the physical experience and her fear that either she would not have orgasm or that if she did, she would convulse and explode into fragments. She closed her eyes and saw oblong geometric forms. During subsequent interviews the forms became rounded and unified as a hand and an arm, tearing at her vagina. She revealed that for years she had awakened at night, clawing her perineum. She was sure she continued to have invisible pinworms from childhood. When stool examinations were negative, she understood the fantasized oblongs in terms of projected sadistic part-objects. She now revealed that she kept her apartment like a pigsty and ate her meals standing up when she was alone. She also found it interesting that she had never learned to wipe herself and always had feces on her perianal hair and underpants. When she deemed this behavior to reflect a continuing wish to be totally taken care of, she felt humiliated and began to straighten up her apartment and keep herself clean.

During an interview in which she recalled the fantasy of the fragmented geometric, dehumanized hand-arm symbols, she returned to the terrifying experience on board ship. She had gone to the head and seen her father having intercourse *a tergo* with a nursemaid. She had been shocked, and she felt that her face had become wrinkled and flat and had then slid off her head, to lie on the floor like an emptied breast (Isakower 1938, Lewin 1946). She recalled also that her father had seen her watching him and looked aghast. His face seemed similarly to disintegrate. She had thought both of them were dissolving. Now she rememberd early childhood episodes of watching her father's masturbation and having experienced a halo effect (Greenacre 1947; Chapter 5, this volume).

She dreamed that she was being decapitated as she was in danger of being swallowed by huge waves. These she equated with her mother's vaginal labia. Her remembered seekings to get into her mother's vagina face-first were recathected. Dressed like a teenage boy, she lay rigid on the couch. She feared she would vomit, ejaculate with her whole body, and that I would cut off her head in retribution for her ambivalent wish to render me impotent by making her treatment a failure. Soon she saw these ideas in terms of an early wish to demasculinize her father as her mother's behavior had effectively done. She became intensely aware of having identified herself with her father's phallus and was both stunned and relieved. She had the fantasy that if she could supplant her father's sexual role with her mother, then her mother would need no one but her and they could live together in an idyllic symbiotic union. On the other hand, such a situation would be dangerous because a fusion with the mother would mean a destructive loss of personal identity.

When she did not regress during my summer absence, she decided to terminate before the annual Christmas separation. During the final six months, she continued to function well, except that she eschewed relationships with men other than the black lover from whom she was detaching herself. She recathected her jealousy of women at work, mother and sister surrogates, but her behavior remained appropriate and her murderous wishes were confined to fantasies. She became relaxed in her relationship with me, which essentially became that of an old friend. While my behavior remained strictly analytic with her, I shared her feelings and her fantasies that when we were apart, we would miss each other and wish each other well.

Just before termination, she brought me a tiny bonsai tree, representing herself, and in the pot was one of the Himalayan shrine stone fragments. She wanted to remain with me, to have me continue to help her mature. She planned to return in another six months, to sit and talk with me as old friends, and perhaps then we would tenderly hold one another. She understood that this wish included an element of finally telling her father she loved and missed him.

During the last interview, she sat on the couch, looking at me through much of the interview, saying she now securely felt herself to be a separate and real person and could view me as a real person. At its end, she hugged me and kissed my cheek. Then she told me she had to touch me during the drunken interview, to be sure I was not the product of her mind, but had some separateness from her.

By the end of treatment she was a vastly changed woman, capable of warm, responsible, calm relationships with the members of her family. She drank socially, had progressed in her work to a position of authority, and was on the verge of obtaining a baccalaureate. She was very proud of herself and happy. However, she had not developed the capacity to have lasting mature relationships with men and had neither completely worked through her idealization of me nor truly mourned the death of her grandfather.

A year after termination, Mrs. B. requested follow-up interviews because she was uneasy about the Christmas season. She had renounced her relationship with the black lover, had begun to have dates with men who were more eligible for marriage, had lost much of her idealization of me, and appeared to have satisfactorily mourned her grandfather. She no longer felt compelled to get her baccalaureate, which she now deemed to have been a goal set with the idea that by achieving it she would be more pleasing to me. Rather, she now took courses solely for her own pleasure. She announced her intention to return for interviews early in the holiday season each year until she felt more secure with her emotional responses to Christmastime.

Discussion

Diagnosis

I view the classical psychoanalytic technique to be the model for the psychological treatment of psychiatric disorders, and the purpose of evaluative interviews is to work out which variations of that technique are necessary for the individual patient. But the early establishment of a diagnosis may tend to predetermine the nature of treatment and to reduce the therapist's plasticity. In my opinion, the therapist should assume that underlying the presenting symptomatology are untapped ego strengths and a capacity for maturation which might allow a working alliance and the development of a technical approach close to the analytic model.

There have been continuing efforts to refine diagnostic categories, which might lead to more suitable therapeutic procedures. Kernberg's (1975a) dynamic definition of the borderline personality disorder is a particularly useful contribution. When the term is used as he advocates, it ordinarily makes the nature of the characterological dysfunctioning more easily comprehensible. His recommendations concerning the modifications of psychoanalytic technique are sound, although, in my opinion, fewer deviations are necessary than he advocates.

The establishment of a diagnostic label for Mrs. B. continues to plague me. It may be that her having been diagnosed as schizophrenic predetermined to some extent the nature of her treatment before I saw her and resulted in her having been denied the opportunity to undergo the therapy which would have led to her improvement. To be sure, there were good reasons to apply that label to her. Her reaction to our first prolonged separation was to try to kill herself so that I would continue to exist. Her surprise that I remained alive although she had not died was dramatic evidence that the self-representation of being a martyr was delusional. She underwent a catatoniclike regression during her teens when she felt deserted by her primitively idealized girlfriend and lived in a withdrawn, almost machinelike state for six years. After her first marriage she passively accepted her husband's attempts to murder her. Later she accepted enemas from her father-in-law. The seriousness of her subsequent regressive behavior, however, was complicated by a toxic brain state from chronic alcoholism.

In Mrs. B. we have a very complicated concatenation of ego structures. She apparently retained from very early childhood split maternal introjects which she then sought to project onto various people in her environment, as evinced by her primitive idealization and devaluation (Volkan 1976). There remained an ego-syntonic drive to fuse with loved ones whom she could equate with the good-mother projection, and her self-worth was enhanced by her self-view as martyr. We can suppose that the persistence of the goal to fuse represents a wish to regain the mother of the symbiotic phase (Mahler, Pine, and Bergman 1975). Her self-identification as martyr may be considered as an attempt to be at one with a primitive ego ideal, a phenomenon which Kernberg (1975a) views as evidence of pathological narcissism. However, she retained an internal bad-mother introject which she sought to externalize.

Her actual life models served to reinforce her primitive split internalized object relations. Her parents served predominantly as bad models with whom to identify in contrast to her grandfather who, before me, provided her sole consistent good model. The imposition of traumatizing primal-scene experiences and her comprehension of those events at the level of her psychosexual maturation (oral-aggressive, fusional, and anal-phallic-sadistic) served as an ego organizer, determining the manifest nature of her need to adjust to the retained split introjects. One root of her faulty sexual identity and ego-syntonic striving to become Christ lay in her striving to achieve a sense of intrapsychic unity and wholeness.

But, although it was easy for her to identify with her autistic son, Mrs. B. did not become an autistic psychotic. She had the capacity to develop a hierarchy of defenses, including rationalization and repression, and object relationships which varied in their levels of maturity.

A case could be made for schizoaffective psychosis, with masked depression stemming from the incomplete mourning of her lost grandfather, combined with cognitive regression. Her fundamental characterological pathology may have had its roots in her relationships with mothering objects in the latter half of her first year of life.

To conclude, the course of her life and transference responses seem to me to indicate the diagnosis of borderline personality organization. Before the introduction of that label I would have said she suffered from a severe hysterical personality disorder with schizoid, depressive, and impulsive trends.

Absences of the Therapist

Separations imposed by the therapist are generally thought to be detrimental to therapy with regressed patients. The topic has been touched on by various writers who usually focus on its adverse effects (Federn 1952), but also on the possibility of useful interpretations resulting from countertransference experiences (Langer 1957) and on the setting of a termination date as an impetus to analysis (Orens 1955).

During all the years of my research in treating regressed patients, I have imposed separations frequently, being absent as a rule at least ten times yearly for periods of a few days to ten weeks at one time. This procedure resulted initially from my involvement in other research, but then I learned that such imposed absences were generally helpful. However, many colleagues feel that emergency contacts between interviews by telephone or actual meetings are necessary. They hold the view that the therapist's role includes "real" good parental caretaking to substitute for the presumed poor past-life experience of their patients (Azima and Wittkower 1956, Federn 1952, Nunberg, 1932, Schwing 1954). But I have not been readily available for emergency contacts, and it is my view that the best substitute parenting one can afford the patient is to hew as closely as possible to the classical analytic model (Giovacchini 1970).

Before the analytic contract has been reached, I inform the potential patient of my planned absences, a move which motivates analysis of reactions to impending separations and their involvement in the transference. From the outset the issue of being deserted is an implicit or explicit focus of investigation. Although most patients respond with anxiety, the forms of which and defenses against which can be studied and used integratively, I have found almost regularly that the patient has heard another message to which he responds with conscious or unconscious encouragement: the therapist does not consider him to be as helpless as he deems himself.

Not infrequently, soon after a patient has been informed of a planned absence, his anxiety takes the form of overt or veiled requests for permission for emergency contacts. In general, it suffices for me to make an interpretation that he wants to be reassured that the therapist still exists. Patients have not usually telephoned me after this interpretation has been made. When such calls have occurred, I have listened long enough to determine whether an actual emergency has arisen; only rarely have I considered the patient in danger of engaging in some harmful acting out which might warrant overt limit setting, or undergoing such a regression that intramural care might be indicated.

In the instances in which I have deemed no true emergency to exist, I have simply asked whether the patient did not feel it would be better to wait until the next interview to discuss the matter in question. This maneuver has regularly occasioned relief and gratitude.

There have been, however, as in the case of Mrs. B., suicide attempts which have been associated with separations. In no such instance had the patient sought telephone contact. The suicide attempt of Mrs. B. came as a total surprise to me and caused me concern and self-searching. I still wonder whether, if I had checked my hunch after the third interview that she had been speaking to me as though I were an actual loved person of her past, material pertaining to the death of her grandfather might have emerged and been subject to analysis. This might possibly have averted her attempt to self-destruction to unite with him and keep me alive.

Personality of the Therapist

The quantitative study of the outcome of the Psychotherapy Research Project of the Menninger Foundation (Kernberg et al. 1972) stressed the importance of both the therapeutic technique and the skill and personality of the therapist in the treatment of patients with serious ego weaknesses, and the need of a "fit" between therapist and patient for a successful outcome.

It has never been established whether a combination of a satisfactory personal analysis, adequate training, and experience are sufficient to enable a therapist to work with seriously regressed patients in a manner which approaches the psychoanalytic model, or whether preconditioning, idiosyncratic life experiences provide an indispensible extra element. For us to know would require publication of confidential information. This is unlikely to happen since it would have to come from training analysts who disclosed confidential data or from a large number of personal autobiographical accounts. I can only speculate.

Early in my psychiatric and later psychoanalytic experience I became aware that I had an unusual capacity to understand primary-process products and simultaneously to retain a degree of objectivity which made me feel comfortable with seriously regressed patients and able to behave in such a manner that they benefited from our contacts. At that time, knowing of my special past, I seriously entertained the idea that reasonably successful survival of a potentially pathogenic childhood might be a prerequisite for such an aptitude.

My subsequent intimate contacts with others who have done successful psychoanalytic work with such patients, combined with extensive teaching experiences, have changed my view. It is my more mature opinion that such an individual past may make the early efforts of trainees less discomfiting and more effective; but a good personal analysis, subsequent training, and experience are entirely adequate as prerequisites for the successful work with borderline and psychotic patients.[3]

Summary

Psychoanalytic treatment with seriously regressed patients is feasible within the framework of the structural hypothesis. Poor results in such treatment can often be traced to the failure of the therapist to use his emotional responses to the patient in his formulations. Success results not only from accurate, empathic, and timely maneuvers which lead to genetic interpretations, but also from the development of the patient's new object relations with the therapist.

Details from the successful seven-and-a-half-year analysis of one patient with a borderline personality disorder are used to illustrate the interaction between the therapist's internal reactions and technique.

While idiosyncratic early life experiences contribute to the relative ease with which some therapists deal with such patients, successful personal analysis and adequate training and experience suffice to prepare the motivated psychoanalyst.

[3]In a personal communication (1983), Dr. O'Neil S. Dillon has made the interesting observation that he had concluded that in order for a psychiatrist or psychoanalyst to successfully treat a borderline patient, he or she must have loved a regressed patient in his or her past.

Part II

Countertransference and the Regressed Patient

8

The Inevitability of a Therapeutic Impasse

Freud was constantly concerned with the impediments to analytic success. Aside from a few papers which dealt with external obstacles (Freud 1917a, 1925), his principal preoccupation was with the forces within the patient which militate against a favorable outcome (A. Freud 1969; Freud 1915a, 1917a). Analysts in general have continued to stress the contribution of the character structure of the patient (Freedman 1972, Kernberg 1972b, Olinik 1970, Stone 1967, Zetzel 1965), the familial environment (A. M. Johnson and Szurek 1964), and other external circumstances to therapeutic difficulties (Rogow 1970; Roszak 1969, Stein 1972).

Freud (1910a) introduced the term "countertransference" a few years before he wrote the bulk of his papers on technique, but he never devoted a special study to it. He considered countertransference, the unconscious responses of the analyst to the patient's productions, in negative terms and felt that the analyst should be able to look within himself enough to eliminate his unconscious reactions to obstacles to treatment. Earlier, Freud had described how Breuer reacted with anxiety to Anna O.'s erotic transference and took a hurried vacation with his wife (Breuer and Freud 1893–1895).

Particularly since 1923 (Stern 1924), other analysts have become increasingly concerned with the therapist's contributions to adverse therapeutic circumstance: the needs, defenses, personality, and style of

---

Peter L. Giovacchini was the coauthor of this chapter.

the analyst have been discussed at length (Carpinacci et al. 1963; Cesio 1963; Giovacchini 1972; Greenson 1966, 1967; Grinberg 1957, 1958, 1963; Langer 1957; Orr 1954; Pinto Ribeiro and Zimmerman 1968; Racker 1957; Searles 1958b, 1959; Siquier de Failla 1966; Spitz 1956; Tower 1956). The analyst's reactions to his patient have been considered not only from the standpoint of how they may lead to impasses but also of how they may be used for analytic resolution (Arlow 1973; Beres 1957; Kohut 1959; Schafer 1959; Searles 1961, 1963a; Winnicott 1947).

In this chapter, the psychoanalytic impasse is treated as a situation in which the analyst feels uncomfortable to the degree that he is tempted to introduce a parameter (Eissler 1953), a nonanalytic procedure, or to discontinue therapy. Such impasses may be encountered during any phase of treatment, and no analysis is free of them. Each function of the mental apparatus can serve the purposes of defense and give rise to resistances which may lead to such apparent therapeutic interferences, and different kinds of impasses will be encountered in the treatment of patients with varying personality structures (Glover 1955). The viewpoint emphasized here is that whether the impasse becomes a therapeutic stepping-stone, even a breakthrough, or an obstacle to treatment often depends on the analyst's reactions to his patient's productions. Some positive and negative aspects of his reactions are discussed in this context.

Therapeutic Philosophies

Depending on the individual therapeutic philosophies of analysts, they will differ in their judgments of what constitute serious impasses and may warrant the introduction of parametric or nonanalytic technical maneuvers or even the termination of psychoanalytic treatment. Identical regressive phenomena will be seen by one analyst as significant impediments but by another as heralding potential progress.

The traditional position regarding treatment follows Freud's stand (1937) that psychoanalysis as a therapeutic procedure should be limited to patients with relatively intact personalities and ego strengths, in whom unconscious conflicts have led to the development of neurotic symptoms or mild to moderately severe characterological disturbances. Such patients are thought to be those who can easily develop true transference neuroses, the analysis of which can result in changes in the structure of the mental apparatus (Stein 1972, Tarachow, 1963). Such transference involves largely the projection of whole object representations.

In this view, patients whose unconscious conflicts are more narcissistic in nature, who have weak ego functions, and whose personality is considerably deformed are to be treated by psychoanalytically oriented psychotherapy, in which transference is permitted to a varying extent to remain uninterpreted as a resistance and the analysis of other types of resistance is to be but partially attempted.

Supportive psychotherapy is to be used with psychotic patients, including those in remission, borderline cases with marked characterological deformities, and other patients with severe narcissistic tendencies. Transference is to remain uninterpreted as a resistance, and other forms of resistance are to remain largely uncovered. The environment is to be manipulated, and the patient's defenses and ego capacities are to be selectively strengthened (Spence 1968).

In the traditional view, the transference relationships of the latter two categories are too unstable to permit the development of the transference neurosis (Freeman 1970, Wexler 1971). They are based for varying periods predominantly on the projections of part-object representations. Some who favor this view use the advent of the development of psychoses during psychoanalysis to support their position. (Bychowski 1966, M. Little 1958, Reider 1957, Romm 1957).

The traditional view largely determines the training of psychoanalytic candidates in the majority of our educational institutions. The prevailing overt attitude is that the application of psychoanalysis to patients other than neurotics and those who suffer from mild characterological disorders is ill-advised and potentially harmful; the covert attitude is that it is akin to "wild" analysis (Freud 1910b) and reprehensible. The psychoanalyst who is trained in this tradition and maintains it tends to feel anxious and guilty when he undertakes the analysis of a patient whom he diagnoses as other than neurotic. He is more apt to feel insecure and to be tempted to change his technique when confronted with serious regressive tendencies in the analytic situation than is his colleague who has either been trained differently or has undertaken individual experimentation for long periods of time with the psychoanalytic treatment of such patients. The latter analyst will usually have come to change his views regarding their analytic treatability and have fewer personal needs to respond to aggressive phenomena in ways which will make analytic obstacles of them.

From the beginning of the use of psychoanalysis as a therapeutic agent, there has been a discrepancy between the traditional viewpoint and actual practice. Although Freud advocated restricting the use of analysis to the care of patients with strong egos, he never clearly defined neurosis or psychosis and failed to integrate his early views concerning them with his structural theory (Arlow and Brenner 1964, Boyer 1967c). Many patients whom Freud analyzed would today be considered as suffering from severe characterological disorders, borderline states, or psychoses (Reichard 1956). It would seem that the very patients with whom Freud had the most difficulty belonged to these categories and that his reactions to such patients partly determined the development of therapeutic obstacles with them. Freud's disciples had similar experiences and conflicts (Boyer 1967b). Two examples of Freud's difficulties with patients follows.

After a long period of therapeutic stagnation when treating the Wolf-Man, whom he considered to be an obsessional neurotic, Freud (1918) introduced two deviations from the model technique. The first constituted the use of the "forcible technical device" of setting an arbitrary termination date. Flarsheim (1972) suggested that Freud's use of that maneuver may have added to the Wolf-Man's difficulty in working through his paranoid transference. In the second device, Freud promised the Wolf-Man a complete recovery of his intestinal activity. Eissler (1953) believed the Wolf-Man to have experienced this as a "definite surrender of the analytic reserve" and as the analyst's admission and promise of omnipotence, "hence the resurgence of the disease when the analyst became sick and proved himself not to be omnipotent" (p. 111).

After some years of relative symptomatic remission, during which at times Freud altruistically provided him with financial aid, the Wolf-Man underwent a frankly psychotic delusional hypochondriacal regression (Gardiner 1971, Jones 1955). Freud then referred him to a female analyst, who saw the Wolf-Man gratis. In his work with her, the patient's residual paranoid transference to Freud came to light, as well as conflict about "alms thrown to a crippled beggar" (Brunswick 1928). Freud's having, in effect, paid the Wolf-Man to be an analytic subject supported his megalomanic fantasies of being an important contributor to psychoanalysis, and Freud's favorite patient "may have contributed two kinds of restrictions while he was seeing Freud: (1) a restriction of the patient's perception of Freud's feelings toward him to positive feelings only; and (2) a corresponding restriction to positive transference reactions" (Flarsheim 1972, p. 115).

It is clear that Freud's behavior contributed to the nature of the complex transference situation, which was not resolved while the Wolf-Man was in analysis with him. We can but speculate on the elements of the countertransference phenomena which, combined with Freud's shifting therapeutic philosophy (Boyer 1967c), led to his various actions toward the Wolf-Man. Did he successfully privately analyze his own hostility toward his patient (Winnicott 1947)? Did he set the time limit primarily for therapeutic reasons or rationalize a wish to get rid of a particularly annoying patient? Did he subsequently subsidize the Wolf-Man through guilt?

Freud once undertook the analysis of a man whom he considered to have "always been psychotic" and who subsequently died of "catatonic fever" (Binswanger 1956, Boyer 1967c). After a period of apparently satisfactory analysis, the patient developed sufficient trust in Freud to be able to reveal some dishonesty by acting out in the consultation room (Zeligs 1957). In Freud's brief absence, the analysand surreptitiously read private notes. He subsequently confessed nefarious business practices. Some analysts today would have been comfortable with the man's regressed behavior and would have believed his behavior indicated analytic progression. Freud reacted by judging the man on the basis of a superego defect, not on the basis of his being psychotic, to be unanalyzable. He immediately abandoned the analytic model. The patient then found reason to leave treatment, probably responding to Freud's change of attitude, apparently to his analyst's relief. It seems likely in this instance that Freud responded to the invasion of his privacy and that his moral sense was offended; he rationalized his wish to be rid of his patient as therapeutically advisable. Freud (1909) in an aside in his case history of the Rat-Man, reported how his spontaneous reaction of moral indignation led to a patient's abrupt cessation of treatment.

Freud's behavior with both of these men led to what various analysts today would consider to be premature cessation of treatment. Perhaps unanalyzed countertransference hostility contributed to the therapeutic judgment to introduce the questionable forcible technical devices with the Wolf-Man and to abandon the basic model technique in the case of the intrusive businessman.

As a result of a vast expansion of child analysis (A. Freud 1959a, Klein 1932) and longitudinal studies of normal and abnormal infants and children and the mother-infant dyad (Bergman and Escalona 1949; S. Brody and Axelrod 1970; Freedman and Brown 1968; A. Freud 1965; Korner 1964; Mahler and Furer 1968; Ritvo and Solnit 1958; Spitz 1957, 1959), an increased emphasis on the analysis of the ego (A. Freud 1936, Hartmann 1939a), and attempts to revise therapy on the basis of changed theoretical concepts (Arlow and Brenner 1964, 1969; Bion 1967; Fairbairn 1941, 1944; Federn 1952; Guntrip 1961; Klein 1957; Kohut 1971; Sullivan 1940), psychoanalysis is now being used as a treatment procedure for an everwidening scope of disturbances (Bullard 1940, Bychowski 1952, Fromm-Reichmann 1950, Jacobson 1971, Lewin 1950, Stone 1954). It is now used by a growing minority of analysts for the treatment of conditions which place them nearer the psychotic end of the continuum of conditions which some consider to extend between the hypothetical states of total psychic normality and total psychosis (Boyer and Giovacchini 1967). The inclusion of such patients has added to the incidence of analytic impasses, both because of the nature of the analysands' regressions and the conscious and unconscious discomforts they create in analysts (Greenson 1972).

Oscillations between regression and progression have been increasingly recognized as necessary aspects of psychological development (A. Freud 1965). The roles of regression and ego disorganization are crucial in the achievement of progressive consolidation of the personality (Loewald 1960). The periods of consolidation around the Oedipus complex and toward the end of adolescence follow phases of regression with temporary ego disorganization.

Regression in general is considered to constitute a return either to a situation of early failure or one of early success (Frosch 1967, Winnicott 1963). The role and function of regression can be seen variously as (1) representing a failure or defect in current modes of mastery; (2) a reactivation of previous modes of adaptation, which were used in earlier life, generally associated with ties to gratifying libidinal objects; or (3) an attempt to master a prior failure, although with techniques inconsistent with current modes of mastery (A. Freud 1936, Freud 1926a, Schur 1953).

The analytic situation itself may bring about new and deeper regressive tendencies with the development of transference (Lorand 1963), which seriously threaten the therapeutic (Zetzel 1956) or working alliance (Greenson 1965).

Some analysts see such regressive tendencies as undesirable and to be eliminated, thereby making therapeutic obstacles of them, whether they are or are not in and of themselves. Others see them as defensive moves against danger arising from the analytic situation (Calder 1958, Holzman and Ekstein 1959), but also as potentially adaptational steps which can lead to mastery of early trauma or perhaps even to unblocking of previously hindered spontaneous maturation and development (Alexander 1956, Bettelheim 1967, Khan 1960). Kris (1950b) viewed psychoanalytic treatment as a creative experience in which the patient's ego has an opportunity to use those regressive experiences which always occur in the service of the analytic work and maturation.

In contrast to the traditional position, there is a growing view that patients should not be denied psychoanalytic treatment on the basis of a phenomenological diagnosis of severe characterological disorder or psychosis, but rather that their treatability should be determined on the basis of a "therapeutic diagnosis" (Winnicott 1955). The therapeutic diagnosis is a statement concerning the patient's capacity to use treatment. It depends principally on two factors. First, can the patient sustain himself between his therapy hours and get to and from his appointments? He may require assistance from his family and, in extreme instances, casework management may be required, not as an inherent part of treatment but to enable the patient to survive between the therapeutic sessions (Flarsheim 1972). The second factor is whether the patient behaves in the office in ways which are tolerable to the analyst. Whether the analyst can be comfortable will depend on his idiosyncratic personal interests and sensitivities, his prior experiences with regressed patients, the ego state and psychopathology of the patient involved, and his unconscious reactions to the patient's behavior and verbal productions (Hoedemaker 1967b).

However, analysts respond differently to both bizarre and fairly ordinary behavior. The patient's silence, which has been discussed from the standpoint of resistance, transference, and countertransference, is a case in point (Bergler 1938, Levy 1958, Loomis 1961, Waldhorn 1959).

Racker (1957) stressed that the patient's words and ideas may serve at times as gratification (nutriment) for the analyst. Zeligs (1960) wrote of the analyst's unconscious retributive hostility because of feelings of deprivation engendered by the patient's silence, a countertransference reaction which can sometimes be removed by self-analysis. Other analysts become so bored and frustrated when dealing with silent patients that they have given up attempting to treat them; no amount of analysis has made them feel comfortable with such patients (E. H. Erikson, personal communication 1948). Flarsheim (1972), analyzed a psychotic man who was frequently mute; one of his silences lasted for three months. He felt the man needed to experience, in a controlled and safe environment, his regressed magical means of control over parental imagos through silence as a manifestation of withholding. Flarsheim's therapeutic philosophy contributed to his comfort during the patient's silences, but he also occupied himself with reading and writing as a means of controlling his own retributive hostility. Eventually, the patient's silence became a means of communication (Arlow 1961, Greenson 1961), which showed how the analysand wanted to be treated, rather than just a magical device to control. Flarsheim's tolerance to the patient's regression had contributed to his development of a more integrated ego.

Analysts differ in their tolerance for various sorts of behavior. Some view pessimistically any type of physiological regression. Others view such regressions at times as necessary steps in the development of a sense of trust and the capacity for dependency on which therapeutic alliance relies. Atkins (1967) stressed that the quality of that alliance reflects to a considerable extent the character of the patient's actual relationships with his early caretakers, and when that capacity is threatened by the existence of fears and distrust of oneself with another, this must be the primary subject for analytic work and interpretation (Lindon 1967).

Fortified with this therapeutic philosophy, Atkins (1967) was able to tolerate the behavior of a patient who misused almost every element of the analytic situation. Invitations to relax his censorship of thoughts and feelings and to communicate through free associations resulted in his mumbling, at times incoherently. Relaxation gradually extended to his sphincters. During asthmatic attacks he produced copious amounts of spit and vomit; he also passed urine and feces, and ejaculated without erection or conscious feelings and fantasies. "During deeply regressed times in the transference he felt himself to be actually his mother, not simply like her" (p. 593). In the third year of analysis, his regression reached its deepest phase and was finally experienced solely as a psychological experience without the usual prior physical concomitants. Despite the severity of the disturbance it was possible to maintain the ordinary analytic situation and to analyze the regressive experience, which was understood to be a reliving of a disturbed mother-child relationship. The regressions during the remainder of the analysis were like the transient ones commonly seen in a transference neurosis. "They were permitted by a relatively secure ego in a situation in which he could trust both himself and the analyst" (p. 596).

We present a final example of a situation which might have been converted into a serious analytic impasse by the therapist's reactions. Instead, it led to a reliving experience in a favorable environment which apparently made possible the release of the innate maturational capacities of a patient who in the past would have been judged unsuitable for analysis.

A girl suffered a catatonoid withdrawal when she left home to attend college (Boyer 1967b; Chapter 5, this volume). To some degree she knew she needed to establish contact with a substitute for her mother, whom she consciously scorned and hated, but she unconsciously feared overt homosexuality and thus did not dare to become close to females. She kept herself relatively psychologically intact and out of the hospital by having her first dates with a young man. She feared and refused intercourse with him but almost immediately began to engage in fellatio; while sucking on his penis she would enter into trancelike states which were later understood to have been associated with nursing fantasies. Eventually the young man demanded intercourse and she became pregnant. They were married and had two children, each of whom she transiently believed to have resulted from parthenogenesis. Partly because she was jealous of her husband's attention to the children, she became sadomasochistically provocative and inordinately demanding of his time and thoughts; he responded first with physical attacks and later by deserting the family, although remaining legally married. She became confused and paranoid and eventually entered psychoanalysis.

Soon after she found that her analyst was able to understand much of her diffuse, primary-process–dominated productions and was apparently unafraid of her leechlike aggression, she began to improve in her everyday life. She was able to get her first paying job and to become self-supporting; then she could divorce her husband. Her life outside of the office became better and better organized, but she became increasingly dreamy and her verbal productions more and more bizarre while she was in the consultation room. For about six months, she lay on the couch fantasizing fellatio on her analyst each day, with a cathexis which was periodically hallucinatory. She was worried about whether her draining his body contents in an effort to fuse with him or take him totally inside her would deprive him of power and substance. There was no doubt that the penis, never erect in the continuing fantasies, which were unaccompanied by sexual excitement, represented a fusion of both her parents. Most of the time, she was quite aware that she was living in a fantasy state but occasionally for various time periods she consciously confused her analyst with one or the other of her parents (Searles 1963b).

During that six months' period, her analyst just waited, while she engaged in what was for her a singularly gratifying experience; one which she said on prompting that she must live through in order to emerge from some stunted stage of infantile development. She was not psychologically sophisticated nor had she read analytic literature. Eventually her reliving and abreactive experience enabled her to recover significant preoedipal and oedipal fantasies and experiences.

Then her genitals became cathected, and for the first time she began to experience sexual excitement which was not associated or confused with urinary or anal excretory sensations. She had matured to a state in which her analyst served as a clear father surrogate and a whole object; after partial analysis of her transference neurosis, she left treatment and married. Five years later she returned for further analysis of a neurotic problem. There had been no further psychotic regression.

The Analyst's Helplessness

As discussed above, disruptive situations in treatment have been viewed alternately as undesirable complications or as potentially therapeutically beneficial. They can be viewed also as inevitable phases of analysis which must emerge in order that fundamental aspects of the patient's personality may be involved in treatment. In our view, many analyses consist of a series of crucial periods which recapitulate traumatic aspects of the infantile environment and the vicissitudes of the early nurturing relationship are relived during therapy. *If the patient's childhood was punctuated by a series of crises, these crises must be re-experienced in analysis. Thus the impasses of early development become impasses in treatment.* They are, however, impasses which are intrinsic to the patient's psychopathology and become obstacles to treatment only when the analyst responds adversely, either because of countertransference reactions or his therapeutic philosophical orientation.

In view of the timelessness of the unconscious, the period which may be involved in an analytic reliving of a developmental impasse can scarcely be forecast. If the analyst is concerned about its duration, the patient is apt to perceive him as impatient; the impatience may be sensed as an intrusion reminiscent of the impatience of others during his formative years.

As children, many patients, and especially those who later suffer from characterological or psychotic disorders, have felt extreme helplessness because of the unattainable, narcissistically derived expectations of their parents. Often, an analytic impasse represents a moratorium to ward off the demands of others so the patient can discover his own expectations of himself. In order to consolidate an aspect of autonomous identity, he may have to seek to project his rage and helplessness onto the analyst. He may need to use various techniques in order to achieve such countertransference state. Such techniques will have been learned in the past or from realistic evaluations of the analyst's aspirations, needs, and conflicts.

While it may not be necessary for the analyst to react to his patient's behavior by actually feeling what the analysand may seek to project onto him, he often does. Self-examination following some impasses reveals the analyst to have defended himself against a patient's attempts to project onto him, usually by denial, reaction formation, and professionalism.

Less experienced analysts who seek consultation are often found to be less defensive and to be able to acknowledge feelings of helplessness more readily. True, they may be unaware that their feelings reflect those of their patients. To the contrary, the less experienced therapist may believe that his feelings are solely the result of his ineptness. This situation is reminiscent of the patient's inability to understand that his feelings toward his analyst involve transference and are not totally realistic. In both of these cases, realistic elements are, of course, also operative.

When the patient seeks to divest himself of some feeling or part of the self and to project it onto the analyst, his attempt is a process which takes place in his own psyche. He only thinks that he has injected psychical elements into the analyst. Nevertheless, the analyst often responds as if something had been put inside of him; he reacts as a *contenido*, as our Latin American colleagues would say. We must always wonder whether the analyst who reacts in a fashion consonant with the patient's productions does so because something intensely personal has been stirred within him, as in Freud's view of countertransference (1910a). Yet helpless feelings are encountered so frequently in the analysis of many patients, and particularly those now included in the broader scope of psychoanalytic applicability, that if idiosyncratic elements are involved, they are sufficiently common to analysts that this particular transference-countertransference situation deserves closer scrutiny.

Patients suffering from helpless and vulnerable self-representations, whose feelings of inadequacy are sometimes overwhelming, are the rule rather than the exception among the regressed people now seen by many analysts. In their experience, as the years have passed and the treatment of such patients has become a fairly routine activity, they are usually able to deal with the deep regressions these patients experience with relative equanimity (Atkins 1967; Flarsheim 1972; Chapter 5, this volume). This was not always true. Earlier, countertransference problems clearly led to therapeutic failures (Chapter 4, this volume). However, from time to time, patients are encountered who create special difficulties which lead to the analytic impasses on which the remainder of this chapter focuses. We wonder whether these patients believe in some distinctive although subtle fashion and if because of certain characterological peculiarities or defensive adaptations they are especially adept at undermining their therapist's equilibrium.

Case Material

A colleague consulted Giovacchini (personal, communication 1973) because he felt anxious and helpless while with a patient and specifically unable to make interpretations. He anticipated each interview with dread and felt furious with his patient, a bright, enterprising, and inventive man in his 30s. He debated terminating the analysis. The therapist was uncertain whether his anxiety and helplessness produced his anger or his rage made him unable to function. He also wondered whether his fury and sense of powerlessness arose from separate sources.

When it was suggested to him that he might be reacting to the content of his patient's productions, the analyst immediately recognized his feeling of impotency as being the counterpart of his patient's feeling of helplessness. Nevertheless, he remained baffled concerning the source of his anger and could not understand why he felt his powerlessness so intensely that he had become functionally paralyzed.

Giovacchini was reminded of other situations in which impasses had arisen during which he felt very angry with patients without knowing why but had been unaware of experiencing helplessness. The situations were not instances of flagrant acting-out behavior nor were the patients obnoxious. By contrast, they were usually mild-mannered, compliant people who talked freely.

There are various reasons why an analyst may feel anger toward his patients. Here we refer to one which we believe to apply to our colleague's analysand and one which is frequently encountered in the therapy of patients who suffer from severe characterological disorders.

The patients of whom Giovacchini was reminded were characterized by two features: (1) they blamed the world for all their difficulties; and (2) they expounded an ideology to which they attributed magical rescuing powers. But such features are commonly found in such patients, especially those with an inclination toward a paranoid orientation. The root of the difficulties appears to be found in the ideology selected by the patients (Giovacchini 1972).

The colleague's patient exploited people in petty ways. Aside from paying his analyst regularly, he was completely unreliable in financial matters. He took women out to dinner and managed to have too little money to pay the check. He was extremely parsimonious and picked up discarded newspapers to save money. His analyst, on the other hand, took money matters very seriously; he was scrupulously honest, perhaps even compulsively so. He was also very generous and often picked up the tab when dining with friends. The patient had been dwelling on his pecuniary manipulations to the exclusion of anything else for some time, and the analyst had been responding with rage and discomfort.

In another instance, one of Giovacchini's patients had expounded the virtue of various nonanalytic schools of psychotherapy and compared psychoanalysis unfavorably to them in order to attack and belittle his analysis and analyst. He had done so at a time when his analyst was feeling some pessimism concerning the value of his work. Both of these patients had basically paranoid cores and often produced bizarre material bordering on the delusional, but it was not their obvious craziness that was disturbing.

In each instance, the analyst reacted to the content of the patient's projections and the analysand had succeeded in undermining the therapist's analytic security. The analyst had become impatient and felt an impasse had been reached. However, the impasses in each case resulted from the analyst's discomfort and anger. Each analyst felt also that the patient was trying to impose something on him which he could not accept and which he felt threatened his autonomy.

Viewed retrospectively, this situation recalls the infantile traumatic environment. Thus, the patient defends himself against the assault on his embryonic identity by producing a similar dilemma within the analyst. Why does he so often succeed? Is it due to some particular idiosyncratic quality in the analyst? Or does this situation permit generalizations? Each point of view can be discussed.

First, one has to consider the form of the patient's material. Both patients mentioned above presented their viewpoints in a logical, rational fashion. The colleague's patient extolled his thrifty viewpoint as reasonable and laudable; if saving money were an ultimate goal, he was an eminent success. Giovacchini's patient's arguments were concise and superficially logical.

In spite of the fact that both analysts understood their patient's exaltations of their viewpoints to be the result of defensive needs to avoid feelings of helpless vulnerability and fears of being assaulted and overwhelmed, each felt threatened. The seemingly rational superstructure presented by each patient obscured problems of delusional proportions. The rationality was the element which disturbed the therapists, who found themselves debating with their patients, using persuasion and argument rather than considering the patients' intrapsychic motivations. With obvious craziness, as was stated earlier, they would have been more comfortable.

Still, the question has not been settled. We might ask again why analysts who are experienced in treating patients with severe psychopathology should find such situations difficult. All paranoid patients seek to construct their delusional systems with as much logical consistency as possible. They may use an enormous amount of secondary-process thinking to cloak their projections and distortions. They are especially adept at selecting situations, persons, or causes that will support their position, and they can be eminently rational and convincing. The external world is often reacted to in a seemingly logical fashion, and at times their beliefs are sensitive and thoughtful.

We believe that in these instances the countertransference difficulties arose because the patients had a propensity to clothe their primary-process projections in secondary-process garments representative of the analysts' *values*. The first analyst's integrity was threatened by his patient's parsimony and pecuniary manipulations. Giovacchini values psychoanalysis and reacted adversely when an aspect of his ego ideal was threatened by his patient's denigrations of psychoanalysis by falsifications of the scientific positions of other therapies. In both cases, the analysts were more threatened by having their value systems attacked in a seemingly logical fashion than they would have been by any direct assault aimed at undermining their self-esteem. Neither analyst was aware that his ego ideal was being encroached on; neither could continue to focus on the delusional core because his patient, by subtle means, had succeeded in upsetting his personal equilibrium and made him feel helpless to a degree. Subsequently, when the analysts became cognizant of the reasons for their countertransference reactions, they were able to rectify their behavior and remove the analytic impasse.

As stated, Giovacchini's patient, by extolling the virtues of other schools of psychology, devalued the analyst's orientation. In retrospect, and even at the time, he understood that the patient sought to project helpless, depreciated aspects of himself onto the analyst, and the analysand adopted an attitude of condescending superiority. This set of circumstances was, of course, the outcome of the unfolding of transference, an inevitable and necessary therapeutic consequence, and one which should not have led to complications. The content of what the patient had used to depreciate, represented an attack on something that mattered to the analyst. The analysand not only impugned the analyst's *modus operandi* but an important aspect of his identity, his professional identity.

This patient threatened his analyst's identity in another fashion as well, one which is found to occur frequently in the treatment of patients who suffer from character problems. During one session, while talking as usual about external factors rather than looking within himself, he mentioned a psychiatrist of whom Giovacchini had never heard. The patient claimed certain knowledge that his analyst disliked the man. The patient viewed the psychiatrist in the same way he saw his emasculated, depreciated father. Giovacchini said he did not know the psychiatrist and suggested that his patient sought to project some of his own attitudes onto his analyst. After a minute's silence, seemingly having ignored his analyst's comment, the patient resumed his discussion of the same school of psychology which had occupied his thinking before Giovacchini's attempt to put matters on an intrapsychic and transference basis. During the next interview, Giovacchini learned from the patient that he had felt irritated after this event and then tended to deal imprudently with the content of the patient's associations. The analyst had not, up to that point, been aware of his hostile response.

Freud (1912) taught us that lifting infantile amnesia through the resolution of the transference neurosis is the essence of psychoanalytic treatment. The technical maneuvers he recommended were learned mainly from the therapy of hysterical neuroses. Dramatic moments in which repressed memories of traumatic events from childhood emerge are uncommon in the psychoanalysis of patients who suffer from severe characterological psychopathology (Lindon 1967; Chapter 5, this volume). Giovacchini's response to having his comments ignored by the patient may be viewed as a situation which approximates the lifting of infantile amnesia, as will be illustrated by the following.

When the patient treated Giovacchini as a nonentity he was repeating one of a series of events which characterized his relationship with his father. During most of his analysis, the patient's associations were focused primarily on his mother, who was described as an intelligent, ambitious woman, quite capable and competent. She was forceful and pushed her son to achieve intellectually. By contrast, the father, who was mentioned rarely, was a poorly educated, financially successful immigrant tradesman, without intellectual interests. The mother taught the patient to regard his father as a nonentity and to use her idealized brother as a male identificatory model. In order to construct a self-image which would please his mother, the analysand consciously pursued his mother's idealization, which included the denial of his father's importance, and, in a sense, of his existence. This was especially difficult because he had never seen his uncle; his mother's version of her brother received no confirmation from reality. When the patient finally met his uncle, he was overwhelmingly disappointed because he in no way corresponded to his mother's descriptions. The exclusion of the father was vitally important in order that he might construct an ideal self-representation. As so often happens, however, what he tried to exclude became the basis of his identity and he sought treatment because of the low esteem associated with the self-image that was, in fact, modeled after his father.

The patient's reactions toward the analyst can now be seen as reenactments of the early situation with his father. What he produced in treatment was not the verbal recall of a repressed infantile memory; instead, within the transference context, he acted out feelings belonging to an early developmental stage. For the moment, the analyst reacted within this frame of reference and felt discomfort and anger when the analysand acted toward him as though he were absent, repeating his behavior with his father. The patient had succeeded in projecting his amorphous, poorly structured self-image onto the analyst. The analyst reacted with what might be considered an existential crisis. The emotional climate of the transference situation, similar to the day residue, linked with unconscious conflicts in the analyst, resulted in a countertransference response which created an analytic impasse. Unlike the patient's father, the analyst could not adjust to being treated as if he did not exist. Once he could stand aside and examine his emotional response, Giovacchini could then understand that the patient was merely reliving an important constellation stemming from his traumatic infantile past and permit the restoration of analytic equilibrium. *For therapeutic purposes, the reenactment of behavior characteristic of early developmental stages is equivalent to the emergence of an infantile memory.* When the stages have been interpreted or spontaneously understood as such by the analysand, sometimes specific confirmatory memories appear and consolidate meaningful insight.

Discussion

The type of psychoanalytic impasse described above is due to a combination of factors which result in a specific kind of interaction between the patient's psychopathology and the analyst's ego ideal and self-representation. In each of cited instances, the impasse was transient because the analysts were able to resolve the countertransference reactions which had created the impasses. *The impasse arose in each instance because the analyst sought to remove his own discomfort by expecting the patient to change the manifestations of his psychopathology.*

The question can be raised whether it is inevitable that the analyst feel disturbed. Because of particular character adaptations, it may be necessary for the patient to seek to provoke certain reactions in the analyst as the transference relationship develops. But should the patient be allowed to succeed? If one were familiar with such situations and could anticipate them, perhaps it would be possible to simply analyze them without feeling personal upheaval.

Some authors (Winnicott 1947) do not believe this is possible. The argument usually given is that in order to be able to evaluate the situation, one has first to experience an emotional response which acts as a spur, so to speak, that then leads to comprehension. Thus, a countertransference response becomes a diagnostic vehicle, a method of gaining understanding (M. Little 1957, Racker 1957).

Ideally, in a psychoanalytic situation, the analyst will be sensitive to all the nuances of the patient's behavior and productions, as well as to his own personal reactions, disruptive or otherwise. Today analysts have generally had long periods of personal psychoanalysis to prepare them to understand their individual personalities as thoroughly as possible. Their adverse reactions that lead to impasses have to be scrutinized in terms of their unanalyzed or repressed conflicts, which constitute blind spots.

To judge from the literature and numerous conversations, blind spots in analysts are as inevitable and varied as are the manifestations of their patient's psychopathology. This is especially true when analysts seek to treat those now included in the broadened scope of analysis and when patients who were accepted in analysis as neurotics undergo unexpectedly deep and continuing transference regressions. However, the incidence and severity of the analyst's blind spots are reduced by experience; when he has gone through situations such as those described, he has learned something about his own sensitivities. At the same time, his prior knowledge that some patients remember through a special kind of reliving in the transference becomes less intellectual. Dealing with such patients becomes less trying as one becomes familiar with the situation and one's countertransference reactions become milder and more easily analyzable.

The necessity for a diagnostic countertransference reaction can be compared to the generation of anxiety. Anxiety as a signal stimulates various responses in the ego's executive system which are designed to master a problem situation (Freud 1926). In some instances, the ego may be so familiar with the problem that anxiety is not felt. One reacts automatically, perhaps reflexively. While analyzing a patient, something similar may occur. The analyst, because he has become so familiar with patients who need to disrupt him, can assess the transference situation without necessarily getting emotionally involved.

However, the patient can be exceedingly subtle and the analytic relationship is difficult at best (Greenson 1966). The question thus raised is whether it is mandatory that the analyst experience adverse countertransference feelings. The question is essentially rhetorical, inasmuch as it pertains to a hypothetically ideal psychoanalyst. Being human includes failings; possibly without such failings there would be no treatment of patients whose psychopathology resulted partly from their having been used to protect others from their own failings.

Summary

In a study of impediments to the success of psychoanalysis as a treatment method, the character structure of the analysand has received the most attention. Psychoanalysis has come to be used for the treatment of an ever widening range of psychopathological states, and analysts have become confronted with a greater incidence and variety of clinical situations which can develop into therapeutic obstacles.

Whether the psychoanalytic impasse will become a therapeutic stepping-stone or an obstacle to treatment often depends on the emotional response of the therapist and his resultant behavior. Accordingly, there has been a heightened interest in the study of countertransference.

Some therapists equate the psychoanalytic treatment of patients with severe character deformations with "wild" analysis and therefore feel needless guilt and anxiety when they attempt to treat patients who suffer from them; thus they increase the likelihood of their becoming therapeutic obstacles. We have considered the psychoanalytic impasse as an inevitable aspect of the analytic sequence and discussed countertransference reactions in this context.

Technical complications resulting from adverse countertransference reactions are examined both in terms of the patient's provocations and responses in the analyst. Among the analyst's responses, three were emphasized: (1) helpless feelings which represent the patient's helplessness and vulnerability; (2) rage reactions; and (3) profound anxiety reactions.

The patient's need to construct an environment similar to the early traumatic environment within the analysis can become a very difficult situation for a therapist. The resolution or at least understanding of these interactions becomes equivalent to the lifting of infantile amnesia, a step which has been considered the essence of psychoanalytic resolution. Thus, adverse reactions can become keys to the gaining of fundamental insights, permitting the analytic process to continue its inevitable course.

9

Analytic Experiences in Work with Regressed Patients

I have used psychoanalysis with few parameters in the treatment of patients whose character structures placed them in or near the psychotic end of the continuum of psychopathological disorders. This treatment was done almost exclusively on an outpatient basis. Early in my work with such patients, I (Chapter 4, this volume) concluded that unresolved countertransference problems constitute a major obstacle to the successful outcome of their treatment. During the past 20 years, I have also come to believe that the therapist's emotional responses to the patient's productions may be used to enhance therapy.

Freud showed an ongoing concern with impediments to analytic success. Although he wrote a few papers that dealt with external obstacles, his principal preoccupation was the forces within the patient which militate against a favorable outcome. One such force was the "adhesive" (A. Freud 1969), or "sticky," libido. In general analysts have continued to focus on the contributions of patients' character structure to psychoanalytic treatment problems.

In 1910(a), Freud cited countertransference as a treatment impediment, but he never devoted a specific study to the phenomenon. He considered countertransference to be roughly the obverse of transference, in that it consisted of the repetition in the therapeutic relationship of the analyst's irrational, previously acquired attitudes. Freud assumed that countertransference was the result of the therapist having been inadequately analyzed. Prior to Hann-Kende's 1933 suggestion that the emotional responses of the therapist could be used as facilitators of the analytic process, psychoanalysts uniformly viewed countertransference in a pejorative light (Ferenczi 1919, Gruhle 1915, Stern 1924). After Hann-Kende, the next therapist to recommend the use of countertransference as an analytic tool was Little (1951).

There is a large literature pertaining to countertransference reactions in the analyses of patients with neurotic transferences, including a number of reviews (Glover 1955, Orr 1954, A. Reich 1960). The most comprehensive recent review is that of Langs (1976), although it is restricted to writings that have appeared in English. During the past quarter of a century, increasing attention has been paid to the role of countertransference in the treatment of regressed patients, both as an impediment to and as a facilitator of the therapeutic process (Adler 1975; Arbiser 1978; Arieti 1955; Bion 1955, 1957; Epstein and Feiner 1979; Fromm-Reichmann 1950; Giovacchini et al. 1975; Hill 1955; Kernberg 1974; Kusnetzoff and Maldovsky 1977; Maltzberger and Buie 1974; Marcondes 1966; Miler 1969; Modell 1963, 1975; Nadelson 1977; Prado Galvão 1966; Robbins 1976; Searles 1965; E. R. Shapiro et al. 1977; M. Sperling 1967; Szalita-Pemow 1955; Volkan 1973, 1976, 1978; Wilson 1970; Zetzel 1971). Therapists who use analytic treatment for regressed patients note that their countertransference responses with these patients differ considerably from those experienced with neurotic patients.

Analysts have long been concerned with the means by which the psychological attributes of one person are assumed by another; many have written about the influence of patients' introjection of analysts' attributes on the transference relationship (Fairbairn 1952; Freud 1917b; Giovacchini 1975a; Guntrip 1961; Hartmann 1939a; Loewald 1960, 1979; Schafer 1968). Fenichel (1945) was the first to note that analysts' countertransferences are largely determined by their introjections of patients' attributes, which may be communicated verbally or nonverbally; subsequent authors have corroborated Fenichel's observation (Federn 1952, Fliess 1953, Weigert 1954).

Primitive Defense Mechanisms of Regressed Patients

The intimate relationships of borderline and other regressed patients are characterized by the use of two closely related primitive defense mechanisms—namely, splitting and projective identification (E. R. Shapiro 1978). Many analysts believe that the regressed patients' tendency to use defenses that involve projection, combined with the introjective aspects of countertransference with such patients, results in countertransferential involvement different in kind and intensity from that commonly experienced in work with neurotic patients.

Splitting

Melanie Klein (1946) hypothesized that in the first months of life the infant has an omnipotent fantasy that unwanted parts of the personality or internal objects can be split, projected onto an external object, and controlled. Kernberg (1975a, 1976b) found that an underlying pattern of sharply polarized relationships is "activated" in the transference of borderline patients and that the polarization is determined by the defensive maneuver of "splitting." That is, the love and hatred associated with internalized relationships are split to avoid the anxiety that would result if they were experienced simultaneously. Patients defend themselves against anxiety by projecting the split-off unwanted personality aspect onto the therapist in the transference relationship.

With the successful negotiation of the rapproachement subphase of separation-individuation, the child develops the capacity for ambivalence and object constancy (Fraiberg 1969, Mahler et al. 1975, Settlage 1979). Although Giovacchini (Boyer and Giovacchini 1980, chap. 9) believes the psychopathology of borderline patients may be rooted in earlier periods of development, most observers think that it lies in patients' failure to traverse the rapproachement subphase successfully (Carter and Rinsley 1977; Mahler 1972; Masterson 1972, 1976; E. R. Shapiro et al. 1975; Zinner and E. R. Shapiro 1975).

Various authors have questioned the validity of characterizing splitting as a primary defense mechanism of regressed patients (Gunderson and Singer 1975, Heimann 1966, Mack 1975, Pruyser 1975, Robbins 1976). Nevertheless, therapists seem to agree that such patients are unable to integrate and modify their impulses and affects, which results in their alternately viewing their therapists as omnipotent and omniscient, and as helpless and ignorant. These patients experience scant dependency on their therapists in the sense of love and concern, but instead, undergo sudden shifts from total need to total devaluation. Therapists who do not expect such treatment by and reactions from regressed patients, or who are dependent on patients' approval for their sense of well-being, are especially susceptible to anxiety-provoking, adverse countertransference reactions.

Projective Identification

The validity, necessity, and utility of the concept of projective identification, the second primitive defense mechanism characteristic of regressed patients, are sometimes questioned by those therapists who do not consider psychoanalysis the treatment of choice for such patients.

The type of material projected by regressed patients is determined by the immature nature of their mental operations, including the selectively deficient modulation of their drives. Many therapists (Fromm-Reichmann 1952, 1958; Hartmann 1953; Klein 1946; Lidz and Lidz 1952; H. A. Rosenfeld 1952a; Winnicott 1960) have noted the central position of conflicts related to the presence of primitive, untamed aggression in borderline, psychotic, and other deeply regressed patients. The vicissitudes of the expression of primitive aggression result in therapist's experiencing eeriness, anxiety, and confusion, sometimes in empathy with patients' experience. Bermak (1979) remarked that "the projective identification type of countertransference occurs characteristically in treating regressed patients . . . I have noticed that the feeling of being affected profoundly and of having a sense of no longer being in contact and of having departed from my well-established analytic ego stance occurs particularly with patients who have borderline features." His comment reflects the subjective experience of an analyst confronted with the pressure of the patient's coercive and seductive primitive projections.

Goldberg's position (1979, p. 347) that "in work with psychotic patients transference and countertransference should not be regarded as separate entities" gives the flavor of the experience of the analyst of the regressed patients. An ever-growing number of analysts (Bion 1956; Carpinacci et al. 1963; Cesio 1963, 1973; Giovacchini 1975b; Grinberg 1957, 1958, 1962; Kernberg 1975a, 1976b; Langer 1957; Novick and Kelly 1970; Ogden 1982; Paz et al. 1975, 1976a, 1976b; D. Rosenfeld and Mordo 1973; H. A. Rosenfeld 1952b, 1954; Searles 1963b; Siquier de Failla 1966; Zinner and R. A. Shapiro 1972) turn to the concept of projective identification to understand their countertransference responses to such patients and to use these responses as facilitators of the analytic process.

Projective identification may be considered an early form of the mechanism of projection (Kernberg 1975a). It frequently has been associated with both splitting and transitional relatedness (Modell 1968, 1975). Uncomfortable aspects of the personality, be they elements of impulse, self-image, or superego, are dissociated and projected onto another person, with whom the projecting person then identifies. According to Schafer (Ogden 1978), the projecting person feels "at one with" the person onto whom he fantasizes he has projected an aspect of himself. Klein (1955) noted that once the split part of the personality has been projected onto another person, it is lost to the subject and an alteration of the object-perception process ensues. Projective identification may involve a nonhuman subject. Anna Freud (1967) wrote of a girl who projected her feelings of loss and sadness onto a cap that she had left at a campsite; she then could grieve, ostensibly for the deserted cap.

In the treatment situation, projective identification creates bewildering situations as patients attempt to evoke feelings and behavior on the part of their therapists that conform to the projection and the therapists consciously or unconsciously accept the projected attributes as parts of themselves (Grinberg 1963, 1976; Malin and Grotstein 1966). Such evocation is particularly characteristic of regressed patients. Many authors have written of the subtlety and effectiveness of such patients' attempts to accomplish this goal and the resulting countertransferential complications.

Patients who use projective identification as a defense are selectively inattentive to the real aspects of their therapists that may invalidate the projection (Brodey 1965). After imbuing their therapists with disclaimed and projected attributes, these patients consciously perceive the therapists to be unlike themselves, but they maintain an unconscious relationship with them in which the projected aspects can be experienced vicariously (Zinner and E. R. Shapiro 1975). The projective aspects of projective identification and projection per se differ in that, in the former, a greater degree of contact is maintained with the part of the personality that has been externalized. Those who use projective identification as a defense are somewhat aware that they are seeking to rid themselves of a property of themselves; in addition, they try to develop relationships with their therapists via the projection, to involve them as collusive partners who conform to the patients' perceptions of them. From the standpoint of countertransference, difficulties arise when therapists unwittingly become such collusive partners.

Racker (1968) wrote of concordant and complementary countertransference identifications. In concordant countertransference identification, analysts identify with the corresponding part of patients' psychic apparatus: e.g., ego with ego, and superego with superego. Under the influence of concordant countertransference identification, analysts experience as their own the central emotion being experienced by patients; they can behave empathically. In complementary transference identification, analysts identify with the internalized transference objects of patients; they have introjected patients' projections unconsciously. These projections stimulate unresolved unconscious conflicts in analysts, causing them to repeat earlier life experiences. Analysts then experience the emotions ascribed to them by patients as transference objects, while patients relive emotions experienced in the past with parental figures. For example, if an analyst identifies with a superego formation connected with a stern, forbidding father figure, he will seek aggressively to control the patient and an impasse may result. Racker (1953) also discussed what he calls "indirect countertransference," that is, therapists' emotional reactions to third persons involved in the treatment program and the latter's adverse effects.

Grinberg (1979) holds that in complementary countertransference identification, analysts always react in ways that correspond to their own conflicts. At times, the analyst takes onto himself a reaction or a feeling that comes from the patient. He calls this phenomenon "projective counteridentification," describes how it may lead to treatment impediments, and cites interpretive steps from his own and Segal's case material (1956) to illustrate how the impediments can be removed once the therapist becomes aware of the problem.

An important but rarely discussed facet of projective identification in the therapeutic situation is the reintrojection by patients of that which they projected. Ordinarily, the projection involves patients' hostility, which they perceive to be exceedingly dangerous. Many regressed patients are particularly interested in how therapists handle their own aggression. These patients often are unusually sensitive to hostility in their therapists and are masters at provoking it. Over time, as patients observe that their therapists' own hostility and/or that which they believe was projected onto them have harmed neither the therapists nor themselves, they come to view hostility as less dangerous. Of course, acquiring the capacity to make such an observation depends on complex interactions in the developing transference and real relationship (Loewald 1960). Patients' observation that hostility will not destroy them or their therapists, combined with a taming of patients' aggression as a result of successful therapy, allows them to reintroject their modified—or, in the words of a patient, "detoxified"—hostility and integrate it into their evolving personalities. Milton Lozoff (personal communication 1979) suggested that patients' improved ability to handle their aggression may be due in part to their identification with analysts' management of *their own* aggression.

In the fifth year of her successful analysis, a severely obsessive-compulsive woman who had had periodic, transient psychotic regressions over many years both in and out of therapy made the following statement:

> I always treasured my anger as a child, but I kept it secret because I was afraid my thoughts, let alone my words, had killed my aunt, made my mother hate me, and my father leave me. I've always been afraid my angry feelings would kill you and the first time you went away, I spent the days and nights on my knees on street corners praying to God that He would protect you from my anger and keep you alive. I know now that for years I've tried to hurt you with my thoughts, words, and actions, although I thought for a long time it was you who were trying to hurt me with yours. Now I know my anger is not dangerous like I thought before.

However, it is not only hostility that may be viewed as magically dangerous by the regressed patient. Giovacchini (1975a), Klein (1946), Searles (1958a), and I have had patients who deemed their love to be destructive. During treatment, these patients had the omnipotent fantasy that they projected their love onto their therapist for safekeeping, with the idea that they would reintroject it when they no longer considered it so potentially harmful. Bion (1956), among others, wrote of regressed patients' projection of their "sanity," or the nonpsychotic portion of their personality, onto the therapist.

I first became aware of the patient's use of the therapist as a repository before I underwent psychoanalytic training. At that time, I was a psychiatrist in the army. A man in a straitjacket was brought to the hospital where I worked. He had been catatonically excited for some weeks. Because I received several hundred new patients along with him, I was initially too busy to give any of them more than cursory attention. I told him that I could not talk with him at length. I asked him to record the experiences he wanted to communicate to me, as I wouldn't be able to see him for a few days. He received no medication and only routine ward care until I saw him a week later. By then, he appeared to have recovered completely. When I invited him into my office, he presented me with two thick notebooks filled with his handwritten account of his aggression-laden hallucinatory and delusional experiences, among others. No apparent regression transpired during the ensuing month; then I asked him why he had recovered. He was surprised and said it was because he had given me his crazy ideas in the notebooks. He had watched me carefully and was amazed that his writings had not visibly affected me.

Some ten years later, I received a letter from him stating that he had remained well; he expressed concern about my mental health. This patient seemed to have used the written word, and then his therapist, as the repository for his mental aberrations.

The "Sticky" Libido

Let us turn to the notion that a "sticky" libido in and of itself may be responsible for an unresolvable psychoanalytic impasse. Early in my clinical experience, the analyses of two female patients with severe characterological disorders were terminated because triadic relationship interpretations of their highly erotized transference reactions were ineffective. I was all too willing to believe that the onus should be placed on the so-called adhesive libido. However, nagging uneasiness and troublesome dreams led me to conclude that countertransference involvement had been responsible for the therapeutic failures. Self-analysis was contaminated by too many scotomas; therefore I reentered formal analysis, during which I discovered that the seductive way these women had presented their conflicts, and the nature of the conflicts themselves, had stirred up unconscious problems of my own. Through Racker's complementary countertransference identification (1968), or the counterreaction Chediak (1979) described as "the analyst's transference to the patient," I had identified these patients with an important person of my past.

I came to understand that hidden behind my patients' view of me as a genitally withholding father surrogate was their projection onto me of bad self-objects and maternal part objects. My impatience over their failure to accept my misdirected interpretations had supported their view that I was sadistically frustrating. Following my own reanalysis, one of them returned to me and was successfully treated.

Interpretation of Dyadic Relationships in the Transference

Partly as a result of my experiences with these two women patients, early in my work with regressed patients I learned to respond only to certain aspects of transference reactions that had oedipal coloring and appeared early in treatment. After some years, I learned that therapeutic impasses commonly followed triadic relationship interpretations of such material. However, focusing on the material's aggressive aspects within the context of dyadic relations avoided such stalemates (Boyer 1966). Such an approach is consonant with the current developmental conceptualization of the nature of the therapeutic action in psychoanalysis (Settlage 1979). The clinical experiences of Atkins (1967), the Ornsteins (1975), H. A. Rosenfeld (1966a), Sperling (1967), Volkan (1978, 1979), and Wilson (1970), among others, corroborate my findings. These clinicians agree that following the mending of the splits and fragmentations of regressed patients' identity via modern representations of their earlier dyadic relationships, analysis with such patients is scarcely different from that with neurotic patients, who typically use preoedipal rather than oedipal material in the service of defense. Only after the dyadic material has been repeated and worked through can investigation of the oedipal transference be fruitful. A clinical example follows.

At one time a young woman came to see me, complaining of genital anesthesia. I was overjoyed at having found what I initially thought was a classical case of hysteria. Soon, however, I had to revise my judgment; after she had been on the couch for a few days, she misunderstood an adventitious noise to mean that I was openly masturbating behind her and she complacently started to rub her own pubis, stating that as a child she had manipulated her genitalia while surreptitiously watching her father masturbate. What appeared to be a floridly erotic oedipal transference ensued for a very short time. I viewed it as a pseudo-oedipal resistance, which turned out to be correct. Her treatment proceeded unusually smoothly for some three years, during which time her projection onto me of bad self-objects and maternal part objects was analyzed.

A year before I was to take a sabbatical to do other work, I informed this patient of my impending absence. Dr. D.'s consultation room adjoined my own, and he then became a fantasized father surrogate for the patient. A few months before I was to depart, she said she wanted to continue her analysis with him after I left. She continued to use me primarily as a maternal surrogate throughout our work together. Her treatment with Dr. D. lasted a year and dealt solely with classical oedipal problems, which Dr. D. considered typical of analyses of hysterical neurotic patients. This woman has shown no regression in the 20-odd years since her termination.

During her analysis with me, which lasted nearly three years, the patient valiantly sought to get me to behave as her mother had behaved during the patient's early childhood. In her studies of psychotic children and their mothers, M. Sperling (1974) found that mothers unconsciously induced psychosis in their children. Wilson (personal communication 1979), who noted that his regressed patients often strove assiduously to get him to repeat the roles and behaviors of their mothers, suggested that success in treatment depends on our analyzing such efforts by patients, rather than identifying with and repeating their mothers' actions.

Analytic Tolerance of Regressive Behavior

Clearly, analysts' capacity to remain objective and empathic is of paramount importance in the treatment of all patients, but such an equilibrium is especially difficult to maintain with regressed patients whose communications are more strongly influenced by the primary process. Kernberg (1975a, 1978) advocated that when one undertakes the treatment of borderline patients, it may be advisable to set formal limits on these patients' behavior and to obtain their permission to be hospitalized should their regression in the analysis lead to behavior that makes it difficult for the analyst to remain objective.

Analysts' tolerance of patients' behavior varies widely. In part, this is due to the nature of their training. Psychoanalysis is being used for an ever widening scope of disturbances, as a result of (1) the vast expansion of child analysis and longitudinal studies of infants, children, and the mother-child dyad; (2) the increased emphasis on the analysis of the ego; (3) therapeutic revisions based on changed theoretical concepts (e.g., the overshadowing of the topographical by the structural hypothesis, with a consequent etiological shift toward viewing psychopathology as the outcome of both developmental deficiencies and conflict); and (4) the growing sophistication of developmental and object-relations theory.

Despite these developments, many training institutes still teach candidates that psychoanalysis should be offered solely to patients with transference neuroses and that other patients should receive supportive therapy or diluted versions of psychoanalytic psychotherapy which largely exclude interpretation of the transference. Since the inception of psychoanalysis as a treatment modality, there has been a gross discrepancy between this traditional view and the actual practice of psychoanalysis (Boyer and Giovacchini 1980, chaps. 2 and 3). Freud analyzed numerous patients who clearly suffered from severe characterological disorders, borderline conditions, and even psychoses (Binswanger 1956, Reichard 1956). Parenthetically, there seems to be no question that failures in the treatment of some of Freud's seriously disturbed patients resulted from countertransference impediments (Chapter 8, this volume).

As a result of this traditional training, some candidates and young psychoanalysts either forego offering analysis to many patients for whom it is optimally suitable or offer it to them with great guilt and anxiety. The state of both their knowledge and their own emotions interferes with the treatment process. Some observers point to another serious deficiency in traditional psychoanalytic education: supervisors who fail to help candidates see that "a countertransference response is often an indication of some need within the patient and can be a guide to a deeper understanding of both the patient and the therapist" (S. Shapiro 1979).

One message included in the traditional training of candidates is that regression to early pregenital states in the transference situation is an indication to abandon psychoanalysis as the treatment of choice. Yet it has been recognized that oscillations between regression and progression are a necessary aspect of psychological development (A. Freud 1965). Regression and ego disorganization are crucial steps in the progressive consolidation of the personality (Loewald 1960). The periods of consolidation around the time of the emergence of the Oedipus complex and toward the end of adolescence often follow phases of regression, at times to the level of dyadic relationships, and ego disorganization. Such regressions are to be expected in insight-oriented treatment of the patient population we have been discussing.

Regression generally constitutes a return to early failure or success (Winnicott 1955). Regression may represent (1) a failure or defect in current modes of mastery; (2) a reactivation of earlier modes of adaptation generally associated with ties to libidinally gratifying objects; or (3) an attempt to master a previous failure using techniques that may be inconsistent with current modes of mastery (A. Freud 1936, Freud 1926, Schur 1953). Such an attempt may be in the service of progression.

The development of transference in analysis may bring about new and deeper regressive tendencies that may seriously threaten the therapeutic (Zetzel 1956), or working (Greenson 1965), alliance. Some analysts see regressive tendencies as undesirable analytic obstacles that must be eliminated. Others see them as defensive moves against the "dangers" of the analytic situation (Calder 1958, Holzman and Ekstein 1959) that may be used to master early trauma and perhaps even to "unblock" arrested maturation and development (Alexander 1956, Bettelheim 1967, Giovacchini 1979b, Khan 1960). Kris (1950a) viewed psychoanalytic treatment as a creative experience in which the patient's ego has an opportunity to use regression in the service of the analytic work and the patient's maturation.

There is a growing minority view that patients should not be denied psychoanalytic treatment on the basis of a phenomenological diagnosis of severe characterological disorder or psychosis. Instead, according to this view, analyzability should be determined on the basis of a therapeutic diagnosis (Winnicott 1955), that is, a statement concerning patients' capacity to use treatment. The therapeutic diagnosis depends primarily on two factors. First, patients must be able to sustain themselves between therapy hours and to get to and from their appointments. They may require assistance from family members and, in extreme instances, adjunctive casework management, to accomplish this (Flarsheim 1972). Second, patients' behavior in therapy hours must be tolerable to their analysts. Analysts' thresholds of discomfort will vary with their idiosyncratic personal interests and sensitivities, their prior experience with regressed patients, the ego state and psychopathology of the patient involved, and their unconscious reactions to the patient's behavior and verbal productions (Hoedemaker 1967b). Giovacchini (1979a) stressed the importance of the last factor: "The judgment whether a patient is treatable . . . depends more upon the analyst's psychic integration than the patient's psychopathology (p. 236).

Analysts respond differently even to fairly ordinary behavior. Patients' silence, which has been discussed from the standpoint of resistance, transference, and countertransference, is a case in point (Bergler 1938, Levy 1958, Loomis 1961, Waldhorn 1959). Racker (1957) stressed that at times patients' words and ideas may serve as needed gratification or "nutriment" for the analyst. Zeligs (1960) wrote of the analyst's retributive hostility engendered by patients' silence. Erikson (personal communication 1948) was so intolerant of silent patients that he gave up treating them. Searles (1961) wrote of analysts' incapacity to tolerate the intimacy of silence; he suggested that their interpretations sometimes serve the defensive function of breaking what patients perceive to be a needed silence, during which time they can fantasize being in a state of symbiotic union with their therapists.

Flarsheim (1972) once analyzed a psychotic man who was frequently mute. Indeed, one of his silences lasted for three months. Flarsheim felt the man needed to experience in a controlled and safe environment his regressed, magical means of control over parental images through silence, as a manifestation of withholding. Flarsheim's therapeutic philosophy contributed to his comfort during the patient's silences, but he also read and wrote to control his retributive hostility. Eventually, the patient's silences became a means of communicating how he wanted to be treated, rather than being merely a magical device to control. Flarsheim's tolerance of his regression had contributed to his development of a more integrated ego.

Some analysts take a pessimistic view of any psychosomatic regression, despite the work of many clinicians (Alexander and French 1950; Bruch 1973; Chiozza 1976, 1978, 1979; Garma 1978; Schneer 1963; M. Sperling 1974, 1978; Thöma 1967; Wilson 1968) who have illustrated so graphically the meanings, uses, and analyzability of psychosomatic disorders. Others see the occurrence of such regressions during the treatment of some patients as a necessary step in the development of trust and the capacity for dependency on which the therapeutic alliance relies. Atkins (1967) stressed that the quality of that alliance reflects to a considerable extent patients' actual relationships with early caretakers; when their capacity for dependency is threatened by fears and distrust, the latter must become a primary focus of analytic work and interpretation.

Fortified with this therapeutic philosophy, Atkins was able to tolerate the extremely regressive behavior of one patient over a period of several years. When he invited this patient to relax his censorship of thoughts and feelings and to communicate through free associations, the patient mumbled, at times incoherently. Relaxation gradually extended to his sphincters. During asthmatic attacks, he produced copious amounts of sputum and vomit; he also passed urine and feces and ejaculated without erection or conscious feelings or fantasies. Atkins (1967) wrote, "During deeply regressed times in the transference he felt himself to be actually his mother, not simply like her" (p. 593). In the third year of analysis, his regression reached its deepest phase and was finally experienced solely as a physiological experience. Despite the severity of the patient's disturbance, it was possible to maintain what Atkins called the "ordinary analytic situation" and to analyze the regressive experience, which was understood to be a reliving of a disturbed mother-child relationship. The regressions during the remainder of the analysis were like the transient ones commonly seen in a transference neurosis.

Case Material

Regression in a Borderline Patient[1]

A married woman in her 20s fit the modern criteria for borderline personality disorder (Gunderson and Kolb 1978, Gunderson and Singer 1975, Kernberg 1975a, Perry and Klerman 1980, Spitzer et al. 1979) very well. When she was permitted to live out her regression, which was limited to the analytic situation, it led to a reliving experience that seemingly made possible the release of innate maturational capacities.

History. The patient suffered a catatonoid withdrawal when she left home to attend college. To some degree, she knew she needed to establish contact with a substitute for her mother, whom she consciously scorned and hated. But her unconscious fear of overt homosexuality made her avoid females. She kept herself relatively intact psychologically by making a mother surrogate of a young man with whom she had her first dates. A virgin, she refused intercourse the first time they went out because she was unconsciously afraid that his phallus would grow to the size of a baby and rip her apart. On their second date, she quite willingly consented to fellatio, a practice which was their customary sexual activity for some weeks. While sucking on his penis, she entered into blissful trances that included fantasies of nursing on the fantasized phallus-nipple of her mother. Eventually, the young man demanded intercourse and she became pregnant.

They married and she left school while her husband continued his studies. She briefly believed that their two children resulted from parthenogenesis. Partly because she was jealous of her husband's attention to the children, she became sadomasochistically provocative and inordinately demanding of his time and attention. She often slept in the bathtub, sometimes in continuously running hot water. As would be expected, she unconsciously equated that experience with a return to the fantasized bliss of intrauterine life. She barely disguised her pleasure when her husband responded to her defiant sleeping in the bathtub by beating her and subsequently raping her, using either her vagina or her mouth. Eventually he left the family, although they remained legally married. After his departure she became confused and paranoid and entered analysis.

[1]See Chapter 5 for further discussion of this patient.

Treatment. Soon after she found that her analyst was able to understand some of her diffuse, primary-process-dominated productions and was apparently unafraid of her leechlike aggression, she began to improve in her everyday life. She was able to get her first paying job and to become self-supporting; she could then divorce her husband. Her life outside of the consultation room became better organized, but during her therapy hours she became increasingly dreamy and her verbal productions became increasingly bizarre. Then, for about six months, she lay on the couch fantasizing that she was performing fellatio on me every day, believing at times that she was actually sucking on my penis. She was worried about draining my bodily contents and depriving me of power and substance in her efforts to fuse with me or take me totally inside her. There was no doubt that the penis, which never was erect in the continuing fantasies that were unaccompanied by sexual excitement, often represented an amalgam of both her parents, but predominantly her mother. Searles (1975) believes that through such fantasies patients reestablish an imagined symbiotic state within the transference.

During that six-month period, I just waited; I was comfortable with my periodic fantasies of merging with her and my transitory oceanic feelings while she engaged in what for her was a singularly gratifying experience, one which she unsolicitedly said she must live through in order to emerge from "some stunted stage of infantile development." She was psychologically unsophisticated and had read no analytic literature. Had I chosen, no doubt I could have focused on the aggressive and defensive aspects of her behavior and shortened her regressive episode. However, as I considered the modified reliving and abreactive experience to be in the service of her psychological development, I did not interfere.

Subsequent to the regressive period, her genitalia became cathected and for the first time she could feel sexual excitement that was not associated or confused with excretory functions. She later matured to a state in which I served as a clear whole-object father surrogate. After partial analysis of what had then become an oedipal transference neurosis, she left treatment and remarried. Five years later, she returned for analysis of a neurotic problem. There had been no subsequent psychotic regression, although a brief one occurred during her second analysis. My philosophical orientation contributed to my tolerance of this patients' regressed behavior and enabled me to avoid adverse countertransference reactions.

The following vignettes illustrate how treatment impasses with severely regressed patients can be turned into therapeutic enhancers by using the countertransference experience productively.

Regression in a Patient with a Severe Impulse Disorder[2]

History. Fifty-three years old when first seen, Mrs. B. was a twice-divorced, friendless white file clerk who lived alone and was almost totally impulse dominated. Under continuous psychiatric treatment of many different kinds for emotional aloofness, impulsivity, and chronic alcoholism for almost 20 years, she had been hospitalized frequently for weeks to months at a time and usually had been diagnosed as schizophrenic. She had been jailed many times and while in the "drunk tank" had masturbated openly, smeared feces and menstrual effluvia, and screamed endlessly. She had lived dangerously, provoking sexual assault by black gangs in ghettos on various occasions. When she came for treatment, she literally believed that she had never had angry impulses and that any behavior which might have been interpreted as such had been motivated by altruism. Her principal stated reason for seeking psychoanalysis was that she had been told by the therapist of her psychotic son that her interactions with him contributed to the continuation of his disturbance; she eagerly had sought a form of treatment that she knew would be very painful in the service of helping him to improve. She had sought psychoanalysis from highly reputable practitioners several times previously, but none had accepted her for such treatment.

Mrs. B. was the child of a self-centered, vain, impulsive, and hypochondriacal mother and a depressed, exhibitionistic, profligate father who committed suicide during her adulthood. His chronic alcoholism had led to the loss of the fortune inherited from his and his wife's families. In her preschool years, Mrs. B. had read and done arithmetic precociously, but after the first year of school, she became barely literate and lost her mathematical abilities. Her failure to pass any examination in all her school years after the first grade did not disturb her parents, whose goal for their four daughters, of whom she was the second, was that they use their grace and beauty to acquire rich husbands, preferably doctors, who would support the family lavishly. During an early session she stated that she thought she had had a secret

[2]See Chapter 7 for further discussion of this patient.

liaison during her grammar school years with a swarthy chauffeur who wore black gloves.

She had had a severe obsessive-compulsive neurosis with strong altruistic features from the age of 7 or 8 until 12, when she was sent to a girls' finishing school where she felt loved by an adored classmate. At 16, she felt deserted by her idol and withdrew to such a degree that she functioned essentially as a robot for almost six years. She had no boyfriends, although she was quite beautiful, and she behaved mechanically at social functions, including her own debut. When she was 21, her older sister seemed to have "hooked" a rich medical student from an elite social level. Mrs. B. was galvanized into action, apparently by her need to be the family savior, and got the man to marry her instead.

Her sexual passivity and frigidity infuriated her self-centered and unfeeling husband, who had many affairs that he flaunted before her in a manner reminiscent of her father. While her husband attended school in another city, she lived with his parents. Her father-in-law, a retired minister, ascribed her passivity to possession by demons, which he sought to exorcise by giving her enemas while she was naked in the bathtub, an action endorsed by her husband and her parents. She was unaware of either anger or sexual excitement, but had fantasies of seducing her father-in-law and destroying him by public exposure and ridicule. Following her husband's graduation, he entered the army and they moved to a distant area. He was soon sent overseas. As a result of her shyness and passivity, she was almost constantly alone. She began to drink in solitude and had drunken autoerotic and vengeful fantasies that were repressed when she sobered up. She bore three children, none of whom she believed to be her own for varying periods after their births. She feared touching them, and a succession of nursemaids was hired to take care of them and her. She began to frequent bars where she picked up men and had short-lived affairs.

Her third child was an autistic, feces-smearing, exceedingly hyperactive boy who was hospitalized when he was 2 or 3 years old. He rarely acknowledged her existence. Her husband divorced her and henceforth had only rare contact with her or the children. She limited her sexual partners to black men, repressing the actual sexual experiences. On the occasional weekends that her son was with her during the next few years, she brought men home with her and submitted to fellatio and sodomy before him, subjecting him to primal-scene traumas that repeated her own early experiences, which she had repressed. She also repressed the behavior to which she exposed her son, learning of her actions only through the nursemaids. After her daughters were taken away from her, her behavior became increasingly irrational, resulting in her being hospitalized and jailed.

During one of her hospitalizations, Mrs. B. met a man who was a chronic alcoholic. They began to live together and eventually got married. As she had uncritically idealized her mother and later her schoolmate, she now idealized him. As would be expected, she uncritically despised certain authority figures, projecting the "bad mother" onto them as she had done earlier with her father. Her new husband was so like her physically that she often wore his clothes. At times they drank together and spent days in bed, performing polymorphous perverse sexual activities to the point of exhaustion while lying in their own excreta. She often experienced bliss, consciously believing they had achieved a symbiotic physical union. They lived on welfare and grudging charity from her relations. A psychiatrist suggested that she would have more self-value if she became employed. She managed to complete a course in practical nursing and had some success in state hospitals, caring for psychotic and senile patients with empathic tenderness. She was fired repeatedly because of drunkenness.

Eventually her husband left her, an action she could not comprehend since she believed that he depended on their fantasized physical and psychological continuity as she did, and because she supported him financially. A few years before beginning treatment with me, she had obtained a job as a file clerk in a place where her inefficiency and instability were tolerated. Her low-cost therapy was financed by an allotment from a deceased family friend.

Treatment. Following an early session to which she came drunk, seeking through bizarre behavior to test my anxiety tolerance, to seduce me, and to establish a symbiotic union through sexual actions, Mrs. B. decided not to come to the office intoxicated. Soon thereafter, she spontaneously vowed to cease going to bars and picking up men or, as she expressed it, "to be a good girl." Nevertheless, during the first four or five months of treatment, on most weekends she drank wine or beer at home and often woke up in the company of some man whom she could not recall having met. She had no memory of their activities. After a time, she was able to recall the intervening step of going to bars to pick up men. I understood her behavior to have the unconscious, symbolic, communicative role of informing me of the meanings of past activities (Ekstein 1976). She was confused by and rejected my initial transference interpretation that I was a surrogate father figure; eventually I comprehended that my transference role was that of an idealized, phallic, surrogate maternal figure.

On Mondays, she often presented dreams or fantasies in which a young animal or child was tortured or unjustly punished. I assumed they were connected to her weekend activities and silently hypothesized that these activities constituted an identification with what she had perceived to be aggression toward her when as a child she had been exposed to parental sexual behavior and had felt tortured or unjustly punished. I knew I would have to wait a very long time to validate my hypothesis. However, retrospectively I believe I had begun effectively to ignore her as an adult and to perceive her only as a kind of puppet. Treatment stagnated and she began to get drunk and pick up men during the week. I felt increasingly incompetent, helpless, and annoyed with her. I now doubted her claim that she had forgotten the actual sexual activities with the various men; she could not have been unaware of my accusing anger.

During one session, after I silently called her a liar, I became sleepy (McLaughlin 1975). While dozing, I pictured myself as a young child whose contradictory wishes to be good and bad controlled me without my will. With a start, I became alert and thought that it must have been necessary for her to subject me to her emotional experience and that my own emotional needs were being satisfied by an empathic response. I briefly recalled Searles's oft-repeated statement that work with severely regressed patients requires *mutual* emotional growth. I then consciously put myself in her place and supposed that she was experiencing similar helplessness in the face of contradictory wishes. I further assumed that she experienced my repeated questions as accusations, that my past actions had supported her externalized self-punitive need, and that she had expected a reward for her vow to be a "good girl" but felt that she had received none.

When I voiced my assumptions, she acknowledged their validity and recognized her disappointment over my previous lack of awareness of what she had been experiencing. She said she must have been trying to put parts of herself into me and thus get rid of them. Soon thereafter, for the first time during her analysis, she recalled a specific detail of her actions in a bar. She had been disappointed when a man refused her advances, saying she was "too old a pussy" for him. She then dreamed that a boy put kerosene on a kitten's tail and lit it; the kitten ran away terrified, although it wanted to claw and bite its tormenter. In association to the dream, she recalled an early interview in which I had refused her sexual advances. She had responded by trying to claw my face and kick my genitals (my "tail"), which she had sought to put "on fire."

After the foregoing material was discussed, Mrs. B. stopped going to bars and became aware of her anger toward the men she picked up, although the sexual interactions remained repressed. It was a large step forward for her to become aware that she *had* anger and angry wishes that could not be rationalized as stemming from altruistic motives. However, she was not yet aware that her various disappointments with me screened angry feelings toward me. Her projection onto me of the forgiven, uncritically idealized good-mother object remained intact.

When I began treating Mrs. B., I informed her that after six months, I would be leaving for a period of several weeks. Periodically during the six months, she recalled vividly that when she had been a child, her mother customarily had gone to Europe alone on the Grand Tour. The patient had been bitterly disappointed and lonely at such times, and had feared that her mother would die or would not return because she did not want her children and despised her husband. Mrs. B. also had believed that mother had left her because of Mrs. B.'s secret malfeasances with the chauffeur and envy of those sisters who got more of mother's attention than she did through their temper tantrums and other disturbing behavior. Mrs. B. had asumed the role of family martyr in part to assuage her guilt. When I left, I felt secure that her separation anxiety had been dealt with adequately.

Upon my return, I was completely surprised to learn that immediately after I had departed she had attempted to commit suicide by taking sedatives she had saved from previous therapy and that her effort had been thwarted quite accidentally. Her suicide attempt had been determined by several unconscious motivations. As a child, she had believed that her parents had a limited quantity of love to distribute among their daughters. She had blamed the emotional upsets of her sisters on her existence, which had diminished the supply of parental love. She had often contemplated altruistic suicide for their welfare. She had also equated her mother's absence with death and had thought that she could reestablish symbiotic union with her mother when she died. But a new element gradually emerged from repression.

We now learned that during her preschool years, the patient's maternal grandfather had been a consistent love object for her; he had held her on his lap, read and told her fairy tales, and admired her reading and mathematical precocity. He had died during her first schoolyear, but she had not been allowed to view his corpse and unconsciously had retained the belief that he was still alive. He had once promised her a white elephant and she had taken him literally. From the Kipling stories he had read to her, she knew that white elephants might be found in India. In later life, she became seriously involved in Eastern religions, unconsciously believing that they would lead her to the white elephant and reunite her with her grandfather. She also retained the idea that if she were to die, she could join him in heaven and reestablish the gratifying relationship she had experienced before. Two additional motives for her attempted suicide were discovered. First, since childhood she had believed that her death would make it possible for her sisters to obtain more love from their parents to whom she ascribed finite love—too little in quantity to be shared by four daughters. Her altruistic thought helped her deny her death wish toward her sisters. Now she believed that her death would enable me to give better care to my other patients, her surrogate sister figures. And second, she unconsciously hoped her suicide would destroy me professionally, to avenge herself for my presumed favoritism for other patients. Even though she talked about her anger toward me, she spoke intellectually; her anger was not experienced consciously. We found that the loss of her capacity to learn, that is, to read and to do mathematics, was based in part on her attempt to deny the knowledge that her grandfather had died.

After much of this material had been worked through, another therapeutic impasse occurred as a result of my unconscious response to disturbing material of which she sought to rid herself by placing it in me. It will be recalled that during her son's home visits as a small boy, he had seen her drunken sexual behavior with men. Sometimes, when she was unconsciously angry with me, she would return to her shameful memories of being confronted by the nursemaids with those actions. For a few weeks, her interviews were dominated by this issue. I did not know why she was angry with me and felt further frustrated because I could not understand why she expressed that repressed anger with seemingly endless repetitions of material that seemed to lead nowhere. I gradually noted that when she began her ruminative iterations, I responded with irritation and sleepiness. She reverted to picking up men in bars and our rapport all but disappeared. For the first time I regretted having accepted her in analysis and wondered why I had done so.

I found myself fantasizing during one hour, but later could not remember my fantasies. Over the years, I have come to the conclusion that the fantasies I have during sessions are often my empathic responses to what patients are trying to tell me or have me experience. Accordingly, I thought that I had forgotten my fantasy because I had needed to defend myself from internal conflicts that our relationship was reawakening. That night, I had a dream that reminded me of my own past. Through my own analysis, I had learned that I had become an analyst with the unconscious motivation of curing an important love object of my childhood who had suffered from a regressive personality disorder. Analysis of my dream made me aware that another reason for my becoming an analyst was that I had sought to protect a younger sib from the effect of that adult's personality disorder. I knew then that I had accepted Mrs. B. in therapy not only to help her but to help her psychotic son as well.

I then became aware that underlying my conscious identification of her with the disturbed love object of my past lay an unconscious identification with her abused son with my sib and myself as children. I was expressing my anger by withdrawal and refusal to recognize her, as her autistic son had done during the first several years of his life. Such knowledge permitted me to regain my objectivity. Finally, I could interpret her wish to provoke my abuse and punishment for her treatment of her son and me. She responded by remembering dreams and hypnopompic fantasies in which she was forced to watch women being raped anally and having huge phalluses shoved into their mouths. This led to the recovery of memories of what had transpired between her and the black-gloved, swarthy chauffeur. She had equated him with a kind black waiter who had once comforted her; following her grandfather's death, she had sat on the chauffeur's lap, seeking to make him a surrogate grandfather figure. However, after initially telling her fairy tales, he had held her head and forced his phallus into her mouth. After this, the themes of her interactions with the chauffeur and her behavior before her own son all but disappeared in the analysis. About three years after the recovery of this memory, when these themes reappeared, they could be interpreted as attempts to master—by action—her theretofore repressed terror and feelings of dissolution when she had watched parental sexual activities.

Regression in a Schizophrenic Patient[3]

The final clinical example illustrates how clinical experience and increasing knowledge have enabled me to turn threatened impasses into analytic facilitators. It seems to me that what transpired in this

[3]See Chapter 6 for further discussion of this patient.

instance can be understood best through use of the concept of projective identification, with its intrapsychic and interpersonal aspects.

In "The Unconscious," Freud (1915c) wrote, "in schizophrenia words are subjected to the same process as that which makes the dream-images out of dream-thoughts" (p. 199). He was referring to the well-known fact that regression sometimes involves the loss of one's capacity to use words as symbols. I have twice observed patients who in the course of interviews underwent regressions during which they used not only words but syllables as concrete objects. Curiously, each of them bisected the same word, table, into the syllables "tay" and "bul."

When I was an anxious new practitioner, a young man who seemed to me to be suffering from an obsessive-compulsive neurosis requested treatment. The first two vis-á-vis interviews proceeded in a routine manner. When he came the third time, he was anxious and after a short period he hesitantly reported a dream, the manifest content of which involved his having been attacked homosexually. He began to slap a small table which abutted the arm of the chair in which he sat. As he did so, he said the word table. Soon his eyes had a glazed appearance and he seemed bewildered. I became frightened and could only think of seeking to help him regain contact with reality. He paid no attention to my calling him by his name nor to my reassurances. Instead, he looked past me as though he were talking to someone behind me and asked if the object he was slapping *were* a table. He then repeatedly yelled the word table but soon repetitively shouted "tay" and "bul." I hospitalized him and he was eventually treated by electroconvulsive therapy, with transient improvement.

History. Many years later, the father of 17-year-old Robert sought analysis for his son as a last resort. Robert had undergone an acute schizophrenic regression two years before and had been treated first with electroconvulsive therapy and then with supportive therapy and antipsychotic drugs, but had shown continuing hebephrenic deterioration. His therapist had become ill and had had to interrupt his practice.

Treatment. Our first four interviews were spaced over a period of some months. Robert was skeptical about changing therapists. During the first interview, I understood some of his incoherent utterances to express symbolically a fear that if he were to leave his hospitalized therapist, that man might die. However, I limited my interpretations to suggesting that Robert's silliness, incoherence, and vagueness were efforts to disguise information that he feared I might use against him. He became briefly lucid and was relieved and intrigued.

In our second meeting, I said I thought he was using hallucinations in the service of secondary gain. He was delighted that I considered the functions and content of his hallucinations interesting data for investigation and said he wanted to become a psychologist like me.

During the third session, I asked if he was afraid that his anger at his therapist had made that man ill. Again, he was relieved. Following that session, he asked his father whether anger was ever justified and was forcefully told that it was not.

The fourth time we met, I indicated that he feared not only intense, hostile feelings but deeply experienced positive ones as well. He then asked me to take him into analysis. I told him I would be willing to undertake such therapy on an experimental basis when time became available, but only if his parents agreed. Accordingly, I met with them. I learned that his schizoid mother had been a virgin until her marriage at 36 and that she considered sexual relations disgustingly intrusive. His father was a severe obsessive compulsive who controlled his aggression in large part by using reaction formations. Although the parents' communications to me were guarded, I surmised that Robert's mother was a domineering and grossly exhibitionistic woman who unwittingly stimulated her sons sexually but thwarted their efforts to be physically affectionate with her once they reached puberty.

Our fifth interview followed two events: (1) Robert had taken a two-week driving trip with his twin brother; and (2) Robert had moved out of the family home for the first time, to live in a college dormitory in a nearby city. Only the first of these events was known to me at the time. In the interview, Robert sat stiffly on the edge of his chair and was suspicious and apprehensive, in contrast to his previous shy but friendly behavior. I assumed that he was projecting hostility and silently recalled his disappointment and regression when his father told him that angry feelings were taboo.

As mentioned earlier, along with Heimann (1950), Racker (1957), and others, I have come to assign increasing importance to the roles of projective identification and counteridentification in the interactions between patients, especially regressed patients, and their therapists. Accordingly, when I think or fantasize about some person who is important to the patient, I wonder whether I may be responding to the patient's need to have me, or fear that I will, assume some role or attribute of that person. With Robert, I suspected the presence of an acute transference psychosis, conjecturing that he might have become unable to distinguish me from his father. I asked him whether he might be thinking of his father. He nodded in agreement, relaxed, and settled back into the chair. After he had looked at me for a minute or so, he focused on the upper part of my face for some time. I was reminded both of the similar behavior of a previous schizophrenic patient and of the watchful behavior of a nursing baby (Chapter 1, this volume). I silently wondered whether he would begin to confuse me with his mother and become fearful of fantasized fusion.

Robert began to rub the wooden arms of his chair rhythmically. I had the sensation that my own arms were being caressed and recalled that wood often symbolizes women in dreams and folklore. I asked whether he was thinking of his mother. He quickly nodded in agreement and then became frightened again. I found myself feeling confused and fearful. Reflection after the interview led me to think that I had empathized with his regression (which may have gone back to the undifferentiated phase of early infancy [Katan 1979]) to such a degree that I had feared loss of my own ego boundaries. During the interview, my uneasiness continued; my worry that he would confuse me with his mother and become lost in me as her surrogate intensified, but I remained silent and watchful.

He suddenly began to hit the desk with his palms and asked me if it was a table. Then he began to say the word "table" every time he slapped the desk. He seemed to enter a dissociated state; I felt I had lost contact with him. He became progressively more frightened and repetitively shouted the word "table," although he had ceased slapping the desk. I felt better after I remembered that the table often symbolizes the mother in dreams and folklore. Freud's dictum about the schizophrenic's use of words came to my mind. Then it occurred to me that Robert had ceased using the word table as a symbol. Now he was only concerned with the word as an object. Soon he was repetitively saying "tay-bul, tay-bul" and then 'tay-tay-tay, bul-bul-bul."

Again, I found myself feeling unreal and I turned to the use of active thinking and recall in the service of regaining my personal sense of integrity. I remembered that before children can speak words, they become actively interested in their vocal utterances as discrete phenomena and that when they learn to speak, they like to play with the sound qualities of their newly acquired words.

I considered the possibility that Robert's regression was being used in the service of defense and that he had begun to use word fragmentation as a primitive representation of body or world destruction. That is, perhaps he had lost his sense of personal identity in an imagined fusion with his mother or me, as a representation of her. Concurrently, I felt somewhat fragmented, but I calmed myself with the knowledge that I could test the validity of my thoughts by questions and interpretations. I remembered that Robert had told me that when he returned from trips and tried to hug his mother, she pushed him away. I recalled both her frustrating exhibitionism and her uneasiness around the boys after they reached puberty, and wondered whether she had projected incestuous wishes onto them and feared overt sexual advances by them.

By this time, I had formulated what seemed to be a rational approach to determining the validity of my assumptions. I asked Robert whether he had missed his mother while on vacation with his brother. He immediately regained his personal integrity and contact with me, nodded in agreement, and cried. After a time he said, "She pushed me away," referring to the mother's response to the boy's return. He then began to speak of his loneliness in the coeducational dormitory.

On the preceding Saturday, he had been frightened by observing interactions between male and female students that indicated to him that they were going to have sexual relations. He had thought that one girl had wanted to have sex with him, but he had heard God's voice say, "Thou shall not commit adultery." (Both of his parents, but particularly his mother, demanded premarital sexual abstinence of their sons.) He had tried unsuccessfully to get superego support from a faculty member and then had driven home, where his parents had greeted him with seeming displeasure. When he had tried to hug his mother, she had been unresponsive. He had been unable to tell his parents why he had to come home, feeling the need for some demonstration of affection before he could confide in them. Later, when his mother had been undressing in her bedroom with the door open, he had approached her, seeking an understanding word or caress. She had reacted with terror, screaming for his father and claiming that Robert wanted to rape her. His father then had reproached him furiously for disturbing his mother and had accused him of incestuous desires.

By the end of the interview, Robert was calm, shy, and friendly and eagerly sought reassurance that our next appointment would be held at its regularly scheduled time.

In subsequent interviews, we retraced the events of this dramatic session in detail and confirmed the accuracy of my various conjectures. Concurrently, it was possible to review in detail the onset of his overt psychosis at the age of 15 and to understand that all the essential elements that had led to that regression had been recapitulated prior to the interview when he had made concrete objects of words and syllables.

Robert subsequently entered psychoanalysis, which continued for about three years. He improved greatly until he became aware of the fact that his mother was becoming more and more paranoid and disorganized as he improved. He then decided to stop treatment so that his younger brothers might have some semblance of a normal home life. Unfortunately, after he stopped treatment, Robert lost many of his therapeutic gains and became a marginally functioning schizoid character. In addition, all three of his brothers were hospitalized at various times for schizophrenia.

Summary

This chapter discusses a number of issues pertaining to the analytic treatment of regressed patients; these issues are illustrated by case material. Foremost among them is the importance of countertransference for the outcome of therapy.

Analysts' responses to regressed patients are often quite different from those experienced with neurotic patients. Such responses are better understood and therefore more manageable when one bears in mind that regressed patients, especially borderline patients, typically use projective identification as a primitive defense mechanism with both intraspychic and interpersonal aspects. A synthesis of analytic ideas pertaining to protective identification is presented, with special emphasis on the role of the reintrojection of patients' projections onto analysts, following the modification of these projections in the treatment process.

Part III

Fantasies and Symbols of the Regressed Patient

10

Sculpture and Depression

Although studies of the prose, poetry, and paintings of psychotic patients are common in the psychiatric literature, correlative investigations of sculpture and personality are unusual. Because such writings as exist are unavailable in readily accessible publications written in English, brief résumés are included in this chapter.

Several authors have reported their observations on collections of plastic productions of psychotic patients:

Réja (1901) described such objects collected from various French psychiatrists. He found that as a rule these works simulated primitive art forms and were stylized in nature of construction.

Ernst (1925) discussed the works of psychotic and feeble-minded criminals who ingeniously utilized wet paper, flour paste, bread, and bits of wire to produce crude common objects, such as animals and pipes.

Vié and Quéron (1933) delineated the plastic productions of a miscellaneous group of patients in the "family colony" of Ainay-le-Château, individuals who had made satisfactory, simple adjustments as farmers, woodcutters, and performers of menial chores about the houses of the peasants who kept them. They included patients afflicted with feeblemindedness, senile dementia, infantile paralysis, and arteriosclerosis and a few cases of schizophrenia and paresis. These productions were simple and unimaginative. They lacked fantastic qualities often seen in psychotic art.

Vaux (1930) described spontaneous art creations of patients in a state asylum. The amateur sculptors made large numbers of objects, many being grotesque and ingenious. Individual patients were found to repeatedly use certain symbols in their productions, such as faces, numbers, and stars. Various materials were employed, including wood, metal, twigs, yarn, paper, wax, and soap. Meticulous, markedly careful work was performed on objects of no apparent value, producing ridiculous designs of worthless materials. Various themes were recurrent; sex, religion, and battle predominated.

Ducoste (1920) depicted a similar collection and attempted to correlate the natures of the objects with the types of psychoses of the patients who produced them. He found that simple dements produced crude, useful objects, paranoid patients made weapons, and certain paranoids, alcoholics, and epileptics produced objects through the use of which they could hope to escape.

A few authors have described the spontaneous productions of individual psychotic patients who had no previous special training in artistic fields:

Villamil (1933) reported the case of an alcoholic manic Spanish farmer who had had "limited education." This patient skillfully executed a large series of wood carvings during the acute phase of his mania. They were strongly religious in character, and Villamil found them to contain numerous Egyptian, Persian, and Catholic symbols. As the mania waned, the farmer's creations lost their artistic nature and became progressively more utilitarian. As he neared recovery, the patient requested to be allowed to do carpentry and to farm. When he was confronted with his prior carvings, he doubted that he had made them. The author presented a Jungian interpretation of the sculptures and claimed that the religious symbols were products of the farmer's "archaic unconscious." Anastasi and Foley (1940) felt perhaps Villamil may have read the symbolism into the products and that the Catholic symbols were explicable by the patient's religious associations.

Morselli (1881) wrote of a 33-year-old paranoid schizophrenic carpenter and cabinetmaker. After this man was hospitalized he continuously carved stylized "trophies" with coats of arms, armor, and varied emblematic figures. The symbols used were found to have special significance for the artist. A cigar which was held in a slanting position in the mouth meant contempt for kings and tyrants.

Hospital (1893) described a wooden panel which had been carved by a painter who suffered a melancholic and hypochondriac condition. The panel was done in bas-relief and was performed with great skill, although certain distortions of perspective and proportion were noted. It resembled the bas-reliefs to be found in medieval abbeys, and its subject matter was the care of the insane by the monks.

There are a few case reports in which the plastic works of psychotic professional artists and artisans are described:

Prinzhorn (1923) delineated in detail the case of a paranoid schizophrenic who had been a builder, decorator, and maker of iron castings, and who had had a hobby of constructing dolls for his children. During his hospitalization he made figurines of bread and whitewash and carved many statuettes and relief-forms from wood. These objects were fairly stereotyped and frequently portrayed fantastic and grotesque combinations of the intermixed features of animals and men or representations of men or animals alone. There were inconsistencies and disproportions but his work was skillful. It resembled certain primitive art forms. Religious and sexual themes were included, and certain figures had distorted sexual organs.

Stärcke (1920, 1921) described "about 40" sketches and models which had been made by a hebephrenic sculptor during his period of commitment. Representations of men and various animals predominated. Portrayals of the head of Christ was included. Stärcke attributed sexual symbolism to the products.

Osario and Monteiro (1927) reported the history of a paranoid schizophrenic Portuguese sculptor and gave an analysis of his drawings and plastic works. The patient had been a fervently religious Catholic, and much Catholic symbolism was apparent.

Kris (1933) reported a thorough study of the life of Franz Xavier Messerschmidt, a 17th century sculptor, and a series of "character heads" which he had skillfully executed while he was becoming paranoid. Kris considered the products to represent the sculptor's portrayal of his varied moods and his attempt to retain sanity.

Laignel-Lavastine (1920) and Vinchon (1924) discussed the case of a 46-year-old sculptress who had a psychotic episode characterized by a suicidal attempt, hallucinations, religious mysticism, and spiritualism. This woman determined to do a bust of the Virgin of the Redemption. She went into a trance during which she made the statue in what seemed to be an automatic manner. She said her arm felt as though it were guided from external forces. The bust was unlike her usual work and resembled Gothic and Florentine Renaissance religious figures. When she later examined the statue she was surprised and found herself unable to complete the product with ease of movement and ideation.

A large number of authors have described the paintings of psychotics. The writings of Séglas (1892), Hrdlička (1899), Dantas (1900), Rogues de Fursac (1905), and Prinzhorn (1923) are representative. Writers generally concede that the artistic creations of psychotics are of inferior quality and usually worthless as works of art. There are some notable exceptions to this generalization, and Réja (1901, 1907) states that some patients who have had artistic training prior to their psychoses do work revealing greater talent and of more artistic value after they have become insane. It is found that paranoid and chronically manic patients produce the majority of paintings and the works with the greatest artistic value. The characteristics of the ilnesses are portrayed: mystic, religious, and erotic symbols are present in profusion; fantastic and grotesque productions with repetitive patterns and themes, and stylized and stereotyped forms are assumed. Primitivism is seen. Perspective and coherence suffer. In demented patients and those of meager intelligence, nonsensical and disorganized or common, unimaginative productions are the rule. Perseveration and absurdities are frequently noted. Very little is written concerning the spontaneous drawings of depressive patients. Karpov (1926) found "the mechanism of creative ability in its fullest development" in manic-depressive psychotics and cited paintings "of considerable artistic merit." He found that depressive patients used darker pigments and were less productive than others. He did not find in their products the bizarre characteristics described as occurring in schizophrenics. Vinchon (1924, 1926) said that depressed patients rarely draw.

The similarities between the graphic and plastic art productions of psychotic patients are amply demonstrated. It is particularly noteworthy that the creations of depressed patients usually portray reality in a doleful way and with fair perspective and coherence.

This chapter is written in an attempt to correlate the life and psychotherapeutic course and the sculpture of a professional sculptress who suffered a psychotic depression. The history is unavoidably and regrettably incomplete. It concerns an artist whose endeavors cncompass poetry, painting, ceramics, and sculpture. The material included here will be limited principally to a simultaneous appraisal of her personality and sculpture.

Case Material

History

Mrs. W., a 57-year-old woman, first interviewed January 14, 1947, complained of fatigue and depression of two and one half years' duration. She said her depression began with the death of her husband, immediately following which she discontinued her heavy social activities and became a recluse. She felt almost unbearably depressed and seriously contemplated suicide. She refused to accept her husband's death as reality. She became restless, insomniac, and anorexic, and lost an undetermined amount of weight. She ceased dreaming. She read in a desultory manner, traveled from one city to another, slept in her clothes in her car or on the ocean beach, and lost interest in her personal appearance and property. After a few months she resumed sculpture and ceramics. She lived with her old dog in a dirty studio and, although she had no need for the money, leased her desirable houses. In the autumn of 1946 she withdrew completely from society and refused to leave her studio. She became apathetic and even ceased to brood over her husband's death. She felt suicide would be too much effort. She had bread, milk, and eggs delivered to her studio and ate nothing else. She spoke to and saw no one. She seldom removed her clothes, cleansed herself, or straightened the studio. She stopped doing sculpture but methodically spent her days making pottery, much of which she emotionlessly destroyed as soon as removed from the kiln. In December she began to dream of her husband. Her dreams, the contents of which she would not reveal to doctors who examined her, disturbed her. She became anxious and restless and eventually sought psychiatric aid.

When she was first interviewed, this woman was dressed in tan corduroy slacks with tight legs and a baggy seat, a white shirt with French cuffs which were not doubled back but flapped down to her fingers, a green velvet jacket, white, pointed oxfords, a white, dangling scarf, and coarse cotton hose. She wore no jewelry or makeup, and her hair was merely brushed back off her face. Her nails were dirty and she had numerous paronychias. Her facial expression was one of apathy and neither sadness nor joy could be elicited. She averred that life was hopeless and that nothing made any difference. She denied self-condemnatory thinking, and no ideas of reference or influence, nor hallucinations or delusions were elicited. She denied previous depressions.

There was no record of mental illness in her family. Her father was a moody, respected country lawyer who had "a terrible tempter at times" and professed atheism. She said that as a young child she had always crawled in his bed on Sunday mornings until once when she was 6 he touched her genitals. Thereafter she could not bear to have him near her. Her mother, a music teacher, was the family disciplinarian and a sentimentally religious "Christian woman." The patient said she loved her mother very much until the period of puberty, subsequent to which she turned more toward her father. There were half-siblings from her father's two earlier marriages, but the patient was never close to any of them or her own 5 siblings. She said her home was unhappy and that, as a result of religious arguments, her parents wouldn't speak to each other for weeks at a time. She did not speak until she was 3 years old. Mrs. W. was a sickly child. She experienced numerous nightmares and, as a young child, had a terrible fear that her mother would die. She spent many nights standing outside her parents' room "listening for my mother's breathing because I had to make sure she was alive." She found schoolwork easy but had "a million whippings" because she daydreamed all the time. She graduated from high school at 16 and then taught for one year in a country school. At 17 she fled from her family and moved from her country town home to a large city where she spent four years studying art. She had no "dates," worked night and day, and "almost starved." She had had no sexual instruction and was frightened at 12 by the onset of menstruation. She denied any interest in sexual matters and had no heterosexual experiences until she met the man who later became her husband. She denied homosexual encounters and masturbation. While she was studying art she met a "dark, vital Russian Jew," a refugee who had been a revolutionary against the czarist regime. He taught languages and eventually became professor at a large eastern university. He was an artist and writer and well known as a translator and critic. He was a notorious philanderer. Their marriage was turbulent because of his frequent affairs. Mrs. W. knew of them but for the most part denied to herself that she cared, schooling herself with the doctrine that "love was above the sins of the flesh." She wanted children and he did not. No contraceptives were used, but there were no pregnancies. Her husband was asthmatic, and among her happiest moments with him were the periods when he was severely ill and dependent on her. She described herself as a dreamer and a "lone wolf." She said she had always been interested in intellectual things. She had numerous acquaintances and few friends. She accumulated a sizeable knowledge of art, literature, and philosophy. She said she was an idealist and a champion of the underdog. She was a self-styled "rebel and liberal." She suffered lifelong "stomach trouble" characterized by belching and sourness and occasional preprandial burning in the epigastrium. At 50 she was certainly diagnosed to have a peptic ulcer and treated with a Sippy regime. She recovered and subsequently suffered only vague epigastrial discomfort. She underwent an asymptomatic menopause at 53.

Physical examination revealed small, soft axillary lymph nodes, complete dentures, a questionable mass in the right lower quadrant, "presumably cecum," moderate varicose veins, and mild thickening of the peripheral vessels; blood pressure 118/72; pelvic examination normal.

Laboratory studies showed normal blood cellular elements, urinalysis, and electrocardiogram; Wassermann test negative. X-rays revealed moderate emphysema of the lungs, moderate osteoporosis of the cervical and thoracic spine, hypertrophic spurs on the 6th and 7th cervical vertebrae, and a presumed gallbladder stone.

Treatment

She reluctantly accepted inpatient care, during which she was restless but usually cooperative. She took an intense dislike to certain people, without apparent reason. She was seclusive and glum. Electroshock therapy was instituted, with three grand mal seizures during the first week. After seven days in the hospital she heard that her old dog refused to eat for the veterinarian and insisted on leaving the hospital to care for him. She had but mildly improved. She vigorously protested each shock but appeared for two outpatient treatments. She then refused further electroconvulsive therapy.

The interval between her first and fifth treatments was 12 days. At the end of that time she had very mild loss of memory for recent events. She was obviously more interested in her surroundings and her appearance, was more alert, but otherwise she was unchanged. It was decided that she should be seen at weekly intervals.

During the first few interviews, Mrs. W. complained of various physical ailments, especially relating to the stomach. She angrily denounced all doctors, particularly me, and refused standard medical symptomatic treatments. Simultaneously, with a marked emotional explosion, she recounted her husband's many philanderings. She described affairs she had had "to get even" and told of two impulsive suicidal attempts with which she had tried to punish her husband ten years after their marriage. She told of youthful Baptist missionary aspirations and her turbulent change of ideologies to what she called "free thinking." She told of her communistic ideas and spent much time eulogizing Eugene Debs, Henry Wallace, and Soviet officials. She told of her husband's severe asthma and related how she had sometimes put allergenic substances in his bed in order to precipitate attacks. When his asthma was severe he required constant care. She said, "The times I was really happy with him were when I was nursing him." She expressed guilt about his death, due to a heart attack, and felt that she had been partly responsible for it. When he died, she lay at his side most of the night, periodically laughing hysterically. At midnight she got up and canned fruit. There were no tears. During the first month of interview treatment I was entirely passive.

Either during the outpatient electroshock therapy or immediately thereafter, the patient made the statuettes depicted in Figure 11, 13, and 15. These figurines were done automatically and impulsively.

In the fifth interview her hostility suddenly diminished, and she began to describe her sexual life in a systematic manner. Her father fondled her genitals when she was 6, and another man did so when she was 8. During her first 18 years she had numerous fantasies of idyllic love affairs but no social contact with men and very little with women. At 18 she met a man who "electrified" her, and 3 days later went to live with him. Six months later they married because he accepted a university appointment. He was passionate, and she was always cold and frequently anesthetic vaginally. She knew of her husband's many affairs but denied resentment concerning them. At the end of the fifth interview she threatened suicide. I took an active role at this point, indicating that she had always previously left doctors before they could help her and had twice tried to punish her husband with suicide. I also felt reassurance was indicated and, when she said I should think her terrible, said that on the contrary I liked her.

During the next month she expressed much hostility toward her husband and at length admitted that she resented his behavior and had wished for his death. In the 9th interview she presented a dream which clearly depicted me as her lover. During the 10th and 11th interviews she compared me to a former lover and found her emotions rekindled concerning that man. She decided to return to him and discontinued therapy. She was subjectively and objectively markedly improved. She was socially active and alert. She had taken her business affairs in hand and resumed her artistic endeavors. She presented me with the statues shown in Figures 3 and 4.

Two weeks later, Mrs. W. called for further appointments. She had not communicated with her friend. She asked to be seen twice weekly. She brought a number of sketches of proposed statues. They consisted of penises and breasts going in opposite directions. She said they represented her and therapist, and that they were going in antipodal directions because "psychoanalysis is artificial." During the next few interviews she told of a marked desire to be a man and to castrate men. She presented sketches in which she had symbolically done so. She told of her husband's great attraction to her breasts and said that from 1930 onward she had fantasized mutilating her breasts to deprive him of them.

During the first 6 resumed interviews she tried very hard to get me to fight with her and depreciated me vigorously. During the next 6 interviews she related with great emotion her lifelong desires to be a mother and brought dreams and drawings in which she fantasized me as father, husband, and lover. Once she brought as a gift 16 books concerning sexual customs and philosophies in many lands. They had been her husband's. She had fantasies of being pregnant by me. In the 24th interview she became relaxed and said she now felt calm and realized her fantasies had been elements of transference; she now considered me a friend and a son. From the 11th through the 24th interviews I was passive and made only superficial interpretations.

During the preceeding weeks Mrs. W. had run a low-grade fever. A medical consultation revealed a probable ovarian carcinoma and she was hospitalized, after five months of psychotherapy, for a laparotomy. It was determined she had a highly malignant embryonic ovarian carcinoma with much intra-abdominal spread. She was not informed of the outcome of surgery, nor did she ask. The consensus of the pathologists and surgeons was that she had but a very few months to live.

During her hospitalization she composed numerous romantic poems which belied her statement of having ceased to picture the psychiatrist as her lover. Her sketches were varied, but an occasional one yet showed a woman holding a baby. One poem depicts her mood best:

When I die
Let me be the wind
Sailing the ships
Finding the moist places
Where the lilies grow—
Fanning the fire
Through the forest
In vengeance—
But—
When the evening comes
. . . . touching the face
Kissing the lips
Caressing the hand
. . . . of you.

She spoke not at all of death, but her mood was sad and her writings and drawings were of death and melancholy.

Therapy was resumed after the interval of a month. She was guarded and talked of the writings of various authors. She dispassionately reviewed much of the previous material but seemed to have no interest in treatment. She was active socially and worked productively with more calm. After half a dozen interviews it was decided that therapy had best be terminated. Soon thereafter I received the following letter:

> Thank you again for freeing me as a patient. I had known for some time the gestation for this period was over, and was waiting, probably unconsciously, for your help. I felt I could not do it alone. I shall always love you. In my soil, few things grow but when they do the roots go deep (God pity me) and however severe the pruning, the shoots *will* come. We will speak of it no more. Once is enough for always.

She was not again seen for treatment. It was considered that her death was near and that further therapy would be too painful to her to warrant it. However, a friendly, social relationship was begun. It was confirmed that she was strongly Russophile and a champion of Communism and fellow travelers. She was markedly anticapitalist and strongly supported labor's every claim, legitimate or not. She stoutly defended minority groups, even when no one opposed her. She displayed a great interest in pessimistic philosophies. She showed great generosity and much appreciation for affectionate consideration. She revealed a love for music, but particularly atonal and bizarre, unorganized music. She showed great patience as a teacher of ceramics. She seemed periodically to retain her newly admitted knowledge that she had greatly resented her husband's doings and had wanted to harm him, but eventually it appeared she had lost all insight into the true state of affairs. She continued to be moody but did not again become psychotically depressed.

Sculpture

Some time after therapy had been discontinued, a colleague suggested that it might be worthwhile to report the case history and correlate it with the sculpture of the patient. Mrs. W. freely collaborated and provided further examples of her sculpture for photography. In the following paragraphs, the figures are explained and partially related to her life.

Figure 1. Maxim Gorky (bronze head cast from a clay model, 1927). This sculpture was produced in Italy, five years after Mrs. W's marriage, to illustrate a published biography. At that time Mrs. W., uninvited, had followed her husband to Europe and felt unwelcome. Referring to the statuette she said, "Gorky was a man who produced optimistic writings about sad subjects." She had an intimate acquaintance with Gorky's appearance, and said, "He wasn't so sad as the portrait." Although she had not consciously incorporated her own sadness into the sculpture she remarked, "It must have been part of my sadness I put into his face."

On a train journey to be with her lover, she found herself drawing, as though in a trance, sketches for the sculptures pictured in Figures 2, 3, 4, and 5.

Figure 2. Diana (bronze, 1930). She commented: "I was repentant. I pictured Diana after she got what she wanted and was sad about it. The bird was dead and she had lost it. I didn't know I was picturing myself, but I see now it was that something had been killed between me and F" (her husband). Another time she called the dead bird a dead phallus.

It is to be noted that, in this statue, the right breast is sunken. Mrs. W. derived this form construction from an artistic theorem that concave and convex surfaces presented the same feeling. However, it was in 1930 she began to fantasy mutilating her breasts to deprive F. of them. This figure was built in one night and later cast in bronze. "I was thinking Diana was a huntress. I was in a trance and didn't know what I was hunting."

Figure 3. Lot's Wife (mahogany, 1930). "She was looking backward at something she had lost. The piece of mahogany wouldn't permit her left arm to point back, so I made the clavicle lines do that. The right arm is hanging limp because she was reluctant to go forward with her husband." This was Mrs. W.'s initial extramarital affair and she found her first real sexual gratification with this lover. "I guess I was looking back at something I had wanted but had not realized with F. Lot's wife had children." It must not be forgotten that she associated the therapist with this lover, and that she spontaneously made a gift of statues 3 and 4 to me before she had analyzed their meaning. She had never previously thought of the sculptures as being herself. The hollow breast again appears.

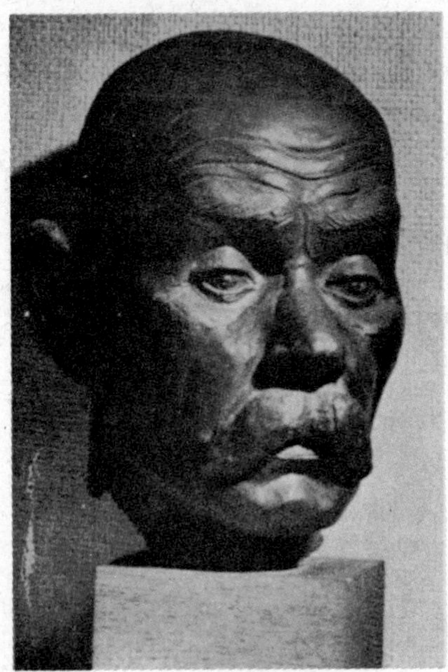

Figure 1. Maxim Gorky

Figure 2. Diana

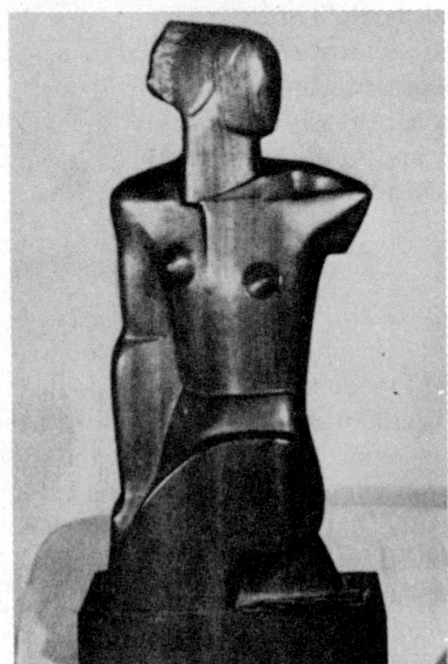

Figure 3. Lot's Wife

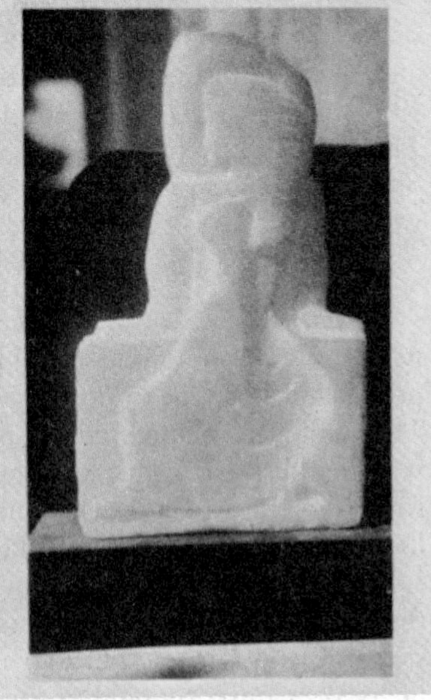

Figure 4. Lot's Wife

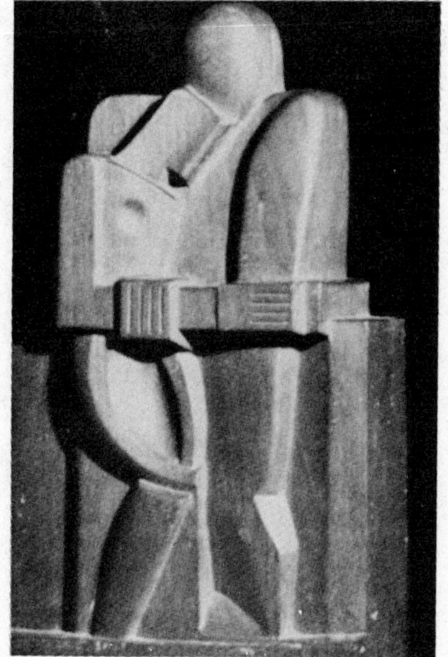

Figure 5. The Lovers

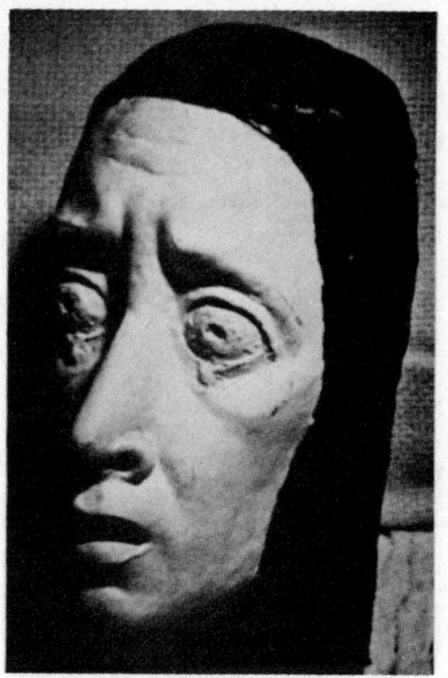

Figure 6. Cassandra

Figure 7. Conflict

Figure 8. Mother and Baby

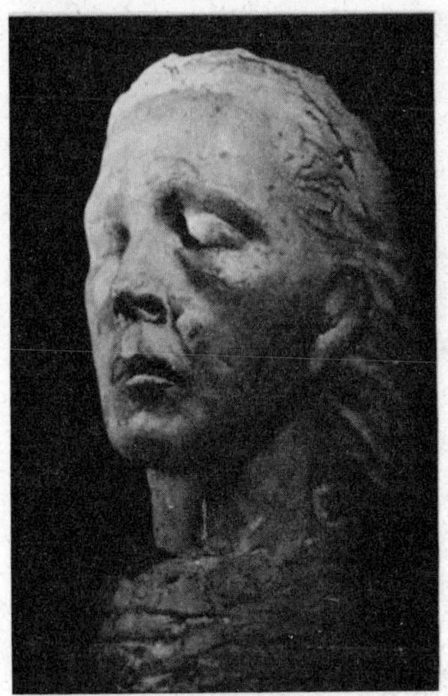

Figure 9. Self-Portrait

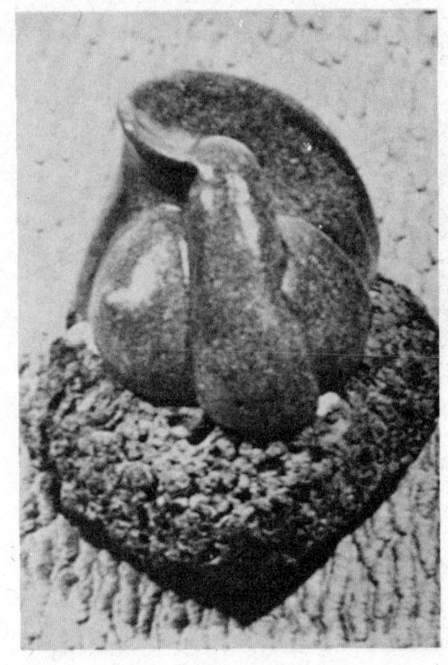

Figure 10. Unnamed

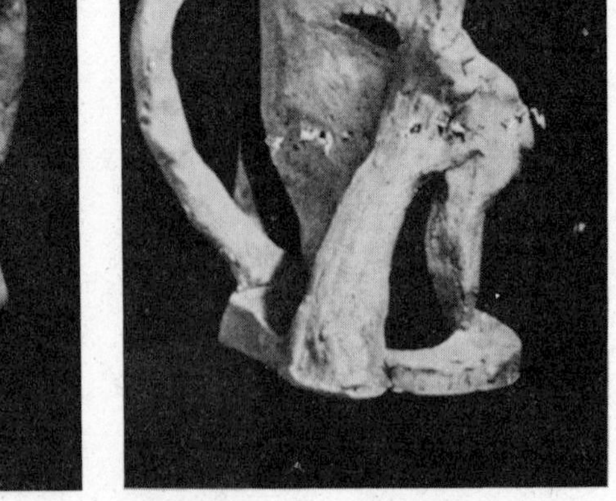

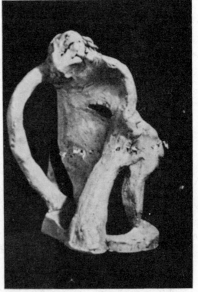

Figure 11. Unnamed

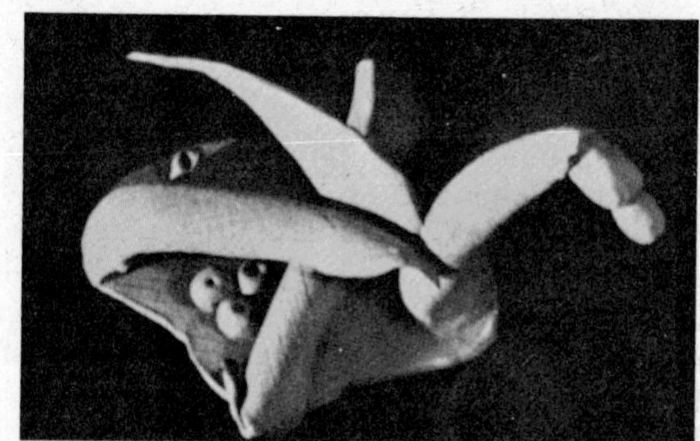
Figure 12. Leaf Insect

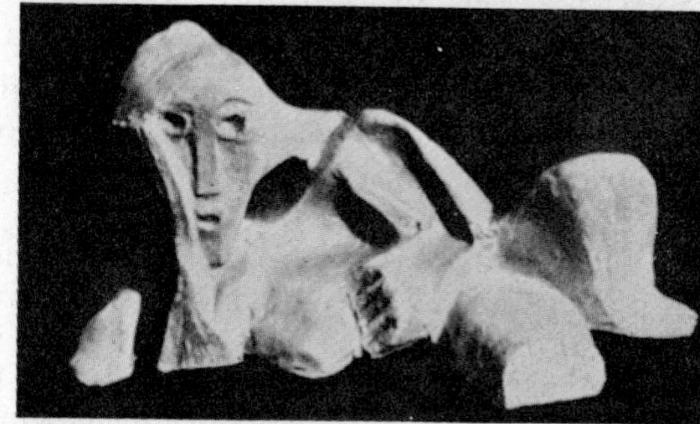
Figure 13. Unnamed

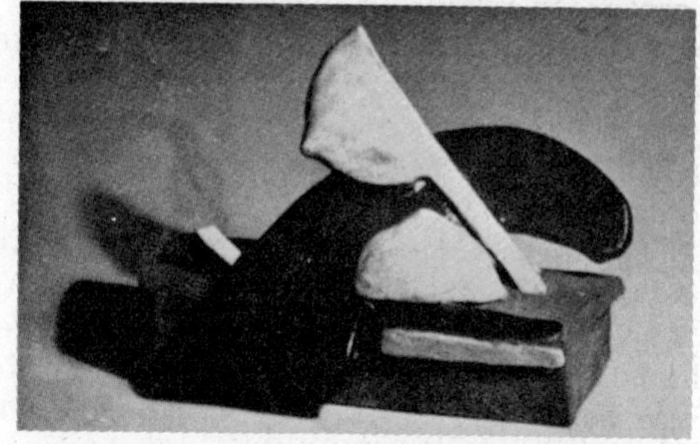
Figure 14. Unnamed

Figure 15. Horse

Figure 4. Lot's Wife (alabaster, 1930). "There is a straight line down the middle. All to the left, from where she has come, is desirable. All to the right, where she is going, is undesirable. Her left arm is down and reconciled. The right arm just hangs, limp. Another arm, hope, is over her head. The left breast is firm and up. The right one is sagging and dead. Lot's wife was going with her husband into a new area." (F. approved of her affair with her lover). The same remarks that apply to Figure 3 apply to Figure 4.

Figure 5. The Lovers (mahogany, 1930). "I had returned to F. I was sorry but not repentant. I wanted F. there and secure. I wished I hadn't begun the affair. When I carved it I didn't think of myself but just thought that a man protects a woman he loves." The hollow breast and hollow thigh are to be noted.

Figure 6. Cassandra (clay, 1939). "I'm sure it's purely political. I did it at the time of Munich. The world was going to war and all was sad. I was much wrought up." As one can see by comparing the head with Figure 9, this too is a self-portrait. The long face, the sensitive mouth, the high forehead, and the attenuated nose with the flare alae are too similar to be mistaken. While the world was in such a state that men should all have been despondent and "wrought up," her personal life was responsible for much of her unhappiness at this time. A strong vein of self-projection was obvious in all her philosophies and interpretations of problems involved.

Figure 7. Conflict (aluminum, 1932). "At that time I lived alone in the studio and he lived alone in the house. At that time I shot at one of his lovers and was tormented. We couldn't get along. I wanted to kill her so he couldn't have what he wanted." She felt the two hemispheres were herself and her husband, separated by conflicting lines and facing opposite directions. The ax-shaped form she merely called "conflict." At the base of the design are three steps, unequally balanced and disjointed by vertical lines. "Those were our lower parts which got together but didn't match." She had been brought up to believe sex was sinful, shameful, and base. She and her husband did not "match" sexually because she did not have orgasm with him. It must be recalled that, as a virgin who had completely rejected any physical contact before she met F., she willingly went to live with him three days after she met him. She maintained this common-law marital relationship for at least six months before their marriage. Such a practice was entirely foreign to her strict upbringing. It seems reasonable to interpret the plaque as her method of saying that the basis of their marriage was sexual and that the reason for their conflict was mismating in the same sphere.

Figure 8. Mother and Baby (red stone, 1933). "It was in the depression. I saw a poor woman and her baby sitting bewildered and alone at the side of the road, not knowing where to go." Mrs. W.'s desire for a child, and her own indecision as to what road to take, must be considered as relevant in connection with this figure.

Figure 9. Self-Portrait (plaster, 1944). This sculpture was made during the first month after her husband died but never finished. "I felt as though life had ended. I couldn't bear to see anyone. I wanted to be alone. I felt nothing. I couldn't bear to finish the head. I hate it. I can't stand to look at it." The immeasurable sadness of "Cassandra" is here replaced by sadness combined with withdrawal. From the sculpture itself better than from the photograph one gets a profound impression of death. Her withdrawal is portrayed by the closed eyes.

Figure 10. Unnamed (clay, 1947). "It's just sex. That was when I wanted you as a lover. It's penises, breasts, and a vagina."

Figure 11. Unnamed (clay, 1947). This figure was made within a few days of the "Horse" (Fig. 15) and also in a "trance." Mrs. W. had no associations except to say, "I knew I had to support it with small hands." The hollow eye reminds one of a death mask. The hollow shell is reminiscent of the hollow "Horse." It might be conjectured that the small hands are a child's hands. At that time she often called the therapist a child. The long nose probably identifies the figure as her own portrait.

Figure 12. Leaf Insect (clay, 1947). "I thought it was just eucalyptus leaves and balls. Now I see it's phalluses and testicles. I guess I got lonesome." This piece was done after therapy was concluded. In other photographs the wing strongly resembles the vagina in Figure 10.

Figure 13. Unnamed (clay, 1947). Mrs. W. had no associations to offer. The face is well-nigh expressionless. The long nose is again present. The left arm is hollow; there is only one breast. (See Fig. 5 with the hollow thigh and the concave breast.) One could read this as a self-portrait and representative of her depression.

Figure 14. Unnamed (clay, 1947). "It's the same as Figure 10."

Figure 15. Horse (clay, 1947). The statuette was done either during electroshock therapy or just after its completion. "I was just working with clay. I seemed to go into a trance and then I made a horse. It's empty and biting its back. I had never made a horse before."

Discussion

A true dynamic formulation of this case would require psychoanalysis. Consequently, this chapter must be restricted to a correlation of Mrs. W.'s sculpture and her personality, as it appeared in the short-term psychotherapeutic interval described.

Throughout the psychological material presented are certain major characteristics: depression, withdrawal, impulsiveness, preoccupation with sexual subjects, self-blame, masochistic attitudes, rebellion against authority, conflict between masculinity and femininity, and overreaction to her conservative, rightist background, resulting in a blind championing of the underdog and the leftists.

Psychotic depressions following the death of loved ones have been depicted as developing in narcissistic, orally fixated people who had marked ambivalence toward the ones who died. Frequently the death has been desired and the death wish has been repressed, leaving a residue of guilt. Fenichel (1945) has said, "The identification with the dead also has a punitive significance: 'Because you have wished the other person to die, you have to die yourself'" (p. 209). Although a detailed analysis of each sculpture is forbidden by space limitations, a study of one figure may serve as a representative illustration. The "Horse" is a particularly interesting figurine. In this small, crude production we find an animal devoid of insides. In my experience, psychotically depressed patients not infrequently present delusions in which their insides, particularly intestines, are absent. I found in the literature no case in which this delusion has been analyzed. On theoretical grounds it might be explained by unconscious denial of the oral incorporation of the love object, as though the patient were saying, "How could I have eaten him and made him a part of me? I have no insides in which to harbor him." The "Horse" is a solitary figure. It is biting its back. Although I am not justified in definitely interpreting the "Horse" without deeper insight into the dynamics of the case, tentative postulations seem warranted. The "Horse" is alone and its interest is directed toward itself. Mrs. W. was markedly withdrawn and interested in no person but herself during her depression. It is biting itself (punishing itself—significantly, orally). Mrs. W. placed allergenic powders in her husband's bed, causing severe asthmatic attacks and perhaps contributing to his death. She later seriously contemplated suicide and punished herself by refusing to eat, and in other ways. Then, the horse is empty. The "Horse" seems to closely depict Mrs. W.'s personality at the time she sculptured the figurine. It was produced automatically and impulsively and would appear to more nearly portray Mrs. W.'s unconscious than some of her more studied sculptures (Goitein 1948).

Depression is objectively flagrant in most of the sculptures portrayed and, in others, is present in her associations. Thus, in "Maxim Gorky" she has accentuated the sadness of a voluntarily chosen sad subject. "Diana" is repentant and rueful. The statues of "Lot's Wife" clearly depict a reluctance to go forward, and sorrow at the necessity. Once again, the subject matter itself is important. The repentant, sad theme is to be seen anew in "The Lovers." One could scarcely imagine a sculpture more representative of sadness than "Cassandra" and again, in the utter melancholy of "Self-Portrait" is graphic depression. Sadness is a part of "Mother and Baby." Depression is obvious in Figures 11 and 13. In the plaque "Conflict," one cannot see depression objectively but her associations are laden with sadness.

Withdrawal is harder to illustrate, or at least to interpret as present in portrayals. Nevertheless, it can be seen in "Diana," the statues of "Lot's Wife," her associations to the plaque called "Conflict," "Self-Portrait," "Horse," the unnamed figures 11 and 13, and probably in "Cassandra."

Preoccupation with sexual subjects is obvious throughout. Breasts are openly depicted in "Diana," the two figures of "Lot's Wife," "The Lovers," "Mother and Baby," and in Figures 10 and 15. The hemispherical forms in the plaque "Conflict" closely resemble breasts. Frank penises are represented in Figures 10 and 14 and in "Leaf Insect." During therapy the patient once associated a horse as being a phallic symbol. She called the dead bird in "Diana" a dead penis. Phallic symbols can be seen in the plaque "Conflict," and she referred to the rectangular, elongated steps as "our lower parts." The birth motif is seen openly only in "Mother and Baby." Sexual themes other than open anatomical depiction are present in all the figures except "Maxim Gorky." "Cassandra" is a self-portrait and pictures her sadness in her marriage, the basis of which was said to be in the mismatched union of their "lower parts."

Impulsiveness is perhaps better demonstrated by the history than the sculptures themselves. We know she impulsively destroyed productions on occasion. After treatment was terminated, she sculpted a head of the therapist. At least twice she suddenly destroyed the work she had done. She impulsively and perhaps automatically drew sketches of or produced "Diana," the statues of "Lot's Wife," "The Lovers," "Cassandra," the plaque "Conflict," "Self-Portrait," Figures 11 and 13, and "Horse." The construction of "Horse" and Figures 11 and 13 is crude and reveals the careless rapidity with which they were made, and thus perhaps illustrates her impulsiveness.

The differentiation between self-blame and masochistic attitudes is probably too fine to be demonstrated plastically. In the figures presented here, we find evidences of self-mutilation in the concave breasts of "Diana," one figure of "Lot's Wife," and "The Lovers," and in the "Horse," which is biting itself. If we consider the dynamics of depression itself to legitimately apply to our interpretation of these sculptures, we may assume that all the figures which depict depression illustrate self-blame.

Rebellion against authority is perhaps more difficult to depict. Certain of her sculptures are intended to accurately and realistically portray the subject matter (*e.g.*, "Maxim Gorky" and "Self-Portrait"). In other figures, although the sculpture pattern is conventional, details disclose rebellion against conservative authority. In the concave breasts of "Diana," "Lot's Wife," and "The Lovers," and the concave thigh in "The Lovers," Mrs. W. was copying Archipenko's then revolutionary theory that concave surfaces could be equivalent to convex surfaces. Other figures lean toward abstractionism. Her own background was markedly conservative. The usage of the wide diversity of materials as sculpture media and her dissatisfaction with conservative sculpture patterns probably limn rebellion against authority.

Conflict between masculinity and femininity is intrinsic in the plaque "Conflict." A majority of the figures are blatantly and solely feminine in context. Some display masculine and feminine symbols intermixed. The lines of "Diana" and her strong, heavy form display her masculine propensity although she is a woman repenting the death of the bird (phallus of her lover). In her associations to certain dreams

Mrs. W. fantasized she had lost a penis of her own. The wide variance of sexual symbols perhaps indicates the disquietude and conflict of the artist. It might even be conjectured that her preoccupation with art is in itself an evidence of her dissatisfaction with her feminine role.

From a theoretical standpoint, one would expect a depictment of retrogression of form and pattern in the sculptures produced during the regressed, psychotic episode. "Self-Portrait" was produced immediately after the death of her husband. Its construction and design are those of a well-integrated artist. Figures 11 and 13 and "Horse" were impulsively constructed as the patient began to be reawakened from the deepest period of her psychosis. These figurines are quite unlike any previous works in their crudity and roughness. As psychotherapy progressed after the termination of electroshock therapy, more polished statuettes appeared, as represented by Figures 10 and 14, and "Leaf Insect."

Summary

The life and psychotherapeutic course of a 57-year-old depressed artist are presented in combination with a random, representative selection of her sculptures. The characteristics of the plastic productions appear to reflect closely the personality patterns and case history of the patient.

Acknowledgments

Drs. Karl M. Bowman, Anna Maenchen, and Alexander Simon have given prized advice. Dr. William F. Boyer did most of the photography. To these colleagues thanks are gladly given.

11

Christmas "Neurosis"

The psychodynamics of depressive reactions which occur at Christmastime have been inadequately studied.

It is my contention here that depressions which occur during the Christmas season are primarily the result of reawakened conflicts related to unresolved sibling rivalries. On the basis of a study of 17 patients who suffered Christmas depressions, I suggest tentatively that partly because the holiday celebrates the birth of a Child so favored that competition with Him is futile, earlier memories, especially of oral frustration, are rekindled.

A Review of the Literature

Jones (1951) felt that Christmas represents psychologically an ideal of resolution of family discord through reunion and that it owes its perennial attraction to the hope that such a goal can be attained. He reminded his audience that all religions attempt to solve on a cosmic stage the loves and hatreds originating in the interactions of children and parents.

Jekels (1952) surmised that the introduction of the festival of Christ's nativity indicated a growing tendency to regard the Son as coequal with the Father. He could see a wish, born of a "grandiose identification" with Jesus, that if the Son be the equal of the Father, there would be neither supremacy nor subordination, and, therefore, because all was unity, equality, and harmony, guilt would cease to exist.

Eisenbud (1941) briefly described the courses of two female patients who reacted adversely to Christmas while they were undergoing psychoanalysis. In each case the woman suffered from intense penis envy. The first arranged during her adulthood Christmastimes to act out a childhood tragedy in which she had been promised by her mother that Santa Claus would bring her whatever she desired. She had chosen to ask for a penis with which she felt she could compete with her favored brother for her mother's love. When she failed to realize her ambition, she was bitterly resentful. Her later Christmastimes were marked by her arranging repeatedly to be disappointed and rejected, as a result of which she felt depressed and anxious. The second woman had a brother also and compared what she would get at Christmastime to what he had to play with. She, too, was depressed and furious that Santa Claus did not bring her a penis. In each of the patients, this central theme, as would be assumed, was surrounded by varied ramifications.

Sterba (1944) illustrated similarities between the mode of celebration of Christmas and the customs surrounding childbirth. He was struck by the long period of preparatory excitement, secret anticipation, the last minute flurry of preparation, the prohibitions about entering the rooms containing the gifts, and the relief of tension afforded by the delivery which characterize both events. He indicated symbolic similarities: Santa Claus brings a bag of gifts down the chimney and delivers them through the fireplace. He felt Christmas stirred up unconscious fantasies of childbirth and unresolved conflicts related to "feelings, wishes, magical fulfilments or frustrations of childbirth," resulting in pathological reactions in the susceptible.

Cattell (1954) described a syndrome persisting, in America, from Thanksgiving until after New Year's Day, characterized by diffuse anxiety, feelings of depression, helplessness, nostalgia, irritability, and wishes for magical resolution of problems, and reaching its zenith at Christmas. He illustrated his thesis that patients suffering from the holiday syndrome have difficulties in establishing close emotional ties, feel isolated, lonely, and bored, and tend toward self-devaluation. They come from disrupted families and have poorly crystallized concepts of self and role.

Ferenczi (1950) contributed to our understanding of psychological reactions to holidays with his penetrating study of the "Sunday neurosis." He reminded his readers that many people suffer headaches and stomach disturbances with regular weekend periodicity, and illustrated the psychogenic nature of the symptoms. In explanation he stated that Sunday is a holiday from both internal and external taboos. One's internal restrictive forces are originally external prohibitions as one has interpreted them, and at times when external limitations are loosened, the internal censors of some people become more lax. Certain neurotically predisposed individuals enter their holidays with excessive wantonness of act or fantasy. They become threatened by a potential unrestricted release of instinctual drives, and untimely depressions or "little hysterical symptoms" result.

Case Material

Case #1

Mrs. V. was a 30-year-old, childless housewife, an inactive Episcopalian. She was a dependent, orally aggressive, exhibitionistic woman who suffered various hysterical and psychosomatic complaints. She was quite unable to believe she was not the center of her parents', husband's, and analyst's thoughts. In her quest for a penis, she had pursued various masculine avocations and engineering as a profession. Although she was in reality an only child, a paternal nephew had resided in the household before her birth, and she had believed him to be her brother. She had always been convinced she was unwanted and had attributed her undesirability to her being female.

During her infancy, her mother had had almost no milk. Mrs. V. was weaned at 3 or 4 months of age and subsequently fed goat's milk, which she was reputed to have detested, even as a small baby.

During an interruption in her analysis one spring, her father died. She displayed little reaction to his death, beyond quickly spending much of her inheritance lest it be taken away from her. She resumed her analysis during the autumn. On the last day of November, I was a few minutes late to an appointment. Her fantasies that I had been killed led to her experiencing the repressed emotions relating to his death. Within a few days, she told me she had made a fruitcake for me. She called it feces and an undesirable child, herself. Her dreams and fantasies dwelt on oral impregnation. During interviews, she reached above her head toward me, clawed the skin of her right hand, and said she was doing so as self-punishment for her desire to get my love by grasping at my penis. She equated penis and breast and wanted semen-milk.

By the middle of December, she had become obviously depressed. She told me that during her childhood Christmastimes, she somehow felt she had lost something. "I used to feel if I didn't find something wonderful that Christmas, I'd find it another year, another Christmas." She had wanted to find the missing penis. She wanted me to give her a penis in order that she would merit being my only child. Although in three previous years of analysis she had revealed no interest in religion, at this time she became preoccupied with religious thoughts. Her ruminations rotated about the theme, "If only I would turn to religion, God would give me a penis." She said that if one couldn't be a Christchild, borne by a woman without sin to be worshiped by all men, one could "make it into a religion."

Three days before Christmas, while she was menstruating, she brought me the cake. It represented her precious feces and a baby boy. She recalled that her father had refused her Christmas offerings to him. He had told her that when she grew up, he wanted her to have a baby boy for him. She understood him to infer he would, in return, give her whatever she wanted. Her basic wish was to be her parents' only child, a child so beautiful that the entire world would love her and give her whatever she wanted without expecting anything in return.

During the period just before and after Christmas, she fought continuously with her husband, with the intent of forcing him to rape her violently. She thought that amid the physical struggle, she could get his penis for herself. Within a few days after Christmas, she had a fantasy that I sired a son for my secretary, took the boy, and gave him to some unknown woman. She then stated bitterly that during her girlhood, Christmastimes had been celebrations for her father. Her anxious depression, with its acting out, dissipated.

Comment. Mrs. V. volunteered the thought that her reaction to my having been late on just that occasion affected her so strongly because she had been brooding about the oncoming Christmas season.

Her overwhelming wish was to be an infant without responsibility or competition. Her childhood sibling rivalry was unrealistic, but intense. In her analysis, it became clear that her fantasized solution to her dilemma (the inability to obtain omnipotent infancy) was to fight physically or professionally with men with the aim of acquiring a penis. With her penis she could have sexual relations with her mother. The expected reward for gratifying her mother sexually was permanently available and full breasts. To get father's penis, first she must give him her son.

During childhood Yuletimes, she imagined God or Santa Claus would bring her the necessary penis. As was revealed through her analysis, her prepubertal unconscious evaluation of her obesity was that she was pregnant. The onset of her menstruation and her adolescent slimming were doubly traumatic.

In adulthood she had been depressed and anxious regularly during the Christmas season. The return of repressed wishes and the anticipation of renewed frustration caused her to act out childhood fantasies in her attempt to rectify the childhood traumata. During one Christmas depression, she consciously considered Christ to be her rival.

Case #2

Miss O., a 34-year-old virgin Episcopalian, was the editor of a newspaper. She was the last of three children. Her brother and sister had been born while her parents were prosperous, and her unwelcome birth had coincided with the loss of the family fortune. She had trained in professional fields usually practiced by men. She competed regularly with men, hoping through defeating them to acquire their penises, supplant her father in sexual relations with her mother, and, as a reward for satisfying her frigid mother genitally, become her favorite baby. She had practiced homosexuality overtly for many years. Although she dressed and acted like a man, she chose directive, maternal partners, and was passive and clinging in her relations with them. In various statistical and executive positions, she almost succeeded in displacing men who held higher positions, but always arranged to lose her job just before accomplishing her aim. When she was discharged, she regularly developed delusions of persecution by the men with whom she had competed.

When her psychoanalytically oriented psychotherapy began, she stopped an affair with M., a female church official, and no longer took part in formal religious activities. For two years she avoided social contacts with her previous lover and largely satisfied her repressed wishes in the transference relationship. However, in November of the third year of her therapy, she became more restless than previously. She returned to M., hoping to reestablish social relations with her. After her overtures were rebuffed, she developed the delusion that M. and the minister of the church were engaged in sexual activities. She became depressed and very tense. She masturbated violently, bruising her legs and scratching them until blood came.

She recalled Christmastimes in childhood. Her mother had been a socialite and her father a brilliantly successful businessman whose alcoholism always crescendoed at the Yule season. Her parents were so involved with their problems they had little time for their children. Miss O. recalled Christmas periods during which her father had had violent hallucinations, and had become delusional. He had run about the house nude, brandishing a loaded revolver and threatening to kill his family. Miss O.'s mother taunted him, but finally she became frightened and persuaded him to come to her bedroom, where she seduced him and quieted his rage.

During December, Miss O. wanted urgently to rejoin her church group. She equated the minister with her father, God, and her therapist, and cried out her desire to be his favorite child. A week before Christmas, she went to him impulsively and denounced her erstwhile lover as a homosexual. Although she was furious that the minister did not banish M. from the church and reward Miss O. by pleading with her to rejoin the fold and be his favorite child, she was clearly relieved when her attempt failed. Then she remembered that during her girlhood, she had been unsuccessful in her desire to obtain mother's favoritism. She had turned to her father with some degree of achievement, because at least she and he commiserated with one another.

Immediately after Christmas, Miss O.'s delusional thinking abated. Her anxiety and depression lifted. She returned to her previous, less intense complaints that her therapist did not love her enough to prove to her that she was his most valuable patient or to leave his wife and children to care for her exclusively. She revealed that during the Christmas period she had thought of the minister as God, and considered herself to be Christ's rival for the position of His favorite child.

Comment. This woman's unconscious aim had been to acquire a penis with which she could satisfy her mother sexually and obtain in return the permanent role of mother's favorite baby, with constant access to a full breast. She had failed in all her attempts to be close to her mother and had striven to become father's favorite child. At Christmastime, she observed his unhappiness and fantasized replacing her mother as his wife. Her goal, however, had been a preoedipal one. She had equated penis and breast and thought that through his penis, she could obtain the coveted milk, the proof that only she had access to his love. When the Christmas season passed, each year she was confronted with the proof that her fantasies were doomed to frustration. During her adulthood, Christmastimes were periods of renewed depression because of the return of repressed wishes which could not be gratified and of reawakened guilt. Her dramatic episodes of acting out were attempts to make those wishes come true. In her religious activities, she displaced the original dramatis personae with members of the church or sought to displace Christ in His position with God.

Case #3

Mrs. Y., a 32-year-old Jewish mother, had entered psychoanalysis immediately following a severe catatonic excitement for which she received electroshock therapy.

In her parents' native home, a Slavic country, her father had been an Hebraic scholar. She had been reared in an attitude of contempt for Christians, in Europe and Palestine until she was 6, and later in the United States. Nevertheless, during her 7th and 8th years, she became interested in Christ and His teachings, and composed prizewinning poetry about Christmas. Such writings were concealed from her parents.

Although there had been extensive acting out during the first ten months of her analysis, she had been rather singularly free of external emotional expression. As Christmas neared, she became overtly depressed. She very much wanted a Christmas tree. Her husband, who had been reared in an orthodox Jewish household, forbade celebration of Christmas. She had equated tree and penis. For the first time she revealed jealousy of her brother. Immediately following Christmas her depression turned to rage against her parents because they were Jews and had deprived her of Christmas celebrations in childhood. If she had been permitted to have visits from Santa Claus, or had been permitted to worship Christ, one of them would have given her the penis she needed to compete with her brother. If only she had had a penis, she could have displaced him as the favorite of her parents and more particularly, of her mother.

The subjects of penis envy and jealousy of her brother were again repressed. Not until the next Christmastime did they reappear. The same pattern was repeated. During early December, she became depressed. Although her husband permitted her to have a tree, she was still inadequate and her parents still preferred her brother. Following that Yuletide, anger again appeared that another Christmas had gone by and she still had no penis. Once more, penis envy and jealousy of her brother were repressed. Before the third Christmas, yet another depression appeared. Following that holiday, she began to talk at length of her period of acute psychosis. Only then did she reveal that during her confinement in seclusion, she had believed that I was God and Death and that she was Christ. When her brother had visited her during that time, she had felt superior to him for the first time in her life.

Comment. Mrs. Y. was an orally fixated woman whose life pattern had been one of dependency and passivity. Her aim had been to avoid responsibility and, through obedience, to become the favored child of parent surrogates. Her concepts of a good mother and father were identical. They would care for her and show their love through supplying all her wants. They would prove their need for her by being dependent on her existence for their happiness, indeed, their lives. However, she was faced with the reality that her brother was their favorite. She concluded that he was their chosen child because he had a penis. During childhood, she felt that if only she could be permitted to have Christmas celebrations like the other children in her environment, Santa Claus or Jesus would give her a penis. Then she could remove her brother and be her parents' (mother's) favorite. During her adulthood, at least during her analysis, each Christmas reminded her that a boy was the chosen child of mankind. Old frustrations returned from the repressed, and depression resulted. Before Christmas, there was again the hope that she would get a penis. After the holiday, when she again found herself to be a girl, she was angry.

Case #4

Mr. Z. was a 29-year-old, childless, married salesman. He was an inactive Baptist. He had been discharged from the military as psychotic, and his Rorschach test indicated he was schizophrenic. Clinically, he presented a borderline state characterized by obsessive traits, severe superego defects, neurotic alcoholism (Simmel 1948), and psychosomatic complaints (chiefly peptic ulcer symptoms, migraine, chronic constipation, and obesity). During the first few months of his psychoanalytically oriented psychotherapy, he soon projected his concept of the ideal father onto me. Concurrently, his migraine,[1] alcoholism, and

[1]The dynamics of the migraine in this case support the thesis presented by M. Sperling (1952).

gastrointestinal complaints disappeared. The anxiety he presented initially was not seen after two or three months of twice weekly vis-á-vis interviews.

His mother had wanted a girl. He was clad in dresses and wore curls until he was 4 or 5. Any aggressive behavior was punished by her withdrawal. Although his father was an openly bawdy, thieving barber, Mr. Z. was not allowed to express interest in sexual matters. So long as he behaved like a quiet, obedient girl, he was coddled by his mother. At the same time, his father ridiculed him.

When he was 3 or 4, a sister was born. Mother's attentions centered on that child. However, the sister died within a few months. Thereafter, Mr. Z. was ignored and maltreated. When he was 6, a brother was born. That child was treated like a little god. Whatever he did was praised. His aggressiveness and sexual curiosity were encouraged. Mr. Z. was required to mother him and repress his original murderous impulses.

Mr. Z.'s attempts to win his mother's and father's approval failed, whether he sought their favor through girlish or boyish behavior. His later turning to various surrogates, whom he sought to please through criminal behavior and homosexuality, failed.

Following his first three months of therapy, Mr. Z. became affectively quite flat. His dreams indicated he had at last found a good mother. However, six months later, during December, he became depressed. His headaches returned. He recalled his hopeless sibling rivalry. Whereas the same material had been recited without emotion during the previous months of interviews, now it was accompanied by feelings of hopelessness, insomnia, and anorexia. In the middle of December, he dreamed of a group of people. "We danced around a skeleton lying on its back on the floor. It had an erect, big penis." He said the dream represented a tribal dance, in which penis worhsip was the major theme. He recalled his father's death. His father had been asthmatic and required constant attention. When Mr. Z. was 11, he was alone with his father one night. Father had an acute asthmatic attack and ordered Mr. Z. to fetch his atomizer. The patient refused to obey, and his father died. After these memories reappeared, Mr. Z. began to awaken at night, sobbing and terrified. He recalled that his migraine had begun with the birth of his brother.

Two interviews before Christmas, Mr. Z. asked me, apparently out of context, to see him Christmas Day. He then revealed he had always dreaded Christmas. At home his brother had been grossly favored with gifts. The evening after he requested the holiday interview, he attended a prostitute and suckled her breasts. He did not attempt intercourse. The interview before Christmas, he cried bitterly. He had previously shed no tears during his hours. He expressed a desire to see me socially. At the end of the interview, I shook his hand and wished him season's greetings. He sobbed loudly and started to hug and kiss me. In the next interview, no depression was discernible.

Just before the Christmas which followed termination of his interviews, he came to the office and presented me with a concrete statue he had made. The sculpture looked like a winged penis. He said he owed it to me.

Comment. Mr. Z.'s therapy enabled him to behave independently. He gave up his amoral attempts to be fed at the expense of others. He renounced his government pension, supported his wife, became a leader rather than a follower in his business, and adopted a child. His dependent behavior disappeared, and his alcoholism, migraine, and gastrointestinal complaints have now been absent for several years. In his follow-up interviews, he has treated me as an equal and been at ease. His relations with his siblings at work and his brother have become realistic, and he has been able to compete without anxiety.

His Christmas depressions were stimulated by the return of the repressed sibling rivalry anxieties. In a sense, Mr. Z. also suffered from penis envy. Again, the possession of a penis was viewed by him to represent the key to obtaining the breast. His fantasies were of nursing with his penis.

Discussion

The reader who wishes to refresh himself concerning the detailed psychodynamics of depression is referred to Abraham (1924a, b, c), Fenichel (1945), Freud (1914, 1915b, 1917b, 1921, 1923), Garma and Rascovsky, (1948), and Lewin, (1950, 1953a). The precipitating agents of depression are diverse. Experiences which precede depressions involve a loss of self-esteem (Fenichel 1945). Failures of prestige or monetary matters, disappointment in love or death of dear ones, incidents which force an individual to feel a sense of inferiority, and even successes which cause people to fear punishment or the imposition of greater and more threatening duties, precipitate depression. A loss of narcissistic gratification is present. The depressed person feels he has lost everything and the world is empty, if his loss of self-esteem is due to a withdrawal of external support, or he feels he has lost everything because he is undeserving, if it is due to a loss of superego support. Some depressives feel they are doomed forever to be failures because their oedipal complexes were inadequately solved (Freud 1914). When a love object is lost, libidinal strivings, which are no longer bound to the object, flood the mourner. The product is anxiety (Freud 1915b). A person predisposed to depression in times of grief retards the detachment rate, frequently retaining the illusion the dead one lives. In order that this may be done, he regresses from object relationships to identification through incorporation (eating and retention). That people take on the qualities of lost loved ones has been widely described (Abraham 1924c, Freud 1914, 1923). Bulimia, unconsciously equated with eating the dead person and reminiscent of totem festivals (Sharpe 1946), is a common component of grief. The folklore of death customs and the reactions of children to death reveal that introjection is a frequent reaction to the loss of love objects (Freud 1921; Money-Kyrle 1939). After the introjection phase of mourning has been established, the ties to the incorporated object are loosened. It has been illustrated amply that people recovering from depression unconsciously equate fecal riddance with removal of the introject (Abraham 1924a). Each tie is slowly dissolved and the erstwhile bound drive energy is then available for attachment elsewhere (Freud 1917b). Identification is to some extent always ambivalent. Requisite for melancholia is marked ambivalence. When libidinal cathexis is withdrawn from a love object, it is directed toward the self which is now subject to the ambivalence of the libidinal and aggressive impulses (Abraham 1924c). When the relationship to the lost object is ambivalent, the incorporation acquires a sadistic meaning. The hated object is both preserved and destroyed. If one hates a person, one wishes for his death. If he dies, one unconsciously believes one's wish killed him. Then one fears retribution from the dead and feels one has to die himself. One goes through rituals to prevent the return of the dead (Freud 1915b). In brief, then, in mourning occurs an ambivalent introjection of the lost object. The feelings originally directed toward the object are now continued toward the introject, and guilt feelings participate throughout.

In the patients observed, various causes of loss of self-esteem occurred at Christmastime. Cash shortage sometimes caused the patients to feel that they were unequal to their rivals, real or fancied. Primarily, however, the loss of prestige they experienced appeared to have been precipitated by the meaning they attached to the anniversary of Christ's birth. In Him they saw a sibling rival with whom they could not possibly compare. This reminded them of what they had perceived to be unsuccessful rivalries with their real or imagined siblings during their childhoods. Their responses were basically depressive. Their reactions were handled in manners which had been peculiarly developed during the courses of their lives. Eisenbud's first patient (1941) acted out her childhood disappointment by arranging to be rejected, in order that she could perceive her depressive feelings to be based in the present and so that she would not be confronted with their original meanings. She also fantasized she had a penis, partly, it would seem, so that she could have the means wherewith to avoid the feelings of loss of narcissistic gratification and successfully compete with her brother for her mother's love. Mrs. V. attempted to rid herself of depression by presenting her analyst with a symbol of a baby which she thought would please her father and cause him to give her the cherished penis, and the feces her mother had demanded as the price for her favors. In addition, she chose more direct methods of obtaining the penis with which she thought she could obtain mother's love, through violent sexual scenes with her husband. Miss O. sought to destroy her mother-sister through banishing her fantasized rival with the minister. Her hope was to enter into a multisided relationship with that father figure. On one level she could enter into sexual relations with him, obtain his penis, and then utilize that precious acquisition in her dealings with her mother, with the aim of thereby removing her siblings in her rivalry for the breast. On another, she had learned that she could get more maternal affection from her father than from her mother, and thus she hoped she would get that love from a presentday father figure. In her near delusional thinking, she identified the minister with God and fancied herself His Son, with whom her brother and sister could not compete. It is probably unnecessary to comment on her identification of her therapist and God-father-minister and her desires to eliminate his loved ones, with the same aims in view. Mrs. Y. strove to obtain a penis either totemically, through possession of a Christmas tree, or from her analyst. She was quite willing to give her sons in return for this favor. She was a Jew who had been taught that the most important contribution of a woman is sons. In addition, there is reason to believe she identified herself with Christ, with the same aim as Miss O. Mr. Z. strove valiantly to get his therapist's love in various ways. His fantasy was that if he could be forgiven for the murder of his father, his new father would give him permission to use the penis he already possessed to bargain with his mother and obtain her approval. His favored brother had lost a leg. Surely, if he had two legs and a penis, he should be able to win out in the preoedipal competition for mother's love.

Each of these patients craved complete oral satisfaction from the mother, that is, a return to the early period of life during which a child perceives his mother to be an extension of himself and under his wishful domination. The presence of father or sibling, or their substitutes, was felt by them to endanger their position in the fantasized ideal situation. The father as well as the brother or sister was a rival for the mother's breast and the patient's wished-for status (Lewin 1950, 1953a, 1954). Throughout the previous case material and discussion, the hostility of the patients described has been implicit and explicit.

Winter solstice celebrations have existed throughout recorded history. Men have always attributed the success of their crops to the existence of the sun. They have feared that because of their misdeeds, the sun would not reappear. Hence, their crops would not again grow and they would starve. To assure themselves of a returning sun and a replenishment of food supplies, they have felt the necessity of atoning for their sins and pleading for divine forgiveness.

According to official Catholic teachings, Christ had no earthly father and no siblings. Whether He had a terrestrial father or the men Jesus chose to call His brothers were literally His brothers, is not an issue so far as popular thought has been concerned. The masses have chosen to believe that there must have been a son so fortunate as to have been the permanently primary object of his asexual mother's love. If we turn our attention briefly to artistic productions, we note that before the birth of Christ, the mother-child theme was rarely portrayed (Bodkin 1949). Subsequently, however, religious paintings and sculptures have commonly employed that symbol of unity as a central topic (Belvianes 1951). The popularity of the madonna paintings which very unusually include any suggestion of father or sibling, illustrates man's preoccupation with that dynamic idea.[2]

The philosophical tenets of Mithraism and Christianity contained wide areas of agreement (Ferm 1945, Leach 1950, Reinach 1930, Taraporewala, 1950). Although the development of the Christian religion out of Judaism has been traced from many logical standpoints (Ferm 1951), one must wonder whether Christianity has succeeded in

[2]I am indebted to Drs. Sandor Lorand and Bertram Lewin, who in their discussions of this essay at the Midwinter Meetings, 1954, suggested that reference be made to religious art as support for the principal theses of the study.

becoming the popular religion of the Western world at least partially because of the unconscious dream in all of us to retain the early belief in the unity of mother and child.

Christmas stemmed originally from festivals onto which Christian coloring was superposed. In recent centuries, man has mastered the preservation of his crops and learned enough about the movements of celestial bodies that worries concerning the reappearance of the sun have been determined to be unrealistic. Nevertheless, his infantile anxieties about starvation have not lessened. Apparently, the celebration of Christmas as a children's holiday is still an acceptable medium through which man can express those fears and attempt to deny their existence. He is able to give his children gifts (food) and, through his identification with children, feel that he himself is fed by a beneficent mother. Perhaps this explains why it has been possible to a varying extent for Santa Claus to displace God as the figure to be worshiped.

Yet Christmas anxieties continue. They can be observed in the masses. Families convene with the hope that old conflicts of various natures can be denied or resolved. Popular literature not infrequently portrays the hostilities which exist at that season (Christie 1952). The angers revolve usually about the theme of who will get the most and whether monetary sacrifices can be tolerated without harm to the givers. "It is more blessed to give than to receive" is an admonition which is necessary only because man's impulses to receive rather than to give are foremost.

Patients under the care of psychiatrists frequently reveal depressions at Christmastime. In the case material presented in this chapter, the dynamics of the depressions illustrated were similar basically. Oral conflicts were reawakened. Previously repressed hostilities toward siblings who were viewed by the patients to have been favored by their mothers (parents) entered the preconscious. The remembrance by the entire populace of the birth date of a Child who was so favored that competition with Him is hopeless reminded these patients that they were unsuccessful in competition with their siblings for the gifts of love from their mothers. These patients had striven to change themselves in whatever manner they had conceived to have been most likely to please their mothers. The three female patients described had concluded that the possession of a penis would qualify them to get the ultimate reward, the breast.

Does the material presented in this essay support the theses offered by the previous psychoanalytic contributors?

Jones' interpretation (1951) that the holiday psychologically represents a period in which an erasure of or a denial of family discords is inferred by the fact that although the holiday is celebrated with gaiety, emotionally predisposed people are rather disturbed by being reminded of two of the great traumata of childhood: sibling rivalry and oral deprivation.

Jekels' contribution (1952) was that Christmas is popular in large part because on that date sons can imagine themselves equal with their fathers and thus deny oedipal strivings and frustrations. The case material available to me indicates that this interpretation is too superficial to explain the depressive reactions. Here, as elsewhere, basically oral traumata are involved. Whether his thesis is applicable to the reactions of individuals who suffer less severe responses to Christmas cannot be stated. Among my patients, identification with Christ at Christmas is not unusual, but the identification is aimed at denying they were not their parents' favorite children rather than that they were not their mothers' husbands.

Eisenbud's observations (1941) seemed to agree fundamentally with those described herein. He found that penis-envy frustrations were accentuated at Christmastime and inferred that the unsatisfied women he treated had wanted phalluses to place them in a position to be favored by their mothers, over their brothers.

Sterba's thesis (1944) that the celebration of Christmas is an acting out of unconscious fantasies about childbirth is neither affirmed nor denied by the productions of the patients described. However, that fantasies of childbirth—in this case of the fact of the birth of a sibling rather than of the method of childbirth—are rekindled and old conflicts are rejuvenated is amply verified. This, however, may not be what Sterba was implying.

Cattell's description of the holiday syndrome (1954), his delineation of the types of patients involved, and his thesis that neurotic reactions to these holidays are based on oral strivings are confirmed.

Is the Christmas "neurosis" comparable to the Sunday neurosis? In common are the periodicity and the holiday atmosphere. As Ferenczi (1950) told us, on Sunday (in America, on the weekend) outer restrictions are lifted and internal ones likewise become more lax. The result is an upsurge of otherwise limited desires and impulses, the nature of which causes, in certain predisposed individuals, various neurotic symptoms. In clinical practice, such symptoms are generally minor in character. The holiday period extending from before Christmas until after New Year's Eve, however, is a relatively continuous period of culturally accepted emotional release. For varying periods in individual households, the pre-Christmas preparations go on. At Christmas Eve or Christmas Day, the family reunion and the revived conflicts surrounding favoritism and receiving and giving are at their height. After a respite of a few days comes the New Year's celebration with its condoned licentiousness. Other conflicts are aroused, especially having to do with the release or potential release of forbidden sexual impulses of all kinds and either overt or covert acts of hostility (symbolically, the murder of Father Time). It is to be expected that the degree of neurotic responses to such an intense holiday release would be more frequent and more severe. This, in clinical experience, is true.

In common with neurotic responses to birthdays, again are prevalent the facets of favoritism as demonstrated through gifts and other partiality.

Various analysts who have practiced abroad have presented contradictory data regarding the incidence of Christmas depressions in Europe. Siegfried Bernfeld (personal communication 1951) indicated that he found his patients in Austria less frequently to suffer depressions at the Yuletide than in America. Berliner (1954) on the other hand emphasized the sharp rise in suicides which occurred in Germany on Christmas Eve. In Europe, the religious aspects of Christmas are more important generally than is true in the United States. Therefore, one would think that if Christ's birth per se is an important stimulus for the revival of sibling rivalries, depressive reactions would be more prominently observed in Europe. However, the fact that in the United States Christmas has become associated with gift giving in a family setting, could result only in a focalizing of oral conflicts. Thus the elements of favoritism become more prominent. It could be that in many patients Santa Claus as a symbol for parents and frustrations resulting from his apportionment of presents plays an important role in precipitating the neurotic responses. It may be recalled at this time that in Russia and Italy Santa Claus is conceived as a woman.

Is Christmas "neurosis" a clinical entity? It cannot be. The depressive reactions which occur at this time of the year are phenomenologically and dynamically the same as those observed at other times. The constellation surrounding Christmas makes it a more important holiday and a more powerful trigger for reactions in the predisposed. It is interesting to consider, nevertheless, the problem of whether there may be a phylogenetic predisposition to depression at the period of year when darkness predominates. The celebrations and mythologies of

Western and Near-Eastern worlds are replete with evidences of uneasy, manicoid reactions to the yearly threatened disappearance of the sun. Our psychologically deduced knowledge that darkness symbolizes separation from the mother notwithstanding, we know that darkness and cold produce physiological changes in animals and men (Berliner 1914). I have heard from nonanalytic observers that depressions are not infrequent at Christmastime in Hawaii and Argentina. If such information is correct, it seems far more tangible to attribute neurotic reactions to emotional than to inherited physiologic tendencies.

Families with a particularly strong religious ethic sometimes produce superego structures of especial severity. It is possible that Christ's birth would remind a patient whose background includes such parents less of sibling-rivalry failure than of the fact of his being an unforgivable sinner by comparison. I do not have case material to confirm or illustrate this hypothesis.

Whether special transference situations prevailed among the patients whose cases are here described is a question which must be considered. Careful analysis of the case material does not reveal such a factor to have been of importance. However, I have experienced Christmas depressions and it is possible that in some manner not perceived by me, certain emotional stimuli were transmitted to the patients studied.

Among the questions which require consideration regarding the possible theoretical significance of the material presented in this, three will be considered briefly.

Dynamics and the Severity of Illness

One must wonder whether patients less seriously disturbed than those here described would present similar fundamental dynamics at the bases of their Christmas depressions. Each of the patients studied in the preparation of this chapter suffered from a psychosis or borderland area disturbance. However, since this study was made, I have observed in detail similar depressions with identical dynamics in four neurotic patients. In three of them, two men and a woman, the rivalry with Christ was explicitly demonstrated. The fourth patient, a woman, again illustrated strikingly the role of sibling rivalry in her recurrent Christmas depressions, but no reference to Christ was made. A number of analysts have been so kind as to inform me that in their practices, Christmas depressions which involved the trigger mechanism of sibling rivalry have been observed in patients whose illnesses were much less severe than those described here. Beckwitt (1968) wrote of a neurotic woman who had recurrent Christmas depressions the origins of which could be traced clearly to a murderous attack on her twin brother at 2 years 8 months of age, when she strove to castrate him and acquire his penis at Christmastime. It seems that we must assume that the same dynamics are involved in patients who have depressive reactions at Christmastime, regardless of the seriousness or nature of their psychological disturbance in toto. There will always be the cardinal theme of reawakened oral conflicts, but the reactions will involve reactions pertaining to different levels of psychosexual maturity and will be of different quantities, depending on the seriousness of the original oral conflict and the maturity of the personality structure.

Role of the Oedipus Complex

There are varied opinions regarding the role of the Oedipus complex in the genesis of schizophrenia. They range between two poles. One group of students believes that schizophrenics are so strongly orally fixated that, because of the failure of psychosexual development, the Oedipus complex is not faced with such anxiety as that of children who have suffered less severe oral traumata. Other psychologists are of the opinion that schizophrenia is, like the neuroses, an affliction which results from regression as a defense against oedipal anxiety. After extensive working through of oral material, these cases revealed oedipal problems not essentially unlike those of neurotics.

Although the answer to this important theoretical question is outside the scope of this chapter, it is my opinion that some data presented in these case histories might be used to help find its ultimate solution. The striking preoccupation of these patients with penis envy is indicative that they did indeed suffer oedipal traumata of significance.

Use of Denial

Is the celebration of Christmas a culturally integrated, group manicoid, defensive reaction meant to obviate guilt related to murder wishes against siblings? The utilization of denial is one of the basic mechanisms stated or inferred by all the previous psychoanalytic writers in their theses concerning the meaning of Christmas to individuals or the masses. Denial is a primary defense utilized by the patients whose histories are abstracted in this chapter. It is my opinion that not only the history of Christmas but the study of individuals' reactions to Christmas will indicate generally the answer to this question in the affirmative. However, the development of the thesis as a result of a historical study will have to wait for a more detailed study than has yet been done.

Summary

Case material derived from patients who were interviewed in psychoanalytically oriented psychotherapy and psychoanalysis revealed that their Christmas depressions were the result of unresolved sibling rivalries. In them the birth of Christ, a fantasized competitor against whom they were unable successfully to contest, reawakened memories of unsuccessful rivalry with siblings, real or fantasized, in their pasts. Oral conflicts were stimulated, and repressed cravings and frustrations were rearoused. They sought uniformly to obtain penises with which they imagined they could woo their mothers to give them the love which they felt had been previously unequally showered upon their siblings. There was some indication that they at times identified with Christ in an attempt to deny their own inferiority and to obtain the favoritism which would be His just due.

Acknowledgments

Thanks are due numerous colleagues for their helpful criticisms during the preparation and after the presentations of this paper. I wish particularly to express my gratitude to Drs. Bernhard Berliner, Siegfried Bernfeld, Anna and Otto Maenchen, Bertram Lewin, Sandor Lorand, and Norman Reider.

12

An Unusual Childhood Theory of Pregnancy

In this chapter I describe a childhood theory of pregnancy which to my knowledge has not been reported previously. Mr. H., a married, childless architect, suffered from a severe obsessive-compulsive personality disorder and at times, both in and out of analysis, regressed into transitory psychotic states. He was the youngest of four children and the only son. His father's vocation had involved the use of both artistic and mechanical skills.

Mr. H. entered psychoanalysis with me some months after his wife's having done so. His conscious motivation was partial impotence, but the driving force was jealousy.

During the third year of the analysis, after his intense ambivalent feelings toward his father had been strongly transferred to me, passive homosexual longings periodically emerged and were immediately subjected to repression. Each time such passive urges briefly appeared, he developed delusions of jealousy which were resolved by a macroscopic tracing to rivalry with his father for the physical attentions of his seductive, domineering mother. The repetitive pattern led to scant microscopic examination, and the analysis seemed to be at a standstill. After perhaps a dozen such episodes, he one day had the unwelcome thought that he would like to have me hold and kiss him. He had never been aware previously of such an idea and could not recall ever having wanted such caresses from his father. Because of his father's unshaved stubble, he remembered with displeasure his father's having held him and kissed him when he was a small child. Within minutes after the occurrence of the unwelcome thought, he forgot its expression and became engrossed with delusions of jealousy. For several interviews his conviction that his wife and I were having an affair was fixed and accompanied by ongoing rage and threats directed toward each of us. He spent evening hours spying into neighbors' houses with a telescope but could see no connection between that behavior and his jealous delusion. Ultimately, in the midst of a tirade against his wife and me, he was able to respond to my inquiry regarding his fantasy about the nature of our sexual relations. He very angrily related visualizing our "French kissing" and then suddenly recalled with intense emotion events he had mentioned many times before but without affect. As he recalled, there had been an after-dinner routine during his early childhood years in which his mother would begin to simper and ask father how much she was worth to him. He would then give her coins or bills, whereon she would sit on his lap and, feigning disgust, they would alternately plunge their tongues into one another's mouth. Mr. H. cried for the first time in his analysis.

When he appeared for the next interview, Mr. H. was incredulous. He revealed a bloodblister on the palm of his left hand. He had worked with tools from early childhood. His father, who frequently worked with chisels, had warned him repeatedly to take care lest he hurt his hands. Mr. H. had been consciously annoyed with such admonitions because he was convinced no harm *could* befall him. Factually, so far as he could recall, he had at no time in his life sustained an injury during his frequent work with tools. On the previous evening he had been tightening screws on the housing of a motor which drove a lathe. He had caused the screwdriver to jump from the groove in the head of a screw and pinch his palm. He recalled how mother had babied father when his hands were injured. He had felt wronged when his wife had paid his mildly damaged hand no heed. He joked about the sexual meaning of the words screw and screwdriver but ridiculed the connection.

On the following day, he presented a dream in which he saw a child peering in a doorway. He saw "a person" lying on his or her side, facing away. On the person's back was a raised, red spot. His associations led to present-day treatments of pneumonia. He broke off his technical medical dissertation with the recollection that on the previous evening he had suffered a sudden attack of anxiety with hyperventilation. He was bewildered by its appearance. Before he slept he had a thought he defined as ridiculous, namely, that the bloodblister would become infected and require surgery. During the remainder of the interview he was preoccupied with material relating to that fear. At the end of the hour he had a "nonsensical" thought: bacteria were living organisms and would kill him.

After a week he again returned to the subject of pneumonia. He discussed treatments for lung infections of various kinds. He recalled having seen pictures of Chinese doctors who used suction cups to draw "infected blood" to the surface, producing blisters which were then lanced. Finally he remembered for the first time that when he was 4, his mother had suffered from pneumonia and had been treated by the use of suction cups. He had been forbidden entrance into the bedroom and had been most anxious to discover what the doctor was doing with his mother. He had thought it most strange that his father had been refused admittance. As he recalled his fantasies, he had imagined the doctor to have been "handling" his mother and that they had exchanged French kisses. He had watched the transportation of boiling water into the bedroom. He had peeked through the keyhole and observed the physician as he placed vials of hot water onto mother's back. He had seen swollen, red areas rise in the cups as they cooled. He thought he had seen the doctor incise the blisters.[1] At the end of the hour, he recalled an addition to the after-dinner routine. Father at times handled mother's breasts during the tonguing procedure. He and his sisters had been titillated and disgusted. As he left the office he remarked, "It was when my aunt was pregnant."

After a few interviews in which he spoke of his work and complained that he was exploited, he found himself talking of pregnancy. As he did so, he repeatedly examined his left palm. The blister had receded, but dried blood remained under the epidermis. He began picking at his skin. When his attention was called to the picking, he felt nervous. He expressed a fear that something was alive there and should be removed. He talked of a trip to the tropics. He had observed tumors which were the result of flies' having laid eggs under the skin of children's legs. The growth of larvae had resulted in swollen, red areas. The treatment for the disorder was the surgical removal of the worms. My suggestion that he had feared that his mother had been sick with pregnancy rather than pneumonia was greeted with scorn. Soon, however, he talked of embryology and remembered a phrase from a biology class, "ontogeny recapitulates phylogeny." A fantasy then emerged that the doctor had come because mother was going to have children which were to emerge from the bloodblisters, and he thought he would want to kill the babies.

[1]He later learned, or relearned, that mother yet bore the scars of the incisions.

As Freud (1908) remarked, as a rule the "child's desire for sexual knowledge arises under the goad of a self-seeking impulse which dominates him when he is confronted by the arrival of a new child—perhaps at the end of the second year" (p. 212). In the present case, the suction-cup episode dated to the fourth year, when an aunt was pregnant. His aunt had a child almost exactly Mr. H.'s age, with whom he empathized. It was as though his cousin's state of tension kindled within him fears that he, too, would be replaced.

During the next few months, much time was spent in the further analysis of the vicissitudes of his sexual curiosity in early childhood. The unfolding of his particular fantasy regarding pregnancy appeared to be a turning point in his analysis. It was determined that his self-injury had been an expression not only of a wish to compete with his father for mother's babying (including tonguing and permission to handle her breasts) but also a variant of a passive wish to be cared for by me as a representative of his father, who had been so concerned with his son's health. After he could view passive longings for father in such a light, the delusional episodes of jealousy disappeared, with the exception of one which shortly preceded the termination of his analysis two years later. It was learned further that his mother had undergone surgery when he was about 3 years old, following which he had seen blood in her bed. He had accurately perceived her to have been pregnant. After he had come to that conclusion without the remembered acquisition of outside information, he inquired of an older sister whether she had known of a pregnancy after his birth. He learned his mother had indeed miscarried at that time, but, in addition, her miscarriage had been a common subject of household talk, although in hushed tones and in the foreign, "secret" language of his immigrant parents, a tongue he understood very well while pretending to be ignorant, during childhood years. His sexual curiosity appears to have arisen from the threat to his position as family idol and baby at the end of his second year or the beginning of his third. The "young scientist" developed the common theory of pregnancy that either the man or the woman ingests something which grows in the bowel and emerges like feces. Although Freud (1908) stated that he had observed only in females the idea that kissing results in pregnancy, the peculiar dinner-time routine of Mr. H.'s parents led to his concluding that French kisses cause pregnancy. This idea proved to be one which frightened him less than thoughts it had replaced, just as the excited and disgusted feelings which had accompanied watching the parents' postprandial sex-play defended against the panic, fear, and rage he had experienced throughout childhood while watching his parents having intercourse in the "grasshopper position."

At some time before he was 4, he had developed the usual, more sophisticated, alternate idea that the baby is born through the navel. When he had inquired regarding the origins of babies, he had been informed that "doctor brings them." He had concluded that surgery is required to obviate the bursting of the abdomen.

The unique pregnancy fantasy has two elements made less mysterious by these data: the swelling of the blister as a displacement of the enlarged abdomen, and the need for the presence of the doctor.

Later in the analysis it became clear that his oral-anal and blood-blister theories of pregnancy had been regressively employed later in childhood to obscure primal-scene observations and anxieties. During a period when his early pattern of torturing insects was under scrutiny, he recalled that he had slept for his first five years in the parental bedroom. While we know that one apparently universal symbolic meaning of insects in dreams is tiny sibling rivals (Boyer 1979), in the case of Mr. H. we might assume that his torturing insects had represented a wish to kill the "grasshopper" parents as well.

Epilogue

Dr. Samuel B. Bloom has called to my attention a short story entitled "Lukundoo," by Edward Lucas White (1949). The essential theme of the story follows:

A white man humiliates an African witch doctor before his tribe. At a later time the Englishman falls ill, physically and mentally. At first he appears to suffer from carbuncles which appear over his knees, shoulders, and chest. However, the swellings prove not to be the result of infection. Instead from the tumors emerge wizened, hideous old men in the form of very small babies. They are omniscient and polyglot. To observers, their heads are reminiscent of those of witch doctors.

It would appear that not only my analysand but others as well have voiced bizarre fantasies of childbirth which are variants of the navel theory.

13

Folktale Variation in the Service of Defense and Adaptation

Early in the practice of their science and art, psychoanalysts discovered that patients introduce folklore data into their "free" associations and use such information as they do other verbal and nonverbal communications. This discovery was one of the major stimuli which focused psychoanalysts' attention on the study of folklore. Subsequently, much oral literature obtained in this manner has been studied systematically in the context of its use by patients. However, to my knowledge no examples exist in the folkloristic, anthropological, or psychological literature of the systematic analysis of folklore data which have appeared in the associations of non-Western patients, although some therapists have presented fragmentary examinations of such information within the context of the prevalent transferential situation within which it appeared (Devereux 1951).

The material which follows was obtained during fieldwork with the Apache Indians of the Mescalero Indian Reservation in south central New Mexico. I have been engaged in such field work in conjunction with anthropologists, primarily my wife, since 1957. We have spent some time on the reservation each year; the longest continuous period of investigation there lasted 15 months in 1959–1960. The ultimate purpose of the research is to define the interactions among social structure, socialization, and personality organization of the Apaches who live there. Dr. Ruth Boyer's principal task has been the delineation of child-rearing patterns; she and other anthropologists, especially Harry W. Basehart, have studied the social structure. My charge has been to study personality organization, and my main research technique for some years was to serve as a psychiatrist whose procedure was to conduct investigative and psychoanalytically oriented psychotherapeutic interviews with Indians who sought them; my therapeutic technique was limited to making interpretations, largely of resistance and transference. Because psychogenic illnesses are traditionally treated by shamans among these Apaches, I was known as a white shaman from the outset of our work.

At one time during my work, a woman[1] and her grandnephew were being seen individually. The great-aunt introduced a folktale, which had been previously unrecorded for the Chiricahuas and Mescaleros, as a "free" association. She subsequently related it to her grandnephew, who later introduced his idiosyncratic version as a part of his associations. This chapter consists of a systematic analysis of their variant presentations of the folktale and demonstrates how they used the prose narrative to express their dominant common and individual intrapsychic conflicts in manners which defended them against disturbing anxiety and guilt.

Better-To-See-You attended psychoanalytically oriented psychotherapeutic interviews lasting an hour each for six months, being seen face to face five times weekly. She was a middle-aged medicine woman whose services had been formerly sought frequently, but her shamanistic status had waned during recent years, following her having begun to drink heavily. She suffered from chronic osteoarthritis and diabetes and had begun to develop cataracts. However, she refused standard medical care because of her conviction that illnesses resulted solely from the retributive resentment of affronted supernatural "powers" or the actions of witches or ghosts. Accordingly, she had sought shamanistic treatment for her physical illnesses, without successful results, both from local faith healers and from renowned practitioners of other Indian tribes.

Several factors had combined to cause her to have lowered self-esteem and perhaps to question her identity as a shaman, and contributed to her regressively seeking solace in excessive alcohol intake; their relative importance cannot be weighed. Her latest husband was younger than she and, finding her progressively less attractive, he had begun to consort with other women and to threaten to divorce her. Her daughters, for whom she had had puberty ceremonies conducted and of whom she had unrealistic positive expectations, had disappointed her with their behavior. The repetitive failures of faith healing treat-

[1]See chapter 14 for further discussion of this patient.

ments for her disorders had led her to have deep-seated doubts concerning the efficacy of shamanism, doubts ordinarily repressed but disturbingly conscious following each fruitless ceremony.

Better-To-See-You's stated motives for seeking interviews were that she was curious about why other Apaches came to talk with me and that she needed the small fee which the researchers were required by the tribe to pay informants. However, one of her relatives was a shaman who came for interviews after he failed to cure a man who subsequently was helped through psychotherapy with me. That shaman thought his reputation had been diminished and stated openly to others that he had come to kill me through witchcraft. Thus it is highly probable that her desire for interviews had also been motivated by a wish for a shamanistic cure for her physical ailments, her drinking problem, and her depression.

During the first few weeks of interviews, she developed a strong transference relationship of a mixed nature. She reacted to me both as an ideal father surrogate and as a son who had received supernatural power but who had yet to be trained in native religiomedical ceremonies. It was in the context of this transference situation that she related the folktale, "The Man Who Turned into a Water-Monster," which provides the raw data of this chapter. She told the tale in such a manner that during much of the first of the two hours of its recitation, I thought she was reporting a dream.

Soon after she came for therapy, her 13-year-old grandnephew, Peter, who lived with her and who was the son of her sister's daughter, also came to see me. He had earlier established a strong transference reaction in which I was an ideal father surrogate, and he was in open competition with one of my sons, a boy of his own age and Peter's classmate, for my favoritism. Soon after Better-To-See-You told me the story, she related it to him and he in turn presented his individual version in his interviews.

A year after their treatment had been terminated by our departure from the reservation and when I was no longer seeing Indians in therapy, I surveyed the incidence of awareness of the story among the reservation Apaches. Until that time, we had not heard the tale from anyone but Better-To-See-You and Peter. Of 51 people who were 51 years of age or older, 27 percent knew a variant of the tale, as did 14 percent of 48 people who were 21 to 50 years old. With two exceptions, the Chiricahuas, Lipans, Mescaleros, and San Carlos Apaches who knew the story believed its protagonists to have been members of their tribe. Probably only one who was 20 years old or younger had known the tale before the survey was begun. The commonest presentation of the story follows:

Two adult male friends were hunting or raiding in Mexico and had lived on berries and occasional rodents for several weeks. They were tired, hungry, and depressed. One evening they made camp by a lake and found some large eggs. One partner warned the other that eating the eggs might be supernaturally dangerous. Nevertheless, his reckless companion roasted and ate one or more of them, without having first performed a little ceremony to avoid affronting the "power" of the eggs.

The following morning he had turned into a black snake some 30 feet long and 2 or more feet thick. The transgressor had become one of the Underwater People and was thus sacred, but, at the same time, he had the ability to perform evil at will. He told his companion to return to their band, to tell the Snake-Man's relatives what had happened, and to inform them that he would remain in the area of his new abode where, if visited by members of the band, he would perform ceremonies to bring them good luck and perhaps confer supernatural power onto some of them.

The partner obeyed the monster's instructions. A brother of the Snake-Man believed the returned companion had committed murder. Accordingly, his kin group went to the site of the alleged transformation. There they found huge snake tracks and exonerated the messenger.

Two endings of the story were of equal incidence: (1) the people who visited the lakeside never found the Snake-Man; they returned home and "forgot" their relative; and (2) the kin group found the Water-Monster, who conferred good luck on them and gave some of them supernatural powers.

After the survey was done, I reviewed the world literature and found variants of the tale to exist in the folklore of many Indian tribes in the United States, in that of some Indian groups in Central America, and perhaps in Tierra del Fuego (Boyer 1975). Analysis of the manifest content of the folktale, based on conclusions drawn from interpretation of the evidence to follow from Better-To-See-You and Peter, indicated that the folktale was used particularly to help individuals defend themselves against anxieties resulting from unresolved sibling-rivalry problems.

The Folktale According to Better-To-See-You

Better-To-See-You essentially introduced herself during her first interviews by spontaneously relating a dramatic life history. According to her personal myth (Kris 1956), her father, a violent, notorious Chiricahua buffalo hunter, had come across her Mescalero mother, then an unmarried teenager, and her mother's sister while they were gathering berries on White Mountain—the imposing 12,000 foot peak which is the central landmark of the Mescalero homeland. He had tied them to trees but otherwise treated them well. After a few days he selected the mother of Better-To-See-You as his bride. He persuaded her to join him and took her into the wilderness of northwestern Arizona. They and their ensuing children had wandered about, avoiding other Indians, since the kidnapper had been banished from his own tribe as a "wild" man, inferentially a cannibal, and they lived on the spoils of his hunting and plundering. He was slain by "Anglos" when Better-To-See-You was 3 or 4 years old, after he had murdered one of their companions while looting their camp. His wife burned his body to a mass of charred bones, which she scattered lest they be found and used for witchcraft purposes. She and her three daughters then arduously trekked southwestward, seeking to return to the reservation. When they reached the Rio Grande it was in flood and they had no way to cross. However, at that time a maternal uncle of Better-To-See-You consulted a shaman, who divined the location of the mother and her children and magically enabled them to cross the river and the waterless White Sands, and, eventually, to return to the Mescaleros. There, the four lived with the mother's brother for a time, and the young girl came to view her uncle as her father. He lovingly reared her after her mother remarried and took her other children with her. When Better-To-See-You was a young adult, a half-brother was shot and killed by an "envious" man.

Better-To-See-You's mother had told this story to each of her children; we were told that each related a variant version. Over the years, we learned information from other sources which modified Better-To-See-You's highly cathected personal myth. According to more objective observers, the violent Chiricahua had abused and kidnapped both of the teenagers. The mother's sister had escaped after they arrived in Arizona and remained on another reservation with a man she met there. Later, the mother had also gotten free and gone with another man. Who actually fathered Better-To-See-You was moot. Subsequently, her mother had become homesick and written to her brother, who went to get her and her children. The "wild" Chiricahua was probably killed by white men after he murdered their companion when he was caught stealing their provisions. When they returned to the reservation, the family included a baby boy who subsequently died. We can assume that the infant was treated by the mother as her favorite. The maternal uncle had not reared Better-To-See-You after she was left with him by her mother. Nevertheless, she often visited her uncle, who always treated her with consideration. He informally adopted her. During her childhood, Better-To-See-You had always been jealous of and hostile toward little boys. There can be no doubt that she had heard all of the data presented above at various times during her life, but her need for a different past had caused her to either deny or repress information contrary to her personal myth, which had become for her a historical reality. Her belief that her uncle reared her required repression of the fact that she had been shifted from family to family.

During the course of her life, Better-To-See-You had sought one father after another; she had hoped that each would perform both fathering and mothering functions. She had been left by two husbands who found her dependency and jealousy intolerable.

It is common among these Indians for a person who "knows" a ceremony to impart it to one of his or her offspring. Better-To-See-You deemed her children to be too immoral and unstable to be shamans, and none had a power dream. She had begun to teach her ceremonies to Peter, through the means of storytelling, but he, too, had had no power dream. Her desire to transmit her knowledge to me was motivated in part by her regarding me as a son to teach. She was one of the shamans who wanted me to accept the new position of chief Apache shaman, in order to have me serve as a good, strict, omniscient father "for all future generations of Apache children." During the early weeks of her therapy, she asked me to learn all the songs of the puberty ceremony (Bourke 1890, R. M. Boyer 1962, Opler 1941), in order that I would be able to serve as the singer for a grandniece during her ceremony, which was planned for nine years thence.

Soon after she asked me to become an Apache, rather than just a white shaman, and to sing for her grandniece, she related the folktale. Her actual rendition involved much redundancy. An abridged recounting follows:

Long ago, two Mescalero guys went to Mexico to hunt buffalo. One night at a lakeside, Grasshopper-Boy ate a *big* egg and turned into a *big* black snake. His partner had warned him not to eat that egg without first performing necessary rites, because it might be (supernaturally) dangerous. The other guy returned to White Mountain and told Grasshopper-Boy's relatives what had happened, but they thought he had murdered his partner. So he took the brother of Grasshopper-Boy down there. The Snake-Man told his brother what had happened.

Some years later the brother of Grasshopper-Boy went to see him again. As he hunted deer, the brother heard a shot. Two Comanches had killed the Water-Monster, so the brother returned home and they all "forgot" about Grasshopper-Boy.

Later some Blackfoot Indians went to Mexico. They found the snake bones and used them for poison for their arrowheads. They went north and attacked a camp of Mescaleros near White Mountain.

Three men, some ladies, and some children got away. They were hurt and poisoned by the bone powder of the snake, but they went to a shaman who made medicine and saved them. Two of his daughters had been kidnapped; the man who got well found and recovered the girls while the Blackfoot Indians were feasting and drinking *tiswin* [a weak beer].

For Better-To-See-You, the telling of the story was at least preconsciously associated with her wish to educate me, and its content was not perceived by her to have any relationship to her life or intrapsychic conflicts. Her mood was largely euphoric, reminding me of a hypomanic reaction; the psychology of such reactions includes denial as a predominant defense (Lewin 1950).

Soon after Better-To-See-You had related the story, she began to talk about the half-brother who had been shot. Her envy of him and particularly his penis was starkly evident, and it was clear that she had had transiently conscious wishes for his death before he was killed. She said another man had shot him because of envy, although the facts were that he was murdered in the course of being robbed of recently acquired money. During the period when she was talking of her half-brother, she was anxious. In fact, she had had little contact with her half-brother, but she was clearly jealous of his having been his mother's apparent favorite. Her ill will toward her sisters and half-sisters who lived with Better-To-See-You's mother and her hostility toward her mother were successfully denied through two rationalizations: (1) her uncle was so fond of her that he would not let her go with her mother; and (2) her mother's new husband was poor and could not afford to take care of so many children. Then she transiently remembered that her younger brother had accompanied the family on their trek to the reservation. It was obvious that she had replaced her jealousy of him by the envy she ascribed to the murderer of the half-brother. In her interviews with me, Better-To-See-You spoke English. It was clear that her use of English often involved direct translation from Apache. The Apaches have but one word for envy and jealousy.

We should remember that the family returned to the reservation when Better-To-See-You was 3 or 4, when we would expect her to have been especially concerned with penis envy and castration anxiety.

It will be noted that her variation of the folktale contains two major additions to the usual version, that involving the Snake-Man's having been shot by Comanches and the sequel which involved the Blackfoot Indians and the shaman. No other informant mentioned either group of Indians in his or her narration. For historical and other reasons which will be omitted here, we must assume that she included the Comanches and the Blackfoot Indians for idiosyncratic reasons.

Although my hypothesis is based on inferential information and not from direct associations to the Comanches and the Blackfoot Indians by Better-To-See-You, I believe she included the former group as substitutes for the white men who shot her father and the Apache who slew her half-brother, and the latter because their name includes black, the color of the snake and the alleged charred bones of her father. As will be seen later, Peter called the latter group "those black-footed Indians."

When we examine Better-To-See-You's presentation, we also find a number of variations of the type Opler designated as fortuitous. Thus, as an example, it was a brother of the man who was turned into the water snake who accompanied the hunting partner to the site of the transformation. For reasons which will be amplified below in the discussion of Peter's version, I believe Better-To-See-You and the others who included a brother in the manifest content of the legend thus exhibited repressed sibling rivalry, discharged safely through the protection of the folktale. Suffice it to say at this point that Grasshopper-Boy was killed in the manifest legend not by fratricide but by tribal enemies. We shall see that Peter conceived of the hunting partners as brothers from the beginning. He was in actual life closer to active sibling rivalry than were the adult informants, and his resultant conflicts were more nearly conscious. It is entirely consistent with the socialization data and considerable information from the case study of Better-To-See-You, omitted here for the sake of brevity, to assume that the original hunting partner was indeed in her mind a sibling surrogate of Grasshopper-Boy. We recall that both her half-brother and her father were shot and that many young Apache children view their fathers in part as rivals for maternal attention.

Factual historical data are sometimes included in legends and even folktales. We do not know to what historical period the tale was ascribed by the informants. Some said "long ago," but the majority dated the occurrence to the middle or latter portion of the 19th century. During that period, not only the Comanches but also the Blackfoot Indians and the Apaches had guns. However, the Comanches had acquired guns much earlier than either of the other two groups, from the French (Clark 1966)—a bit of information which may have been learned at some time by Better-To-See-You and then "forgotten." She dated the time of the event to "before the days of the reservation." Can we not assume that her giving the guns only to the Comanches and her choice of having the Snake-Man killed by gunshot stem from insecurely repressed sibling rivalry?

The Blackfoot Indians found the bones of the dead Water-Monster and used them for witchcraft purposes, which were subsequently neutralized or overpowered by the workings of the Mescalero shaman. Why did she not have the Blackfoot Indians appear sooner after the demise of the Snake-Man and use some other part of his corpse for witchcraft purposes? Let us remember that in her personal myth her own father was burned so that only his bones remained; her mother scattered those bones so that they would not be found and used for witchcraft. We believe these data give credence to the supposition that Better-To-See-You equated the buffalo-hunting Grasshopper-Boy with her notorious buffalo-hunting father. Her legend version was the only one in which the companions were hunting bison. Her father was a "wild man"; wild men were always thought to possess supernatural power which they used for evil purposes. Again, during prereservation days, most if not all Apaches were thought to possess powers, or at least ceremonies which might themselves carry power.

She never explained why she called the protagonist of the legend "Grasshopper-Boy," but her interview associations indicated that she chose that name because her father was one who "jumped" from place to place.

Better-To-See-You went through life seeking a replacement for her dead father. Why then should she equate a dead shaman with her father, since we would expect her to restore her father and rejoin him in her legend version? She was "adopted" by a much loved uncle after her return to the reservation. She grieved greatly at his death, which occurred in her adulthood, and during a long period of her interviews she spoke of him in such terms that it was clear that her cherished uncle, the first father surrogate, still lived in her mind. She married and lost two husbands whom she had striven to make into father replacements. In the folktale Blackfoot raids, three Mescalero men got away. Can we not assume that her choice of the number three refers to those three men? This is partly conjectural, but soon after she related the legend she introduced the subject of her dissatisfaction with her third husband, whom she partly wished to be dead, and her relative satisfaction with her uncle and two previous husbands. Perhaps in her individual legend variation she thus restored the three loved-and-lost former father surrogates.

The return of the mother and daughters to the reservation after the death of her father was, in her personal myth, due to the workings of a shaman. In the folktale as she presented it, it was a shaman who saved the three men (as well as others). However, we then find a curious statement, namely, that two daughters of the shaman himself had been kidnapped and found through his employment of supernatural powers. In fact, one of the conditions of his practicing shamanism for the poisoned camp members was that the men promise to return his daughters to him. The mother and maternal aunt of Better-To-See-You were kidnapped. In a sense, Better-To-See-You and her sister were too, since their proper place was with the Mescaleros. This would seem to form an unmistakable link between Better-To-See-You's account of the legend and her personal myth. If so, we have then the undoing of the death of Grasshopper-Boy, who became a shaman and, in her mind, her father. At the end of the legend, she, as one of the recovered daughters, was reunited with her father.

The Folktale According to Peter

The following is a verbatim account of Peter's rendition of the folktale, omitting only repetitions:

Two guys went to a pond. One of them ate an egg and turned into a big black snake. The other guy went home. Ten years later two brothers went hunting buffalo. One of them went off and got killed. The other was scared he'd done something that had killed his brother. He went to a medicine man to learn how his brother had died. The medicine man told him to carry an eagle's stomach filled with water so he'd never be thirsty and so his brother's ghost wouldn't kill him. He said the boy's father had been killed by a mountain lion. He went home.

Two other guys went out hunting. They came to that pond. The snake talked to them and scared them. One of them dropped that stomach full of water. Then the snake told him, "You are my boy."

Two Comanches killed that snake. Ten years later, those black-footed Indians found the bones and made poison of them. There were only three men and one woman left after they raided the Mescaleros. They went to a medicine man and he told them the whole story. He made medicine and those men got well and got his two sons while those black-footed Indians were feasting.

Having been abandoned by their parents over a year previously, Peter, 13, and his two brothers, aged 2 and 4, lived with their maternal great-aunt. During his first interview Peter had falsified grossly his past and present lives. He said his parents lived happily together in a nearby town where they lovingly cared for him and his brothers. According to his story, he lived alone with his great-aunt during the school year and idyllically spent summers with his parents and brothers. He said his parents had given him a bicycle, factually nonexistent, identical to one owned by my son.

During the first seven interviews, three themes emerged: (1) his longing and seeking for a powerful and nurturant father; (2) his rivalry with his brothers for their great-aunt's attention; and (3) his ambivalent rejection of his mother. One manifestation of his competition with his brothers for the great-aunt's favoritism was his attempt to have a "power dream," which would qualify him to become a shaman.

In the eighth interview he expressed the desire to be adopted by white parents who had a son of his age and to move with them to California, where he knew my family has our regular home. He also related a hypnogogic experience, dating it to a year earlier when he had thought his father dead. In it, he had seen the ghost of an Indian man and feared the ghost would kidnap him in a bag made of bed sheets. When I questioned a maternal aunt as to whether she had known of his "dreams,"she said she had, but he had not mentioned the bag made of bed sheets. In the ninth interview he presented a recent frightening hypnopompic experience in which the ghost of an Indian commanded him to jump rope, an activity which was being learned by his 4-year-old brother. Then he related the legend.

As mentioned, Peter longed for a father and competed with his brothers for their great-aunt's attention. The "dream" of the man with the bed sheet was recognized by him to be a veiled wish to be taken away by his father. The intimacy of the desired relationship is indicated by the presence of bed linen. Sheets were not used in Peter's family at that time, but he knew them to be used by mine. The second "dream" is more obscure. Peter wanted a strong father who would support his attempts to be a good boy. He knew me to be relatively strict with my son. One of Peter's brothers adored me and his affection was returned. Perhaps the rope-jumping represented a desire to regress and compete on the level of that younger brother, in addition to a wish to be made to behave well. The first interpretation is the product of Peter's associations, but the second is conjectural.

Peter's distortions of the legend from the version presented to him by Better-To-See-You reflect the same intrapsychic conflicts as had emerged during the first seven interviews. In her version, the theme of finding the lost father appeared only in the latent content, and that of hostility toward the mother was absent. In the manifest content, there was a hint of sibling rivalry. Grasshopper-Boy's brother accused the companion of murder but then abandoned and "forgot" Grasshopper-Boy. Let us examine Peter's version. There, the cardinal psychological theme of the manifest content is the finding of the lost father. In addition, there is obvious sibling rivalry. A hunter is killed and his brother accuses himself of murder, that is, reveals his guilty wish that his brother be dead. However, the ego defense mechanism of undoing finds expression in Peter's having an externalized superego figure, the shaman, absolve the guilty brother of the murder by stating that the death resulted from the actions of a puma. We shall return to this detail later. A second example of the need to undo the unconscious wish to murder the rival follows.

In the manifest content of Peter's rendition, a second set of brothers goes hunting. However, the presence of the eagle's stomach identifies them as being the first pair. Thus, the murdered brother has been revivified. The wish that the sibling had been eliminated is fulfilled, however, because the snake-father then claims only one son as his own. We find further that men, women, and children survived the massacre. In Peter's story no children live, since he first says there are only three men and one woman left alive. At a later time he reverses the implicit denial of living children by stating that two boys survive. As we remember, Peter has two younger brothers. There is but a hint of distortion, which coincides with his ambivalent rejection of his mother. First he reduces the number of surviving women to one; then he says, "He made medicine and those men got well." The one woman who was left is thus eliminated.

Peter's variant production of the tale related to him by his great-aunt presents a thinly veiled confession of and resolution of some of his personal conflicts. It was clear he wished to be the son who lived and refound his father. Let us examine one facet in some detail. The shaman who absolved one brother of the murder of his rival can be equated with the father, because the Snake-Man who said "you are my son" had become a shaman, a personage who lived partially in the spirit world and had supernatural powers he could use volitionally for good or evil purposes. The shaman avowed that the mountain lion had killed the unwanted brother. Every Apache with whom we spoke about pumas, including Peter, preconsciously equated those cultural bogeys with women, presumably dangerous mother surrogates to whom oral aggression had been projected.

Peter's use of the puma as the murderer, then, can be understood to be a distorted way of saying that a neglectful, greedy woman, surely reminiscent of his own mother, had slain his sibling. It seems more than fortuitous that he chose to have a carnivore kill his rivals. Cougars kill by biting and clawing. The individual who has not yet resolved his oral-dependent conflicts is wont to dream of removal of his enemies by oral-aggressive means. In the unconscious thinking of all patients with whom I have dealt, whether white, yellow, black, or brown of skin, teeth and nails or claws are equated. In Peter's version the father was a shaman. It is probably relevant that I was regularly accorded the position of shaman.

Discussion

It will be noted that the interpretation offered for the legend version presented by Better-To-See-You is less completely convincing than that for Peter's. I believe this can be explained on the basis of the great-aunt's having been older and having had much more time to defend herself against the psychological problems which have been demonstrated to have motivated portions of her legend variation, and to use the products of conflict solution for adaptive purposes. Peter was still in the regressive period of his puberty, and stimuli continued to activate conflicts against which his defenses were less adequate. Thus the evidences of his unsolved conflicts were more apparent, because less successfully distorted.

Two major problem complexes resulting from child-rearing practices of the Apaches are those produced by the psychologically unsatisfying father and insecurely repressed sibling rivalry. These problems were reflected in the legend variations that were produced by the informants who had the opportunity to provide easily validatable free associations. Additionally, there were demonstrated some of the manners in which the legend served as a self- and societal-protective device, which enabled individuals to discharge strivings which had been suppressed or repressed and thus to live with unconscious or preconscious conflicts without feeling overwhelming anxiety and guilt.

The unconscious fantasy life and wishes demonstrated in the legend which has been presented here are common in the mental life of children who have been displaced early in life by younger siblings. A few examples will suffice:

1. It can be no coincidence that the egg was associated with water, a constant female symbol in dreams. Various Apaches revealed a wish to kill unborn rival siblings. The symbolic unborn younger child was killed by being eaten, by the use of teeth, the first effective means by which the young child can inflict actual harm.
2. The wish to reenter the mother and thereby be in close contact with her in a state of symbiosis is represented by the disappearance of the snake into the water. I do not wish to minimize the obvious fact that the snake is a phallic symbol. Our clinical data make clear that these Indians use their so-called "genital sexuality" in large part to resolve oral problems.
3. The fear of retaliation, which in our culture is reflected frequently as the main determinant of cancer phobia, is represented in the folktale by the fear of ghosts, witches, and the snake.
4. The fear of being poisoned by the remnant of the destroying sibling is a logical corollary of (3).

Epilogue

The psychotherapeutic interviews of Better-To-See-You and Peter resulted in a sharp reduction of their intrapsychic conflicts pertaining to the dominant problems which were expressed in their legend recitations. It is probable that this was due in part to the stories' being brought into the treatment situation and analyzed as though they had been dreams. Is is of interest that when Better-To-See-You first introduced the legend, I was confused for the better part of an interview as to whether she were relating a dream.

Better-To-See-You was able to decathect to some degree her search for a father. She was able to extricate herself from a most unsatisfactory marriage to which she had previously clung because of her desperate quest for a loving and supporting father. No doubt her actively divorcing her husband helped her repress her hostility toward me for deserting her and contributed to her ability to partially resolve her split transference relationship with me and develop an abiding friendship.

Additionally, sibling rivalry with other shamans lost its intensity. She was able to face her decreasing shamanistic status with more equanimity and to give up the active practice of shamanism, coming to restrict her activities to those of practicing herbalism with little implication of the involvement of supernatural power. She continued to utter appropriate incantations when administering everyday native medicines but could acknowledge that they were merely necessary form statements. She continued to be in demand as a chaperone at the girls' puberty ceremony but now considered herself simply an educator who gave instructions to the debutantes as to how to live a good and useful life.

Peter's quest for a father lost its urgency and he was able to become more self-dependent, apparently as a result of his internalization of qualities and attitudes he observed to exist in me and others, more idealized, which he had projected onto me. The intensity of his sibling rivalry was sharply reduced and he renounced his ambivalent attachment toward his mother, who had deserted her children. Twenty-one years later he remains one of the few young men of his generation who has never been jailed and has not become a drunkard. He works steadily and consistently looks after his needy relatives. His transference relationship with me has also resolved itself into a continuing friendship.

14

Understanding the Patient through Folklore

Transcultural psychiatric research has sought to determine the influence of social structure and socialization practices on the etiology and symptomatology of personality disorders and to establish general principles which might assist psychotherapists in their efforts to better understand and more successfully treat people from divergent sociocultural backgrounds. Such research has become worldwide in its scope and its latest efforts can be assessed from perusal of *Transcultural Psychiatric Research Review*. Recent unpublished studies of the psychological illnesses of immigrants into the United States of members of lower socioeconomic groups have indicated that their form and dynamics can best be understood in terms of the folklore of their native lands. Thus, a common psychopathological constellation found in Philadelphia among Italians is clearly a derivative of the *malocchio* (evil eye) beliefs and a condition found among Puerto Ricans stems from the *ataqué* syndrome (D.M.A. Freeman, personal communication 1976).

During the past 30-odd years, increasing attention has been paid to the sociopsychological problems of North American Indians. In the course of this research, it has become obvious that those who seek individuals of non-European derivation to do research with must undergo training (1) that will rid them of ethnocentric prejudices which lead inevitably to countertransferential problems (Boyer 1964c); and (2) that they must acquaint themselves with the specific bases which determine their patients' culturally bound modes of communication. Various

Ruth M. Boyer was the coauthor of this chapter.

studies have been devoted to demonstrating the utility of learning about native folklore elements, such as traditional oral literature and ceremonies, in an effort to understand their influence on communication styles used by Indian patients (Boyer et al. 1974, R. M. Boyer and Boyer 1977, Devereux 1951, L. B. Johnson and Proskauer 1947).

This chapter presents a fortuitous clinical vignette which would have been quite incomprehensible to a clinician who was not deeply cognizant of the folklore bases of a patient's efforts to make herself understood.

Case Material

She-Who-Uses-A-Cane was an elderly Mescalero Apache woman who had long suffered from diabetes but had eschewed standard medical care because of her retention of the old-time religiomedical orientation of her people that all illnesses result from hostile actions of affronted supernatural "powers," witches, or ghosts and the conviction that shamanistic intervention was necessary for the removal of physical and psychological ailments (Boyer 1964b). Almost totally blind and afflicted with chronic degenerative osteoarthritis, she had fallen a few months previously and sustained an abrasion to her left foot, for which she refused to follow the medical instructions of local Indian Health Service physicians.

She-Who-Uses-A-Cane had formerly been accorded the status of shaman and had practiced shamanism successfully until she had begun to drink heavily. Her imbibing to excess resulted from a series of factors the relative importance of which cannot be weighed. One factor was the disappointment she experienced when she sought shamanistic cures for her diabetes, osteoarthritis, and slowly developing cataracts, first from local native practitioners and then from renowned Indian faith healers from other tribes. In 1968 she had begun to consider seeking help of the white faith healer Oral Roberts. In 1973, she had become convinced that he could cure her without her actually going to see him. She reasoned that since witches could cause illness by shooting invisible "witches' arrows" from great distances, he could treat her by correspondence and accordingly sent him money to cure her from afar. His written blessings had proved ineffective but her faith remained undiminished.

The abrasion on her foot became infected and gangrene developed. Although she was warned by local hospital physicians that she should receive immediate attention, she went alone, without an appointment and against all advice, from New Mexico to Oklahoma, for treatment by Oral Roberts. She did not see him. She returned home and her leg was amputated at the knee. After some months, it was possible to fit her with a prosthesis.

The senior author of this chapter is a psychoanalyst and the junior, a cultural anthropologist. Since 1957, we have been engaged with other anthropologists and psychologists in a study of the interactions of social structure, puericultural practices, and personality development among the erstwhile hunting, gathering, and raiding Apaches of the Mescalero Indian Reservation in south central New Mexico. We lived on the reservation with other members of the investigating teams for a period of over 14 months in 1959 and 1960. A principal aspect of my research method was to engage in psychiatric practice, using psychoanalytically oriented investigative interviews.

She-Who-Uses-A-Cane was one of my informants for many months, being seen vis à vis four times weekly in sessions of an hour each. She volunteered to be an informant because she was curious and knew that research subjects were paid modestly for their time. She quickly became a regular patient, although she never clearly identified verbally what therapeutic goals she had in mind. Soon she developed a strong, complex transference relationship in which I was simultaneously envisioned as a son being trained by her in shamanistic practices and as an idealized father surrogate. During one period she related a folktale as though it were a dream. Her rendition of the story titled "The Man Who Turned into a Water-Monster" (Boyer 1975) constituted the first time that tale had been recorded as being a part of the folklore stock of any Apachean group except that of the Jicarillas (Mooney 1898). (See Chapter 13.)

A synthesis of the story as known to a few old Mescalero and Chiricahua Apaches of the reservation follows:

Two brothers were hunting deep in Mexico. They had been unfortunate and were starving. They came to the shore of a lake and found a huge egg which they knew to be the mundane representative of a supernatural power and that they would have to perform a small ritual, requesting permission to use it for food, in order to avoid the revenge of the power. The younger brother rashly cooked and ate the egg without having first performed the obeisance. The next morning, he had turned into a huge snake, become a fearsome denizen of the underwater world. He instructed his brother to return to their homeland and tell their relatives what had happened. However, the family assumed that fratricide had occurred and traveled to the lakeside to check their suspicion.

There they found the "tracks" of the Snake-Man, absolved the brother of guilt, returned home and "forgot" their deceased relative.

In traditional Apachean thinking, to remember a dead person, to speak or even think his name, will call his ghost. The shade, either because it is lonely or wishes to avenge itself for past factual or fancied wrongs, is apt to make a living individual extremely ill or to drive him insane, causing him to either commit suicide or behave foolishly so that he gets killed. The condition of the person so-afflicted is known as "ghost sickness."

The main psychological purpose served by the typical version of "The Man Who Turned into a Water-Monster" is to support individual efforts to deal with unresolved problems related to sibling rivalry. The tale is widespread among North and Central American Indian tribes. The idiosyncratic version presented by She-Who-Uses-A-Cane, to be presented below, was found to reflect most of her manifold psychological problems and to serve defensive purposes which helped her to allay anxiety and guilt pertaining to them (Boyer 1964a, Boyer and Boyer 1968–1971).

When we learned of She-Who-Uses-A-Cane's recent amputation, we decided to determine whether another rendition of the same tale, obtained 17 years after the first, might include new elements which would reflect her current concerns and her efforts to cope with them (cf. Eggan 1955). On arriving at the reservation, we found her to be a patient in the Bureau of Indian Affairs Hospital in Mescalero, learning to use her prosthesis. Members of the staff said she had at times been disoriented as to time and place during the night and that she had then talked in Apache, which none of them understood, to apparently hallucinated individuals. She was in a private room and received no external stimuli but for occasional noises in the hallway. No confusion had been observed during the daytime. She was receiving no medications.

As will be seen in the following vignette, during our conversation She-Who-Uses-A-Cane became quickly regressed. In her everyday life, she was almost constantly with relatives and small children and in complete contact with reality. When her kin were briefly absent, at times she lapsed into altered ego states during which her fantasies served to defend her against loneliness, feelings of helplessness, and various fears. During the 17 years of our contacts with her, the complex transference relationship of her treatment months had continued unabated, although we had also an abiding, deep friendship. She had come to view Dr. Ruth Boyer as predominantly a good mother surrogate. We had been with her dozens of times over the years and during each visit, she had communicated with us as though we were factual relatives who were totally aware of Apache history and lore.

After we greeted her and were warmly welcomed, I said we had learned that she had gone to see Oral Roberts. She responded:

He called me over there seven and a half years ago and when I went, he and his wife were together and she was a nice-looking lady but they didn't do anything for me. I didn't know anything until now but now I know everything.

She turned immediately to speaking of her present difficulties:

That C. H. [a female to whom she was distantly related through her father] came to my house. I was in my kitchen, cooking good food: pancakes, hamburgers, onions. My granddaughter had gone to a movie at the center. She hadn't wanted to go. I fell down and I couldn't get up. I was lying alone on the kitchen floor. Then John [C. H.'s son] came and put his face right against mine. It was all white. [She touched her cheek with the palm of her hand.] I don't know why he done that. I don't know if he was alive or dead.

She asked us:

Is he dead?

and continued,

I don't know why he done that because I never harmed anyone, never killed anyone.

At this point, she became preoccupied with trying to get us to take her to her house, to show us exactly what had happened. She complained that her granddaughter was to have come to take her home several hours earlier but had not done so.

I asked her then if she remembered the story of the two men who went to Mexico and found the egg. She nodded agreement and said the story had been told to her by Old Lady W.

Old Man W. had two daughters, no, two wives. The ladies had trouble between them and they left him. Each lady fell in love with someone else and they went away.

Without transition she referred to her own life story, which will be presented later.

My mother came back from over there with my father. Poor thing. She brought back four people with her: a boy, Alfie; a girl, S.; me; and another girl I can't remember.

Without pause she went on:

When I was in school I had a dream of two men, God and Jesus. I was just sick. I was over there in the house by the underpass. There was no roofing. The sun was bright. It was about this big.

As she spoke, she first made a circle about 7½ inches in diameter and then moved her fingers rhythmically, indicating that the image was pulsating.

Then it got all cold and dark and then the sun came back. I felt myself all covered with ashes. It was all bright.

I asked whether she was referring to the ashes when her mother burned her father's bones. She agreed. Then, referring again to John, she asked:

Did he die? I was lying in the ashes in the black coals. There was no roofing. The sun came up. Morning was the color of [red] clouds. Soon I saw the sun clearly. The father of Jesus.

Again without temporal discontinuity she went on:

I dreamed I was on top of East Mountain in *this* bed [pointing to the hospital bed]. Two boys was talking. Then both of them fell on the ground and this bed was right there. I was in bed with the two boys. The sun was bright, right on top of East Mountain, talking to me. "Hi, hi," he said. He was laughing. He said, "You are going to be all right. You are going to get well and live a long time." I was dreaming. I woke up. The sun was [she made the pulsating movements with her fingers] and laughing. It was a dream I had a long time ago. I was 6 or 7 years old. I'm all right. I told you, "You are going to live." I was in school. Through all the clothes, steps, smothered me to death. East Mountain, on top. Someone calling me, Oral Roberts calling me. He said, "Get up!" Does she remember me? I was in the hospital. I dreamed that way. Roberts brought me the book and I was just reading it.

Again without pause she said:

There was two bees. Sunflowers. Bees, red and yellow. You know their name?

I asked if she meant bumblebees, since the only bees on the reservation which have red on them are bumblebees. She shook her head no.

They was fighting.

I asked if they had brought her (supernatural) power. She nodded yes.

I was really unhappy. I was going down. My uncle came. He took me outside. The bees were fighting real hard for me. They came and brought me sweet stuff like candy, honey. They put the honey in the palm of my (left) hand where they were fighting. They were eating meat.

I asked her to describe the bees again; she made it clear they were now wasps, biting little pieces of flesh from her palm.

They foretold I would spend half of my life in bed. I was just praying and praying. Then I got sick again. S. P. was married to my mother. Then it was the same thing again. The butterflies were fighting. They were big yellow butterflies, with black on the edges, beautiful, yellow. One bee was dead. One buttterfly, he flew away, safe, and didn't get hurt. The other one was killed. The butterfly came from the east. Yellow is for happiness.

She spent some time repeating this material in various ways, making it clear that one bee killed the other while fighting "over" or "for" her and that one butterfly did the same to the other. Although the interview was being recorded in shorthand, she mumbled now and spoke so softly and rapidly that we do not have a verbatim account for a period. However, our understanding of what she said was that she had been raped by two boys on East Mountain while she was a girl and had had a nightmare recollection of the experience the previous night, while in the hospital. Then she spoke more clearly again.

The school children all got sick. The girls got in fights. There was no hospital. Influenza. Just go off and die. We went to see God. Lots of things happen I dream about. I got a vision that came to me. My uncle L. A. came to me on a porch. He sat with me. It's about the beehive.

I, recognizing that we had just heard what was undoubtedly a "power dream," the birth of the acquisition of supernatural power, inquired of her how she had used the bee power after she accepted it. Rather disgustedly, she replied:

I told you before [a factually false statement]. I know lots of things, but I hold myself back. I could become . . . I saw a picture of me. I am not dead, but I have no head.

I asked if her ownership of bee power enabled her to put herself and others back together when they were in parts. She nodded yes. Then she hummed briefly, as though she were a bee, and said:

The beehive is really good but the butterfly is really bigger and more beautiful than the wasp.

She differentiated between bees and wasps, saying bees brought honey and wasps eat raw meat. Then she said the bee was trying to kill the butterfly.

But she got away.

At this point, she became acutely uncomfortable and would not continue to talk about bee power and its acquisition nor did she refer again to "The Man Who Turned into a Water-Monster." She sought again to have us take her home. We informed her we were not permitted to do that, after having been forbidden to do so by a nurse in her presence. As we said goodbye, she looked frightened and said:

Not goodbye.

She rubbed the black sleeves of Dr. Ruth Boyer's blouse, now noticing its color for the first time. Startled, she asked:

Why did you wear that? You go home and wash it white.

As we left, she asked again why John had touched her cheek with his white face.

Discussion

Supernatural Power

The basic concept of Apache religion is that diffuse power floods the universe and renders even ostensibly inanimate objects potentially animate. The virtue of this power is its potency and it is intrinsically neither good nor evil. To become effective, it must "work through" humankind, and it uses familiar animals, plants, natural forces, and inanimate objects to initiate such contact. When contact has been made during some type of ordeal or altered ego state in the form of a power dream which may occur during sleep or hallucinatorily, the power appears in a personified guise and offers a ceremony or supernatural power to the person approached. If the latter chooses to accept the responsibilities of power possession, he may then elect to use his power either for good or evil purposes.

The possession of supernatural power enables the owner to perform beneficent shamanistic functions, to counteract affronted powers, witches, or ghosts in his efforts to cure individuals of their illnesses. However, the shaman often views himself and is viewed by others also as a fearsome or evil person, a witch. An affronted supernatural power remains vengeful and the shaman's actions serve solely to deflect its hostility from the particular individual who is being treated; someone must still die. Ordinarily, the person who must die is the shaman himself or someone who is dear to him, often a relative.

Although some Apaches hold that all powers have equal potency, whether they take the form, for example, of sun, star, lightning, or other celestial phenomena, or any of the fauna or flora, others hold that lightning and snake power are more potent than others. To our knowledge, no Apache had ever been said to have possessed bee power, and its possible functions had never been mentioned.

Theoretically, the possession of any supernatural power endows a shaman with the ability to cure all illnesses, whether they are assumed to have resulted from the actions of affronted powers, witches, or ghosts. The possession of some powers makes the shaman especially likely to be able to heal specific conditions. Thus, the person who possesses bear power is particularly fit to cure "bear sickness," and he who owns snake or lightning power is sought after for the treatment of "snake sickness" (Boyer 1964b). The only power She-Who-Uses-A-Cane ever claimed to own or was accredited with possessing was that of the butterfly. Butterfly power is unique in that it can be used to make someone "love sick," that is, irresistably attracted to the sexual advances of the person who hires the shaman who possesses it. She-Who-Uses-A-Cane had formerly been employed to use it for that purpose but she had also used her butterfly power in the treatment of various illnesses, predominantly "ghost sickness" and various gastrointestinal disorders. When she treated the latter, she not only made incantations invoking the intervention of her power, but administered native medicinal herbs as well.

Personal History

In 1959, She-Who-Uses-A-Cane related the following:

Her father, a wild, violent Chiricahua Apache buffalo hunter, had kidnapped her Mescalero mother as a young teenager and wandered with her and their ensuing children, hunting, plundering, and murdering. He remained in areas remote from the reservation since, as a "wild man," a cultural bogey, he was thought to be a cannibal and were he to be seen by a reservation member, he would be subject to execution. When She-Who-Uses-A-Cane was 3 or 4 years old, he had been slain by whites who were avenging his having murdered one of their companions. His widow had burned his body to a mass of charred black bones and scattered them, lest they be found and used as poison on "witches' arrows." Despite great hardship, the widowed mother and her three daughters were able to return to the reservation, through the aegis of a shaman who had been hired by a relative, She-Who-Uses-A-Cane's uncle, L. A. When She-Who-Uses-A-Cane was an adult, a younger half brother was killed by a gunshot by someone who was envious of him.

Information obtained subsequently from more objective informants gave a significantly modified picture. The "wild man" had kidnapped not only the mother of She-Who-Uses-A-Cane but her sister as well. The sisters got along badly with their captor-husband and both left him for other men. When the mother of She-Who-Uses-A-Cane left her second husband and returned to the reservation, she brought not only three small daughters but also a son, who died in early childhood. That brother's name was John, although during the vignette She-Who-Uses-A-Cane had miscalled him Alfie.

When the mother returned to the reservation, she lived with her brother, "my uncle L. A.," for some unknown period before remarrying and taking all of her children but She-Who-Uses-A-Cane with her. Although the little girl continued to call L. A. her uncle, she thought of him as her father. After a few years, he too deserted her, placing her in the care of another family.

She-Who-Uses-A-Cane sought one father surrogate after another throughout her life. One (unspoken) reason she had sought therapy was that her latest husband had tired of her expecting him to be her eternally giving father and was leaving her; she was fearful and lonely.

At the time in her treatment when she introduced the story, she was dealing simultaneously with several problems: very strong sibling rivalry with the brother who was murdered, the wish to acquire a penis, intense dependent wishes directed toward idealized father surrogates, and a new awareness of intense hostility toward her mother, whom she had viewed formerly solely as a victim of circumstance, a "poor thing." The timing and method of recitation of the tale was reminiscent of the relation of a dream by a patient in psychoanalysis. The following presentation is a faithful abstract of a recounting which occupied two full hours. For a detailed analysis of its content and defensive uses, the reader is referred to Chapter 13. For our present purposes, it suffices to state that all of the problems mentioned above were expressed and defended against by her version of the story with its idiosyncratic modifications.

She-Who-Uses-A-Cane's Idiosyncratic Version of "The Man Who Turned into a Water-Monster"

Long ago two guys went to Mexico to hunt buffalo. One night at a lakeside, Grasshopper-Boy ate a big egg and turned into a *big* black snake, maybe thirty feet long and a foot and a half thick. His partner had warned him not to eat the egg without praying first, because it might be dangerous. The other guy returned to White Mountain (the imposing 12,000-foot peak on the reservation which is the central landmark of the Mescalero homeland) and told Grasshopper-Boy's relatives what had happened, as he had been told to do, but they thought he had murdered his partner. So he took the brother of Grasshopper-Boy down there. The Snake-Man told his brother what had happened. Some years later the brother of Grasshopper-Boy went to see him again. As he hunted deer, he heard a shot. Two Comanches had killed that Water-Monster, so the brother returned home and forgot all about Grasshopper-Boy.

Later, some Blackfoot Indians went to Mexico. They found the snake bones and used them as poison for their arrowheads. They went north and attacked a camp of Mescaleros. Three men, some ladies, and some children got away. They were hurt and poisoned by the bone powder of the snake, but they went to a shaman who made medicine and saved them. Two of his daughters had been kidnapped; the man who got well found and recovered the girls while the Blackfoot Indians were feasting and drinking *tiswin* [the corn beer of the Apaches].

Analysis of the Clinical Vignette

After I said we had heard she went to see Oral Roberts, She-Who-Uses-A-Cane replied he had called her to see him some seven years previously. It was then that she first began to think about seeking him out as her faith healer. It is unlikely she expected that her message would be taken literally. It is frequent for a prospective client of a shaman to state that he has had a vision in which the shaman called to him to apply for succor, although such actual visionary claims are almost always fictional and recognized as such. Some seven years previously she had dreamed that we had called to her to visit us and when we went to see her some months later, said the dream had forecast our coming to see her and that she had hoped that I would cure her of her various ills in the shamanistic role which was generally ascribed to me. Her disappointment and only partially hidden anger because no cure had occurred appears to have persisted and to have been expressed in her statement, "I didn't know anything until now, but now I know everything." In point of actual fact, the year before, she had prepared a dinner for us without letting us know she expected us and knew that we had spent our time that day with a sister surrogate whom she hated. She-Who-Uses-A-Cane had pouted like a neglected child despite our apology. Such manifest evidence of her ambivalent feelings toward us was not new even then. She had previously had us to "lunch," taking great pains to cook "good food," and had come to demand that we visit her *first* when on the reservation. When we did not do so, she sometimes whiningly complained and on occasion, she had temporarily refused to visit with us when we did call on her.

After she said, "Now I know everything," she spoke about a distant female relative toward whom she felt intense ambivalence. C. H. had been her expected guest when she was cooking the "good food," but had not appeared. Had she done so, C. H. could have looked after She-Who-Uses-A-Cane who could not get up from the floor when she fell, being too drunk. Just as we had neither cured her nor prevented her developing further blindness and arthritis and had failed to come for the meal she had prepared, so too C. H. had failed her.

John, C. H.'s son, was alive and healthy although She-Who-Uses-A-Cane repeatedly expressed fear that he was a ghost. John was also the name of the little brother who had died after their return to the reservation and of whom she had been intensely jealous. During the course of her treatment, she became aware of persisting death wishes toward him and of her apprehension that his ghost would harm her. She misremembered her brother as Alfie rather than John, a phenomenon surely in the service of defense. It will be recalled that in the life story she had given in 1959, she had omitted that brother's having come with her, along with her mother and sisters, to the reservation. During times when she was feeling hostile toward C. H., whose favorite child was her son John, She-Who-Uses-A-Cane had sometimes "feared" that he would be harmed, in order that C. H. would miss him. It seems clear that C. H.'s son John was equated during the vignette with She-Who-Uses-A-Cane's sibling rival when she was 3 or 4 years old.

She responded to the question concerning whether she remembered the story of "The Man Who Turned into a Water-Monster" by stating it had been told to her by Old Lady W. Then came a slip of the tongue in which she equated Old Man W.'s wives and daughters. In her treatment period, she had once made the same parapraxis, calling her mother her father's daughter. We were unable to determine whether Old Man W.'s wives had deserted him in fact, but we remember that other informants told us that the sisters who were kidnapped by the "wild man" left him.

Then followed a revision of her life history as given in 1959. She said "My mother came back from over there with my father. Poor thing." In fact, the mother had returned with her brother, whom She-Who-Uses-A-Cane thought for a time to have been her father. It seems likely that her own feeling like a "poor thing" immediately following her surgery allowed her to rerepress her hostility toward her mother, hostility which was now ambivalently displaced onto C. H. and us.

During this recitation She-Who-Uses-A-Cane promptly turned to a dream she claimed to have had at age 6 or 7, in which two men, God and Jesus, appeared. It was at that period of her life when her beloved uncle turned her care over to a different family; the day school she so reluctantly attended was located "by the underpass" at the foot of East Mountain. It was then that she was introduced to Christianity and taught that God and Jesus were fathers in the sky who loved and would save their mortal children. As the interview continued, it became apparent that she had certainly had the dream during the previous night, whether she did in fact have it during her childhood or not. However, it seems reasonable to assume that she had had such a dream during her childhood and that it may well have occurred repetitively during times of stress. Apparently one such dream-plea for rescue had occurred when she was raped as a small child, whether that rape actually occurred or was only desired and feared. Sexual assaults on small girls by teenage boys are common today and, according to our data, took place then as well although apparently less often than at the present time.

However, we can guess that at least one other element contributed to her dreaming that she was found sexually attractive during the previous night. She had always been a sexually active, bawdy woman and had been deprived of sexual relations for several years. She must have felt particularly unattractive following her amputation. There is little reason to doubt that her granddaughter had not come to see her because she was on a sexual assignation. We recall how she sought to deny her hostility toward that promiscuous girl earlier in the interview when She-Who-Uses-A-Cane had asserted that she was absent against her will at the time of the drunken mishap.

Symbolic significance of the sun. At least in cultures in which the main deity is conceptualized as male, regressed patients often equate the sun with God; a famous example is to be found in the Schreber case (Freud 1911). However, She-Who-Uses-A-Cane was without doubt alluding also to the puberty ceremony for girls, which traditionally has taken place on the reservation at the foot of East Mountain.

During the puberty ceremony, a man who knows relevant ritual songs is hired to sing them for the maiden whose "coming into womanhood" is being celebrated and sanctified. Although he may not be accorded the status of shaman at other times, during that period of five days and four nights he is so deemed, because of the "power of his songs." On the morning of the fifth and the most sacred day, a picture of the sun is painted in yellow pollen outlined by black on the singer's left palm. He holds his palm up toward East Mountain at the moment of sunrise, and the representation on his hand is thought by some to make the sun rise.

The girl who is "coming out" also has a female attendant who instructs her in the lore of the ceremony and supervises her ritual behavior which must be impeccable for the successful outcome of the ceremony which is designed to make her become a moral woman, a good wife and mother, and to give her fertility, and a long, healthy and happy life.

On the fifth morning, when the sun appears over East Mountain, the girl is symbolically reborn as *itsúneglezh*, White Painted Lady. In Apache mythology, *itsúneglezh*, a virgin, born *tubajíshchineh*, Child of the Water, after being impregnated by rain from *yusn*, God. *Tubajíshchineh* is the culture hero who subjugated the Apache-speaking faunal monsters who ate *indéh*, the people, and made them agree to serve as food for Apaches. The female attendant forbids the girl to bathe during the four previous days and nights and tells her to keep her legs close together, lest she become pregnant. At the same time, she drinks only through a cylindrical tube, a bone or a hollow reed, an object which is about six inches long. On the final morning, the maiden is briefly accorded the shamanistic status; she blesses many people and paints the tops of their heads and their cheeks with yellow pollen and/or white clay. Some of them are thought to be cured of or protected against various afflictions as a result of her blessing. Part of the girl's face is colored with white clay; her cheeks are painted with a ring of red superposed on which is a spot of yellow pollen.

Let us return more directly to the clinical vignette. The significance of the sun's pulsating can be but conjectured. Extrapolating from information from analytic patients from our culture, we must wonder whether she was symbolically depicting preconsciously experienced vaginal sensations as she referred to the dream of being sexually assaulted by two boys. Her having mentioned them immediately after she spoke of dreaming of God and Jesus leads us to suspect that the dream had a disguised incestuous element.

Another phenomenon may be applicable as well. In the lives of young Apache children, it is scarcely possible for them not to see their fathers' erections. Greenacre (1947) noted that little girls of our culture, when seeing an adult erection, sometimes see pulsating bright lights. We do not have information concerning this among the Apaches, but the possibility is worth considering.

Bee and Butterfly Power. By now, she had ceased alluding directly to the tale of "The Man Who Turned into a Water-Monster." However, its associative links to what followed clearly include the themes of sibling rivalry and magical rescue from death, symbolized by dismemberment. She went directly from reciting her dream to talking about the acquisition of bee and butterfly power.

As mentioned earlier, supernatural power is acquired during an ordeal and/or when one has a power dream or hallucination. Her "I was really unhappy. I was going down," can be understood to represent an internal experience of an ordeal. In her life history and at various times during her treatment period she had viewed her uncle as one who rescued through magical means, a representative both of God and her father. The vignette material was confusing as to when she had the power dreams which endowed her with bee and butterfly power. However, since we had known her very well and she had never previously mentioned possessing bee power, we must assume that its presumed acquisition had occurred in the very recent past, perhaps during the previous night, if, indeed, it did not occur during our being with her. She may have preconsciously conceptualized me to be her singer-shaman and Dr. Ruth Boyer to be her attendant.

We can ascribe the sequential acquisition of the new bee and the old butterfly power to the condensation and negation of the existence of time which are typical of unconscious thinking.

Let us turn to the subject of the bees. At first they were red and yellow; later they were yellow and black. We note the similarity to the colors used on the singer's palm when the sun was painted on it and also to the colors painted on the maiden's face and infer that there may be a connection between these phenomena. While the color red has no special symbolic meaning to the Apaches, a red paste or clay is important in certain aspects of the puberty ceremony and it is sometimes thought that the red-tinged early morning clouds herald a good day and "good luck." Earlier in the vignette She-Who-Uses-A-Cane had said, "Morning was the color of clouds." Yellow, as she mentioned, customarily represents happiness and "good luck" and is equated with the pollen which is used to bless the maiden and which she uses to bless people on the first and fifth mornings of the puberty ceremony. Such pollen is to be found in the medicine bags of shamans and others and is always sprinkled on the person who is being treated for an illness. Black has two meanings. It is an unlucky color and when it occurs in dreams, is thought to herald misfortune. At the same time, one of the four "gifts" required by the shaman before he undertakes a healing ceremony is a black object, usually a black-handled knife, and the products of fire, ashes which were first black and later gray, are always used in the treatment of ghost sickness and ailments which are thought to have resulted from witchcraft. Black neck scarves were worn by many elderly Apaches in the past as a precaution against evil, misfortune, and ghosts.

But red is also the color of blood and in the context of the vignette, we must wonder whether its early inclusion should be connected with the bleeding which is to be expected when the wasps were eating her flesh—"They were eating meat"—and during childbirth.

In is of interest that she did not speak of the acquisition of wasp power but referred only to bee or beehive power. The bees/wasps were both good and bad agents, reminding us of the good and bad aspects of Apache shamans who, while they are rescuers, are latently witches. The shaman and the witch of many cultures are thought by various observers to constitute societally acceptable good and bad mother projections. The bees both brought her honey, good food, and ate her flesh. They can be understood to indicate the psychological developmental stage to which she had partly regressed, that involving oral dependency and oral sadism.

But why did She-Who-Uses-A-Cane fuse the acquisition of bee and butterfly powers? In the vignette she said, "I saw a picture of me. I am not dead, but I have no head" and then affirmed my interpretation that bee power gave her the capacity to restore dismembered bodies. From my previous experience with her, I knew that she coveted the possession of a penis. The following material makes clear her equation of omniscience and powerful thought, with such possession.

When She-Who-Uses-A-Cane was in therapy, a man's hour always succeeded hers. On the first day of her relating the story of the Water-Monster, I permitted her to overstay her allotted time a few moments. The jealous man knocked, opened the double doors, and, very uncharacteristically, just walked in. Part of their straight-faced interchange in Apache follows. He said, "Excuse me. I didn't know you were here." She replied, "I thought you knew everything, since your third leg hangs to the ground."

Taking into consideration the regressive pictorial representation of ideas which is characteristic of the dream (Freud 1900), we can view her statement during the vignette "but I have no head" to denote the amputated leg. This must surely be the final clue that her new acquisition of bee power was her wishful statement in terms of Apache folklore that she had the capacity to regain her lost member. Considering overdetermination of symbols, we conjecture that she sought simultaneously to solve several problems, including her long-sought acquisition of a penis, the possession of which would hopefully remove for her the guilty and fearful aspects of her sibling rivalry.

She-Who-Uses-A-Cane had never told me how or when she had acquired butterfly power. However, her services as a shaman had been sought from the time she was about 40, within a year after she lost her second husband to another woman. She had presented no clear details of how she came to lose him, but once alluded to a belief he had left her for a woman who had hired a shaman to use butterfly power on him and cause him to have love sickness. We may guess that at that time, during another intrapsychic ordeal, she hallucinated the acquisition of butterfly power in the service of wishful restitution of an external love object as she apparently believed during the vignette that she had acquired bee power to wishfully replace another love object, a body part.

Let us deal with but four further aspects of the vignette. First, following her indication that the possession of bee power hopefully gave her the power to reconstitute her body as entire, she said, "The beehive is really good, but the butterfly is really bigger and more beautiful than the wasp." Bee power has now been changed to beehive power.

When a beehive appears in the dream of a western analysand, it often symbolizes pregnancy. Among the Amazonian Kagwahiv, to dream of a pregnant woman is interpreted traditionally to mean that honey will be found; conversely, to dream of finding honey symbolizes a pregnant woman (Kracke 1977). Additionally, honey in a dream symbolizes both semen and oral impregnation. To dream of a wasp indicates the wish to be kissed by a woman, and a dream in which a woman is kissing a man denotes the threat of being stung by a wasp. She-Who-Uses-A-Cane used the word wasp to designate a flesheater, no doubt a symbolic representation of a projected cannibalistic wish.

When we studied the potlatch ceremony of Alaskan Athabaskans, we learned that their cannibalistic wishes directed toward mother figures represented, in part, a wish to regain fantasized symbiotic reunion (Boyer et al. 1974).

Both the western analysand and the Kagwahiv use the beehive to symbolize pregnancy partly because of the larvae which teem inside the beehive which has the shape of a pregnant abdomen. While such symbology has not been discovered explicitly among the Apaches, its presence can be inferred from one belief which rationalizes their traditionally murdering one of twins soon after their birth: twins are thought to result either from witchcraft or from immoral behavior on the part of the mother, who is thought to have indulged in "too much sex" or in intercourse with more than one man. Each of these latter acts would involve the presence of excess semen. Apache children frequently conceptualize their mothers to be constantly pregnant. Taking these data into consideration, it seems reasonable to assume that the larvae inside the beehive may well be equated both with semen and with intrauterine babies. An occasional Apache has wondered whether semen were homunculi. Depsite their obvious ambivalence toward babies, Apache mothers usually consciously want them and refer to them as "sweet."

We can, then, assume with some degree of confidence that She-Who-Uses-A-Cane, with her allusion to the puberty ceremony, one function of which is to make the girl fertile, referred to a wish to have the capacity to become pregnant as well as to be reborn.

The statement that the beehive is good but the butterfly is bigger and more beautiful than the wasp is highly condensed. It implies that the capacities to make dismembered bodies whole and to become fertile-pregnant via ordinary intercourse, the result of "lovesickness," are perhaps differentiated from the forbidden wish to become orally impregnated. During her therapy, it was evident that She-Who-Uses-A-Cane feared taking a penis into her mouth lest she bite it off.

She-Who-Uses-A-Cane then said the bee was trying to kill the butterfly but *she* got away. It was clear at that moment that she had identified with her supernatural power, as she did when she hummed. Again we can but offer suppositions. Perhaps she feared that the acquisition of bee power would remove repression of cannibalistic wishes and displace her butterfly power, the use of which surely depicts a more acceptable, less regressed phase of psychosexual development. But She-Who-Uses-A-Cane indicated at various times during her therapy that she retained the common Apache fear that sexual relations were potentially damaging to either partner, particularly to the female.

It is very likely that She-Who-Uses-A-Cane feared continuing to talk about bee power for two reasons. Other shamans have refused to complete their recitations of their experiences of power acquisition because they feared that telling the whole story would endow the hearer with the power and thereby result in shared ownership and a lessening of the quantum of power held by the relater. At the same time, they have sometimes ceased their recitations in order to protect the listener. Thus, Old-Lady-With-A-Sash would not complete a tale she was telling Dr. Ruth Boyer about her bat power because "If I told you all of it, you would hang to the ceiling like a bat." (Boyer and Boyer 1981).

Ghosts and death. At the end of the vignette, when our separation was imminent, She-Who-Uses-A-Cane associated our departure with death. It was *not* to be goodbye. Her thought of death became associated with the newly noticed black sleeves which were to be washed white, as though their change of color would magically undo the separation-death threat. But she had an insoluble dilemma. Earlier in the interview she had designated the face of the ghost to be white. Apaches do not generally picture ghosts as being white but rather black or gray. In the Apache language, the word *indáh* means both enemy and white man. It is our conjecture that the ghost of the son of her distant female relative, which we have shown to be equated with the ghosts of her two dead brothers, became fused with us and the hostility she had projected onto us. Thus, whether the sleeves were black or white, her fear of death through separation would have remained unsolved.

Physical ailments. Apache folklore abounds with stories which encompass most of the basic expectations evinced by She-Who-Uses-A-Cane in her quest to regain her health, to be cured of her blindness and arthritis, and to regain her lost leg. The Apaches of yore were ignorant of the existence of diabetes, and today's aged people are unable to understand either its existence or physiological origins. A few examples will suffice.

According to a well-known story, in the remote past, a blind boy carried a legless boy to a mountain where they hoped to be made whole by the Mountain Spirits. After undergoing an ordeal, each was cured of his disability (Hoijer 1938).

Long ago, an old woman was deserted because she was becoming blind and deaf. She sought the help of the Mountain Spirits and after she had undergone an ordeal, she could not only see and hear well but was endowed with supernatural power (Hoijer 1938).

In a modern version of an old story with many variants, one of which has been interpreted psychoanalytically (Boyer 1965), two boys set out in quest of supernatural power. They were taken into a holy cave and subjected to a series of ordeals by the Mountain Spirits. During the fourth night, they were totally dismembered, probably as the result of being eaten by sibling representates. On the fifth morning, they emerged from the cave, symbolically reborn, not only completely reconstituted, but possessing supernatural power.

Two months after we recorded the clinical vignette concerning She-Who-Uses-A-Cane, we were again on the reservation. We learned from the granddaughter who lived with and looked after her and from a devoted grandson who lived next door that she had not mentioned her acquisition of bee power to them. Each said, "She must want to keep that private for herself." Such secret retention of self-assigned supernatural powers is common among these Apaches. They had heard her ask occasionally and without explanation, "Why did that boy's ghost come to me?" She-Who-Uses-A-Cane denied to us that she had experienced further power dreams or contact with ghosts. We learned that she had returned from Oklahoma very angry with Oral Roberts and denounced him and his curative powers. Subsequently, however, she had resumed her attitude of adulation toward him and was again praying to him for renewed health and longevity.

Summary

We have aimed in this chapter to illustrate the constant interplay between the total environment of a society, particularly its expressive modes of communication, and the idiosyncratic thinking and behavior of the individual participant within that culture. To understand in fullest richness the content of the conscious and unconscious motivations, activities, and fantasies of a patient of differing ethnic background from that of the psychotherapist, it is essential that the latter become thoroughly familiar with the sociocultural bases of the person seeking aid.

Sourcenotes

Chapter 1 first appeared in *The Psychoanalytic Study of the Child* 11(1956): 236–256. Reprinted by permission of International Universities Press. Other versions appeared in *Adolescent Psychiatry* 1(1971):363–378 and *La Revista de la Sociedad Argentina de Psiquiátria y Psicología de la Infancia y Adolescencia* 3(1972):211–223, and were presented, under the title "On the Stimulus Barrier and Schizophrenia," before the East Bay Psychiatric Association, November 1955, and the Midwinter Meeting of the American Psychoanalytic Association, December 1955.

Chapter 2 first appeared in *Archives of Criminal Psychodynamics* 2(1957): 541–571. Other versions were presented before the West Coast Psychoanalytic Societies, Seattle, Washington, August 1956; the San Francisco Psychoanalytic Society, November 1956; the Winter Meeting of the American Psychoanalytic Association, New York, December 1956; and the Grupo Mexicano de Estudios Psicoanalíticos, Mexico City, July 1957.

Chapter 3 first appeared in *International Journal of Psycho-Analysis* 41(1960): 114–122. Reprinted by permission. Other versions were presented before the Grupo Mexicano de Estudios Psicoanalíticos, Mexico City, July 1957; the San Francisco Psychoanalytic Society, October 1957; the Joint Meeting of the Western Division of the American Psychiatric Association and the West Coast Psychoanalytic Societies, Los Angeles, November 1957; and the Fall Meeting of the American Psychoanalytic Association, New York, December 1957.

Chapter 4 first appeared in *International Journal of Psycho-Analysis* 42(1961): 389–403. Reprinted by permission. A version was presented before the

Asociación Psicoanalitica Mexicana, Mexico City, July 1958. Other versions appeared in *Acta Psiquiátrica y Psicológica de América Latina* 11(1965):147–155; *Revista de Psicoanálisis* 23(1965):287–317; *Rivisti di Psicoanálisi* 12(1966):3–22; *Psychoanalytic Forum* 1(1966):337–356; *Die psychoanalytischer Behandlung Schizophrener*, by L. B. Boyer, pp. 143–177. Munich: Kindler Verlag, 1976; and *Revista de la Sociedad Colombiana de Psicoanálisis* 5(1980):59–76.

Chapter 5 first appeared in *International Journal of Psycho-Analysis* 52(1971): 67–86. Reprinted by permission. Presented at the Fall Meeting of the American Psychoanalytic Association, New York, December 1967, and subsequently at other meetings. Other versions appeared in *Tactics and Techniques in Psychoanalytic Therapy. II. Countertransference*, ed. P. L. Giovacchini, A. Flarsheim, and L. B. Boyer, pp. 341–373. New York: Aronson, 1975; *Prácticas Psicoanalíticas Comparadas en las Psicosis*, ed. L. Grinberg, pp. 15–57. Buenos Aires: Editorial Paidós, 1977; *Psychotherapies: A Comparative Casebook*, ed. S. J. Morse and R. L. Watson, pp. 71–89. New York: Holt, Rinehart and Winston, 1977.

Chapter 6 first appeared in *Adolescent Psychiatry* 4(1976):371–386. Presented at the Annual Meeting of the American Psychoanalytic Association, Honolulu, May 1973. Another version appeared in *Cuadernos de Psicoanálisis* 9(1976):53–66. Reprinted by permission of Jason Aronson, Inc.

Chapter 7 first appeared in *The Psychoanalytic Quarterly* 46(1977):386–424. Reprinted by permission. Other versions appeared in *La Revista de la Asociación Psicoanalítica de Buenos Aires* 1(1979):361–406; and were presented before the American Psychotherapy Seminar Center, New York, December 1975; the Los Angeles Psychoanalytic Society and Institute, May 1976, and other groups. Other versions will appear in *Cuadernos de Psicoanálisis* and *Psyche*.

Chapter 8 first appeared in *International Journal of Psychoanalytic Psychotherapy* 4(1975):25–47. Another version appeared in *Revista de Psicoanálisis* 32(1975):143–176. Reprinted by permission of Jason Aronson, Inc.

Chapter 9 is a synthesis and expansion of papers that appeared in *Countertransference: The Therapist's Contribution to the Therapeutic Situation*, ed. L. Epstein and A. H. Feiner, pp. 533–574. New York: Aronson, 1979; and *Psicoanálisis Actual: Caracter, Transferencia y Contratransferencia, Fantasía y Realidad*, ed. F. Cesarman. Mexico City: Asociación Psicoanalítica Mexicana, 1978; and presentations made at the Twelfth Latin American Psychoanalytic Congress, Mexico City, February 1978; at 1979 meetings of the San Diego, San Francisco, and Southern California Psychoanalytic Societies; and as the Fifth Melitta Sperling Memorial Address, New York, 1979.

Chapter 10 first appeared in *The American Journal of Psychiatry* 106(1950): 606–615. Copyright © 1950, the American Psychiatric Association.

Chapter 11 first appeared in *The Journal of the American Psychoanalytic Association* 3(1955):467–488. Reprinted by permission of International Universities Press. Presented to the East Bay Psychiatric Society, November 1953; the San Francisco Psychoanalytic Society, May 1954; the West Coast Psychoanalytic Societies, Coronado, California, October 1954; and the Midwinter Meeting of the American Psychoanalytic Association, New York, December 1954.

Chapter 12 first appeared in *The Journal of the Hillside Hospital* 8(1959): 279–283. Reprinted by permission of International Universities Press.

Chapter 13 is adapted from papers that appeared in *Psychopathologie Africaine* 3(1967):333–372; *Cuadernos del Instituto Nacional de Antropología* (*Buenos Aires*) 7(1968–1971):111–138; and *The Psychoanalytic Study of Society* 6(1974):100–133.

Chapter 14 was originally published in *Contemporary Psychoanalysis*, Journal of the William Alanson White Institute and William Alanson White Psychoanalytic Society, 1977, 13:30–51. Reprinted by permission.

References

Abraham, K. (1913). Restrictions and transformations of scoptophilia in psychoneurotics, with remarks on analogous phenomena in folk-psychology. In *Selected Papers on Psychoanalysis*, pp. 169–234. London: Hogarth, 1948.

——— (1924a). Melancholia and obsessional neurosis: two stages of the sadistic anal stage of the libido. In *Selected Papers on Psychoanalysis*, pp. 422–432. London: Hogarth, 1948.

——— (1924b). Notes on the psychogenesis of melancholia. In *Selected Papers on Psychoanalysis*, pp. 453–463. London: Hogarth, 1948.

——— (1924c). Object loss and introjection in normal mourning and in abnormal states of mind. In *Selected Papers on Psychoanalysis*, pp. 433–441. London: Hogarth, 1948.

Adler, G. (1975). The usefulness of the "borderline concept" in psychotherapy. In *Borderline States in Psychiatry*, ed. J. E. Mack, pp. 29–40. New York: Grune and Stratton.

Aichhorn, A. (1925). *Wayward Youth*. New York: Viking, 1948.

Alexander, F. (1931). Schizophrenic psychoses: critical consideration of the psychoanalytic treatment. *Archives of Neurology and Psychiatry* 26:815–828.

——— (1956). Two forms of regression and their therapeutic implications. *Psychoanalytic Quarterly* 25:178–196.

Alexander, F., and French, T., eds. (1950). *Psychosomatic Medicine*. New York: Norton.

Anastasi, A., and Foley, J. P., Jr. (1940). A survey of the literature on artistic behavior in the abnormal. III. Spontaneous productions. *Psychological Monographs* 52(6).

Aray, J. (1968). Discussion of chapter 5 at the meeting of the Grupo Venezolano de Estudios Psicoanalíticos, Caracas.

Arbiser, A. (1978). Patología de la contratransferencia en los tratamientos interminables. *Revista de Psicoanálisis* 34:753–765.

Arieti, S. (1955). *Interpretation of Schizophrenia.* New York: Brunner/Mazel.

Arlow, J. A. (1952). Discussion of Dr. Fromm-Reichmann's paper, "Some aspects of psychoanalytic psychotherapy with schizophrenics." In *Psychotherapy with Schizophrenics*, ed. E. B. Brody and F. C. Redlich, pp. 112–120. New York: International Universities Press, 1954.

——— (1961). Silence and the theory of technique. *Journal of the American Psychoanalytic Association* 9:44–45.

——— (1973). Reflections on empathy. Paper presented at the meeting of the San Francisco Psychoanalytic Society, March.

Arlow, J. A., and Brenner, C. (1964). *Psychoanalytic Concepts and the Structural Theory.* New York: International Universities Press.

——— (1969). The psychopathology of the psychoses: a proposed revision. *International Journal of Psycho-Analysis* 50:5–14.

Atkins, N. B. (1967). Comments on severe psychotic regressions in analysis. *Journal of the American Psychoanalytic Association* 15:584–605.

Aubry, J. (1955). The effects of lack of maternal care: methods of studying children aged one to three years, placed in institutions. In *Emotional Problems of Early Childhood*, ed. G. Caplan, pp. 293–306. New York: Basic Books.

Avenburg, R. (1962). Modificaciones estructurales en un paciente esquizofrénico a través del primer mes de análisis. *Revista de Psicoanálisis* 19: 351–365.

Azima, H., and Wittkower, E. D. (1956). Gratification of basic needs in treatment of schizophrenics. *Psychiatry* 19:121–129.

Balint, M. (1959). *Thrills and Regressions.* London: Hogarth.

Barchilon, J. (1959). Beauty and the beast: from myth to fairy tale. *Psychoanalytic Review* 46:19–29.

Beach, F. A. (1954). Ontogeny and living systems. In *Group Processes*, ed. B. Schaffner, pp. 9–74. New York: Josiah Macy, Jr., Foundation.

Beckwitt, M. C. (1968). On the vicissitudes of sibling penis envy in a girl twin. *Israel Annals of Psychiatry and Related Disciplines* 6:13–29.

Bellak, L., and Hurvich, M. (1969). A systematic study of ego functions. *Journal of Nervous and Mental Disease* 148:569–585.

Belvianes, M. (1951). *La Vierge par les Peintres.* Paris: Editions de Varenne.

Beres, D. (1957). Communication and the creative process. *Journal of the American Psychoanalytic Association* 5:408–423.

Bergler, E. (1938). On a resistance situation: the patient is silent. *Psychoanalytic Review* 25:170–186.

Bergman, P., and Escalona, S. K. (1949). Unusual sensitivities in very young children. *Psychoanalytic Study of the Child* 3/4:333–352.

Berliner, B. (1914). Der Einfluss von Klima, Wetter und Jahreszeit auf das

Nerven- und Seelenleben auf physiologischer Grundlage dargestellt. In *Grenzfragen des Nerven- und Seelenlebens,* vol. 99. Wiesbaden: J. F. Bergman.

——— (1940). Libido and reality in masochism. *Psychoanalytic Quarterly* 9:322–333.

——— (1947). On some psychodynamics of masochism. *Psychoanalytic Quarterly* 16:459–471.

——— (1954). Discussion of chapter 11 at the Meeting of the West Coast Psychoanalytic Societies, Coronado, California, October.

——— (1956). Discussion of chapter 2 at the Meeting of the San Francisco Psychoanalytic Society, November.

Bermak, G. E. (1979). Discussion of chapter 9 at the Meeting of the San Francisco Psychoanalytic Society and Institute, September.

Bettelheim, B. (1967). Regression as progress. In *The Empty Fortress: Infantile Autism and the Birth of the Self,* pp. 290–298. New York: Free Press.

Binswanger, H. (1956). Freuds Psychosentherapie. *Psyche* (Heidelberg) 10: 357–366.

Bion, W. R. (1955). Language and the schizophrenic. In *New Directions in Psycho-Analysis,* eds. M. Klein, P. Heimann, and R. E. Money-Kyrle, pp. 220–230. London: Hogarth.

——— (1956). Development of schizophrenic thought. *International Journal of Psycho-Analysis* 37:344–346.

——— (1957). Differentiation of the psychotic from the nonpsychotic personalities. *International Journal of Psycho-Analysis* 38:266–275.

——— (1967). *Second Thoughts: Selected Papers on Psychoanalysis.* London: William Heineman Medical Books.

Blank, H. R. (1954). Depression, hypomania and depersonalization. *Psychoanalytic Quarterly* 33:20–37.

Bodkin, T. (1949). *The Virgin and Child.* New York: Pitman.

Bourke, J. G. (1890). Notes on Apache mythology. *Journal of American Folklore* 3:209–212.

Boyer, L. B. (1956). Ambulatory schizophrenia: some remarks concerning the diagnosis. *Kaiser Foundation Medical Bulletin* 4:457–460.

——— (1964b). Folk psychiatry of the Apaches of the Mescalero Indian Reservation. In *Magic, Faith and Healing: Studies in Primitive Psychiatry Today,* ed. Ari Kiev, pp. 384–419. Glencoe, Ill.: Free Press.

——— (1964c). Psychoanalytic insights in working with ethnic minorities. *Social Casework* 45:519–526.

——— (1965). Stone as a symbol in Apache mythology. *American Imago* 22:14–49.

——— (1966). Office treatment of schizophrenic patients by psychoanalysis. *Psychoanalytic Forum* 1:337–365.

——— (1967a). Author's reply. *Psychoanalytic Forum* 2:190–195.

——— (1967b). Historical development of the psychoanalytic therapy of the schizophrenias: contributions of the followers of Freud. In *Psychoanalytic Treatment of Schizophrenic and Characterological Disorders*, ed. L. B. Boyer and P. L . Giovacchini, pp. 80–142. New York: Science House.

——— (1967c). Historical development of the psychoanalytic therapy of the schizophrenias: Freud's contributions. In *Psychoanalytic Treatment of Schizophrenic and Characterological Disorders*, ed. L. B. Boyer and P. L. Giovacchini, pp. 40–49. New York: Science House.

——— (1972). A suicidal attempt by an adolescent twin. *International Journal of Psychoanalytic Psychotherapy* 1:7–30.

——— (1975). The man who turned into a water monster: a psychoanalytic contribution to folklore. *Psychoanalytic Study of Society* 6:100–133.

——— (1976a). *Die psychoanalytische Behandlung Schizophrener*. Munich: Kindler Verlag.

——— (1976b). Meanings of a bizarre suicidal attempt by an adolescent twin. *Adolescent Psychiatry* 4:371–381.

——— (1977). Mythology, folklore and psychoanalysis. In *Encyclopedia of Neurology, Psychiatry, Psychology and Psychoanalysis*, vol. 7, ed. B. B. Wolman, pp. 423–429. New York: Van Nostrand Reinhold and Aesculapius.

——— (1978a). Countertransference experiences while working with severely regressed patients. In *Psicoanálisis Actual: Caracter, Transferencia y Contratransferencia, Fantasía, y Realidad*, ed. F. Cesarman. Mexico City: Asociación Psicoanalítica Mexicana.

——— (1978b). Countertransference experiences with severely regressed patients. In *Countertransference: The Therapist's Contribution to the Therapeutic Situation*, ed. L. Epstein and A. H. Feiner, pp. 533–574. New York: Aronson.

——— (1978c). On aspects of the mutual influences of anthropology and psychoanalysis. *Journal of Psychological Anthropology* 1:265–296.

——— (1979). *Childhood and Folklore: A Psychoanalytic Study of Apache Personality*. New York: Library of Psychological Anthropology.

——— (1980). Folklore, anthropology and psychoanalysis. *Journal of Psychoanalytic Anthropology* 3:259–279.

——— (1982). *Kindheit und Mythos*. Stuttgart: Klett-Cotta.

Boyer, L. B., and Boyer, R. M. (1967). A combined anthropological and psychoanalytic contribution to folklore. *Psychopathologie Africaine* 3: 333–372.

——— (1968–1971). Un aporte mixto, antropológico y psicoanalitico al folklore. *Cuadernos del Instituto Nacional de Antropología, Buenos Aires* 7:111–138.

——— (1972). El uso del test de Rorschach como un adjunto de investigación en el estudio de los Apaches en la Reservación India Mescalero. *Revista Argentina de Psicología* 3:69–102.

Boyer, L. B., Boyer, R. M., Brawer, F. B., Kawai, H., and Klopfer, B. (1964).

Apache age groups. *Journal of Projective Techniques and Personality Assessment* 28:337–342.

Boyer, L. B., Boyer, R. M., and DeVos, G. A. (1983). On the acquisition of the shamanistic status: a clinical and Rorschach study of a specific case. In *Die Wilde Seele. Kritische Aufsätze zur Ethnopsychiatrie George Devereux*, ed. Hans Peter Dürr. Frankfurt: Syndikat (in press).

Boyer, L. B., Boyer, R. M., and Hippler, A. E. (1974). The Alaskan Athabaskan potlatch ceremony: an ethnopsychoanalytic study. *International Journal of Psychoanalytic Psychotherapy* 3:343–365.

Boyer, L. B., Boyer, R. M., Kawai, H., and Klopfer, B. (1967). Apache "learners" and "nonlearners." *Journal of Projective Techniques and Personality Assessment* 31:22–29.

Boyer, L. B., Boyer, R. M., Klopfer, B., and Scheiner, S. (1968). Apache "learners" and "nonlearners." II. Quantitative signs of influential adults. *Journal of Projective Techniques and Personality Assessment* 32:146–159.

Boyer, L. B., DeVos, G. A., Borders, O., and Tani-Borders, A. (1978). The "burnt child syndrome" among the Yukon Eskimos. *Journal of Psychological Anthropology* 1:7–56.

Boyer, L. B., DeVos, G. A., Boyer, R. M., and Goldstine, T. L. (1983). A longitudinal study of three Apache brothers as reflected in their Rorschach protocols. *Journal of Psychological Anthropology* 6:125–162.

Boyer, L. B., and Giovacchini, P. L. (1967). *Psychoanalytic Treatment of Schizophrenic and Characterological Disorders*. New York: Aronson.

——— (1980). *Psychoanalytic Treatment of Schizophrenic, Borderline and Characterological Disorders*. 2nd ed., rev. and exp. New York: Aronson.

Boyer, L. B., Klopfer, B., Brawer, F. B., and Kawai, H. (1964). Comparisons of the shamans and pseudoshamans of the Mescalero Indian Reservation. *Journal of Projective Techniques and Personality Assessment* 28:173–180.

Boyer, R. M. (1962). *Social Structure and Socialization Among the Apache of the Mescalero Indian Reservation*. Unpublished doctoral dissertation, University of California, Berkeley.

Boyer, R. M., and Boyer, L. B. (1981). Apache lore of the bat. *Psychoanalytic Study of Society* 9:263–300. New York: Psychohistory Press.

Braatøy, T. (1954). *Fundamentals of Psychoanalytic Technique*. New York: Wiley.

Brenman, M. (1952). On teasing and being teased. *Psychoanalytic Study of the Child* 7:264–285.

Breuer, J., and Freud, S. (1893–1895). Studies on hysteria. *Standard Edition* 2:1–252. London: Hogarth, 1955.

Brodey, W. M. (1965). On the dynamics of narcissism: I. Externalization and early ego development. *Psychoanalytic Study of the Child* 20:165–193.

Brody, E. B. (1952). The treatment of schizophrenia: a review. In *Psychotherapy with Schizophrenics*, ed. E. B. Brody and F. C. Redlich, pp. 39–88. New York: International Universities Press, 1954.

Brody, S., and Axelrad, S. (1970). *Anxiety and Ego Formation in Infancy.* New York: International Universities Press.

Bruch, H. (1973). *Eating Disorders: Obesity, Anorexia Nervosa and the Person Within.* New York: Basic Books.

Brunswick, R. M. (1928). A supplement to Freud's "History of an infantile neurosis." *International Journal of Psycho-Analysis* 9:439–476.

Bullard, D. M. (1940). Experiences in the psychoanalytic treatment of psychotics. *Psychoanalytic Quarterly* 9:493–504.

Burlingham, D. T. (1952). *Twins.* New York: International Universities Press.

Bychowski, G. (1952). *Psychotherapy of Psychosis.* New York: Grune and Stratton.

——— (1966). Psychosis precipitated by psychoanalysis. *Psychoanalytic Quarterly* 35:327–339.

Calder, K. T. (1958). Panel report: technical aspects of regression during psychoanalysis. *Journal of the American Psychoanalytic Association* 6: 552–559.

Carpinacci, J. A., Liberman, D., and Schlossberg, N. (1963). Perturbaciones de la comunicación y neurosis de contratransferencia. *Revista de Psicoanálisis* 20:63–69.

Carter, L., and Rinsley, D. B. (1977). Vicissitudes of "empathy" in a borderline patient. *International Review of Psychoanalysis* 4:317–326.

Cattell, J. P. (1954). The holiday syndrome. Paper presented before the Meeting of the American Psychoanalytic Association, St. Louis.

Cesio, F. R. (1963). La comunicación extraverbal en psicoanálisis. Transferencia, contratransferencia e interpretación. *Revista de Psicoanálisis* 20: 124–127.

——— (1973). Los fundamentales de la contratransferencia: el yo ideal y las identificaciones directas. *Revista de Psicoanálisis* 30:5–16.

Chediak, C. (1979). Counterreactions and countertransference. *International Journal of Psycho-Analysis* 60: 117–130.

Chiozza, L. A. (1976). *Cuerpo, Afecto, y Lenguaje: Psicoanálisis y Enfermedad Psicosomática.* Buenos Aires: Editorial Paidós.

——— ed. (1978). *Ideas para una Concepción Psicoanalítica del Cancer.* Buenos Aires: Editorial Paidós.

——— (1979). *La Interpretación Psicoanalitica en la Enfermedad Somática en la Teoría y en la Práctica Clínica.* Buenos Aires: Universidad de Salvador.

Christie, A. (1952). *A Holiday for Murder.* New York: Avon.

Clark, L. H. (1966). They Sang for Horses. The Impact of the Horse on Navaho and Apache Folklore. Tucson: University of Arizona Press.

Dantas, J. (1900). Pintoras e poétas de Rilhafolles. *Medicina Contemporanea* (Lisbon) 3 (Series 2):220–221.

Day, R., Boyer, L. B., and DeVos, G. A. (1975). Two styles of ego development:

a cross-cultural, longitudinal comparison of Apache and Anglo school children. *Ethos* 3:345–379.

Deutsch, F., and Murphy, W. F. (1955). *The Clinical Interview*. New York: International Universities Press.

Deutsch, H. (1933). Zur Psychologie der manisch-depressiven Zustände, insbesondere der chronische Hypomanie. *Internationale Zeitschrift für Psychoanalyse* 19:338–351.

——— (1942). Some forms of emotional disturbance and their relationships to schizophrenia. *Psychoanalytic Quarterly* 11:301–321.

Devereux, G. (1951). *Reality and Dream: Psychotherapy of a Plains Indian*. New York: International Universities Press.

Dewald, P. A. (1976). Transference regression and real experience in the psychoanalytic experience. *Psychoanalytic Quarterly* 40:213–230.

Dickes, T. (1975). Technical considerations of the therapeutic and working alliance. *International Journal of Psychoanalytic Psychotherapy* 4:1–24.

Ducoste, M. (1920). Outils, armes, pièce d'étoffe, tissé exécutés par des aliénés. *Bulletin de la Société Clinique de Médecine Mentale* 13:147–151.

Eaton, J. W., and Weil, R. J. (1955). *Culture and Mental Disorders: A Comparative Study of the Hutterites and Other Populations*. Glencoe, Ill.: Free Press.

Eggan, D. (1955). The personal use of myth in dreams. *Journal of American Folklore* 68:445–453.

Eidelberg, L. (1933a). Zur Metapsychologie des Masochismus. *Internationale Zeitschrift für Psychoanalyse* 19:615–616.

——— (1933b). Zur Theorie und Klinik der Perversion. *Internationale Zeitschrift für Psychoanalyse* 19:620–621.

——— (1934). Beitrage zum Studium des Masochismus. *Internationale Zeitschrift für Psychoanalyse* 20:336–353.

Eisenbud, J. (1941). Negative reactions to Christmas. *Psychoanalytic Quarterly* 10:639–645.

Eisler, M. J. (1922). Pleasure in sleep and disturbed capacity for sleep. *International Journal of Psycho-Analysis* 3:30–42.

Eissler, K. R. (1953). The effect of the structure of the ego on psychoanalytic technique. *Journal of the American Psychoanalytic Association* 1:104–143.

Ekstein, R. (1976). General treatment philosophy of acting out. In *Acting Out*, eds. L. E. Abt and S. L. Weissman, pp. 162–171. New York: Aronson.

Ekstein, R., and Caruth, E. (1966). Psychotic acting out: royal road or primrose path. In *Children of Time and Space, of Action and Impulse*, ed. R. Ekstein, pp. 298–308. New York: Appleton-Century-Crofts.

Epstein, L., and Feiner, A. H. (1979). *Countertransference: The Therapist's Contribution to the Therapeutic Situation*. New York: Aronson.

Erikson, E. H. (1950). *Childhood and Society*. New York: Norton.

Ernst, W. (1925). Plastische Arbeiten verbrechernischer Geisteskranker. *Archiv für Psychiatrie und Nervenkrankheiten; vereinigt mit Zeitschrift für die gesamte Neurologen* 74:838–842.

Escalona, S. K. (1953). Emotional development in the first year of life. In *Problems of Infancy and Childhood*, ed. M. J. E. Senn. New York: Josiah Macy, Jr., Foundation.

Fairbairn, W. R. D. (1941). A revised psychopathology of the psychoses and psychoneuroses. *International Journal of Psycho-Analysis* 22:250–279.

——— (1944). Endopsychic structure considered in terms of object relationship. *International Journal of Psycho-Analysis* 25:70–93.

——— (1952). *An Object Relations Theory of Personality*. New York: Basic Books.

Federn, P. (1952). *Ego Psychology and the Psychoses*. New York: Basic Books.

Fenichel, O. (1945). *The Psychoanalytic Theory of Neurosis*. New York: Norton.

Ferenczi, S. (1919). On the technique of psycho-analysis. IV. The control of the countertransference. In *Further Contributions to the Theory and Technique of Psycho-Analysis*, pp. 186–189. London: Hogarth.

——— (1950). *Further Contributions to the Theory and Technique of Psycho-analysis*, 2nd ed. London: Hogarth.

Ferm, V. (1945). *Encyclopedia of Religion*. New York: Philosophical Library.

——— (1951). The fountainhead of Western religion. In *The Hebrew Impact on Western Civilization*, ed. D. D. Runes. New York: Philosophical Library.

Flarsheim, A. (1972). Treatability. In *Tactics and Techniques in Psychoanalytic Therapy*, ed. P. L. Giovacchini, pp. 113–131. New York: Science House.

Fliess, R. (1951). *The Revival of Interest in the Dream*. New York: International Universities Press.

Fliess, W. (1953). Counter-transference and counter-identification. *Journal of the American Psychoanalytic Association* 1:268–284.

Fraiberg, S. (1969). Libidinal object constancy and mental representation. *Psychoanalytic Study of the Child* 24:9–47.

Freedman, D. A. (1972). On the limits of the effectiveness of psychoanalysis: early ego and somatic disturbances. *International Journal of Psycho-Analysis* 53:363–370.

Freedman, D. A., and Brown, S. L. (1968). On the role of coenesthetic stimulation in the development of the psychic structure. *Psychoanalytic Quarterly* 37:418–438.

Freeman, T. (1970). The psychopathology of the psychoses: a reply to Arlow and Brenner. *International Journal of Psycho-Analysis* 51:407–415.

Freud, A. (1936). *The Ego and the Mechanisms of Defense*. New York: International Universities Press, 1946.

——— (1949). Aggression in relation to emotional development. *Psychoanalytic Study of the Child* 3/4:37–42.

——— (1959a). *The Psychoanalytic Treatment of Children*. New York: International Universities Press.

——— (1959b). The therapeutic process. Paper presented at the Meeting of the San Francisco Psychoanalytic Society, April.

——— (1965). *Normality and Pathology in Childhood.* New York: International Universities Press.

——— (1967). About losing and being lost. *Psychoanalytic Study of the Child* 22:9–19.

——— (1969). *Difficulties in the Path of Psychoanalysis.* New York: International Universities Press.

Freud, S. (1900). The interpretation of dreams. *Standard Edition* 4/5. London: Hogarth, 1957.

——— (1905). Three essays on the theory of sexuality. *Standard Edition* 7: 123–245. London: Hogarth, 1953.

——— (1908). On the sexual theories of children. *Standard Edition* 9:205–226. London: Hogarth, 1959.

——— (1909). Notes upon a case of obsessional neurosis. *Standard Edition* 10: 151–320. London: Hogarth, 1955.

——— (1910a). The future prospects of psycho-analytic therapy. *Standard Edition* 11:139–151. London: Hogarth, 1957.

——— (1910b). "Wild" psycho-analysis. *Standard Edition* 11:219–227. London: Hogarth, 1957.

——— (1911). Psycho-analytical notes on an autobiographical account of a case of paranoia (dementia paranoides). *Standard Edition* 12:1–82. London: Hogarth, 1958.

——— (1912). Recommendations to physicians practising psycho-analysis. *Standard Edition* 12:109–120. London: Hogarth, 1958.

——— (1913). The occurrence in dreams of material from fairy tales. *Standard Edition* 12:279–287. London: Hogarth, 1958.

——— (1914). On narcissism: an introduction. *Standard Edition* 14:67–102. London: Hogarth, 1957.

——— (1915a). Observations on transference-love (further recommendations on the technique of psycho-analysis III). *Standard Edition* 12:157–171. London: Hogarth, 1958.

——— (1951b). Thoughts for the times on war and death. *Standard Edition* 14: 273–302.

——— (1915c). The unconscious. *Standard Edition* 14:159–215. London: Hogarth, 1957.

——— (1917a). A difficulty in the path of psycho-analysis. *Standard Edition* 17:135–144. London: Hogarth, 1955.

——— (1917b). Mourning and melancholia. *Standard Edition* 14:237–258. London: Hogarth, 1957.

——— (1918). From the history of an infantile neurosis. *Standard Edition* 17: 1–122. London: Hogarth, 1955.

——— (1919). A child is being beaten: a contribution to the study of the origin of sexual perversions. *Standard Edition* 17:175–204. London: Hogarth, 1924.

——— (1920a). *Beyond the Pleasure Principle.* London: Hogarth, 1948.
——— (1920b). The psychogenesis of a case of homosexuality in a woman. *Standard Edition* 18:145–172. London: Hogarth, 1955.
——— (1921). Identification. In *Group Psychology and the Analysis of the Ego.* London: Hogarth, 1948.
——— (1923). The ego and the superego (ego-ideal). In *The Ego and the Id.* London: Hogarth, 1948.
——— (1924). Neurosis and psychosis. *Standard Edition* 19:147–153. London: Hogarth, 1961.
——— (1925). The resistances to psycho-analysis. *Standard Edition* 19:211–222. London: Hogarth, 1961.
——— (1926). Inhibitions, symptoms and anxiety. *Standard Edition* 20:75–175. London: Hogarth, 1959.
——— (1930). Civilization and its discontents. *Standard Edition* 21:57–145. London: Hogarth, 1961.
——— (1937). Analysis terminable and interminable. *Standard Edition* 23: 209–253. London: Hogarth, 1964.
——— (1940). An outline of psycho-analysis. *Standard Edition* 23:139–207. London: Hogarth, 1964.
Fries, M. E. (1944). *Some basic differences in newborn infants during the lying-in period.* (Teaching film with guide). New York: New York University Film Library.
Fromm-Reichmann, F. (1939). Transference problems in schizophrenics. *Psychoanalytic Quarterly* 8:412–426.
——— (1950). *Principles of Intensive Psychotherapy.* Chicago: University of Chicago Press.
——— (1952). Some aspects of psychoanalytic psychotherapy with schizophrenics. In *Psychotherapy with Schizophrenics,* eds. E. B. Brody and F. C. Redlich, pp. 89–111. New York: International Universities Press, 1954.
——— (1958). Basic problems in the psychotherapy of schizophrenia. *Psychiatry* 21:1–6.
Frosch, J. (1964). The psychotic character: clinical psychiatric considerations. *Psychiatric Quarterly* 38:81–96.
——— (1967). Severe regressive states during analysis: summary. *Journal of the American Psychoanalytic Association* 15:606–625.

Galvin, J. A. V. (1955). Mothers of schizophrenics. Paper presented at the First Western Divisional Meeting of the American Psychiatric Association, a joint meeting with the West Coast Psychoanalytic Societies, San Francisco, October 28.
Gardiner, M. (1971). *The Wolf Man, by the Wolf Man.* New York: Basic Books.
Garma, A. (1943). Sadism and masochism in human conduct. *Journal of Clinical Psychopathology and Psychotherapy* 6:355–390, 1944.

——— (1955). Vicissitudes of the dream screen and the Isakower phenomenon. *Psychoanalytic Quarterly* 22:369–382.

——— (1958). *El Dolor de Cabeza.* Buenos Aires: Editorial Nova.

——— (1968). Discussion of this chapter at the meeting of the Asociación Psicoanalítica Argentina, Buenos Aires.

——— (1977). The theory of curative factors and its incidence in psychoanalytic technique. Unpublished manuscript.

——— (1978). *El Psicoanálisis: Teoría, Clínica y Técnica,* 3rd ed. Buenos Aires: Editorial Paidós.

Garma, A., and Rascovsky, A. (1948). *Psicoanálisis de la Melancolia.* Buenos Aires: Librería y Editorial "El Ateneo."

Gelinier-Ortigues, M.-C., and Aubry, J. (1955). Maternal deprivation, psychogenic deafness and pseudo-retardation. In *Emotional Problems of Early Childhood,* ed. G. Caplan, pp. 231–247. New York: Basic Books.

Giovacchini, P. L. (1958). Some affective meanings of dizziness. *Psychoanalytic Quarterly* 27:217–225.

——— (1969). The influence of interpretation upon schizophrenic patients. *International Journal of Psycho-Analysis* 50:179–186.

——— (1970). Modern psychoanalysis and modern psychoanalysts, a review. In *Psychoanalysis of Character Disorders,* ed. P. L. Giovacchini, pp. 292–315. New York: Aronson.

——— (1972). Technical difficulties in treating some characterological disorders. *International Journal of Psychoanalytic Psychotherapy* 1:112–128.

——— (1975a). *Psychoanalysis of Character Disorders.* New York: Aronson.

——— (1975b). Self-projections in the narcissistic transference. *International Journal of Psychoanalytic Psychotherapy* 4:142–166.

——— (1979a). Countertransference with primitive mental states. In *Countertransference: The Therapist's Contribution to the Therapeutic Situation,* eds. L. Epstein and A. H. Feiner, pp. 235–265. New York: Aronson.

——— (1979b). *Treatment of Primitive Mental States.* New York: Aronson.

Giovacchini, P. L., Flarsheim, A., and Boyer, L. B., eds. (1975). *Tactics and Techniques in Psychoanalytic Therapy, Vol. II: Countertransference.* New York: Aronson.

Glover, E. (1955). *The Technique of Psychoanalysis.* New York: International Universities Press.

Goitein, L. (1948). *Art and the Unconscious.* New York: United Book Guild.

Goldberg, L. (1979). Remarks on transference-countertransference in psychotic states. *International Journal of Psycho-Analysis* 60:347–356.

Gordon, R. (1965). The concept of projective identification: an evaluation. *Journal of Analytic Psychology* 10:127–149.

Graber, G. H. (1925). Die Schwarze Spinne: Menschheitsentwicklung nach Jeremiah Gotthelfs gleichnamiger Novelle, dargestellt unter besonderer Berücktigung der Rolle der Frau. *Imago* 11:254–334.

Green, A. (1975). The analyst, symbolization and absence in the analytic setting (on changes in analytic practice and analytic experience). *International Journal of Psychiatry* 50:1–22.

Greenacre, P. (1945). The biological economy of birth. *Psychoanalytic Study of the Child* 1:31–51.

——— (1947). Vision, headache and the halo. In *Trauma, Growth and Personality*, pp. 132–148. New York: Norton, 1952.

——— (1967). Discussion of chapter 5 at the Meeting of the American Psychoanalytic Association, New York.

——— (1975). On reconstruction. *Journal of the American Psychoanalytic Association* 23:693–712.

Greenson, R. R. (1961). On the silence and sounds of the analytic hour. *Journal of the American Psychoanalytic Association* 14:9–27.

——— (1965). The working alliance and the transference neurosis. *Psychoanalytic Quarterly* 34:155–181.

——— (1966). The "impossible" profession. *Journal of the American Psychoanalytic Association* 14:9–27.

——— (1967). *The Technique and Practice of Psychoanalysis*, Vol. 1, New York: International Universities Press.

——— (1972). Beyond transference and interpretation. *International Journal of Psycho-Analysis* 53:213–318.

Grinberg, L. (1957). Perturbaciones en la interpretación por la contraidentificación proyectiva. *Revista de Psicoanálisis* 14:23–28.

——— (1958). Aspectos mágicos en la transferencia y en la contratransferencia. *Revista de Psicoanálisis* 15:15–26.

——— (1962). On a specific aspect of countertransference due to the patient's projective identification. *International Journal of Psycho-Analysis* 43: 436–440.

——— (1963). Psicopatología de la identificación y contraidentificación proyectivas y de la contratransferencia. *Revista de Psicoanálisis* 20:112–123.

——— (1965). Contribución al estudio de las modalidades de la identificación proyectiva. *Revista de Psicoanálisis* 21:263–278.

——— (1976). *Teoria de la Identificación*. Buenos Aires: Editorial Paidós.

——— (1979). Countertransference and projective counteridentification. *Contemporary Psychoanalysis* 15:226–247.

Grinker, R. R., Sr., Werble, B., and Dry, R. C. (1968). *The Borderline Syndrome: A Behavioral Study of Ego-Functions.* New York: Basic Books.

Gruhle, W. W. (1915). Selbstschilderung und Einfühlung; zugleich ein Versuch der Analyse des Falles Bantung. *Zeitschrift für die Neurologie und Psychiatrie* 28:148–231.

Gunderson, J. G., and Kolb, J. E. (1978). Discriminating features of borderline patients. *American Journal of Psychiatry* 135:792–796.

Gunderson, J. G., and Singer, M. T. (1975). Defining borderline patients: an overview. *American Journal of Psychiatry* 132:1–10.

Guntrip, H. J. S. (1961). *Personality Structure and Human Interaction: The De-*

veloping Synthesis of Psychodynamic Theory. New York: International Universities Press.

Haak, N. (1957). Comments on the analytical situation. *International Journal of Psycho-Analysis* 38:183–195.

Hallopeau (1889). Alopecia par grattage (trichomania ou trichotillomania). *Annales de Dermatologie et Syphilologie* 10.

Hann-Kende, F. (1933). On the role of transference and countertransference in psychoanalysis. In *Psychoanalysis and the Occult*, ed. G. Devereux, pp. 158–167. New York: International Universities Press, 1953.

Hartmann, H. (1939a). *Ego Psychology and the Problem of Adaptation.* New York: International Universities Press, 1958.

——— (1939b). Psychoanalysis and the concept of health. In *Essays on Ego Psychology: Selected Problems in Psychoanalytic Theory*, pp. 3–18. New York: International Universities Press, 1964.

——— (1950). Psychoanalysis and developmental psychology. *Psychoanalytic Study of the Child* 5:7–17.

——— (1952). The mutual influences in the development of ego and id. *Psychoanalytic Study of the Child* 7:9–30.

——— (1953). Contribution to the metapsychology of schizophrenia. *Psychoanalytic Study of the Child* 8:177–198.

Hartmann, H., and Kris, E. (1945). The genetic approach in psychoanalysis. *Psychoanalytic Study of the Child* 1:11–30.

Hartmann, H., Kris, E., and Loewenstein, R. M. (1946). Comments on the formation of psychic structure. *Psychoanalytic Study of the Child* 2:11–38.

——— (1949). Notes on the theory of aggression. *Psychoanalytic Study of the Child* 3/4:9–36.

Heilbrunn, G. (1953). Fusion of the Isakower phenomenon with the dream screen. *Psychoanalytic Quarterly* 22:200–204.

Heimann, P. (1950). On countertransference. *International Journal of Psycho-Analysis* 31:81–84.

——— (1966). Discussion of "Structural derivatives of object relationships" by Otto F. Kernberg. *International Journal of Psycho-Analysis* 47:254–260.

Hill, L. B. (1955). *Psychoanalytic Intervention in Schizophrenia.* Chicago: University of Chicago Press.

Hoedemaker, E. D. (1956). Discussion of chapter 2 at the Meeting of the West Coast Psychoanalytic Societies, Seattle.

——— (1967a). Intensive psychotherapy of schizophrenia: an initial interview. *Canadian Psychiatric Association Journal* 12:253–261.

——— (1967b). The psychotic identification in schizophrenia: the technical problem. In *Psychoanalytic Treatment of Schizophrenic and Characterological Disorders*, eds. L. B. Boyer and P. L. Giovacchini, pp. 189–207. New York: Science House.

Hoijer, H. (1938). *Chiricahua and Mescalero Apache Texts.* Chicago: University of Chicago Press.

Holzman, P. S., and Ekstein, R. (1959). Repetition-functions of transitory regressive thinking. *Psychoanalytic Quarterly* 28:228–235.

Horney, K. (1935). The problem of feminine masochism. *Psychoanalytic Review* 22:241–257.

Hospital (1893). L'art chez l'aliénés curieuse sculpture sur bois, par un pensionnaire de l'asile d'aliénés de Montredon. *Annales Médico-psychologiques* 18:250–255.

Hrdlička, A. (1899). Art and literature in the mentally abnormal. *American Journal of Insanity* 55:385.

Isakower, O. (1938). A contribution to the psychopathology of phenomena associated with falling asleep. *International Journal of Psycho-Analysis* 19:331–345.

——— (1954). Spoken words in dreams. *Psychoanalytic Quarterly* 23:1–6.

Jackson, D. D. (1954). Some factors influencing the Oedipus complex. *Psychoanalytic Quarterly* 23:566–581.

——— (1958). Family and sexuality. In *Psychotherapy of Chronic Schizophrenic Patients*, ed. C. A. Whitaker, pp. 110–143. Boston: Little, Brown.

Jacobson, E. (1943). Depression: the Oedipus conflict in the development of depressive mechanisms. *Psychoanalytic Quarterly* 12:541–560.

——— (1954a). Contribution to the metapsychology of psychotic identifications. *Journal of the American Psychoanalytic Association* 2:239–262.

——— (1954b). On psychotic identifications. *International Journal of Psycho-Analysis* 35:102–108.

——— (1954c). Transference problems in the psychoanalytic treatment of severely depressed patients. *Journal of the American Psychoanalytic Association* 2:595–606.

——— (1957). On normal and pathological moods. *Psychoanalytic Study of the Child* 12:73–113.

——— (1971). *Depression: Comparative Studies of Normal, Neurotic and Psychotic Conditions.* New York: International Universities Press.

Jekels, L. (1952). The psychology of the festival of Christmas. In *Selected Papers of Ludwig Jekels*, pp. 142–158. New York: International Universities Press.

Johnson, A. M. (1953). Factors in the etiology of fixations and symptom choice. *Psychoanalytic Quarterly* 22:475–496.

Johnson, A. M., and Szurek, S. (1964). Etiology of antisocial behavior in delinquents and psychopaths. *Journal of the American Medical Association* 154:814–817.

Johnson, L. B., and Proskauer, S. (1974). Hysterical psychosis in a prepubescent Navajo girl. *Journal of the American Academy of Child Psychiatry* 13:1–19.

Jones, E. (1951). The significance of Christmas. In *Essays in Applied Psychoanalysis*, Vol. 2, pp. 212–224. London: Hogarth.

—— (1955). *The Life and Works of Sigmund Freud* 2:273–278. New York: Basic Books.

Kanzer, M. (1954a). Manic-depressive psychosis with paranoid trends. *International Journal of Psycho-Analysis* 35:119–128.

—— (1954b). Observations on blank dreams with orgasm. *Psychoanalytic Quarterly* 23:511–520.

—— (1975). The therapeutic and working alliances. *International Journal of Psychoanalytic Psychotherapy* 4:48–73.

Kaplan, L. B. (1963). Snow White: a study in psychosexual development. *Bulletin of the Philadelphia Association for Psychoanalysis* 13:49–65.

Karpov, P. I. (1926). The creative activity of the insane and its influence on the development of science, the arts and technics. *Educational Monographs*, Moscow: First Exemplary Typography, Sovereign Publisher. (In Russian.)

Katan, M. (1979). Further exploration of the schizophrenic regression to the undifferentiated state: a study of the "assessment of the unconscious." *International Journal of Psycho-Analysis* 60:145–176.

Kepecs, J. G. (1952). A waking screen analogous to the dream screen. *Psychoanalytic Quarterly* 21:167–171.

Kernberg, O. F. (1967). Borderline personality organization. *Journal of the American Psychoanalytic Association* 15:641–685.

—— (1972a). Critique of the Kleinian School. In *Tactics and Techniques in Psychoanalytic Therapy*, ed. P. L. Giovacchini, pp. 62–93. New York: Aronson.

—— (1972b). Treatment of borderline patients. In *Tactics and Techniques in Psychoanalytic Therapy*, ed. P. L. Giovacchini, pp. 254–290. New York: Aronson.

—— (1974). Further contributions to the treatment of the narcissistic personality. *International Journal of Psycho-Analysis* 55:215–240.

—— (1975a). *Borderline Conditions and Pathological Narcissism*. New York: Aronson.

—— (1975b). Transference and countertransference in the treatment of borderline patients. *Strecker Monograph Series* 10. Philadelphia: Institute of Pennsylvania Hospital.

—— (1976a). Introduction to *Primitive Internalized Object Relations: A Clinical Study of Schizophrenia, Borderline and Narcissistic Patients* by V. D. Volkan. New York: Aronson.

—— (1976b). *Object Relations Theory and Clinical Psychoanalysis*. New York: Aronson.

—— (1976c). Seminar on Borderline Personality Disorders. San Francisco Psychoanalytic Society, March.

——— (1978). Contrasting approaches to the psychotherapy of borderline conditions. In *New Perspectives on Psychotherapy of the Borderline Adult*, ed. J. F. Masterson, pp. 75–104. New York: Brunner/Mazel.

Kernberg, O. F., Burstein, E. D., Coyne, L., Appelbaum, S. A., Horwitz, L., and Voth, H. M. (1972). Psychotherapy and psychoanalysis: final report of the Menninger Foundation's Psychotherapy Research Project. *Bulletin of the Menninger Clinic* 36(whole numbers 1 and 2).

Khan, M. M. R. (1960). Regression and integration in the analytic setting. *International Journal of Psycho-Analysis* 41:130–146.

Klein, M. (1932). *The Psycho-Analysis of Children*. London: Hogarth, 1950.

——— (1946). Notes on some schizoid mechanisms. *International Journal of Psycho-Analysis* 27:99–110.

——— (1955). On identification. In *New Directions in Psychoanalysis*, eds. M. Klein, P. Heimann, and R. E. Money-Kyrle, pp. 309–345. London: Tavistock.

——— (1957). *Envy and Gratitude: A Study of Unconscious Sources*. New York: Basic Books.

Klimpfinger, S. (1950a). *Der Kindergarten als familiensoziologisches Problem*. Vienna: Bundesverlag.

——— (1950b). *Zur Psychologie des Kleinkindalters*. Vienna: Bundesverlag.

Klopfer, B., and Boyer, L. B. (1961). Notes on the personality structure of a North American Indian shaman: Rorschach interpretation. *Journal of Projective Techniques and Personality Assessment* 31:22–29.

Kohut, H. (1959). Introspection, empathy and psychoanalysis. *Journal of the American Psychoanalytic Association* 7:459–483.

——— (1971). *The Analysis of the Self: A Systematic Approach to the Psychoanalytic Treatment of Narcissistic Personality Disorders*. New York: International Universities Press.

Kolb, L. C. (1956). Psychotherapeutic evolution and its implications. *Psychiatric Quarterly* 30:579–597.

Korner, A. F. (1964). Some hypotheses regarding the significance of individual differences at birth for later development. *Psychoanalytic Study of the Child* 19:58–72.

Kracke, W. (1977). Dreaming in Kagwahiv: dream beliefs and their psychic uses in an Amazonian Indian culture. *Psychoanalytic Study of Society* 8: 119–174. New Haven: Yale University Press.

Kris, E. (1933). *Psychoanalytic Explorations in Art*. New York: International Universities Press, 1952.

——— (1950a). Notes on the development and on some current problems of psychoanalytic child psychology. *Psychoanalytic Study of the Child* 5: 24–46.

——— (1950b). On preconscious mental processes. *Psychoanalytic Quarterly* 19:540–560.

——— (1954). Chairman, problems of infantile neurosis, a discussion. *Psychoanalytic Study of the Child* 9:16–71.

—— (1956). The personal myth: a problem in psychoanalytic technique. *Journal of the American Psychoanalytic Association* 4:653–681.

Kubie, L. S. (1952). Problems and techniques of psychoanalytic validation and progress. In *Psychoanalysis as Science*, ed. E. Pumpian-Mindlin, pp. 46–124. Stanford, Calif.: Stanford University Press.

Kusnetzoff, J. C., and Maldovsky, D. (1977). Aportes al estudio de una paciente borderline de base esquizóide: análisis componencial y consideración de los "lugares psíquicos." *Revista de Psicoanálisis* 34:803–842.

Laforgue, R. (1930). On the erotization of anxiety. *International Journal of Psycho-Analysis* 11:312–326.

Laignel-Lavastine, M., and Vinchon, J. (1920a). Délire mystique et sculpture automatique. *Revue Neurologique* 27:824–828.

—— (1920b). Un cas de sculpture "automatique." *Bulletin de l'Académie de Médecine* (Paris) 83:317–319.

Langer, M. (1957). La interpretación basada en la vivencia contratransferencial de conexión o desconexión con el analizado. *Revista de Psicoanálisis* 14:31–38.

Langford, W. S. (1955). Disturbance in mother-infant relationship leading to apathy, extranutritional sucking and hair ball. In *Emotional Problems of Early Childhood*, ed. G. Caplan, pp. 57–76. New York: Basic Books.

Langs, R. J. (1975). Therapeutic misalliance. *International Journal of Psychoanalytic Psychotherapy* 4:77–105.

—— (1976). *The Therapeutic Interaction. II. A Critical Overview and Synthesis*. New York: Aronson.

Langs, R., and Searles, H. F. (1980). *Intrapsychic and Interpersonal Dimensions of Treatment: A Clinical Dialogue*. New York: Aronson.

Leach, M., ed. (1950). *Dictionary of Folklore, Mythology and Legend*, Vol. 2. New York: Funk and Wagnalls.

Levy, K. F. (1958). Silence in the analytic session. *International Journal of Psycho-Analysis* 39:50–58.

Lewin, B. D. (1932). Analysis and structure of a transient hypomania. *Psychoanalytic Quarterly* 1:43–58.

—— (1933). The body as phallus. *Psychoanalytic Quarterly* 2:24–47.

—— (1946). Sleep, the mouth and the dream screen. *Psychoanalytic Quarterly* 15:419–434.

—— (1948). Inferences from the dream screen. *International Journal of Psycho-Analysis* 29:224–231.

—— (1950). *The Psychoanalysis of Elation*. New York: Norton.

—— (1953a). The forgetting of dreams. In *Drives, Affects, Behavior*, ed. R. M. Loewenstein, pp. 191–202. New York: International Universities Press.

—— (1953b). Reconsideration of the dream screen. *Psychoanalytic Quarterly* 22:174–199.

—— (1954). Sleep, narcissistic neurosis, and the analytic situation. *Psychoanalytic Quarterly* 23:487–510.

Lewinsky, H. (1956). The closed circle. *International Journal of Psycho-Analysis* 37:290–297.

Lewis, N. D. C. (1933). Studies on suicide. I. Preliminary survey of some significant aspects of suicide. *Psychoanalytic Review* 20:241–273.

Lidz, R. W., and Lidz, T. (1952). Therapeutic considerations arising from the intense symbiotic needs of schizophrenic patients. In *Psychotherapy with Schizophrenia*, ed. E. B. Brody and F. S. Redlich, pp. 168–178. New York: International Universities Press.

Lindon, J. A., ed. (1967). Report on regression: a workshop. *Psychoanalyic Forum* 2:293–316.

Little, M. (1951). Counter-transference and the patient's response to it. *International Journal of Psycho-Analysis* 32:32–40.

——— (1957). "R"—the analyst's total response to his patient's needs. *International Journal of Psycho-Analysis* 38:240–254.

——— (1958). On delusional transference (transference psychosis). *International Journal of Psycho-Analysis* 39:134–138.

——— (1966). Transference in borderline states. *International Journal of Psycho-Analysis* 47:476–485.

Little, R. B. (1966). Oral aggression and spider legends. *American Imago* 23: 169–179.

——— (1967). Spider phobias. *Psychoanalytic Quarterly* 36:51–60.

Loewald, H. W. (1960). On the therapeutic action of psychoanalysis. *International Journal of Psycho-Analysis* 41:16–33.

——— (1979). Reflections on the psychoanalytic process and its therapeutic potential. *Psychoanalytic Study of the Child* 34:155–167.

Loewenstein, R. M. (1940). A special form of self-punishment. *Psychoanalytic Quarterly* 21:377–400.

——— (1950). Conflict and autonomous ego development during the phallic phase. *Psychoanalytic Study of the Child* 5:47–52.

——— (1956). Some remarks on the role of speech in psychoanalytic technique. *International Journal of Psycho-Analysis*, 37:460–468.

——— (1957). A contribution to the psychoanalytic study of masochism. *Journal of the American Psychoanalytic Association* 5:197–234.

Long, R. T. (1968). Discussion of Chapter 5 at the meeting of the Psychoanalysts of the Southwest, San Antonio, Texas.

Loomis, L. S. (1961). Some ego considerations in the silent patient. *Journal of the American Psychoanalytic Association* 9:56–78.

Lorand, S. (1963). Regression: technical and theoretical problems. *Journal of the Hillside Hospital* 12:67–80.

Lorand, S., and Console, W. A. (1958). Therapeutic results in psycho-analytical treatment without fee. *International Journal of Psycho-Analysis* 39:59–63.

Lorenz, E. F. (1931). Hänsel und Gretel. *Imago* 17:119–125.

Lubin, A. J. (1967). The influence of the Russian Orthodox Church on Freud's Wolf-Man: an hypothesis. *Psychoanalytic Forum* 2:145–174.

Mack, J. E., ed. (1975). *Borderline States in Psychiatry.* New York: Grune and Stratton.

Maenchen, A. (1968). Object cathexis in a borderline twin. *Psychoanalytic Study of the Child* 23:438–456.

Mahler, M. S. (1963). Thoughts about development and individuation. *Psychoanalytic Study of the Child* 18:307–324.

——— (1972). A study of the separation-individuation process and its possible application to borderline phenomena in the psychoanalytic situation. *Psychoanalytic Study of the Child* 26:403–424.

Mahler, M. S., and Furer, M. (1960). Observations on research regarding the "symbiotic syndrome" of infantile psychosis. *Psychoanalytic Quarterly* 29: 317–327.

——— (1963). Certain aspects of the separation-individuation phase. *Psychoanalytic Quarterly* 32:1–14.

——— (1968). *On Human Symbiosis and the Vicissitudes of Individuation,* Vol. 1. New York: International Universities Press.

Mahler, M. S., and LaPerriere, K. (1965). Mother–child interaction during separation–individuation. *Psychoanalytic Quarterly* 34:483–498.

Mahler, M. S., Pine, F., and Bergman, A. (1975). *The Psychological Birth of the Human Infant: Symbiosis and Individuation.* New York: Basic Books.

Mahler, M. S. and Settlage, C. (1959). Severe emotional disturbances in childhood: psychosis. In *American Handbook of Psychiatry,* vol. 1, ed. S. Arieti, pp. 816–839. New York: Basic Books.

Malin, A., and Grotstein, J. S. (1966). Projective identification in the psychotherapeutic process. *International Journal of Psycho-Analysis* 47:26–31.

Maltzberger, J. T., and Buie, D. H. (1974). Countertransference hate in the treatment of suicidal patients. *Archives of General Psychiatry* 30:625–633.

Mangham, C. A., and Tjossem, T. D. (1955). Locomotor behavior in young children, relationship to mother and child interaction. Paper presented at the First Western Divisional Meeting of the American Psychiatric Association, a joint meeting with the West Coast Psychoanalytic Societies, San Francisco, October 28.

Marcondes, D. (1966). A regressão na contratransferencia. *Revista Brasileira de Psicanálise* 2:11–21.

Martin, P. A. (1959). The cockroach as an identification: with reference to Kafka's *Metamorphosis. American Imago* 16:65–71.

Masterson, J. F. (1972). *Treatment of the Borderline Adolescent: A Developmental Approach.* New York: Wiley.

——— (1976). *Psychotherapy of the Borderline Adult: A Developmental Approach.* New York: Brunner/Mazel.

McLaughlin, J. T. (1975). The sleepy analyst: some observations on states of consciousness in the analyst at work. *Journal of the American Psychoanalytic Association* 23:363–382.

Menninger, K. A. (1931). Psychoanalytic aspects of suicide. *Archives of Neurology and Psychiatry* 25:1369.

Milner, M. (1969). *The Hands of the Living God: An Account of Psychoanalytic Treatment.* New York: International Universities Press.

Mintz, T. (1969–1970). The meaning of the rose in *Beauty and the Beast. Psychoanalytic Review* 56:615–620.

Modell, A. H. (1956). Some recent psychoanalytic theories of schizophrenia. *Psychoanalytic Review* 43:181–194.

——— (1963). Primitive object relationships and the predisposition to schizophrenia. *International Journal of Psycho-Analysis* 44:282–292.

——— (1968). *Object Love and Reality.* New York: International Universities Press.

——— (1975). A narcissistic defense against affects and the illusion of self-sufficiency. *International Journal of Psycho-Analysis* 56:275–282.

Mohr, G. J., Richmond, J. B., Garner, A. M., and Eddy, E. J. (1955). A program for the care of children with psychosomatic disorders. In *Emotional Problems of Early Childhood,* ed. G. Caplan, pp. 251–268. New York: Basic Books.

Money-Kyrle, R. (1939). Totemism. In *Superstition and Society,* p. 56. London: Hogarth.

Mooney, J. (1898). The Jicarilla genesis. *American Anthropology* 40:198–209.

Morrow, T., Jr., and Loomis, E. A. (1955). Symbiotic aspects of a seven-year-old. In *Emotional Problems of Early Childhood,* ed. G. Caplan, pp. 337–361. New York: Basic Books.

Morselli, E. (1881). Intagli ideografici di un alienato. *Archivio di Psichiatria, Scienze Penali, e Antropologia Criminale* 2:421–425.

Nadelson, T. (1977). Borderline rage and the therapist's response. *Archives of General Psychiatry* 134:748–751.

Novick, J., and Kelly, K. (1970). Projection and internalization. *Psychoanalytic Study of the Child* 25:69–95.

Nunberg, H. (1920). On the catatonic attack. In *Practice and Theory of Psychoanalysis,* pp. 3–23. New York: International Universities Press, 1955.

——— (1921). The course of the libidinal conflict in a case of schizophrenia. In *Practice and Theory of Psychoanalysis.* New York: International Universities Press, 1955.

——— (1932). *Principles of Psychoanalysis: Their Application to the Neuroses.* New York: International Universities Press, 1956.

O'Connor, W. A. (1948). Some notes on suicide. *British Journal of Medical Psychology* 21:222–228.

Ogden, T. H. (1978). A developmental view of identifications resulting from maternal impingements. *International Journal of Psychoanalytic Psychotherapy* 7:486–506.

——— (1982). *Projective Identification and Psychotherapeutic Technique.* New York: Aronson.

Olinick, S. L., Reporter (1970). Negative therapeutic reaction. Panel discussion of the American Psychoanalytic Association, Fall Meeting, New York, December 1969. *Journal of the American Psychoanalytic Association* 18: 655–672.

Opler, M. E. (1941). *An Apache Life-Way.* Chicago: University of Chicago Press.

Orens, M. H. (1955). Setting a termination date—an impetus to psychoanalysis. *Journal of the American Psychoanalytic Association* 3:651–665.

Ornstein, A., and Ornstein, P. H. (1975). On the interpretive process in schizophrenia. *International Journal of Psychoanalytic Psychotherapy* 4:219–271.

Orr, D. W. (1954). Transference and countertransference: a historical survey. *Journal of the American Psychoanalytic Association* 2:621–670.

Osario, C., and Monteiro, J. P. (1927). *Contribuição ão estudo do simbolismo mistico nos alienados* (*Um caso de demencia prococe paranóide, n'um antigo esculptor*). Sao Paulo: Oficinas da Editorial Helios Limitada. (Abstracted by R. de S. in *Revue Française de Psychanalyse* 2:205, 1928.)

Paz, C. A. (1963). Ansiedades psicóticas: complejo de édipo y elaboración de la posición depresiva en un borderline. Paper presented at a meeting of the Asociación Psicoanalítica Argentina, Buenos Aires.

Paz, C. A., Pelento, M. L., and Olmos de Paz, T. (1975). *Estructuras y/o Estados Fronterizos en Niños, Adolescentes y Adultos. I. Historia y Conceptualización.* Buenos Aires: Editorial Nueva Visión.

——— (1976a). *Estructuras y/o Estados Fronterizos en Niños y Adultos. II. Casuística y Consideraciones Teóricas.* Buenos Aires: Editorial Nueva Visión.

——— (1976b). *Estructuras y/o Estados Fronterizos en Niños y Adultos. III. Investigación y Terapéutica.* Buenos Aires: Editorial Nueva Visión.

Perry, J. C., and Klerman, G. L. (1980). Clinical aspects of the borderline personality disorder. *American Journal of Psychiatry* 137:165–173.

Pichon Rivière, E. (1951). Algunas observaciones sobre la transferencia en los pacientes psicóticos. *Revista de Psicoanálisis* 18 (1961):131–138.

Pinto Ribeiro, R., and Zimmerman, D. (1968). Notes sobre la contratransferencia. *Revista de Psicoanálisis* 25:847–862.

Pious, W. L. (1949). The pathogenic process in schizophrenia. *Bulletin of the Menninger Clinic* 13:152–159.

Prado Galvão, L. de A. (1966). Contratransferencia frente a regressão. *Revista Brasileira de Psicanálise* 2:22–34.

Prinzhorn, H. (1923). *Bildnerei der Geisteskranken: ein Beitrag zur Psychologie und Psychopathologie der Gestaltung.* Berlin: Julius Springer.

Pruyser, P. W. (1975). What splits in "splitting?" *Bulletin of the Menninger Clinic* 39:1–46.

Racker, E. (1952). Observaciones sobre la contratransferencia como instrumento técnico: communicación preliminar. *Revista de Psicoanálisis* 9: 342–254.

——— (1953). A contribution to the problem of countertransference. *International Journal of Psycho-Analysis* 34:313–324.

——— (1957). The meanings and uses of countertransference. *Psychoanalytic Quarterly* 26:303–357.

——— (1959). Countertransference and interpretation. *Journal of the American Psychoanalytic Association* 6:215–311.

——— (1968). *Transference and Countertransference.* New York: International Universities Press.

Rado, S. (1933). Fear of castration in women. *Psychoanalytic Quarterly* 2: 425–475.

——— (1951). Psychodynamics of depression from the etiological point of view. *Psychosomatic Medicine* 13:51–55.

Rangell, L. (1955). Panel report: the borderline case. *Journal of the American Psychoanalytic Association* 3:285–298.

Rapaport, D. (1951a). The conceptual model of psychoanalysis. *Journal of Personality* 20:56–81.

——— (1951b). *Organization and Pathology of Thought.* New York: Columbia University Press.

Reich, A. (1956). Discussion of Chapter 2 at the meeting of the West Coast Psychoanalytic Societies, Seattle, April.

——— (1960). Further remarks and countertransference. *International Journal of Psycho-Analysis* 41:389–395.

Reich, W. (1933). *Character Analysis.* New York: Orgone Institute Press, 1945.

Reichard, S. (1956). A re-examination of "Studies in hysteria." *Psychoanalytic Quarterly* 25:155–177.

Reider, N. (1957). Transference psychosis. *Journal of the Hillside Hospital* 6: 131–149.

Reinach, S. (1930). *Orpheus.* New York: Liveright.

Réja, M. (1901). L'art malade: dessins de fous. *Revue Universelle* 1:913–915, 940–944.

——— (1907). *L'Art Chez les Fous.* Paris: Société du Mercure de France.

Remus-Araico, J. (1957). Discussion of Chapter 3 at the meeting of the Grupo Mexicano de Estudios Psicoanalíticos, Mexico City, July.

Resnik, H. L. P. (1972). Erotized repetitive hanging: a form of self-destructive behavior. *American Journal of Psychotherapy* 26:4–21.

Ripley, H. S., Ax, A. F., Dorpat, T. L., Strand, G. T., Jr., Kogan, W. S., and Quinn, R. D. (1955). Multiple psychophysiological responses in psychiatric patients and in control subjects. Paper presented at the First Western Divisional Meeting of the American Psychiatric Association, a joint meeting with the West Coast Psychoanalytic Societies, San Francisco, October.

Ritvo, S., and Solnit, A. J. (1958). Influences of early mother-child interaction on identification processes. *Psychoanalytic Study of the Child* 13:64–85.

Robbins, M. B. (1976). Borderline personality organization: the need for a new theory. *Journal of the American Psychoanalytic Association* 24:831–853.

Rogow, A. A. (1970). *The Psychiatrists.* New York: G. P. Putnam's Sons.

Rogues de Fursac, J. (1905). *Les Écrits et les Dessins dans les Maladies Nerveuses et Mentales.* Paris: Masson.

Róheim, G. (1953). Hansel and Gretel. *Bulletin of the Menninger Clinic* 17: 90–92.

Romm, M. E. (1957). Transient psychotic episodes during psychoanalysis. *Journal of the American Psychoanalytic Association* 5:325–341.

Rosenfeld, D., and Mordo, E. (1973). Fusión, confusión, simbiosis, e identificación proyectiva. *Revista de Psicoanálisis* 30:413–423.

Rosenfeld, H. A. (1952a). Notes on the psycho-analysis of the super-ego conflict of an acute catatonic schizophrenic patient. *International Journal of Psycho-Analysis* 33:111–131.

——— (1952b). Transference phenomena and transference analysis in an acute catatonic woman. *International Journal of Psycho-Analysis* 33:457–464.

——— (1954). Considerations regarding the psycho-analytic approach to acute and chronic schizophrenia. *International Journal of Psycho-Analysis* 35: 135–140.

——— (1966a). Discussion of "Office treatment of schizophrenic patients" by L. B. Boyer. *Psychoanalytic Forum* 1:351–353.

——— (1966b). Una investigación sobre la necesidad de "acting out" en los pacientes neuróticos y psicóticos durante el análisis. *Revista de Psicoanálisis* 23:424–437.

Roszak, T. (1969). *The Making of the Counterculture.* New York: Doubleday.

Rubenstein, B. O. (1955). The meaning of the Cinderella story in the development of a little girl. *American Imago* 12:197–205.

Ruesch, J., and Bateson, G. (1951). *Communication: The Social Matrix of Psychiatry.* New York: Norton.

Rycroft, C. (1951). A contribution to the study of the dream screen. *International Journal of Psycho-Analysis* 2:252–254.

Sarnoff, C. (1976). *Latency.* New York: Aronson.

Savage, C. (1958). Problems and countertransference of the analyst in the treatment of schizophrenia. Paper presented at the meeting of the American Psychoanalytic Association, San Francisco, May.

Schafer, R. (1959). Generative empathy in the treatment situation. *Psychoanalytic Quarterly* 28:342–373.

——— (1968). *Aspects of Internalization.* New York: International Universities Press.

Schechtmann, J. (1968). Discussion of Chapter 5 at a meeting of the Asociación Psicoanalítica Argentina, Buenos Aires.

Schmideberg, M. (1959). The borderline patient. In *American Handbook of Psychiatry*, vol. 1, ed. S. Arieti, pp. 398–416. New York: Basic Books.

Schneer, H. I., ed. (1963). *The Asthmatic Child.* New York: Harper and Row.

Schneider, D. E. (1954). The image of the heart and the synergic principle in psychoanalysis (psychosynergy). *Psychoanalytic Review* 41:197–215.

Schur, M. (1953). The ego in anxiety. In *Drives, Affects, Behavior*, vol. 1., ed. R. M. Lowenstein, pp. 67–103. New York: International Universities Press.

Schwing, G. (1954). *A Way to the Soul of the Mentally Ill.* New York: International Universities Press.

Searles, H. F. (1958a). Positive feelings in the relationship between the schizophrenic and his mother. In *Collected Papers on Schizophrenia and Related Subjects*, pp. 216–253. New York: International Universities Press, 1965.

——— (1958b). The schizophrenic's vulnerability to the therapist's unconscious processes. In *Collected Papers on Schizophrenia and Related Subjects*, pp. 192–215. New York: International Universities Press, 1965.

——— (1959). Oedipal love in the countertransference. In *Collected Papers on Schizophrenia and Related Subjects*, pp. 284–303. New York: International Universities Press, 1965.

——— (1961). Phases of patient-therapist interaction in the psychotherapy of chronic schizophrenia. In *Collected Papers on Schizophrenia and Related Subjects*, pp. 521–559. New York: International Universities Press, 1965.

——— (1963a). The place of neutral therapist-responses in psychotherapy with chronic schizophrenic patients. In *Collected Papers on Schizophrenia and Related Subjects*, pp. 626–653. New York: International Universities Press, 1965.

——— (1963b). Transference psychosis in the psychotherapy of chronic schizophrenia. In *Collected Papers on Schizophrenia and Related Subjects*, pp. 654–716. New York: International Universities Press, 1965.

——— (1965). Feelings of guilt in the psychoanalyst. *Psychiatry* 29:319–323.

——— (1975). The patient as therapist to his analyst. In *Tactics and Techniques in Psychoanalytic Therapy. II. Countertransference*, ed. P. L. Giovacchini, A. Flarsheim, and L. B. Boyer, pp. 95–151. New York: Aronson.

——— (1979). *Countertransference and Related Subjects: Selected Papers.* New York: International Universities Press.

Sechehaye, M. D. (1951). *Symbolic Realization.* New York: International Universities Press.

Segal, H. (1956). Depression in the schizophrenic. *International Journal of Psycho-Analysis* 37:339–343.

——— (1967). Melanie Klein's technique. *Psychoanalytic Forum* 2:197–227.

Séglas, J. (1982). *Les Troubles du Langage Chez les Aliénés.* Paris: Ruef et Cie.

Seitz, P. F. D. (1950). Psychocutaneous conditioning during the first two weeks of life. *Psychosomatic Medicine* 12:187–188.

Settlage, C. F. (1979). Clinical implications of advances in developmental theory. Paper presented at the 31st International Psycho-Analytic Congress, New York, August.

Shapiro, E. R. (1978). The psychodynamics and developmental psychology of the borderline patient: a review of the literature. *American Journal of Psychiatry* 135:1305–1315.

Shapiro, E. R., Shapiro, R. L., and Zinner, J. (1977). The borderline ego and the working alliance: indications for family and individual treatment in adolescence. *International Journal of Psycho-Analysis* 58:77–87.

Shapiro, E. R., Zinner, J., Shapiro, R. L., and Berkowitz, D. A. (1975). The influence of family experience on borderline personality development. *International Review of Psycho-Analysis* 2:399–411.

Shapiro, S. (1979). Discussion of Chapter 9 at the San Diego Psychoanalytic Association Symposium on the Borderline Syndrome, January.

Sharpe, E. F. (1946). From *King Lear* to *The Tempest*. *International Journal of Psycho-Analysis* 27:19–30.

Simmel, E. (1948). Alcoholism and addiction. *Psychoanalytic Quarterly* 17:6–31.

Simmonds, C. (1968). Discussion of Chapter 5 at the meeting of the Psychoanalysts of the Southwest, San Antonio, Texas, September.

Siquier de Failla, M. J. (1966). Transferencia y contratransferencia en el proc-esso psicoanalítico. *Revista de Psicoanálisis* 23:450–467.

Spence, D. P., ed. (1968). *The Broad Scope of Psychoanalysis: Selected Papers of Leopold Bellak*. New York: Grune and Stratton.

Sperling, M. (1946). Psychoanalytic study of ulcerative colitis in children. *Psychoanalytic Quarterly* 15:3023–3029.

——— (1952). A psychoanalytic study of migraine and psychogenic headache. *Psychoanalytic Review* 39:152–163.

——— (1955). Psychosis and psychosomatic illness. *International Journal of Psycho-Analysis* 36:320–327.

——— (1957). The psycho-analytic treatment of ulcerative colitis. *International Journal of Psycho-Analysis* 38:341–349.

——— (1967). Transference neurosis in patients with psychosomatic disorders. *Psychoanalytic Quarterly* 36:342–355.

——— (1974). *The Major Neuroses and Behavioral Disorders in Children*. New York: Aronson.

——— (1978). *Psychosomatic Disorders in Childhood*. New York: Aronson.

Sperling, O. (1957). A psychoanalytic study of hypnagogic hallucinations. *Journal of the American Psychoanalytic Association* 5:115–123.

Spiegel, L. A. (1956). Discussion of Chapter 2 at the Midwinter Meeting of the American Psychoanalytic Association, New York, December.

Spitz, R. A. (1945). Hospitalism: an inquiry into the genesis of psychiatric conditions in early childhood. *Psychoanalytic Study of the Child* 1:53–74.

——— (1946). The smiling response: a contribution to the ontogenesis of social relations. *Genetic Psychology Monographs* 34:57–125.

——— (1947). Hospitalism: a follow-up report. *Psychoanalytic Study of the Child* 2:113–117.

——— (1949). The role of ecological factors in emotional development in infancy. *Child Development* 20:145–155.

——— (1950). Anxiety in infancy: a study of its manifestations in the first year of life. *International Journal of Psycho-Analysis* 31:138–143.
——— (1954). Genèse des premieres relations objetales. *Revue Française de Psychanalyse* 18:479–575.
——— (1955a). A note on the extrapolation of ethological findings. *International Journal of Psycho-Analysis* 36:162–165.
——— (1955b). The primal cavity: a contribution to the genesis of perception and its role for psychoanalytic theory. *Psychoanalytic Study of the Child* 10:215–240.
——— (1956). Countertransference: comments on its varying role in the analytic situation. *Journal of the American Psychoanalytic Association* 4:256–265.
——— (1957). *No and Yes: On the Genesis of Human Communication*. New York: International Universities Press.
——— (1959). *A Genetic Field Theory of Ego Formation*. New York: International Universities Press.
Spitzer, R. L., Endicott, J., and Gibbon, M. (1979). Crossing the border into borderline personality and borderline schizophrenia. *Archives of General Psychiatry* 36:17–24.
Stärcke, A. (1920). Demonstratie van een 40-tal teekeningen en boetseerwerken, door een licht hebephreen geworden beeldhouwer vervaardigt tijdens zijn verblijf in een gesticht (Autoreferat). *Nederlandsch Tijdschrift voor Geneeskunde* 64:103–104.
——— (1921). Aanvullende mededeelingen bij de demonstratie eener artistieke productie. *Nederlandsch Tijdschrift voor Geneeskunde* 65:897–898.
Stein, A. (1972). Causes of failure in psychoanalytic psychotherapy. In *Success and Failure in Psycho-Analysis and Psychotherapy*, ed. B. Wellan, pp. 37–52. New York: Macmillan.
Sterba, R. F. (1944). On Christmas. *Psychoanalytic Quarterly* 13:79–83.
Stern, A. (1924). On the counter-transference in psychoanalysis. *Psychoanalytic Review* 11:165–174.
Stone, L. (1954). The widening scope of indications for psychoanalysis. *Journal of the American Psychoanalytic Association* 2:567–594.
——— (1967). The psychoanalytic situation and transference. *Journal of the American Psychoanalytic Association* 15:3–57.
Strupp, H. H. (1958). The psychotherapist's contribution to the treatment process. *Behavioral Science* 3:34–67.
Sullivan, H. S. (1940). *Conceptions of Modern Psychiatry*. Washington: William Alanson White Psychiatry Foundation, 1947.
Szalita-Pemow, A. B. (1955). The "intuitive process" and its relation to work with schizophrenics. *Journal of the American Psychoanalytic Association* 3:7–18.
Szurek, S. (1955a). Childhood schizophrenia, psychotic episodes and psychotic maldevelopment. Paper presented at the Meeting of the San Francisco Psychoanalytic Society, May 16.
——— (1955b). Concerning the sexual disorders of parents and their children. *Journal of Nervous and Mental Disease* 120:369–378.

Tarachow, S. (1963). *An Introduction to Psychotherapy.* New York: International Universities Press.

Taraporewala, I. J. S. (1950). Mithraism. In *Forgotten Religions,* ed. V. Ferm, pp. 205–214. New York: Philosophical Library.

Teruel, G. (1968). Discussion of Chapter 5 at the meeting of the Grupo Venezolano de Estudios Psicoanaliticos, Caracas, July.

Thöma, H. (1961). *Anorexia Nervosa,* trans. E. Brydone. New York: International Universities Press, 1967.

Tjossem, T. D., Leider, A. R., Deishner, R. W., Holmes, T. H., and Ripley, H. S. (1955). Psychophysiological studies of skin temperatures in young children. Paper presented at the First Western Divisional Meeting of the American Psychiatric Association, a joint meeting with the West Coast Psychoanalytic Societies, San Francisco, October.

Tower, L. A. (1956). Countertransference. *Journal of the American Psychoanalytic Association* 4:224–255.

Vaux, C. L. (1930). Some results of unguided occupations. *Occupational Therapy and Rehabilitation* 9:63–68.

Vié, J., and Quéron, P. (1933). Productions artistiques des pensionnaires de la colonie familiale d'Ainay-le-Château. *Aesculape* 23:266–271.

Viederman, M. (1976). The influence of the person of the analyst on structural change: a case report. *Psychoanalytic Quarterly* 45:231–249.

Villamil, J. P. L. (1933). Matiz intenso de religiosidad en el contenido inconsciente del psiquismo humano. *Los Progresos de la Clínica* 41:106–109.

Vinchon, J. (1924). *L'Art et la Folie.* Paris: Stock.

——— (1926). Essai d'analyse des tendances de l'art chez les fous. *L'Amour de l'Art* 7:246–248.

Volkan, V. D. (1973). Transitional fantasies in the analysis of a narcissistic personality. *Journal of the American Psychoanalytic Association* 21: 351–376.

——— (1976). *Primitive Internalized Object Relations: A Clinical Study of Schizophrenic, Borderline and Narcissistic Patients.* New York: International Universities Press.

——— (1978). The night of the living dead. Paper presented at the meeting of the American Psychoanalytic Association, New York, December.

——— (1979). The "glass bubble" of the narcissistic patient. In *Advances in Psychotherapy of the Borderline Patient,* ed. J. LeBoit and A. Capponi, pp. 405–431. New York: Aronson.

——— (1982). A young woman's inability to say no to needy people and her identification with the frustrator in the analytic situation. In *Technical Factors in the Treatment of the Severely Disturbed Patient,* ed. P. L. Giovacchini and L. B. Boyer, pp. 439–465. New York: Aronson.

Waldhorn, H. F., Reporter (1959). Panel report. The silent patient. *Journal of the American Psychoanalytic Association* 7:548–560.

Wallerstein, R. S. (1967). Reconstruction and mastery in the transference psychosis. *Journal of the American Psychoanalytic Association* 15:551–583.

Wangh, M. (1955). Discussion of Chapter 1 at the Midwinter Meeting of the American Psychoanalytic Association, New York, December.

Weigert-Vowinckel, E. (1954). Counter-transference and self-analysis. *International Journal of Psycho-Analysis* 35:242–246.

Wexler, M. (1951a). The structural problem in schizophrenia: therapeutic implications. *International Journal of Psycho-Analysis* 32:157–166.

——— (1951b). The structural problem in schizophrenia: the role of the internal object. *Bulletin of the Menninger Clinic* 15:211–235.

——— (1957). Discussion of Chapter 3 at the Joint Meeting of the Western Division of the American Psychiatric Association and the West Coast Psychoanalytic Societies, Los Angeles, November.

——— (1971). Schizophrenia in conflict and deficiency. *Psychoanalytic Quarterly* 40:83–100.

White, E. L. (1949). Lukundoo. In *The Pocket Week-End Book*, ed. P. v. D. Stern, pp. 169–186. New York: Pocket Books.

Wilson, C. P. (1968). Psychosomatic asthma and acting out: a case of bronchial asthma that developed *de novo* in the terminal phase of analysis. *International Journal of Psycho-Analysis* 49:330–335.

——— (1970). Theoretical and clinical considerations in the early phase of analysis of patients suffering from severe psychosomatic symptoms. *Bulletin of the Philadelphia Association for Psychoanalysis* 20:71–74.

Winnicott, D. W. (1947). Hate in the countertransference. In *Collected Papers: Through Pediatrics to Psycho-Analysis*, pp. 194–203. New York: Basic Books, 1958.

——— (1955). Metapsychology and clinical aspects of regression within the psycho-analytic setup. *International Journal of Psycho-Analysis* 36:16–26.

——— (1960). Countertransference. *British Journal of Medical Psychology* 33: 17–21.

——— (1963). Dependence on infant care, in children and in the psychoanalytic setting. *International Journal of Psycho-Analysis* 44:339–344.

Wolf, K. M. (1953). Observations of individual tendencies in the first year of life. In *Problems of Infancy and Childhood*, ed. M. J. E. Senn, pp. 97–137. New York: Josiah Macy, Jr., Foundation.

Wolfenstein, M. (1966). How is mourning possible? *Psychoanalytic Study of the Child* 21:93–123.

——— (1969). Loss, rage, and repetition. *Psychoanalytic Study of the Child* 24:432–460.

Zeligs, M. A. (1957). Acting in: a contribution to the meaning of some postural attitudes observed during psychoanalysis. *Journal of the American Psychoanalytic Association* 5:685–706.

——— (1960). The role of silence in transference, countertransference and the psychoanalytic process. *International Journal of Psycho-Analysis* 41: 407–412.

Zetzel, E. R. (1956). Current concepts of transference. *International Journal of Psycho-Analysis* 37:369–376.

——— (1965). The theory of therapy in relation to a developmental model of the psychic apparatus. *International Journal of Psycho-Analysis* 46:39–52.

——— (1971). A developmental approach to the borderline patient. *American Journal of Psychiatry* 128:867–871.

Zilboorg, G. (1936). Differential diagnostic types of suicide. *Archives of Neurology and Psychiatry* 35:270–291.

——— (1937). Considerations on suicide, with particular references to the young. *American Journal of Orthopsychiatry* 7:15–31.

Zinner, J., and Shapiro, E. R. (1975). Splitting in families of borderline adolescents. In *Borderline States in Psychiatry*, ed. J. E. Mack, pp. 103–122. New York: Grune and Stratton.

Zinner, J., and Shapiro, R. A. (1972). Projective identification as a mode of perception and behavior in families of adolescents. *International Journal of Psycho-Analysis* 53:523–530.

Index